Between the Public and Private in Mobile Communication

Mobile devices' impact on daily life has raised relevant questions regarding public and private space and communication. Both the technological environment (operating systems, platforms, apps) and media ecosystems (interface design, participatory culture, social media) influence how users deal with the public and private, intimate and personal spheres. Leading researchers in communication, art, computer engineering, education, law, sociology, philosophy, and psychology here explore current methodologies for studying the dichotomy of the public and private in mobile communication, providing a foundation for further research.

Ana Serrano Tellería is Assistant Professor at University of Castilla La Mancha, Spain; a Postdoctoral Researcher at LabCom.IFP, University of Beira Interior, Portugal; Media Consultant, R+D+i Project Manager; and a journalist and artist-performer.

Routledge Studies in New Media and Cyberculture

For a full list of titles in this series, please visit www.routledge.com.

Between the Public
and Private in Mobile
Communication

Edited by Ana Serrano Tellería

Routledge
Taylor & Francis Group

LONDON AND NEW YORK

First published 2017 by Routledge

2 Park Square, Milton Park, Abingdon, Oxfordshire OX14 4RN
52 Vanderbilt Avenue, New York, NY 10017

Routledge is an imprint of the Taylor & Francis Group, an informa business

First issued in paperback 2019

Library of Congress Cataloging-in-Publication Data

Names: Serrano Tellería, Ana, editor.
Title: Between the public and private in mobile communication / edited by Ana Serrano Tellería.
Description: New York: Routledge, 2017. |
Series: Routledge studies in new media and cyberculture |
Includes bibliographical references and index.
Identifiers: LCCN 2017018904
Subjects: LCSH: Interpersonal communication—Data processing. | Mobile communication systems—Social aspects. | Mobile computing—Social aspects. | Social media. | Privacy, Right of.
Classification: LCC HM1169 .B48 2017 | DDC 302.23/1—dc23
LC record available at https://lccn.loc.gov/2017018904

ISBN: 978-1-138-22555-8 (hbk)
ISBN: 978-0-367-88495-6 (pbk)

Typeset in Sabon
by codeMantra

Contents

Editor's Note

I, the editor, coordinated this volume after receiving Routledge's expression of interest. Routledge offered me the chance to develop a book project as a result of organizing the final conference (March 2015) of the "Public and Private in Mobile Communications EU FEDER project" (2013–2015). This project was developed at LabCom.IFP Research Laboratory in Beira Interior University (Portugal) where I was hired as Postdoctoral Researcher (coordinator of Ph.D. candidates).

Acknowledgments

To all authors involved; for their effort, valuable contribution, and support.

To Scott Campbell, for his assistance in the review process.

To Cristina García Escudero, for her assistance in the English review of the proposal.

To Tom Williams, for his assistance in the English review of the final manuscript.

To LabCom.IFP Research Laboratory at Beira Interior University in Portugal, where I, the editor, was hired as Postdoctoral Researcher (coordinator of Ph.D. candidates) in the "Public and Private in Mobile Communications EU FEDER project" (2013–2015).

To my dear family and friends, for their unconditional support.

Introduction

Ana Serrano Tellería

Mobile devices have impacted daily life as a technology that has raised relevant questions regarding core paradigms of communication: space and time. Both the technological environment (OS, platforms, apps, etc.) and the media ecosystems (interface design, participatory culture, social media, etc.) influence, in an interdependent process, how users deal with the public and private, intimate and personal spheres. A liquidity or diluted border can be perceived in users' management of these spheres within a fluid media ecology (Bauman, McLuhan and McQuail).

The main objective of this book is to delve into this hardly explored field, mostly from a communication science approach and perspective. It will be complemented by other related disciplines such as art, computer engineering, education, law, sociology, philosophy, and psychology, due to the nature of this interdisciplinary field. Authors will cover highlighted current issues, from reframing the theoretical background and the methodologies applied to the main consequences of managing the public and private, intimate and personal spheres.

Within this framework, the volume covers an in-depth analysis of big data; new codes of communication; the relevant relationship between user profile and digital identity and the diverse and ongoing transformation of mobile content; copyright challenges; geodata and localization; the increasing use of images and video; digital and mobile literacy as well as an 'Education for Privacy' syllabus proposal; user empowerment and its implications for active citizenship participation; user engagement, participatory culture, social media, social movements, and journalism; and mobile sociability with a special focus on children and young people.

Authors come from various disciplines, have extensive experience in professional and research fields (leading pioneers in their area), and, thus, offer an enriching international review: James E. Katz, Rich Ling, Leopoldina Fortunati, Naomi Baron, Derrick de Kerckhove, Amparo Lasén, Larissa Hjorth, Lev Manovich, Leslie Haddon, Kenichi Ishii, Ishita Shruti, Javier Díaz Noci, Juan Miguel Aguado, Inmaculada J. Martínez, Laura Cañete, João Carlos Correia, Sharon Meraz, Cheryll Ruth Soriano, Maria Luisa Branco, Koldo Meso, Simón Peña, Heitor Costa Lima da Rocha, Elisabeth Thomas Croker, Sandra Carina Guimarães, Ruepert Jiel Cao and myself, the editor, Ana Serrano Tellería.

Statement of Aims

Due to the increasing incorporation of mobile devices into our daily lives and the profound implications they have for human communication, this authoritative reference book has the aim of fulfilling an urgent lack of understanding and management of the dichotomies between public and private, intimate and personal spheres. Online and mobile communication have been studied for more than a decade; however, our knowledge and comprehension of the specific effects of mobile devices on our daily lives concerning these dichotomies between spheres, being always on and perpetually connected, are still in an early stage.

Technologies have changed and continue to evolve communication conditions, access to information, socialization, and behavior. Furthermore, in the particular case of mobile technological environments and mobile media ecologies, outstanding differences can be seen among the various devices people use to access the internet: computers, tablets, and smartphones. It means that core differences have arisen when analyzing and studying users' actions, activities, animations, behaviors, knowledge, perceptions, performances, and understandings.

The objective of this highly innovative volume is to examine the implications of mobile communication in the public and private, intimate and personal spheres as well as its consequences when delimiting these dichotomies. It is also to explore current research and methods and provide a foundation for the further development models of human behavior in an ever-changing technological environment and in mobile media ecologies full of affordances and risks, in which media are described as artifacts, activities, and arrangements (Deuze's *Media Life*) and users' behaviors in the form of actions, animations, and performances.

This cutting-edge volume therefore discusses and addresses the differences and challenges that emerge when humans communicate via mobile devices and how they impact their conceptions about these spheres. It will provide the latest research in online and mobile communication theories, findings, emerging trends, and support decisions and the creation of best practices. It will provide an essential volume to make sense of the defining aspects and cardinal dynamics of mobile communication, integrating the most significant and pioneering new material to create an indispensable research tool and pedagogic resource. Authors will delve into the relevant issues described below, based on the correlation between the features of the mobile technology environment and McLuhan's laws describing the ecological approach method to "old" and "new" media, along with Bauman's metaphor of modern liquid life. Furthermore, beyond the correlation between the impact of mobile technology and characteristics of the liquid society, mobile media particularly fit the fluidization parameters of the technological, institutional, and cultural dimensions of the media previously described by McQuail.

A wide range of challenges must be faced. First, whether or not the academy should consider a different approach to its state of the art review and the research methods to apply. Second, how mobile devices may be analyzed not only as a technology that enables certain potential but also as a probe for research and the ethics involved. Two outstanding and internally recognized academics will cover this controversial area: Rich Ling and Derrick de Kerckhove, who will offer their extensive and leading experience.

Thereafter, the volume will delve into crucial questions and tendencies that surround communicative models and practices. They include new and mixed codes and modes of communication, different kinds of media practices, and visual communication with a special focus on images and video, geodata, and localization. Prominent pioneers in these fields will discuss their ongoing innovative research: Leopoldina Fortunati and Naomi Baron; James E. Katz and Elisabeth Thomas Crocker; Cheryll Ruth R. Soriano and Ruepert Jiel Cao; Ishita Shruti; Amparo Lasén; Larissa Hjorth; and Lev Manovich.

The following stage collects and gathers together the matters mentioned above, other possible content and data together with the users' actions, animations, and performances that may be afforded by mobile devices with two relevant configurations that feature user behavior: social media, user profile and digital identity. Kenichi Ishii will start with social media and Juan Miguel Aguado; Inmaculada J. Martínez and Laura Cañete will establish the relationship between performance of the Self and mobile content. Thereafter, Javier Diaz Noci will accurately describe the international perspective on copyright issues and user-generated content for mobile devices, specifically including news, entertainment, and multimedia.

An "Education for Privacy" syllabus proposal for primary and secondary education will be introduced by Ana Serrano Tellería, Maria Luísa Branco, and Sandra Carina Guimarães. Their research is based on the EU FEDER project "Public and Private Communications" (2013–15), combining the fields of communication, education, and psychology. Meanwhile, Leslie Haddon member of the EU Kids Online multinational research network, will explore online sociability whereas Lev Manovich will delve into the perceived characteristics and features of this mobile generation in close relation to instagram photography.

Media literacy and communicative affordances, social innovations, journalism, and political participation for active citizenship will be discussed by Koldo Meso and Simón Peña; Sharon Meraz; João Carlos Correia, Heitor Costa Lima da Rocha, and Ana Serrano Tellería. On an international scope mostly covering the EU and the US, these experienced scholars will inquire into how these technologies and devices can reframe the structural meaning of news media, bearing in mind users' actions, animations, and performances reflected in new forms and models such as citizen journalism, crowdsourcing, and social media like Twitter.

All these highly innovative contributions will present a variety of possible answers to be able to go a step forward in this brand new field that requires an international, intersectorial, and interdisciplinary scope.

Part I
Reframing Theories and Methods

1 The Phases of Mobile Communication Research

Rich Ling

Introduction

Our understanding of the telephone as a focus of research has evolved. The unit of analysis and the function of the device have been in flux through the history of research on telephony. There have been changes in both our estimations of the social unit that it represents and our understanding of it as a representation of social interaction. This evolution parallels phases in the development of the technology itself. This chapter has four major sections. The first will examine changes in what researchers can consider as a unit of analysis in their investigation of mobile communication. The second will discuss the "social consequences" line of mobile communication research. The third section will examine the mobile terminal as a type of data-gathering probe, and the final section will consider the paradox posed by the previous two phases.

Starting with the first issue, a major line of research has been changes in what researchers can consider the telephonic unit of analysis. Starting with the landline phone, it was often the household consisting of several individuals. With the diffusion of mobile communication, there was the progressive refinement of what researchers examine. In many cases, this became, and still is, the individual. The mobile phone has become a proxy for how we interact and move about in society. This model, however, is changing. There are an increasing number of multi-SIM[1] phones—that is, phones that allow the user to have several subscriptions. This is particularly the case in the Global South. In addition, the increasing ubiquity of computing means that the mobile phone is no longer a unitary device. Rather, it is a hub that might coordinate a variety of other devices and gadgets such as exercise monitors, watches, sound systems, alarms, and home management systems (Donner 2015).

Mobile communication research has a tradition of examining the social consequences of the mobile telephony. The transition from the shared landline phone to an individual device has meant that we have alternative ways of being available to one another. The individual nature of the device means that we can coordinate, nurture, and interact with other individuals as needed. There is not the need to seek out the number of a phone that is near them. They are, de facto, available so long as they have a phone that is charged up and turned on. The examination of social consequences afforded by this individual addressability (Ling 2012) has been the central focus of research in the subdiscipline. This research has helped us to better understand social processes when confronted with new technology.

In a second approach, there is a different conceptualization of mobile communication. In this newer tradition, the mobile terminal functions as a type of probe that gathers data. It is also a device that leaves traces (e.g., phone calls, text messages, location markers) through which the researcher can study social dynamics and indeed a collection of other processes. At one level, the analysis of call data records (CDRs) assumes that the phone is a proxy for the individual. It allows the researcher to trace a person's position in a social network. It is a way to examine their media and communication consumption behaviors and/or as a marker of their physical mobility.

This has its positive sides as seen in the analysis of epidemiology and urban travel patterns and insight into the flux of social interactions. In addition, it means that we can examine society using other units of analysis, e.g., instead of only examining individuals we can examine dyadic, triadic, and even networks as units. Looking somewhat further at the "probe" conceptualization of the device, the functionality of smartphones can be employed to gather information that is integrated into crowd-sourced applications. In this case, smart phones can be used to, for example, supplement weather maps, gather environmental information, and help drivers get traffic information.

There are also problems with the assertion that one subscription is the same as one individual. There is the issue of "thin" data. That is, we often only have behavioral information and no attitudinal information. Tracking of individuals and their digital traces also shows that there are major privacy issues at stake.

Finally, there is a paradox in the development of mobile communication research. On the one hand, there is wide confirmation of how the mobile phone has changed social interaction. The individual addressability of the device has restructured. It has changed the way that we coordinate interaction and the organization of everyday logistics. Indeed, this is the broad theme of many papers in this area. The paradox is that we are also using the data gathered via the device to actually study society. We are starting to use the CDRs to study broad-scale social dynamics. In this, there is the assumption that the traces of a mobile phone are a proxy for social interaction. The paradox is that, on the one hand, the mobile phone has changed social interaction, while we are using it as a data collection system to study that changed society, on the other. Examining this issue is taken up in the last part of this chapter.

The Evolution of a Telephonic Unit of Analysis

The first approach to understanding the role of mobile communication in research is to examine how the device has, in some cases, become a proxy for the individual. In much of the mobile communication research done between the late 1990s and the first decade of the new millennium, there was a tacit assumption that the individual was represented by one mobile phone subscription. This assumption was perhaps not critical when thinking of qualitative and survey research, where the individual was asked to comment on their total use. However, when seen from the perspective of CDRs, it is more crucial.

Landline Telephony

If one conceptualizes the telephone, and now the mobile phone, as a system of links connecting various nodes, it is possible to examine changes in the structure of the nodes since the earliest telephones were installed. The earliest phones were often installed in businesses and, like fax machines that came later, were a link between the office and the factory or between different branches of an organization. According to Fischer (1992, 36), some businesses would lease pairs of phones to provide two-way contact between the buildings of a business or between a business location and the home of the owner. Phones also were installed in public locations such as drug stores (Fischer 1992, 50) and in homes. According to Fischer (1992), in 1912, about 20% of non-farm and about 30% of farm homes had a telephone in the US. In 1920, about 40% of farm homes had a telephone, but this fell off in the next years because of the Great Depression. Non-farm homes had a pre-Depression peak of approximately 45% in 1930. While there is interesting sociological insight to be gleaned from use of the telephone by these different social groups, the point here is somewhat different. At the time of early landline telephony, the unit of analysis was difficult to specifically understand. It might have been a business, a home, some quasi-public site, or some combination of all these.

After the Second World War, it become more common for a home to have a phone. This meant that the unit of analysis became somewhat more well defined, a situation that lasted through the golden age of landline telephony. That said, there was still an indeterminacy in just who was using the phone. There were various strategies used to deal with this. Johannesen (1981), for example, reported on studies done in the 1960s for Norwegian Televerket where individuals were asked to keep diaries of telephonic traffic. Individuals were largely filling out the diaries for their own activity, but they were, at the same time, providing information as though it pertained to all the members of their household. Thus, it is not immediately clear if the material was being gathered using the individual or the entire household as a unit. The analysis indicates, for example, that 15% of the 321 homes included in the sample had a secondary contact point, 8% of the sample had one secondary phone, and 1% had more than one "secondary" phone. The analysis went on to examine, among other things, whether the person/household wanted other types of telephone equipment, whether they were familiar with the different tariffs, and what they thought of the billing system. It is not clear whether this is an individual desire, that of the entire household, or eventually the desire of the person paying the bills. Thus, analysis conflated the physical instillation of the phone in the home, calling behavior, and the attitudes and insights of the individual.[2]

To grasp a comprehensive understanding of the landline telephone in the home meant that the researcher needed to understand the social composition of the household. The use of an elderly couple will be different from that of a home with teens. The telephone might mean something different to the parents of teens and to the teens. The decomposed meaning of individuals using a common subscription was difficult to attach to specific behaviors since there was not the ability to similarly decompose use patterns. The attitudes and behavior of the individual are hopefully traced by the questionnaire. However, since that individual shares their telephonic connection with others, and since the individual perhaps shares attitudes about billing, access, placement of the device, etc. with others, then the unit of analysis becomes less distinct.

At about the same time, Brandon (1981) went beyond the analysis of the household as a unit and broke down telephone traffic by the type of household. In her work, she was able to examine the total traffic generated by a home and then to examine that based on the sociodemographic structure of the home. She found that the heaviest users were homes with female adults and both male and female teens. In many ways, the work of Brandon represented the state of the art with regard to examining individual telephonic activity.

Individual Addressability: The Paradigm Shift of Mobile Telephony

The mobile phone represented a paradigm shift. At its core, it meant that we called to an individual rather than to a location. This is a fundamental change. Indeed, it is the idea of individual addressability (Ling 2008b; Ling and Donner 2009). Once the individual is the unit of analysis, it is possible to think of telephony, the analysis of our use, and its social consequences in a different light.

The technical shift did not mean, however, that our conceptualization of the phone changed immediately. There was a cultural lag (Ogburn 1950) associated in the reconceptualization of telephony's place in society. Early in the transition from landline to mobile telephony, there was the sense that location-based telephones were adequate. Indeed, some people asserted that a phone at work and a phone at home was enough. In interviews from Norway in 1995, a respondent, Frank,[3] noted,

> An important question I ask myself, do I really need this telephone? That is the most important question. I won't spend 1,000 kroner for something that I do not need. [...] I am in an office and there I have a telephone all the time. And at home there is a telephone and that covers my needs. It takes me twenty minutes to come home, and I do not need to call home to say that I am on the way. Then I can call right from the office.

Frank did not see the need for mobile telephony since the spheres of his life were covered via landline communication. In his estimation, there was little to be gained by having a mobile telephone, particularly given the price. Another informant, David, had a slightly different, and perhaps more accommodating, understanding of mobile telephony.

> Perhaps you have a cheap used phone that you have at the cottage, the few times that you go to the cottage, it is there as security at the cottage. I think it is ok to have one that you can buy for 500 kroner or 1,000, and you can leave it at the cottage. And you can use it to call from there the few times I have a need for that or if the kids at home need to call me or you can call and check on your elderly mother or father.[4]

The interesting point with the comments of David, when contrasted with those of Frank, is that while David is more open to the notion of using a mobile phone, he still sees it as essentially a fixed-location device. Indeed, he notes that it is inexpensive enough that "you can leave it at the cottage." To be fair to David, the mobile phones of 1995 were only starting to be pocket-sized devices.

The next step in this development was the individualization of devices. As is seen in these comments, David had a phone that was technically mobile, but he conceptualized it as having a fixed location (Nordal 2000). It was a feature that was available to all the people at the cottage; just like the sink or the couch. In a technical sense, he was living in the mobile era, but culturally he was in the era of the landline. He had not assimilated the notion that each individual could have a phone.

The notion of one phone per person was only starting to develop. Indeed, in the same series of interviews in 1995, the notion was voiced, albeit skeptically, by Harald, who noted,

> I actually don't want a phone that is more expensive than the normal [landline] telephone, normal subscription price like that. You almost

need to have two telephones in a way. I am married and live with my wife. It is not necessary to have a mobile phone because then everybody has a telephone in a way. We have to have one in the house and so it would be an additional [one] regardless of how you look at it. So you buy two mobile phones [and] then it is almost a necessity that it is as cheap as a normal telephone.

While Harald couched his comments in economic terms, he is noting the idea that, taken to what he saw as its extreme, mobile telephony would mean that everyone has a device. This is indeed the core idea that the individual and their phone number are one.[5] Seen in an academic light, there is the notion that the mobile phone becomes the proxy for the individual. As noted by Harald, there are moral and economic issues to be addressed. At about that time, Nordal (2000) noted that it was seen as legitimate for business people to have a phone, but it was another thing for teens to have one.

From this point, the transition from several people associated with a single phone to each person being individually available went through different phases. First, there might be a single mobile phone in the home that was loaned to the person who needed it at the moment. Here, the assumption was that an individual would take the mobile phone in order to call home when they needed to be picked up. Teens that were active in sports, for example, might take their parents' phone with them and call when it was time to be picked up. This system of loaning to a teen for calling the parental taxi service was seen as more efficient than the parents guessing when to show up. It was also a step in the direction of extending individual availability.[6] During the 1990s and then somewhat later in the Global South, mobile phones expanded into all corners of society.

It is at this point that there was the implicit assumption that a subscription represented an individual. This facilitated research on mobile communication since it let the researcher assume that they were examining the use of an individual person when looking at the CDRs or when examining their responses to a questionnaire on mobile communication. During the period, up until the real growth of mobile internet, the researcher could assume that a large portion of an individual's telephonic communication was indeed that individual.

From Single- to Multi-SIM Phones

In the Global North, it is still largely the case that an individual has a single phone number. In the Global South, however, this assumption is not always (or often) viable. This is due to the rise of dual-SIM or multi-SIM phones. Starting in the early years of the new century, users in the Global South became increasingly innovative in using two or more subscriptions through the same phone. The motivation was to save money and/or to gain better coverage. In many cases, one operator would, for example, have less expensive service during the daytime and another would be cheaper in the evening. If the user had two or more SIM cards—that is, two subscriptions—they could swap them in order to exploit a less expensive subscription at different points of the day. The same issue holds in terms of coverage. If one operator has better coverage in a city and the other has better coverage in the countryside, the user might simply have two SIM cards and swap them as they move into the two respective areas. From a user's perspective, this means that the person's interlocutors may need to manage two or more different phone numbers as they switch between the different SIM cards.

The technology for SIM switching has matured. The earliest versions of SIM switching were done by simply opening up the phone and replacing one card with another.[7] With time, there were different informal systems of integrating two SIM cards onto the same physical chip, and eventually, handsets with two SIM slots and various ways of switching back and forth were developed. Multi-SIM handsets were slow in developing due to the resistance from operators who preferred to tie the customer to their company. Indeed, in the US, it was often not possible to switch SIM cards since the subscription is attached to the handset and not a SIM card. Thus, if a person wanted to adopt a second subscription, they needed to also purchase a second phone.

It has been estimated that one quarter of all Android-based phones can house more than one SIM (Mirani 2015). These are largely in the Global South. In addition, there are a variety of innovative ways to convert single-SIM phones so as to accommodate more than one subscription simultaneously (Chipchase 2008).

Referring back to the unit of analysis issue, the development of multi-SIM phones underscores the changing unit of analysis dynamics. Where landline subscriptions encompassed the activities of several persons behind a single subscription, multi-SIM phones fragment the person into several different phases. As users migrate to multi-SIM devices, it becomes difficult to trace which portion of their life is being described by their phone use. This issue is further complicated by the migration of use away from traditional mobile voice telephony/SMS to IP-based[8] communication channels such as Facebook Messenger, SnapChat, Line, WeChat, and WhatsApp. The sum total of this is that researchers are getting only a portion of an individual's communication behavior if they focus on any one of these channels. There are applications that facilitate more careful analysis of mobile behavior (Wagner, Rice, and Beresford 2014). These are often resident on an individual's phone and, with their permission, record the activities carried out on the device. The advantage is that they provide insight into the variety of things that the user does. The disadvantage is that they do not provide system-wide information on all users that would allow the development of social network dynamics.

The "Social Consequences" of Mobile Communication Paradigm

Just as with the evolution of the unit of analysis, there has been an evolution in the focus of mobile communication research studies. Preliminary work was often descriptive. There has been a trend toward more refined models and theoretical development. That said, the broad focus has been to understand the consequences of introducing the technology to a particular context.

According to Woolgar (2005, 41), the mobile phone provided us with a "Garfinklian moment," in that it was a type of breaching experiment writ large. Their sudden appearance in society set into contrast many issues that we thought were quite set. As it entered into society, it shifted our sense of what it meant to be available to one another and it caused us to rethink what types of behaviors are acceptable in public. Teens suddenly had their own personal communication channel. They were no longer tied to the landline phone, while impatient fathers urged them to stop "blocking the line" (Ling 1998; Ling and Helmersen 2000; Ling 2008a). We could call and seek help *in situ* from various types of minor and not-so-minor accidents (Ling 2004). People in the Global South had access to mobile phones. This was, in many cases, the first time that they had used mediated communication. Research showed innovative uses (Donner 2007) as well as adjustments in entrepreneurial activities (Jensen 2007; Jagun, Heeks, and Whalley 2008; Donner and Escobari 2010). We could manage and coordinate our daily activities in a far more granular way (Ling and Yttri 2002), and we could engage in a flowing interaction with others throughout the day (Licoppe 2004). Finally, work done by a range of scholars has examined how people use mobile devices to layer meaning onto public places (Humphreys 2007; De Souza e Silva and Sheller 2014). In sum, the mobile phone provided a way for us to interact and to bring together the various portions of our social sphere. Indeed, research seems to indicate that the mobile phone has helped to increase the cohesion of the closest ties (Ling 2008b; Campbell 2014).

With time, mobile communication has taken on dimensions of being a Durkheimain social fact (Ling 2012). That is, mobile communication is reciprocally expected. We assume mobile access to others, just as they assume it from us. We are not free not to have our phones with us. This would violate our responsibilities to those with whom we are closest. In everyday life, this would complicate the organization of daily activities. Indeed, if we are somehow "off line," that is, if we do not have our phone at ready, there are fewer ways to contact one another and to work out our plans. In this way, mobile communication is being structured into the functioning of daily life.

Thus, at several levels, the mobile phone has had social consequences. It is used to facilitate the flux of daily life. It is an instrument through which we develop and maintain social cohesion with our closest social sphere. Use of mobile communication has blurred boundaries between the different phases of life since individual addressability means that many different publics can reach us whenever and wherever we might be. Finally, it is becoming a structural feature of daily life.

The Mobile Phone as a Probe

In addition to seeing mobile communication as the causal factor in social dynamics, an alternative view is to see the mobile phone and, increasingly, other devices as probes through which it is possible to glean understanding of social processes. In this approach, there is an alternative understanding of the mobile phone. In essence, the researcher strips away the efficacy of the mobile phone. The important thing is not how it changes social interaction, but how it is possible to use the traces and the sensors of the phone as a lens through which to observe social, as well as other, phenomena. In this approach, the researcher treats the mobile phone as a proxy for the individual and the individual's social interaction.

Mobiles and CDRs as Proxies for Social Interaction

The individualization of telephony has allowed researchers to assume that the mobile phone is, in some ways, a proxy for social interaction. Based on this assumption, the mobile phone becomes a device through which it is possible to understand social processes. Clearly, there are nuances and modifications to this. Our social interactions are far deeper and more complex than those that are recorded by our phones. In addition, there are major portions of our lives that are not a part of the telephonic record. The simple counting of calls to different "ties" does not tell us about the nature of the tie, our relationship with the person at that number, or any number of significant social and psychological dimensions of that relationship. It might be that our most called number is our endeared partner, or it might be the pizza guy. This is not always clear from the raw data.

That said, the mobile data traffic records, so-called call data records (CDRs), provide a unique lens on social interaction. Rather than examining the individual-level activities, this material allows insight into large-scale social dynamics. This is seen, for example, in the examination of people's reaction to catastrophic events such as the July 22 bombings in Oslo. Examination of call patterns in the immediate wake of the bombing shows the operation of strong ties. Indeed, the data show that in the minutes after the explosion, there was a sequencing calls that followed the tie-strength ranking of the individual (Sundsøy et al.

2012). Analysis of CDRs shows that there was a peak of people calling their strongest telephonic partner approximately 25 minutes after the explosion. A second peak came to the people's second strongest link 30–45 minutes after the event, and the third, fourth, and fifth links saw peaks that were more diffuse after this.

This macro-level analysis would not be possible using other approaches. A quick-moving researcher might have been able to get a questionnaire into the field within a week after the event. The questionnaire could have asked the respondent to report on whom they had called after the bombing and about how long it took them to have made the calls. However, this would not have had several shortcomings. The material would have been based on recalled estimates, not actual calling behavior. Survey data would not have had the temporal resolution of the CDR data that indeed is measured in seconds. Finally, and most importantly, survey analysis would not have allowed the researcher to determine the tie strength of the interlocutors since this requires a universal sample.

Looking at the material geographically, in the period after the bombing, there was a surge of calls both into and out of Oslo in the hour after the bombing. Interestingly, there was also a surge of calls between people living near one another outside of Oslo. Again, survey data would not have provided the same level of insight. As with the tie-strength analysis, the granularity and breadth of view cannot be matched by survey material. CDR analysis can be used for tracing the spread of disease (Wesolowski et al. 2015), tracking the flow of automobile traffic in urban settings to facilitate throughput (Caceres et al. 2012), studying social affinity (Motahari et al. 2012), and understanding the movement of people in large crowds, such as the Indian Kumbh Mela, which is a gathering of as many as 100 million people in India (Onnela and Khanna 2015). The insight afforded by CDRs is quite literally not possible to bring together using other forms of research.

Taking up the "unit of analysis" issue noted above, these types of research move the focus away from examining single individuals to the examination of broad social movements and trends. Rather than examining the individual, the use of CDRs and social network analysis reconceptualize the unit of analysis as a whole society or as a broad social network. It is this "unit" that is being examined for its various properties.

A threat to the validity of CDRs is the weakening assertion that a phone number/subscription is a proxy for an individual. As noted above, there has been, in some countries, a progression from understanding one subscription to represent one person to where the subscription represents only a portion of the individual's activities. Thus, while the "unit of analysis" is often the individual, this is not always the case, particularly in the Global South.

Thick as Opposed to Thin Analysis

As with any tool used to understand social interaction, CDRs have advantages and drawbacks. The advantage of using CDRs is that they provide a breadth of insight that is not possible when using other approaches. As illustrated by the work noted in the previous section, there are indeed insights that are literally not possible without CDRs. There are, however, limitations. While the traces of mobile communication help the researcher to understand the total social network, they reduce society to a collection of nodes and links. This material is comprehensive, but it also does not include any sense of opinion, attitude, or contextual behavior. CDRs give insight into large swaths of society, but at the price of only providing what might be called "thin" data.

Staying within the context of big data, an alternative is those types of material that go into great depth with regard to the individual, but at the expense of the breadth of coverage. Examples of this include the work by Eagle and Pentland in their reality mining project (2006), the work of Falaki et al. looking into the diversity of smartphone usage (2010), and that of Böhmer et al. that examine app use (2011). In these cases, there is more comprehensive knowledge about a sample of users. One app that affords this type of insight is called Device Analyzer (Wagner, Rice, and Beresford 2014) that was developed at Cambridge University. Users download the app onto their phones, and with the users' permission, the app gathers information on a variety of smartphone-based activities. These activities include things such as when the phone itself is on or off, when calls are made and texts are sent, which apps are used, when Bluetooth and Wi-Fi devices are near the phone, and the location of the phone. Indeed, many more functions are tracked. This results in a rich database showing various types of user behavior.

Experience Sampling

The mobile phone can also be used to gather information from people "in the moment." Thus, rather than relying on the automatically logged traces left by a subscription as described above, the user is asked to provide information about their situation or their feelings. The mobile phone becomes a data collection terminal for what Csikszentmihalyi et al. (1977) and Csikszentmihalyi and Larson (1987) called experience sampling. This technique has since been used in a variety of settings (Csikszentmihalyi and Larson 1987; Kubey, Larson, and Csikszentmihalyi 1996; Kahneman et al. 2004; Hektner, Schmidt, and Csikszentmihalyi 2007; Hicks et al. 2010; Baxter and Hunton 2011). In its earlier formulation, people noted down feelings or activities in a paper diary at certain times of the day. In some cases, the subjects used preprogramed stopwatches to prompt them when to make an entry.

Eventually, pagers were also used in this context (Hektner, Schmidt, and Csikszentmihalyi 2007).

More recently, the mobile phone and the smartphone have also become devices that are used to prompt the individuals. These devices have the advantage of also being a data collection terminal (Cherubini and Oliver 2009; Kobayashi et al. 2015; Verduyn et al. 2015). This work has employed the original conceptualization of experience sampling. It has enhanced the original approach by automatically collecting the material without the need to transcribe notebooks, etc.; in addition, it has allowed the researcher to trigger the data collection based on activities associated with the smartphone. For example, a user might receive a short questionnaire of three or four questions that are prompted by a call or after a mobile Facebook session. Thus, the mobile phone becomes a probe to gather information from the user on movements, activities, etc.

The Mobile Phone as "Witness"

Moving beyond the use of the mobile phone or smartphone to gather data for social analysis, there are also a wide range of apps that use the device to gather information with which to address social needs. In some cases, it is the user that enters the information, and in other cases, the on-board instrumentation of the smartphone is used. These are often crowd-sourced apps that feed information back to the community of users. These include apps that determine the flow of traffic, keep track of the weather, and map crime and other social problems. Examples include the following:

- Placemeter[9] asks individuals to use a suction cup to attach a smartphone to a window, with which to capture the activity on the street. This, along with other video material, is used to model the type, intensity, and flow of cars, pedestrians, and other actors who move past the camera. The material can then be used in urban-based policy decisions.
- Pressurnet[10] and WeatherSignal[11] are applications that use the on-board barometer and eventually the thermometer to turn the phone into an ad hoc weather station. This information is sent to a central server and is used to enhance the granularity of weather prediction.
- There are apps such as Harassmap[12] and Ushahidi.[13] The latter app started as a tool with which to map violence in the wake of the 2007 Kenyan presidential election. Since then, it has been used to support rescue efforts after the 2010 earthquakes in Haiti and Chile and the 2011 earthquake in New Zealand. It has also been used to document the effect of the Deepwater Horizon oil rig explosion and a variety of other applications.

- Waze[14] is an automobile traffic map that gathers the GPS location and the speed of the phone (presumably in a car). It matches this with the posted speed of the particular stretch of road to determine if the car is moving as expected. If not, the app reports to the central server that there may be a traffic jam. This information is then directed to the app's map, thereby alerting other drivers to the eventual problem. Drivers can also report in accidents, speed traps, and slowdowns, thereby further enriching the material that is fed back out to other users.

In each case, the sensors on the smart phone or perhaps an interaction between the user and their phone gathers information that is then sent to a server and again out to all users. A common issue with all of these is that an optimal deployment requires a critical mass of users (Ling and Canright 2013). If there is, for example, only one person using Waze in an area, the information provided by that person will be sparse and not of much use. However, as the number of users increases, the granularity of the information is better and the utility to all users increases.

These services bring up an important issue with regard to the discussion of public use of telephonic information. On the one hand, the storage of our private activities on remote servers means that the digital traces we produce can be hacked by people who mean us harm or, for example, monetized in ways that are a threat to us or with which we are uncomfortable.

It is a serious side of the discussion. In addition, however, mining of these traces can result in broad-scale social good. These mobile traces can help us trace the spread of disease, map access to important resources in disasters, help to identify the location of social violence, illuminate the ebb and flow of traffic, help to plan social protest, give us better weather reporting, identify urban problems, bring attention to environmental issues, and a wide variety of other social goods. There is, correctly so, a discussion of how to maintain privacy in the ever more digital world. This discussion is permanently linked, however, to the potential for negative uses of the very digital traces that can also be used for social good.

Conclusion: The Mobile Paradox

The mobile phone has changed the organization of society. In addition, it has grown into a tool that can be used to gather information on the functioning of society as well as a variety of other domains. The transition from the landline phone to the often near-universal ownership of mobile phones has provided us with an individual addressability (Ling 2012) that has not heretofore been seen. As noted above, this has changed the way that we coordinate interaction. It has changed how we react to emergencies. It has changed the emancipation process of teens, and it has changed the way in which we feel we need to be available for one another. In short, the mobile phone has changed society in some fundamental ways.

In addition, the mobile phone is a probe through which we can gather information and examine, among other things, the ebb and flow of the public/private spheres of social life. CDRs provide us with, for the first time, the ability to map out social networks. We can see the way that some people are more central and others are more remote. We can see the tight friendship clusters, and we can see how interaction takes place through the day. The mobile phone allows us to track mobility and to predict the spread of contagious diseases. In addition, the mobile phone gives us a probe with which we can gather information, in real time, with regard to our activities and our feelings.

There is a paradox in this. While the individual addressability provided by the mobile phone restructures society, it is also a probe with which we seek to study that restructured society. The paradox is that the mobile phone is both a cause of social change and the device we can use to study that change. It is a Gordian knot consisting of the coevolution of society and the tools used for social analysis (Reichel 2011). The one cannot, in any real way, be understood without the other. Some insight into this issue— and perhaps a resolution of the paradox—can be examined by looking into variation of network density and clustering based on mobile activity. Large-scale examination of general use by individuals and the clustering of their links can provide some clues. However, this is not a conclusive disentangling of the two. The social clusters with this highest clustering and density can be the result of telephonic contact and not organic sociation. Treating these elements as variables helps some, but not conclusively.

Stepping back from this perhaps irresolvable paradox, mobile communication has changed the nature of interpersonal interaction. Furthermore, mobile communication research has examined both the social consequences of our adoption of mobile phones and it has seen the development of the mobile handset as a probe that allows us insight into social interaction. As mobile communication and indeed mobile information collection continue to evolve, researchers will be able to glean insight into many new areas of social interaction. These new areas of research necessarily need to proceed cautiously while observing the need for privacy.

Notes

1 SIM stands for Subscriber Information Module. In the GSM system, the purchase of the handset and the subscription are two separate issues. The SIM card represents the subscription. The physical SIM card is inserted in the phone, and it gives the user access to the network of the operator.

2 Some of the same lack of clarity can be seen in the analysis of early PCs and in particular TV. These technologies are (or were) often a part of the

common technical structure of the home, just as the oven, the refrigerator, or the washing machine. While each household member has a different use pattern, it is not a completely individualized technology.

3 The names of all informants have been changed to protect their identity.

4 Both of these quotes come from Telenor interviews from 1995.

5 Interestingly, this idea had been suggested by Harold Osborne, the recently retired chief engineer of AT&T, in 1954 (Conly 1954, 88). He noted that the developments of transistors would allow people to be assigned a phone number at birth that would be theirs through life.

6 Interestingly, pagers were also popular in the period immediately before mobile phones became available. These provided some, but not all, of the functionality of mobile phone. In addition, they were relatively inexpensive. Unfortunately, they only provided for one-way communication. The return contact relied on finding a telephone to call back.

7 See http://www.gsmarena.com/dual_sim-review-154.php for a review of dual-SIM phones.

8 Internet protocol.

9 www.placemeter.com.

10 https://www.pressurenet.io/.

11 http://weathersignal.com/.

12 http://harassmap.org/en/.

13 http://www.ushahidi.com.

14 https://www.waze.com/.

References

Baxter, R. J. & Hunton, J. E. (2011). Capturing affect via the experience sampling method: Prospects for accounting information systems researchers. *International Journal of Accounting Information Systems*, *12*(2), 90–98. doi:10.1016/j.accinf.2010.12.002.

Böhmer, M., Hecht, B., Schöning, J., Krüger, A., & Bauer, G. (2011). Falling asleep with Angry Birds, Facebook and Kindle: A large scale study on mobile application usage. In *Proceedings of the 13th International Conference on Human Computer Interaction with Mobile Devices and Services* (pp. 47–56). Stockholm: Mobile HCI. Retrieved from http://dl.acm.org/citation.cfm?id=2037383.

Brandon, B. B. (1981). *The effects of the demographics of individual households on their telephone usage*. Cambridge, MA: Ballinger Publishing Company.

Caceres, N., Romero, L. M., Benitez, F. G., & del Castillo, J. M. (2012). Traffic flow estimation models using cellular phone data. *IEEE Transactions on Intelligent Transportation Systems*, *13*(3), 1430–1441.

Campbell, S. W. (2014). Mobile communication and network privatism: A literature review of the implications for diverse, weak, and new ties. *Review of Communication Research*, *3*. doi:10.12840/issn.2255-4165.2015.03.01.006.

Cherubini, M. & Oliver, N. (2009). A refined experience sampling method to capture mobile user experience. In *International Workeshop on Mobile User Experience*, edited by Y. Nakhimovsky, D. Eckles, and J. Riegelesberger. Boston, MA: CHI. Retrieved from http://arxiv.org/abs/0906.4125, accessed November 5, 2015.

Chipchase, J. (2008). *Dual SIM*. April 29. Retrieved from http://janchipchase.com/2008/02/sustainability-summit-download/.

Conly, R. L. (1954). New miracles of the telephone age. *National Geographic Magazine*, July, 87–119.

Csikszentmihalyi, M. & Larson, R. (1987). Validity and reliability of the experience-sampling method. *Journal of Nervous*, 175(9), 526–536.

Csikszentmihalyi, M., Larson, R., & Prescott, S. (1977). The ecology of adolescent activity and experience. *Journal of Youth and Adolescence*, 6(3), 281–294.

De Souza e Silva, A. & Sheller, M. (Eds.). (2014). *Mobility and locative media: Mobile communication in hybrid space.* New York: Routledge.

Donner, J. (2007). The rules of beeping: Exchanging messages using missed calls on mobile phones in Sub-Saharan Africa. *Journal of Computer Mediated Communication*, 13(1), 1–22.

Donner, J. (2015). *After access: Inclusion, development, and a more mobile Internet.* Cambridge, MA: MIT Press.

Donner, J. & Escobari, M. X. (2010). A review of evidence on mobile use by micro and small enterprises in developing countries. *Journal of International Development*, 22(5), 641–658.

Eagle, N. & Pentland, A. (2006). Reality mining: Sensing complex social systems. *Personal and Ubiquitous Computing*, 10(4), 255–268.

Falaki, H., Mahajan, R., Kandula, S., Lymberopoulos, D., Govindan, R., & Estrin, D. (2010). Diversity in smartphone usage. In *Proceedings of the 8th International Conference on Mobile Systems, Applications, and Services, San Francisco, California* (pp. 179–194). New York: ACM.

Fischer, C. (1992). *America calling: A social history of the telephone to 1940.* Berkeley, CA: University of California.

Hektner, J. M., Schmidt, J. A., & Csikszentmihalyi, M. (2007). *Experience sampling method: Measuring the quality of everyday life.* Thousand Oaks, CA: Sage.

Hicks, J., Ramanathan, N., Kim, D., Monibi, M., Selsky, J., Hansen, M., & Estrin, D. (2010). AndWellness: An open mobile system for activity and experience sampling. In *Wireless Health 2010* (pp. 34–43). New York: ACM. doi:10.1145/1921081.1921087.

Humphreys, L. (2007). *Mobile sociality and spatial practice: A qualitative field study of new social networking technologies* (Unpublished Doctoral Dissertation). University of Pennsylvania, Pennsylvania.

Jagun, A., Heeks, R., & Whalley, J. (2008). The impact of mobile telephony on developing country micro-enterprise: A Nigerian case study. *Information Technologies and International Development*, 4(4), 47–65.

Jensen, R. (2007). The digital provide: Information (technology), market performance and welfare in the South Indian fisheries sector. *The Quarterly Journal of Economics*, 122(3), 879–924.

Johannesen, S. (1981). *Sammendrag Av Markedsundersøkelser Gjennomført for Televerket I Tiden 1966–1981.* Kjeller: Televerkets Forskninginstitutt.

Kahneman, D., Krueger, A.B., Schkade, D.A., Schwarz, N., & Stone, A.A. (2004). A survey method for characterizing daily life experience: The day reconstruction method. *Science*, 306(5702), 1776–1780.

Kobayashi, T., Boase, J., Suzuki, T., & Suzuki, T. (2015). Emerging from the cocoon? Revisiting the tele-cocooning hypothesis in the smartphone era. *Journal of Computer-Mediated Communication.* doi:10.1111/jcc4.12116/full.

Kubey, R., Larson, R., & Csikszentmihalyi, M. (1996). Experience sampling method applications to communication research questions. *Journal of Communication*, 46(2), 99–120. doi:10.1111/j.1460–2466.1996.tb01476.x.

Licoppe, C. (2004). Connected presence: The emergence of a new repertoire for managing social relationships in a changing communications technoscape. *Environment and Planning D: Society and Space* 22(1), 135–156.

Ling, R. (1998). *'It rings all the time': The use of the telephone by Norwegian adolescents*. 17/98. Kjeller, Norway: Telenor R&D.

Ling, R. (2004). *The mobile connection: The cell phone's impact on society*. San Francisco, CA: Morgan Kaufmann.

Ling, R. (2008a). Mobile communication and teen emancipation. In G. Goggin & L. Hjorth (Eds.), *Mobile technologies: From telecommunications to media* (pp. 50–61). New York: Routledge.

Ling, R. (2008b). *New tech, new ties: How mobile communication is reshaping social cohesion*. Cambridge, MA: MIT Press.

Ling, R. (2012). *Taken for grantedness: The embedding of mobile communication into society*. Cambridge, MA: MIT Press.

Ling, R. & Canright, G. (2013). *Perceived critical adoption transitions and technologies of social mediation*. Cell and Self Conference, Ann Arbor, MI.

Ling, R. & Donner, J. (2009). *Mobile communication. Digital and media society series*. London: Polity.

Ling, R. & Helmersen, P. (2000). *'It must be necessary, it has to cover a need': The adoption of mobile telephony among pre-adolescents and adolescents*. The Social Consequences of Mobile Telephony, edited by Rich Ling and Per E. Pedersen (pp. 1–21), Oslo, Norway: Telenor, 2000. doi:10.13140/RG.2.1.2827.8244.

Ling, R., & Yttri, B. (2002). Hyper-coordination via mobile phones in Norway. In *Perpetual contact: mobile communication, private talk, public performance* (pp. 139–169). Cambridge, UK: Cambridge University Press.

Mirani, L. (2015). One quarter of all android users have dual-SIM phones. *Quartz*. Accessed November 5, from http://qz.com/334930/one-quarter-of-all-android-users-have-dual-sim-phones/.

Motahari, S., Mengshoel, O. J., Reuther, P., Appala, S., Zoia, L., & Shah, J. (2012). The impact of social affinity on phone calling patterns: Categorizing social ties from call data records. *Proceedings of the Sixth Workshop on Social Network Mining and Analysis*. Beijing, China: ACM.

Nordal, K. (2000). *Takt Og Tone Med Mobiltelefon: Et Kvalitativt Studie Om Folks Brug Og Opfattelrer Af Mobiltelefoner*. Universitetet i Oslo, Institutt for sosiologi og samfunnsgeografi.

Ogburn, W. F. (1950). *Social change*. New York: Viking.

Onnela, J.-P., & Khanna, T. (2015). Investigating population dynamics of the Kumbh Mela through the lens of cell phone data. http://arxiv.org/abs/1505.06360.

Reichel, A. (2011). Technology as system: Towards an autopoietic theory of technology. *International Journal of Innovation and Sustainable Development*, 5(2–3), 105–118.

Sundsøy, P. R., Bjelland, J., Canright, G., Engo-Monsen, K., & Ling, R. (2012). *The activation of core social networks in the wake of the 22 July Oslo Bombing*. 2012 IEEE/ACM International Conference on Advances in Social

Networks Analysis and Mining (ASONAM), Istanbul, Turkey (pp. 586–590). doi:10.1109/ASONAM.2012.99.

Verduyn, P., Lee, D. S., Park, J., Shablack, H., Orvell, A., Bayer, J., Ybarra, O., Jonides, J., & Kross, E. (2015). Passive Facebook usage undermines affective well-being: Experimental and longitudinal evidence. *Journal of Experimental Psychology: General, 144*(2), 480.

Wagner, D. T., Rice, A., & Beresford, A. R. (2014). Device analyzer: Understanding smartphone usage. In *Mobile and ubiquitous systems: Computing, networking, and services* (pp. 195–208). Lecture Notes of the Institute for Computer Sciences, Social Informatics and Telecommunications Engineering 131. Springer International Publishing. doi:10.1007/978-3-319-11569-6_16.

Wesolowski, A., Qureshi, T., Boni, M. F., Sundsøy, P. R., Johansson, M. A., Rasheed, S. B., Engø-Monsen, K., & Buckee, C. O. (2015). Impact of human mobility on the emergence of dengue epidemics in Pakistan. *Proceedings of the National Academy of Sciences, 112*(38), 11887–11892.

Woolgar, S. (2005). Mobile back to front: Uncertainty and danger in the theory-technology relation. In R. Ling & P. E. Pedersen (Eds.) *Mobile communications: Re-negotiation of the social sphere* (pp. 23–44). London: Springer-Verlag.

2 Mobile Culture in Singapore

From *Democrature* to *Datacracy*

Derrick de Kerckhove

> The more they know about you, the less you exist.
> —Marshall McLuhan

The smartphone in our pocket is our principal identity marker. It is much more so than our passport, our bank card, or our birth certificate. It contains everything about each one of us and is always ready to divulge it to anyone who cares to know and has the technical, if not necessarily the legal, means to do so. For all intents and purposes, our smartphone makes each one of us potentially more vulnerable than if we were to walk bare naked in the street.

The grapevine says that the microphone on our smartphones continues to operate even after we have terminated an oral transaction (such as with the iPhone's Siri, for instance). Our oral discussions with others and the sounds surrounding our movements are recorded. Extreme as this may appear, since the appearance of the Internet, we have begun to lose possession—if not control—of our utterances, whether written or spoken, and soon perhaps, also our thoughts. Our smartphone is both our best friend and our worst enemy because it leaves traces of our every move. All of it goes into databases for further reference. This may seem frankly scandalous, but it may also be part of destiny. Indeed, what seems to be happening since the global adoption of Internet is a gradual erosion of the kind of civil liberties and guarantees we associate with Western democracies. Privacy vanishes faster in societies where such guarantees were never there in the first place.

Singapore, capital of the world's highest penetration rate of smartphones, has also put its population under permanent surveillance. There are good reasons for that and bad ones, too. Whatever one may think of it, one thing certain is that Singapore is designing a new model of social engineering that may soon be applied elsewhere, particularly in large human agglomerations such as Paris or favored tourist destinations under the threat of terrorism such as Nice or Tunis. The techno-ethical model may not be ideologically correct, but it is coherent. What follows is a case study that takes Singapore as one of the forerunners of urban control via surveillance, Big Data, and smartphones.

Mobile Culture in Singapore

> The ownership of smartphones has grown exponentially in Asia in recent years. Singapore is one of the countries with the highest penetration rate in the world. We wanted to discover precisely how and why consumers are using digital devices through the survey.
>
> James Rogers, Managing Director,
> APAC, Toluna

An omnibus survey by Toluna revealed that Singapore consumers are increasingly addicted to their smartphones. While as high as 91% of users see technology as a source of happiness, three-quarters (76%) also see it as a source of stress, which highlights the contradictory relationship that Singaporean consumers have with connected devices.[1]

As well as seeking to uncover consumer feelings toward technology, the study, which questioned a representative sample of 500 Singaporean Internet users, also aimed to discover which devices consumers use to access the internet and which activities they undertake using specific devices. A comparative study was also carried out in Australia.

The results highlighted the rising phenomenon of smartphone addiction in Singapore, with 84% of internet users keeping their smartphone by their bed and nearly half of them (47%) checking it if they wake up during the night (compared with 69% and only 29%, respectively, in Australia).

Smartphones are used for very specific online activities among Singapore Internet users, mostly for entertainment purposes—such as streaming music (57%), playing games (52%), and reading the news (49%). Meanwhile, activities such as online banking still tend to be completed on desktop devices (52% on desktop, compared to 42% on smartphones).

Other key findings from the study include the following:

- Singaporean consumers are more mobile when compared to Australian consumers. In Singapore, smartphones (93%) and laptops (90%) are the most common way of accessing the Internet, compared to Australia, where 78% connect using laptops and 76% connect using PCs.
- 74% of Singapore Internet users access the web using a tablet, indicating that this is a popular channel. A tablet is most likely to be used to play games and watch videos.
- Multiscreen behavior is common practice among Singapore consumers, as high as 73% reporting that they have experienced using two devices simultaneously.
- 60% surf the Internet for more than 3 hours each day. TV is no longer the most common form of media interaction in Singapore, with 30% (66%) watching more than 3 hours of TV every day.

The data speak to the fact that Singaporeans, as most of us, spend a large part of their waking life in front of a screen, leaving traces of their whereabouts, as well as verbatim transcriptions of what they write or say. Every mobile is traceable and is being traced. The Singapore civil administration has decided unabashedly to make full use of that information to ensure that the people behave and that the city is clean.

Singapore under Democrature

I have been in Singapore a few times, the first time in 1975. Although the Raffles Hotel still stood up to its proud reputation, it was a little shabby and so was the city. In fact, the city was very shabby, the famous river bend very polluted with Chinese junks half-sunk and a general sense of "oh well, this is just another third-world city". Coming back in 2004, I was flabbergasted by the difference in the city's appearance. It was clean, orderly, and thriving with impressive architectural hotels, elegant venues, and office buildings. The river was circled by restaurants, mostly fast food, but perfectly maintained.

After a short while of puzzlement, I remembered that when I had been there first, I had been struck, not to say amused, by road signs threatening a 50-dollar fine to anyone who threw rubbish on the street and failed to pick it up. A few yards away, another sign would recommend not throwing chewing gum, another, cigarette butts, and many other warnings not to act in an uncivil manner. I had read that Singapore's first Prime Minister Lee Kuan Yew had instituted draconian rules to clean up the city and to manage tensions flaring between the four ethnic groups populating it. What I didn't foresee, then, is how draconian he would be in applying them. Here is a sampling of the rules he instituted[2]:

- Selling chewing gum is forbidden (Singapore takes cleanliness seriously, and apparently gum causes too much of a mess to be sold in the country. This doesn't mean that you can't bring a little with you—just make sure you don't spit it on the floor; otherwise, you can face a hefty fine).
- Do not spit anywhere. Along with throwing cigarette butts on the street, spitting is banned in Singapore. Both infractions come with significant fines and are routinely enforced. As with similar prohibitions, these laws are in place to maintain Singapore's reputation for cleanliness.
- You can get fined for not flushing public toilets (there is clearly a trend in Singapore about keeping things clean, and this extends to the bathroom as well). If you're caught failing to flush a public toilet after using it, you can expect a *fine of around $150*. There do not appear to be detectors, but apparently police officials have been known to check.

- If you graffiti, you will get caned.
- Respect for public property is taken seriously in Singapore, so it should be no surprise that vandalism is really despised—so much so that if you are caught vandalizing, you will receive a mandatory caning.

So much for public cleanliness, how about private conduct:

- No pornography of any kind is allowed. There is a lot of censorship in Singapore, and this includes the ban on pornography in all forms, from pictures to DVDs. Magazines that discuss sex, like Cosmopolitan, are allowed, *but require special "parental warnings" on their covers.*
- Gay sex is illegal and comes with a 2-year jail term (sexual relationships between two members of the same gender are forbidden in Singapore, although the law is not nearly as strictly enforced as some of the other laws on this list). Formerly, oral sex was also illegal until the ban was lifted in 2007.
- It is illegal to walk around your house naked. Singapore culture is intent on prohibiting many personal rights, the government reason for which is that it creates harmony in a conservative and culturally diverse country. Thus, you can't walk around your house naked, according to Singapore law, because it is considered a form of pornography, but it is unclear how a law like this is enforced.

If the above hints of dictatorship, it is not one that has found much resistance on the part of the citizens. Lee's principal objective to harmonize an ethnically very diverse and volatile population was achieved and probably could not have been possible without both a ruthless justice system and a supportive citizenry. Singapore's justice system is different from the US's, as certain laws can have mandatory sentences. Furthermore, Singapore courts do not have juries, only judges.

One could call this kind of regime a democrature, that is, a muscular system of law and order, but that most—if not all—stakeholders accept for its evident benefits. If "when in Rome, do as the Romans," the same goes for any sovereign nation.

Datacracy or "Government by Algorithms"

It is clear that Singapore has taken the international lead in turning genuinely smart. This entails knowing everything possible and useful about not just the city itself but also about its inhabitants. Indeed, when Lee Hsien Loong, son of Lee Kuan Yew, came to power in 2004, not only did warning street signs, such as "no kissing" or "no spitting", proliferate, but so did Argus-like surveillance cameras over those signs in practically all public venues. The real difference between father and son is that the second, albeit not quite a "digital native," was nevertheless the right age group and mindset to adopt the current fashion for "smart cities." However, instead of reserving data collection to strictly urban affairs, his IT teams sourced their guidance and software from MIT and applied it to the citizens themselves. The networks, of course, were making this possible, as well as the arrival of data analytics, but more than that was the adoption by Singaporeans of more smartphones per capita than anywhere in the world. It ranks today as the most interconnected city in the world.

That being said, what Lee Hsien Loong has done is to replace demo-crature with datacracy, "government by algorithm," that is, by data collection, analysis, reporting, and execution. To wit, *The Wall Street Journal* has reported that as part of its Smart Nation Platform (SNP) launched by Prime Minister Lee Hsien Loong, new sensors and cameras deployed across Singapore will scoop up data and information, allowing the government to monitor all facets of the city, spanning everything from cleanliness of public spaces, smoking rates, to density of crowds and the precise movements of all locally registered vehicles. Surveillance is complete; data are culled from smartphones, social media, sensors, and the public cameras. It is correlated everywhere and can provide an instant x-ray vision of anything happening within the city and of any network of connections outside it. The permanent surveillance is both technological and human. For example, where we can doubt that cameras are hidden in residences, neighbors are counted upon to report any misbehaviors such as walking nude in the living room, presumably having forgotten to pull the drapes. The overall effect is to make people transparent and to hold them accountable for eventual misdeed or misdemeanor. The system ensures instant judgment, verdict, and execution of punishment (fines or worse).

By and large, the people seem to be content with this situation. It ensures, as well as peace, order, cleanliness, and investment. Health and as much well-being as possible under the circumstances are guaranteed to the very end of life.

A report in *The Wall Street Journal* says that Singapore's federal government will also harness private companies to place sensors in senior homes to monitor residents' activity levels, including bathroom use. Families can access the data to know the actions of the subject in real time.

A research team from the *Singapore Management University*[3] is conducting a pilot project aimed at enhancing elderly monitoring systems with the use of data analytics. By monitoring behavioral patterns over time, the system can better identify any signs of potential health or social issues and provide timely alerts to caregivers.[4]

There is a sense of social harmony that Singaporeans take pride in.[5] In a corporate promotional material, this is what the government communications department is imagining:

> In 2025, we envision a Singapore transformed for the better by infocomm media. It will be a nation where people live meaningful and fulfilled lives enabled by technology, and where there are exciting opportunities for all. It will be a place where infocomm media enables a better quality of life for our people through world-class connectivity, compelling local content, and technologies to make everyday lives smoother and more convenient. (https://www.ida.gov.sg/About-Us/Corporate-Publications/Infocomm-Media-2025)

Initiatives for social and economic development abound:

> The recently launched co-working space, Hub@Cuppage will provide more than just resources and workspaces for start-ups! Hub Singapore will also be partnering IDA Hive to create more networking platforms for start-ups with tech expertise, to develop more meaningful digital services for the public good.[6]

Including a visionary projection for knowledge distribution and sharing:

> Libraries have been evolving... With the advent of technology, there is now lesser need to spend time and money traveling to the library to look for information, which is easily accessible online, anytime, anywhere! Coupled with the application of IoT, Robotics, and data analytics, libraries can increasingly become more than just a physical space for reading or research.[7]

However, the situation is not entirely blissful, according to a number of critics of the system.

There is a fringe of dissent, and it is itself under close watch.[8]

What the critics say:

- Using the Internet is not safe.
- People tend to self-censor and prefer to keep their mouths shut.
- Dissident bloggers are prosecuted: Amos Yee (16 years old) has been in jail since May 2015 for making offensive remarks on his blog.
- NGOs and Alternate Press are discouraged (there is a state monopoly on television and strong control of the press).
- There is a lot of Newspeak about intercultural harmony in the media, but racism continues in hiring practices.
- The sense of place, or of its past are being are constantly eroded by development (the government pays lip service only to valued and storied areas).

- The past is edited in schoolbooks to suit state propaganda.
- Access to public government archives is restricted (indeed, formerly granted citizen access to government files has been discontinued, a new measure that was taken only last year).

Hence, one has no access to one's own files, a privilege that should be the first citizen right in the datacracy. None of this is encouraging, but eventually the question may become irrelevant. What is happening is not merely a strictly local format of social or political policy, it's a radical change of ground, comparable only to what happened during the European Renaissance. However, this time, it is global. As Marshall McLuhan explained time and again, the new ground is electricity:

> Electrical information devices for universal, tyrannical womb-to-tomb surveillance are causing a very serious dilemma between our claim to privacy and the community's need to know. The older, traditional ideas of private, isolated thoughts and actions—the patterns of mechanistic technologies—are very seriously threatened by new methods of instantaneous electric information retrieval, by the electrically computerized dossier bank, that one big gossip column that is unforgiving, unforgetful and from which there is no redemption, no erasure of early "mistakes". We have already reached a point where remedial control, born out of knowledge of media and their total effects on all of us, must be exerted.[9]

And, he adds,

> How shall the new environment be programmed now that we have become so involved with each other, now that all of us have become the unwitting workforce for social change.

This charged sentence needs unpacking. Since its beginning, electricity has been in constant mutation from the telegraph to Big Data. By going digital, it has entered its cognitive phase. Everything is becoming transparent, instant, connected, and public. The social effects, among others, are the externalization of human psychology and personality on screens and networks. All barriers, all walls, are crossed by different aspects of electricity, including those of the body and the mind. The big social consequence is that interconnectivity is retribalizing people, but on different grounds and distributed, not congregated in single places. In a world victimized by terrorism, nobody knows where the next tragedy will strike. So, to ensure security, individuality and privacy will be sacrificed to community interests.

The question of programing the social sphere and finding a livable equilibrium between private and social needs will eventually emerge as the critical political issue. What would be the consequences on social behavior and the people's welfare? In view of all the above, one could conceivably imagine a new ethics developing where community interests will prevail over individual ones. Manners will change too, adapting to the transparent conditions. People will have to reconcile and manage two identities: one is public, shared in many different profiles, and the other is private and self-conscious, wondering how long it can continue pretending it is safe and still private. Possibly, the focal point of the social and psychological transformation of society worldwide is precisely the age-old problem of identity. Being transparent means exchanging one's private identity for a public one, even as we all pour ourselves into social networks and multiply the features of our digital unconscious in big databases.

There is more than one meaning in the concept of transparence. It is not the same as transparency, which is related to accountability. There is a see-through factor in transparence that deals with the milieu of transparency. With Big Data, it's the whole environment itself that is transparent. In a datacracy, that is, a government by algorithms, every citizen is transparent. The government isn't necessarily so and is usually tempted to remain opaque. The question is precisely how to negotiate an open agreement between the ruled and the rulers behind the great firewall of data. Transparency goes both ways. Trust is still the basis of good government, so mutual trust should be the objective. The other thing is that if we are becoming transparent, so is the world. News in all forms and manners assault us from their media artillery. In a world where everything is known instantly from anywhere on demand, it is all of humanity that puts pressure on each one of us. The first step to a proper governance in an era of universal transparence is to make transparency (financial and regulatory) mutual on anything to do with public and civil service.

More questions than answers arise from this extreme situation. The principal one would be, is datacracy here to stay, not only in Singapore but also in the whole world? Forced by rising worldwide insecurity, will cities such as Paris or Rome, or any other human agglomeration, not feel obliged to follow Singapore's example simply to protect its citizens?

What are the conditions for a datacracy to run smoothly and be sustainable? The really big questions have not yet found satisfactory answers:

- What benefits does datacracy bring?
- What dangers?
- Should datacracy be resisted?
- Can datacracy be resisted? How?
- When and under what circumstances should it be resisted?
- Should European cities adopt datacracy?
- Under what conditions could it be acceptable?

- Can transparency go both ways?
- Whose responsibility is it to assess?
- Whose responsibility is it to implement?
- What sort of political order can be legitimized under datacracy?
- What level of responsibility should data software creators and data analytics managers recognize and keep in mind?

Reading Marcus Gee's conclusion to an opinion piece in Toronto's *Globe and Mail*, a kind of informal obituary for Lee Kuan Yew said,

> So praise Lee Kuan Yew, by all means. He deserves the accolades he is getting for making his country such an unlikely success story. But don't pretend he is a model. Strongman government without true democratic accountability usually ends in failure.[10]

The assessment, for obvious reasons, does not include reference to datacracy, the new version of "soft authoritarianism," but I cannot help asking myself if this dictatorship is more benevolent than the other as regards potential tyranny from a Big Data government. Another question to ask is whether, for better or for worse, we still have any choice in the matter.

Notes

1 https://www.researchgate.net/publication/278968446_A_Systemic_Approach_to_Understand_Smartphone_Usage_in_Singapore/figures.
2 http://aseanup.com/anticipating-singapores-future-to-foster-innovation/.
3 https://www.facebook.com/sgsmu/.
4 Ibid.
5 https://www.youtube.com/watch?v=TFNWAFicGW4 (Promotional tape by Singaporean government).
6 https://www.facebook.com/SmartNationSG/.
7 "Smart Libraries for Tomorrow" #TanKokYam... https://www.facebook.com/SmartNationSG/.
8 I prefer not to quote anyone in particular, for obvious reasons.
9 Marshall McLuhan, *The Medium Is the Massage*, Bantam Books, 1967, page 51.
10 http://www.theglobeandmail.com/opinion/lee-kuan-yew-gave-singapore-independence-and-the-world-a-bad-idea/article23610260/.

Part II
Revisiting Traditional Issues

3 Evolving Patterns of Mobile Call Openings and Closings

Leopoldina Fortunati and Naomi S. Baron

Introduction

While there is a substantial body of research on texting with mobile phones (e.g., Pertierra et al., 2002; Faulkner & Culwin, 2005; Baron & Ling, 2007; Baron, 2008; Rettie, 2008; Ling et al., 2014), scholars have paid less attention to the oral modality of mobile communication (Fortunati, 2001). This chapter focuses on one aspect of oral communication, namely openings and closings of conversations (here, in Italy), a topic earlier discussed in the literature in the context of traditional landline telephony research (e.g., Schegloff & Sacks, 1973; Houtkoop-Steenstra, 1991; Lindström, 1994; Schlegoff, 2002) and body-to-body (that is, face-to-face) conversations (Anolli, 2002).

Conversations are characterized mainly by three phases: the beginning phase (opening), the developmental phase (in which one or more themes are developed), and the phase of leave-taking (closing). Openings initiate the conversation, with one of the two participants typically using more or less set formulas. Opening formulas negotiate the way in which a dialogic event takes place, are shaped by defined rules of courtesy, establish the level of formality, and enable reciprocal identification (Schegloff, 1967). When using telephones, the opening formula is particularly relevant because it helps establish mutual grounds and agreements for communication in a context lacking visual cues (Rutter, 1984). Such openings enable shared circumstances between people communicating at distance, encouraging a relation of mutual accountability and potentially trust (Weilenmann, 2003; Hamill & Lasen, 2005). Closing formulas serve to manage the end of the conversation, paving the way for a separation of the interlocutors. Usually, a smooth conclusion takes place through the use of symmetric adjacent pairs (for example, Speaker A: "Goodbye for now." Speaker B: "See you later."). Often a symmetrical repetition of parting phrases is used to manage the time of the closure and the consequent experience of separation (Anolli, 2002).

Openings and closings respond to different logics: openings are more regulated, as they serve to establish a conversation in the absence of many body-to-body cues, while closings are less rigidly formulaic and depend on the ability of interlocutors to manage terminal exchanges.

In the literature so far, telephone studies have approached the opening and closing formulas of mobile calls for two reasons. The first was for capturing the structure and dynamics of mobile conversations; the second, for approaching this topic in terms of etiquette (Laufer, 1999). In this second case, they have focused on the social skills interlocutors have for handling such conversations (Fortunati, 1995; Plant, 2001). As Erving Goffman pointed out, "a conversation has a life of its own and makes demands on its own behalf. It is a little social system with its own boundary-maintaining tendencies; it is a little patch of commitment and loyalty with its own heroes and its own villains" (1967, p. 113). This approach, while a good start, has remained underdeveloped from a sociological point of view and has not been enhanced by conversational studies, which in recent decades have focused largely on turn-taking.

Turn-taking (or turn alteration) describes the dynamics of the conversation: within a two-party exchange, Speaker A begins talking but at some point grants Speaker B the opportunity to respond. (Alternatively, Speaker B might simply interrupt Speaker A and seize the floor.) This pattern is repeated until the end of the conversation. During the conversation, turns continue to alternate, sometimes marked by small breaks in between. The amount of overlap between interlocutors tends to be low—according to Anolli (2002), about 5%.

In the contemporary literature, analysis of opening and closing formulas, which are equally vital components of conversations, has been developed mainly through qualitative research studies (Weilenmann, 2003; Decuypere, Masschelein & Simons, 2012, regarding SMS; Laursen & Szymanski, 2013) and has focused on describing the structure and the sequences of mobile phone interactions. The present chapter presents a quantitative study that examines mobile phone call openings and closings from a sociological perspective. Additionally, we contrast mobile phone openings and closings with body-to-body conversations and with landline openings and closings, drawing upon an Italian corpus of 1,477 opening and closing conversational events. Our goal is to better understand how mobile conversations differ from earlier modes of spoken communication. We suggest that mobile openings and closings are significantly shaped by relevant social processes and technological factors, including the everyday ecology of information and communication technology usage and remodeling of public versus private spheres.

Our exploratory study attempts to answer three research questions:

RQ1: What are the most frequent openings and closings in mobile calls?

RQ2: To what degree do mobile phone openings and closings differ from formulas and lexical choices used in body-to-body conversations and landline (also sometimes called "fixed") calls?

RQ3: What changes have taken place in recent years (here, between 2012 and 2015) in openings and closings used in mobile calls?

For the diachronic analysis, we will be particularly interested in seeing whether public expression of personal closeness (rather than reliance on formulaics or location requests) is more frequent in a 2015 mobile phone corpus than in a 2012 mobile corpus.

The chapter is structured as follows. In the 'Mobile Communication Evolution' section, we use a sociological lens to examine evolving practices of use of mobile phones in public spaces. Next (in the 'Methods' section), we describe our methodology. In the Results section, we describe our results, and the chapter ends with the Discussion and Closing Remarks section.

Mobile Communication Evolution

Since their large-scale adoption beginning in the 1990s, mobile phones have undergone three major functional transformations, along with a fourth transformation that has come from increased familiarity of users with the device.

From Oral Communication to Multifunctional Device

The first transformation of the mobile phone was from a tool for oral communication to a personal technology. Users began individualizing their devices through, for example, mobile phones' ringtones, choice of cases and opening screen photos, and early use of stickers or straps. Such personalization, along with the fact that many users carry their phones on their physical person (e.g., in pockets, in waist holsters), has produced an increasingly close relationship between the phone and the human body, with implications for the intimate sphere of emotion and affection. This process has surely enriched the modes of communication conveyed by this device. With the introduction and appropriation of SMS in the early 1990s, mobile phones could be used not simply for oral communication but for written exchanges as well. Over time, the written functions expanded to include email, instant messaging, blogs, and communication over social networks. In fact, by the end of 2007, use of texting had surpassed voice calls in the US (Keane, 2008).

Written forms of mobile communication have been successful in part because they are less direct and invasive than speech. The more the volume of communication reaching the individual has grown (especially with the explosion not only of texting but also of such platforms as Facebook and Twitter), the less personally intrusive mobile phone communication has become. This shift has been made possible for various reasons: because of the degree of distance between interlocutors that written communication affords, because it can be asynchronous, and because it can be ignored more easily than a voice call.

The transformation from being primarily a speech device to primarily a writing instrument has significant implications for the ways in which conversational openings and closings take place when using mobile phones. As we shall see, one of the major effects of this transformation has been a shift away from the conventional formulaics used to open or close spoken telephone conversations.

Changing Level of Intimacy Expressed in Public Space

The second transformation in mobile phone communication has been an increase in the level of personal closeness that interlocutors are willing to express in public space. In earlier years, the management of interpersonal relationships in public entailed a precise etiquette that dictated the way in which sociability should take place and in which the communication should be performed, avoiding expression of intimate information (see, for Italy, Fortunati, 1995). Nowadays, the kind of social intimacy that used to be reserved for conversations in domiciles (such as during visits to friends or family) or office settings (with colleagues) is finding its way into mobile phone conversations taking place in the public arena. Through the mobile phone, concerns of private life are casually conveyed in public. As a consequence, public space has been reshaped through speech patterns more typical of private life. Similarly, the fixed formulas that had been typical of social ritualization taking place in public spaces have diminished (Fortunati, Taipale, & de Luca, 2013). Furthermore, thanks to the explosive use of social networks and GPS, interlocutors now commonly know considerable amounts about the details of the lives of friends and family, including their location. As a result, it has become less necessary to inquire about these sorts of details (including location of the person called) when communicating on a mobile phone.

Internet Access through Mobile Phones

The third transformative element is the addition of Internet access through mobile phones. If it is true that the mobile phone has become the digital device through which the Internet is most frequently accessed (Vincent & Harris, 2008), it is also true that availability of the Internet has permeated mobile phone use. The presence of social networks such as Facebook and Twitter has made superfluous many phone calls or questions since the desired information about friends or family members is already available on these social networks. It becomes easier to first check online what a person is doing before calling. In the same way, applications such as WhatsApp enable users to send, for free, messages and photos or videos, thereby making superfluous many SMSs or emails. Moreover, when using the messaging function in many of these social networking systems, the user automatically learns the interlocutor's location without needing to explicitly ask.

Changes in User Familiarity with Mobile Phones

A final transformation has resulted from users' growing familiarity with mobile phones. In the early days of diffusion of the mobile phone, people tended to feel the need to be in perpetual contact (Katz & Aakhus, 2002). That is, as was the case in the early days of the land-line phone, people felt obligated to answer the mobile phone whenever it rang. Today, users increasingly feel more empowered than in the past to manage when (and whether) to respond to vocal or written mobile communications. For example, we make use of caller ID, decide whether to switch off our mobile, choose which modality to activate (voice call, email, SMS, instant message), or have the option of using multiple mobiles or distinctive ring tones to distinguish callers before even looking at the phone. Such increased control available to us with mobile phones has implications for the way we open mobile phone conversations. For instance, knowing in advance who is calling (through caller ID) or seeing a WhatsApp alert on who has written a message to us affords users new places in which to enter the conversational stream. No longer do we need to begin the call with reciprocal recognition or investigation as to whether the interlocutor is available to have a conversation with us.

Methods

To study the evolution of telephone phone communication patterns with respect to openings and closings, we gathered pilot data on mobile phone and landline conversations at two points in time: 2012 and 2015. Italian undergraduate student research confederates were asked to observe mobile phone conversations as well as landline and body-to-body conversations, paying particular attention to openings and closings. Other data collected (where possible) on the interlocutors included gender, age (clustered in three age groups: age 9–20, age 21–35, and age 39 and older), activity (worker, unemployed, student, nonretired person who stays at home, retired). In addition, we gathered information on the relational identity with the interlocutor (family members and relatives, friends, acquaintances, colleagues, and unknown), the communication role of the interlocutor (caller and person called), and location of the conversation (e.g., while on public transportation, in a restaurant or bar, while walking in public space, at home, or in an office). Where data could not be gleaned by direct observation, the student researchers made inquiries of the person whose conversation was being observed. Due to space limitations in

Table 3.1 Corpus of conversations

	2012 BASE = 419	2015 BASE = 1,058	Total BASE = 1,477
Variable	Absolute number and %	Absolute number and %	Absolute number
Conversation typology			
Mobile	200 (18.1)	903 (81.9)	1103
Body-to-body	0	91 (100.0)	91
Landline	219 (77.4)	64 (22.6)	283
Total N	419 (28.4)	1058 (71.6)	1477
Gender			
Male	0	493 (100.0)	493
Female	0	455 (100.0)	455
Total N	0	948 (100.0)	948
Age			
9–20 years (youngers)	0	330 (100.0)	330
21–35 years (youth)	0	361 (100.0)	361
35 and more (older)	0	348 (100.0)	348
Total N	0	1039 (100.0)	1039
Activity			
Worker	0	138 (100.0)	138
Houseperson	0	6 (100.0)	6
Unemployed	0	7 (100.0)	7
Retired	0	14 (100.0)	14
Student	0	149 (100.0)	149
Total N	0	314 (100.0)	314
Communication role			
Caller (initiator)	21 (5.1)	393 (94.9)	414
Person called	43 (11.6)	328 (88.4)	371
Total N	64 (8.2)	721 (91.8)	785
Social role			
Family member, relative	4 (4.8)	79 (95.2)	83
Friend	14 (3.6)	375 (96.4)	389
Acquaintance	9 (10.3)	78 (89.7)	87
Colleague	6 (25.0)	18 (75.0)	24
Unknown	6 (1.9)	308 (98.1)	314
Total N	39 (4.3)	858 (95.7)	897
Place			
Means of transportations	0	8 (100.0)	8
Shops	0	52 (100.0)	52
Public spaces (shops, parks, church, etc.)	0	70 (100.0)	70
Home, office	0	13 (100.0)	13
Total N	0	143 (100.0)	143

Note: By "Base" we mean the number of conversations collected: 419 in 2012 and 1,058 in 2015.

this chapter, we do not report here on the influence of sociodemographic variables on openings and closings of mobile calls compared to landline and body-to-body.

As this was a pilot study, our protocols for data collection evolved between 2012 and 2015. For the mobile call observations, we gathered information on gender, age, activity, and place for the 2015 study but not for the 2012 study. Data on body-to-body conversational openings and closings were only gathered in 2015.

The total corpus consisted of 1,477 mobile, landline, and body-to-body conversations. Table 3.1 summarizes these data with respect to multiple categories.

Coding of Openings and Closings

Content analysis was used to analyze the conversational openings and closings. Data are reported in Italian and, where an English translation exists, with an English translation. Table 3.2 summarizes the content of categories and macrocategories of openings and closings of conversations.

Locutions were broken down into discourse categories in order to capture the most relevant discursive frames (Altheide, 1996). In most cases, we then built macrocategories by including in that single category all the opening or closing formulas with a similar or adjacent meaning. Note that in reviewing our findings, it is important to keep in mind that conversational formulaics in Italian and English are sometimes different. An English translation of an Italian word may not adequately convey the meaning expressed in Italian. Similarly, a word borrowed from English may not have the same meaning in Italian. For example, in English, the words "Hey," "Hi," and "Hello" are often used interchangeably (though with different levels of formality). When used in Italian, the most similar corresponding words, namely "Hey," "Ciao," and "Pronto," have different meanings from one another (see discussion below).

Openings

We begin with the macrocategory *Ehi*. "Ehi" and the analogous forms included in this macrocategory are Italian interjections that are used in spoken language between individuals who are personally very close (Table 3.2).

A second macrocategory is *Ciao*. "Ciao" is an informal greeting commonly used in body-to-body encounters. Compared with "Ehi," the word "Ciao" implies a lower degree of personal closeness between

Table 3.2 Categories of openings and closings

	Content
Openings category	
Ehi (M)	"Ehi" and analogous forms such as "Hey," "Ohi," "Hei," "Oh," "Oi," "Uei," "We," "Eh," "Ou," "Ah," and "Oo"
Ciao (M)	"Ciao" (Hello), "Salve" (Literally: Hail)
Greeting openings (M)	"Buongiorno" (Good day), "Buonasera" (Good evening)
Excuse me (M)	"Mi scusi" (Excuse me), "Disturbo?" (Am I bothering you?)
Pronto	"Pronto" (literally: Ready)
Sì	"Sì" (Yes)
Sono	"Sono" (I am)
Posso?	"Posso?" (May I?)
Dove sei?	"Dove sei?" (Where are you?)
Closings category	
Ciao (M)	"Ciao" (Hi), "Saluti" (Hail)
Bridge closings (M)	"Arrivederci" (Bye bye), "Incontriamoci," "Ci incontriamo" (Let's meet, We meet), "Stiamo in contatto," "Rimani in contatto" (Let's stay in touch. Stay in touch), "Vediamoci" (See you)
Temporal forms (M)	"Dopo" (After), "Domani" (Tomorrow), "Tra un attimo" (In a minute)
Affective closings (M)	"Baci" (Kisses, Smack), "Bella" (Beautiful), "Bello" (Good looking), "E' stato un piacere" (It was a pleasure), "Stammi bene" (Take care), "Caro/a" (Darling), "Tesoro" (Sweetheart), "Stella" (Star)
Good wishes (M)	"Buonasera" (Good evening), "Buonanotte" (Good night), "Buongiorno" (Good day), "Buon lavoro" (Good work)
Excuse me	"Ti disturbo?," "Disturbo" (Am I bothering you?)
Verbal forms (M)	"Arrivo" (I arrive), "Aspettami lì" (Wait there), "Saluti a tutti" (Greets everyone), "Ti chiamo" (I call you), "Ti chiamo più tardi" (I will call you later), "Aspetterò" (I will be waiting)
Thanks	"Grazie" (Thanks)

Note: "M" indicates a macrocategory.

interlocutors. Note that in Italian, the word "Ciao" is used both as a conversational opening and as a way of closing a conversation. The Hebrew "Shalom" similarly fills these dual roles. Also included in this macrocategory was the word "Salve," which in Italian has a similar meaning.

A third macrocategory is *Greeting Openings*. Included here are "Buongiorno" (Good day) and "Buonasera" (Good evening). In the fourth macrocategory, *Excuse me*, we included "Mi scusi" (Excuse me), along with such expressions such as "Disturbo?" (Am I bothering you?). Generally, these forms are used in more formal circumstances than "Ciao."

Finally, there were opening formulaics that constituted their own category. The Italian word "Pronto" literally means "Ready," a term that made sense in the early days of landline telephony, as it signaled that the interlocutor was ready to engage in conversation. That notion of readiness, which, according to Schegloff (1971, p. 35), is an answer to 'the summons'—the ringing of the telephone—no longer has meaning in landline conversations. The Italian "Pronto" then passed into mobile communication as a conversational opener, though it did not appear in body-to-body communication. The term "Pronto" (from its landline origins when responding to a potentially unknown interlocutor) is not used between people who are personally close.

Other openings that constitute stand alone categories are *Sì* (Yes), *Sono* (I am) (a formula of self-identification), and *Posso?* (May I?), which are relatively formal. The final category *Dove sei?* (Where are you?) only appears in the mobile phone conversations because these are the only circumstances in which interlocutors may not know the location of the other, including, as Laurier stresses (2001), conversations involving mobile office workers traveling by cars.

Closings

As to the closing formulas, in the macrocategory *Ciao*, we included not only the Italian "Ciao," but also the similar expression "Saluti." In the macrocategory *Bridge closings*, we included all the expressions that serve to build bridges for continuation of the interlocutors' relationship. Expressions like "Arrivederci" (Bye bye) and "Incontriamoci" (Let's meet) have the function of attenuating possible displeasure in closing the conversation, in that they imply that separation is only temporary. The same logic underlies the macrocategory *Temporal forms*, such as "Dopo" (After), "Domani" (Tomorrow), and "Tra un attimo" (In a minute), which indicates that the period before the next communication will be brief. Thus, this category also contains expressions that reaffirm the continuation of the relationship between the interlocutors.

The macrocategory *Affective closings* includes expressions such as "Baci" (Kisses) and "Bella" (Beautiful), which reaffirm the affective value of the relationship activated through the conversation. The macrocategory *Good wishes*, which includes "Buonasera" (Good evening), "Buonanotte" (Good night), "Buongiorno" (Good day), and "Buon lavoro" (Good work), expresses sentiments long-characteristic of spoken language used when parting. The macrocategory *Excuse me* represents a kind of *captatio benevolentiae* (a rhetorical technique aimed to capture the goodwill of the interlocutor), while the macrocategory *Verbal forms* stresses the description of particular actions that one of the interlocutors will take with the purpose to coordinate with the other interlocutor. Button (1991) defines these formulas used to place the conversation on a closing track as "projecting future activities." The only mono-categorical closing is *Thanks*.

The frequencies of these categories were calculated using SPSS, and the most frequently occurring categories were identified. Those categories with relatively low frequency but possible importance for clarifying some points of our analysis were also retained and discussed, as Silverman (1997) advises. This procedure allowed us to trace a conceptual map of participants' conversational openings and closings and to build a classification scheme, which provides an analytical description of the most important issues. This style of content analysis is a notably nonintrusive and flexible methodology (McNeill & Chapman, 2005).

The analysis of conversations reported here is based on descriptive statistics, chi-square tests, and standardized residuals. We approached the openings and closings by means of bi- and trivariate cross tabulations, involving them and the main variables considered: the year in which the conversations were collected (2012 and 2015), the typology of communication (mobile, landline, or body-to-body), age, gender, activity of the communicator, the interlocutor's role in the conversation (initiator or recipient), and the place where the conversations took place. To these cross tabulations, we applied the chi-square test. When the relationship between the two variables was significant, we looked at the standardized residuals (stand. res.), which are statistically significant when the absolute value is higher than 2.0.

Results

We begin this section by looking at the results for conversational openings, and then moving subsequently to closings. In both instances, we compare mobile versus landline and body-to-body usages.

Openings of Mobile Calls Compared with Landline and Body-to-Body

Table 3.3 presents our findings for conversational openings. The nine contingency tables derive from crossing the nine main opening formulas with the three typologies of conversation (mobile, body-to-body, and landline). The purpose was to investigate the use or not of each formula. Thus we had nine tables with yes or no answers, showing if a formula was used or not for each of the three typologies of conversation. In the summarizing table, we report only the number of conversations in which, for example, *ciao* was used in mobile, body-to-body, and landline (thus, we reported only the numbers corresponding to the answer yes).

The chi-square values reported in the table refer to each single contingency table related to the associations of the two variables. Note that more than half of the conversations have more than one opening. Taking into account that 182 conversations in the corpus have no openings and that 569 conversations have only one opening, we see that 716 conversations (55.7%) have more than one opening. In sum, while the total number of conversations collected was 1,477, the total number of openings was 1,586.

An example of multiple openings forming a sequence is "Pronto, ciao, sono..." (Hello, hi, I am...). The frequent use of such opening sequences suggests a need to strengthen the way in which we address our interlocutor, by merging the different logics underlying various communicative strategies (e.g., identification or recognition).

In the overall corpus, several opening categories were of high frequency: *Ciao* (30.7%), *Pronto* (26.9%), *Ehi* (15.8%), *Good wishes* (Good morning, evening) (12.2%), and *I am* (12.2%). However, frequency varied according to the type of call. For mobile phone calls, the most frequent opening category was *Ciao* (33.0%), followed by *Pronto* (28.0%) and *Ehi* (17.9%). In body-to-body conversational openings, the most frequent categories were *Ciao* (52.7%), followed by *Good wishes* (Good morning, evening, day, and so on) (33.0%) and *Ehi* (22.0%). With landline conversations, the most frequent category of opening was *Pronto* (30.4%), followed by *I am* (21.2%) and *Ciao* (14.8).

One interesting finding in the corpus of conversational openings concerns use of "where are you?" (dove sei?) for mobile phone calls (Puro, 2002). It is sometimes assumed that because users of mobile phones could be anywhere geographically, "where are you?" would be a commonly used opening. However, in our data, only 1.5% of mobile calls began with the words "where are you?".

While some of the same conversational openings appeared in all three conversational conditions, there were noteworthy differences between usage in mobile call, body-to-body, and landline openings. For example, *Ciao* was used significantly more in body-to-body conversations (stand. res. = 3.8). By contrast, there were not significant frequency differences for use of *Pronto* and *Ehi* for mobile versus body-to-body versus landline conversations. The opening *Good wishes* (Good morning, good evening) was used significantly more often in body-to-body conversations (stand. res. = 5.7), while *Sono* (I am) and *Sì* (Yes) were more used in landline calls (stand. res. = 4.3 and 2.7, respectively). Thus, we did not find openings particularly characteristic of mobile phone use. However, some openings typical of landline and body-to-body conversations also appeared in mobile conversations.

Table 3.4 presents our findings regarding changes in the use of mobile openings compared to landline and body-to-body in 2012 and 2015. We constructed a table summarizing nine contingency tables to triple

Table 3.3 The most frequent opening categories, by conversational typology

	Conversation typology				
Opening categories	Mobile BASE = 1,103	Body-to-body BASE = 91	Landline BASE = 283	Total BASE = 1477	χ^2
Ciao	364 (80.2%) (33.0%)	48* (10.6%) (52.7%)	42 (9.3%) (14.8%)	454 (100.0%) (30.7%)	χ^2=56.951,df2, p<0.0001
Pronto	309 (77.6%) (28.0%)	3 (0.8%) (3.3%)	86 (21.6%) (30.4%)	398 (100.0%) (26.9%)	χ^2=28.198,df2, p<0.0001
Ehi	197 (84.5%) (17.9%)	20 (8.6%) (22.0%)	16 (6.9%) (5.7%)	233 (100.0%) (15.8%)	χ^2=28.065,df2, p<0.0001
Greeting openings	111 (61.7%) (10.1%)	30* (16.7%) (33.0%)	39 (21.7%) (13.8%)	180 (100.0%) (12.2%)	χ^2=42.038,df2, p<0.0001
Sono (I am)	116 (64.4%) (10.5%)	4 (2.2%) (4.4%)	60* (33.3%) (21.2%)	180 (100.0%) (12.2%)	χ^2=28.198,df2, p<0.0001
Sì (Yes)	44 (61.1%) (4.0%)	4 (5.6%) (4.4%)	24* (33.3%) (8.5%)	72 (100.0%) (4.9%)	χ^2=9.846,df2, p<0.01
Excuse me	43 (86.0%) (3.9%)	1 (2.0%) (1.1%)	6 (12.0%) (2.1%)	50 (100.0%) (3.4%)	n.s.
Dove sei? (Where are you?)	16 (88.9%) (1.5%)	1 (5.6%) (1.1%)	1 (5.6%) (0.4%)	18 (100.0%) (1.2%)	n.s.
Posso? (May I?)	0 (0.0%) (0.0%)	0 (0.0%) (0.0%)	1(100.0%) (0.4%)	1 (100.0%) (0.1%)	n.s.

Note: The first percentage has been calculated by row and the second, by column. The asterisks indicate the significant standardized residuals.

entry (year, typology of conversation, and opening). For every typology of conversation (mobile, body-to-body, and landline), Table 3.4 only reports the frequencies of calls in which opening formulas were observed in both 2012 and 2015. The p values reported in the table refer to the chi-square test applied to each single contingency and are related to the association of the included variables, conditioned by the affirmative answers given to one of these variables, that is, the conversation openings. Since no body-to-body conversations were collected in 2012, we cannot analyze body-to-body openings diachronically.

Table 3.4 Comparison of most frequent categories of mobile openings with landline and body-to-body in 2012 and in 2015

Category of opening	Year 2012 BASE = 419 MOB = 200 BTB = 0 LAND = 219	Year 2015 BASE = 1058 MOB = 903 BTB = 91 LAND = 64	Total BASE = 1477 MOB = 1103 BTB = 91 LAND = 283	p<
Ciao				
Mobile	43 (11.8)	321 (88.2)	364	0.0001
Body-to-body	0	48 (100.0)	48	
Landline	31 (73.8)	11 (26.2)	42	n.s.
Total	74 (16.3)	380* (83.7)	454	0.0001
Pronto				
Mobile	26 (8.4)	283 (91.6)	309	0.0001
Body-to-body	0	3 (100.0)	3	
Landline	61 (70.9)	25 (29.1)	86	n.s.
Total	87 (21.9)	311 (78.1)	398	0.0001
Ehi				
Mobile	28 (14.2)	169 (85.8)	197	n.s.
Body-to-body	0	20 (100.0)	20	
Landline	8 (50.0)	8* (50.0)	16	0.05
Total	36 (15.5)	197* (84.5)	233	0.0001
Sono (I am)				
Mobile	7 (6.0)	109 (94.0)	116	0.0001
Body-to-body	0	4 (100.0)	4	
Landline	38 (63.3)	22 (36.7)	60	0.01
Total	45 (25.0)	135 (75.0)	180	n.s.
Greeting Openings				
Mobile	6 (5.4)	105 (94.6)	111	0.0001
Body-to-body	0	30 (100.0)	30	
Landline	29 (74.4)	10 (25.6)	39	n.s.
Total	35 (19.4)	145 (80.6)	180	0.01

(*Continued*)

Category of opening	Year 2012 BASE = 419 MOB = 200 BTB = 0 LAND = 219	Year 2015 BASE = 1058 MOB = 903 BTB = 91 LAND = 64	Total BASE = 1477 MOB = 1103 BTB = 91 LAND = 283	p<
Sì (Yes)				
Mobile	1 (2.3)	43 (97.7)	44	0.01
Body-to-body	0	4 (100.0)	4	
Landline	4 (16.7)	20 (83.3)	24	0.0001
Total	5 (6.9)	67 (93.1)	72	0.0001
Excuse me				
Mobile	6 (14.0)	37 (86.0)	43	n.s.
Body-to-body	0	1 (100.0)	1	
Landline	4 (66.7)	2 (33.3)	6	n.s.
Total	10 (20.0)	40 (80.0)	50	n.s.
Dove sei? (Where are you?)				
Mobile	1 (6.3)	15 (93.8)	16	n.s.
Body-to-body	0	1 (100.0)	1	n.s.
Landline	1 (100.0)	0 (0.0)	1	n.s.
Total	2 (11.1)	16 (88.9)	18	n.s.
Posso? (May I?)				
Mobile	0 (0.0)	0 (0.0)	0	n.s.
Body-to-body	0	0 (0.0)	0	n.s.
Landline	1 (100.0)	0 (0.0)	1	n.s.
Total	1 (100.0)	0 (0.0)	1	n.s.

Note: The percentages have been calculated only by row. The asterisks indicate significant standardized residuals.

We first consider the openings in mobile calls. Of the 364 mobile calls collected in 2012 and 2015 combined, frequency of the macrocategory *Ciao* increased significantly over time (2012: 21.5%; 2015: 35.3%). A similar increase occurred with "Pronto" as a mobile call opener (2012: 13.0%; 2015: 31.3%). Use of *Greeting Openings* (Good morning, evening) increased from 3.0% in 2012 to 11.6% in 2015; similarly, the opening *Sono* rose from 3.5% in 2012 to 12.1% in 2015. By contrast, the opening *Sì* only grew from 0.5% in 2012 to 4.1% in 2015.

For landline calls, use of the macrocategory *Ehi* increased significantly (2012: 3.7%; 2015: 12.5%, stand. res. = 2.3). Significant increase also occurred with the category *Sì*, from 1.8% in 2012 to 31.3% in 2015 (stand. res. = 6.3). Finally, the opening *Sono* rose from 17.4% in 2012 to 34.4% in 2015 (stand. res. = 2.3). The openings *Excuse me, Dove sei*, and *Posso* do not show noteworthy changes diachronically.

Closings of Mobile Calls Compared with Landline and Body-to-Body

Table 3.5 presents our findings for conversational closings. The same procedure as before is behind the table summarizing the eight closing formulas. The table summarizes eight contingency tables to double entry and reports for every typology of conversation (mobile, body-to-body, and landline) only the frequencies of the calls in which the various closing formulas have been observed. In the total corpus, 45.4% of conversations (N = 389) had no closings. Another 494 had a single closing. The remaining 594 conversations (54.6%) had more than one closing. In sum, while the total number of conversations collected was 1,477, the total number of openings was 1,088.

An example of multiple closings is "Ciao, ciao, ciao" (roughly translatable as "See you soon, bye"). The frequent use of more than one closing seems to reflect a desire to strengthen affective expression as we take leave from our interlocutor.

Considering the database as a whole, the order of closing frequencies was *Ciao* (34.5%), *Bridge closings* (20.0%), *Thanks* (9.7%), *Good wishes* (6.4%), *Affective closings* (3.8%), *Temporal forms* (3.1%), *Verbal forms* (1.2%), and *Excuse me* (0.5%). Looking only at mobile phone calls, the most frequent closings were *Ciao* (36.4%), followed by *Bridge closings* (20.1%) and *Thanks* (6.6%). In body-to-body conversational closings, we found the following distribution: *Ciao* (45.1%), followed by *Thanks* (30.8%) and *Bridge closings* (20.9%). As for landline closings, *Ciao* was the most frequent (23.7%), followed by *Bridge closings* (19.4%) and *Thanks* (14.8%).

Comparing the mobile closings to the body-to-body and landline, it emerged that *Ciao* was used more often as a body-to-body closing (45.1%) than in mobile conversations (36.4%) or landline calls (23.7%). Similarly, *Temporal forms* were used proportionally more often in body-to-body closings (stand. res. = 2.5) than in mobile and landline calls (7.7% vs. 2.4% and 4.2%). Moreover, the closing category *Good wishes* was used more often with body-to-body than in mobile and landline calls (11.0% vs. 5.4% and 8.8%). *Thanks* appeared significantly more often in body-to-body and landline closings (stand. res. = 6.5 and 2.8), while *Verbal forms* were more prevalent in landline closings (stand. res. = 2.1).

Similarly, the macrocategories *Temporal forms* (stand. res. = 2.5; 7.7% vs. 2.4% and 4.2%), *Good wishes*, and *Thanks* (stand. res. = 6.5 and 2.8) were used proportionally more often in body-to-body closings than with mobile and landline calls (respectively, 11.0% vs. 5.4% and 8.8%). By contrast, *Verbal forms* were more prevalent in landline closings (stand. res. = 2.1). These findings indicate that as of now, there do not appear to be closings that are especially typical in mobile phone conversations. By contrast, several closings emerged as significantly more prevalent in landline or body-to-body conversations.

Table 3.5 The most frequent categories of mobile closings compared with landline and body-to-body in 2012 and in 2015

	Conversation typology				
Closing category	Mobile BASE = 1103	Body-to-body BASE = 91	Landline BASE = 283	Total BASE = 1477	χ^2
Ciao	401 (78.8%) (36.4%)	41 (8.1%) (45.1%)	67 (13.2%) (23.7%)	509 (100.0%) (34.5%)	χ^2 = 20.852,df2, p<0.0001
Bridge closings	222 (75.0%) (20.1%)	19 (6.4%) (20.9%)	55 (18.6%) (19.4%)	296 (100.0%) (20.0%)	n.s.
Thanks	73 (51.0%) (6.6%)	28* (19.6%) (30.8%)	42* (29.4%) (14.8%)	143 (100.0%) (9.7%)	χ^2 = 66.728,df2, p<0.0001
Good wishes	60 (63.2%) (5.4%)	10 (10.5%) (11.0%)	25 (26.3%) (8.8%)	95 (100.0%) (6.4%)	χ^2 = 7.658,df2, p<0.05
Affective closings	42 (75.0%) (3.8%)	5 (8.9%) (5.5%)	9 (16.1%) (3.2%)	56 (100.0%) (3.8%)	n.s.
Temporal forms	27 (58.7%) (2.4%)	7* (15.2%) (7.7%)	12 (26.1%) (4.2%)	46 (100.0%) (3.1%)	χ^2 = 9.133,df2, p<0.05
Verbal forms	10 (58.8%) (0.9%)	0 (0.0%) (0.0%)	7* (41.2%) (2.5%)	17 (100.0%) (1.2%)	χ^2 = 5.989,df2, p<0.05
Excuse me	6 (75.0%) (0.5%)	0 (0.0%) (0.0%)	2 (25.0%) (0.7%)	8 (100.0%) (0.5%)	n.s.

Note: The first percentage has been calculated by row and the second, by column. The asterisks indicate significant standardized residuals. Also note there is a total of 110 body-to-body closings, since in 19 cases, two closings formulas were used in the same conversation.

Consider now diachronic changes in closings used in 2012 versus 2015. Table 3.6 summarizes eight contingency tables to triple entry (year, typology of conversation, and closing). For each typology of conversation (mobile, body-to-body, and landline), the table reports only frequencies of the encounters in which the various closing formulas were observed in both 2012 and 2015. The p values reported in the table refer to the chi-square tests applied to each single contingency table and are related to the association of the included variables, conditioned by the affirmative answers given to one of these variables, that is, the conversation closings. Since no body-to-body conversations were collected in 2012, we cannot analyze body-to-body closings diachronically.

Table 3.6 Comparison of most frequent categories of mobile closings with landline and body-to-body in 2012 and in 2015

Closing category	Year 2012 BASE=419 MOB=200 BTB=0 LAND=219	Year 2015 BASE=1058 MOB=903 BTB=91 LAND=64	Total BASE=1477 MOB=1103 BTB=91 LAND=283	p<
Ciao				
Mobile	28 (7.0)	373* (93.0)	401	0.0001
Body-to-body	0	41 (100.0)	41	
Landline	22 (32.8)	45* (67.2)	67	0.0001
Total	50 (9.8)	459* (90.2)	509	0.0001
Bridge closings				
Mobile	34 (15.3)	188 (84.7)	222	n.s.
Body-to-body	0	19 (100.0)	19	
Landline	44 (80.0)	11 (20.0)	55	n.s.
Total	78 (26.4)	218 (73.6)	296	n.s.
Thanks				
Mobile	3 (4.1)	70 (95.9)	73	0.0001
Body-to-body	0	28 (100.0)	28	
Landline	19 (45.2)	23* (54.8)	42	0.0001
Total	22 (15.4)	121 (84.6)	143	0.0001
Good wishes				
Mobile	6 (10.0)	54 (90.0)	60	n.s.
Body-to-body	0	10 (100.0)	10	
Landline	16 (64.0)	9 (36.0)	25	n.s.
Total	22 (23.2)	73 (76.8)	95	n.s.
Affective closings				
Mobile	7 (16.7)	35 (83.3)	42	n.s.
Body-to-body	0	5 (100.0)	5	
Landline	5 (55.6)	4 (44.4)	9	n.s.
Total	12 (21.4)	44 (78.6)	56	n.s.

(Continued)

Closing category	Year 2012 BASE=419 MOB=200 BTB=0 LAND=219	Year 2015 BASE=1058 MOB=903 BTB=91 LAND=64	Total BASE=1477 MOB=1103 BTB=91 LAND=283	p<
Temporal forms				
Mobile	7 (25.9)	20 (74.1)	27	n.s.
Body-to-body	0	7 (100.0)	7	
Landline	3 (25.0)	9* (75.0)	12	0.0001
Total	10 (21.7)	36 (78.3)	46	n.s.
Excuse me				
Mobile	0 (0.0)	6 (100.0)	6	n.s.
Body-to-body	0	0 (0.0)	0	
Landline	2 (100.0)	0 (0.0)	2	n.s.
Total	2 (25.0)	6 (75.0)	8	n.s.
Verbal forms				
Mobile	6* (60.0)	4 (40.0)	10	0.01
Body-to-body	0	0 (0.0)	0	
Landline	3 (42.9)	4 (57.1)	7	0.05
Total	9 (52.9)	8 (47.1)	17	0.05

Note: The percentages have been calculated only by row. The asterisks indicate significant standardized residuals.

Table 3.6 shows that only minor changes in conversational closings occurred over our time interval. *Ciao* is one of the few closings showing significant changes with both mobile and landline calls. In the case of mobile calls, between 2012 and 2015, the percentage by column rose from 14.0% to 41.3% (stand. res. = 2.5), and for landline it rose from 11.9% to 43.4% (stand. res. = 4.9). Similarly, the closing *Thanks* showed an increase from 2012 to 2015 for mobile calls (from 1.5% to 7.8%), but a much higher increase for landline calls (from 8.7% to 35.9%, stand. res. = 4.4). For *Temporal forms*, the only significant shift in use between 2012 and 2015 was with landline calls, whose percentage by column grew from 1.4% to 14.1% (stand. res. = 3.8). Finally, use of *Verbal forms* showed a decrease for mobile calls from 2012 to 2015 (from 3.0% to 0.4%, stand. res. = 3.1), but an increase in the case of landline calls (from 1.4% to 6.3%).

Discussion and Closing Remarks

Our study confirmed some common assumptions about the ways in which speakers open and close mobile phone conversations. However, they also added new results, including comparisons with landline and body-to-body conversational openings and closings.

Discussion of the Data

Our first research question asked, "What are the most frequent openings and closings in mobile calls?" Interestingly, the classic mobile phone opening *Where are you?* (Italian "Dove sei?"), which was quite common during the early years of mobile phone diffusion (Cooper et al., 2002; Green, 2002, p. 32; Puro, 2002; Ferraris, 2005),[1] appeared very infrequently in our corpus, being replaced by a variety of more speech-like openings. In earlier mobile phone use, the formulaic *Where are you?* enabled the caller to ascertain where the called interlocutor was in order to infer availability (Goliama, 2011). In the shift from fixed to mobile telephony, use of *Where are you?* as an opening formula was motivated by the fact that mobile communication structurally entails lack of knowledge of the interlocutor's place and context. As Laursen and Szymanski underscore (2013), the person called could talk about location by indicating a specific location or transit status. By contrast, communication using landlines prototypically takes place with interlocutors at known locations (de Sola Pool, 1977), with the exception of calls made from pay phones or someone else's fixed line.

In our corpus, only 1.5% of the mobile calls opened with *Where are you?*. Instead, the most frequent mobile call opening was *Ciao* (33.0%), an opening commonly used in body-to-body conversation. If we add to *Ciao* the macrocategories *Ehi* (17.9%) and *Greeting openings* (e.g., "Good morning") (10.1%), we account for more than half of the openings of mobile calls. Openings of mobile phone conversations are now tending to approximate informal openings in body-to-body communication, replacing the earlier formulaics with landlines and then mobiles.

The use in public spaces of expressions that convey a personalized tone (rather than reliance on traditional formulaics or location requests) is substantiated in our corpus of mobile phone conversation data. The word *Pronto*, which was the classic opening of the landline calls in Italy, was carried over to mobile telephony, appearing in our data as the second most frequent mobile call opening. When we combine use of *Pronto* with the opening *Sono* and *Sì*, which are also part of the opening practices of landline conversations, the openings that transmigrated from landline to mobile total 42.5%, that is, less than half of the total openings. This finding reinforces the notion that traditional telephone formulaics do not combine well with personalization of the mobile phone and its close relationship with the human body.

We turn now to conversational closings. For mobile phone calls, *Ciao* was the most frequent form (36.4%), further confirming the use of expressions that are both personal and informal in mobile calls. Looking at the macrocategory *Bridge closings*, which accounted for 20.1% of mobile phone closings, we see evidence suggesting mobile phone interlocutors feel a need (consciously or unconsciously) to propose continuation of the conversation after the end of the call. Less frequent mobile phone closings included *Thanks, Good wishes,* and *Affective closings.*

Our second research question asked to what degree openings and closings of mobile calls differ from the openings and closings of body-to-body conversations and landline calls. We found significant differences across communication contexts with regard to conversational openings such as *Ciao, Pronto, Ehi, Good wishes, Sono,* and *Sì,* as well as with respect to closings, such as *Ciao, Thanks, Good wishes, Temporal forms,* and *Verbal forms.*

The opening *Ciao* was used more frequently in body-to-body conversations, while *Pronto* was more dominant in landline calls. *Ehi,* along with all openings connected to *Good Wishes,* was used most in body-to-body encounters. The opening *Sono* (I am), along with *Sì* (Yes), was found in landline calls.

Regarding closings, five types—*Ciao, Thanks, Good wishes, Temporal forms,* and *Verbal forms*—were found to differ significantly across conversational venue. The openings *Ciao, Thanks, Good wishes,* and *Temporal forms* were used more in body-to-body conversations than in the other two modalities, while *Verbal forms* appeared more in landline calls. These results suggest that presently there are not openings and closings particularly characteristic of mobile phone conversations, while for landline or body-to-body conversations, such characteristic uses appeared. In the case of body-to-body conversations, there were intimate formulas, while with landline calls, the formulas were more formal.

Our third research question asked what changes have occurred over time regarding use of openings and closings for mobile calls. We also compared these diachronic findings with changes in landline openings and closings over the same period. Comparing data from 2012 and 2015, we found differences in the way conversational openings were used for both mobile and fixed telephony.

As for *mobile phones,* informal and confidential *openings* such as *Ciao* and *Good wishes* show a significant increase over time. (For "Ciao": from 21.5% to 35.5%; for *Good wishes:* from 3.0% to 11.6%). By contrast, during our 3-year interval, the macrocategory *Ehi,* which includes the most intimate and personalized opening formulas, did not show any significant increase (only from 14.0% to 18.8%). This pattern suggests that the process of development of mobile communication is a highly personalized form of interaction, but is not driven only by technological evolution.

Regarding *openings* on *fixed telephones (landlines),* we also note change over time. The traditional fixed telephone opening formula *Sono* grew from 17.3% to 34.4% and *Sì* increased from 1.8% to 31.2%. Considering other openings used with landline phones, use of *Ehi* also increased from 3.6% to 12.5%. These shifts suggest that even the openings in landline telephone today can be characterized as lying somewhere between the language of formality and that of close personal interaction.

We move now to the issue of change over time in conversational closings. Looking first at *closings* of *mobile calls*, we found fewer changes than in the case of openings. Between 2012 and 2015, there was a significant increase in use of *Ciao* as a closing (from 14.0% to 41.3%), suggesting a higher level of personal linguistic closeness for mobile phone closings than for openings. Other diachronic changes in landline closings were less dramatic, such as the increase in use of *Thanks* from 1.5% to 7.7% and decrease in use of *Verbal forms* from 3.0% to 0.4%.

In the case of *closings* used with *landline phones*, the significant changes over the 3-year span involve *Ciao*, *Temporal forms*, *Thanks*, and *Verbal forms*. The closing *Ciao* increased in use from 11.0% to 49.8%, while *Temporal forms* increased only from 1.5% to 10%. These changes appear to indicate that the more personal language of body-to-body communication, which has made its way into mobile communication, has also influenced closings of landline calls. By contrast, the closings *Thanks* and *Verbal forms* decreased from 9.5% to 2.5% and from 1.5% to 0.4%, respectively.

Closing Remarks

While the results of our study are suggestive of longitudinal shifts in conversational openings and closings, the research had several clear limitations. First, our corpus represented a convenience sample, not a random sample. Second, the corpus had many missing data points. Third, the research was limited to conversations conducted in Italy and in Italian. It remains to be seen whether our results will be confirmed with more robust corpora and in different cultural and linguistic contexts.

Nonetheless, the strength of the current study is that it poses the question of how conversation is shaped by physical presence versus mediation (here, by landline or by mobile phones), as well as by the particular form of mediation (that is, landline vs. mobile). Future research will be needed to better track, both synchronically and diachronically, how technology is reshaping communication patterns across a range of sociodemographic variables. Our goal has been to initiate this exploration.

Note

1 There are not, however, country-specific or cross-cultural studies that support this widespread assumption. Furthermore, Weilenmann (2003) found in her Swedish research that the most common opening was "What are you doing?"

References

Altheide, D. L. (1996). *Qualitative media analysis*. Thousand Oaks, CA: Sage.

Anolli, L. (Ed.) (2002). *Psicologia della comunicazione*. Bologna, Italy: Il Mulino.

Baron, N. S. (2008). *Always on: Language in an online and mobile world*. New York: Oxford University Press.

Baron, N. S., & Ling, R. (2007). Text messaging and IM. Linguistic comparison of American college data. *Journal of Language and Social Psychology*, 26(3), 291–298. doi:10.1177/0261927X06303480.

Button, G. (1991). Conversation-in-a-series. In D. Boden & D. H. Zimmerman (Eds.), *Talk and social structure: Studies in ethnomethodology and conversation analysis* (pp. 251–277). Cambridge, UK: Polity Press.

Cooper, G., Green, N., Murtagh, G. M., & Harper, R. (2002). Mobile society? Technology, distance and presence. In S. Woolgar (Ed.), *Virtual society? Technology, cyberbole, reality*. Oxford, UK: Oxford University Press.

Decuypere, M., Masschelein, J., & Simons, M. (2012). 'Where are you?' Cell phones and environmental self-understanding amongst students. *International Journal of Qualitative Studies in Education*, 25(6), 705–722.

de Sola Pool, I. (Ed.). (1977). *The social impact of the telephone*. Cambridge, MA: The MIT Press. doi:10.1080/17450100802095346.

Faulkner, X. & Culwin F. (2005). When fingers do the talking: A study of text messaging. *Interacting with Computers*, 17(2), 167–185. doi:10.1016/j.intcom.2004.11.002.

Ferraris, M. (2005). *Dove sei? Ontologia del telefonino*. Milano, Italy: Bompiani.

Fortunati, L. (Ed.) (1995). *Gli italiani al telefono*. Milano, Italy: Angeli.

Fortunati, L. (2001). *The mobile phone between orality and writing*, in ICUST, 12–14 June, Paris, E-usages. 3rd International Conference on Uses and Services in Telecommunications, Parigi, France Telecom (pp. 312–321).

Fortunati, L., Taipale, S., & de Luca, F. (2013). What did happen to body-to-body sociability? *Social Science Research*, 42(3), 893–905. doi:10.1016/j.ssresearch.2012.12.006.

Goffman, E. (1967). Alienation from interaction. In E. Goffman (Ed.), *Interaction ritual: Essays in body-to-body interaction* (pp. 113–136). Chicago, IL: Aldine.

Goliama, C. M. (2011). *Where are you Africa? Church and society in the mobile phone age*. Bamenda, Camaroon: Langaa Research & Publishing.

Green, N. (2002). Who's watching whom? Monitoring and accountability in mobile relations. In B. Brown, N. Green, & R. Harper (Eds.), *Wireless world: Social and interactional aspects of the middle age* (pp. 32–45). London: Springer.

Hamill, L. & Lasen, A. (Eds.) (2005). *Mobile world: Past, present and future*. New York: Springer.

Houtkoop-Steenstra, H. (1991). Opening sequences in Dutch telephone conversations. In D. Boden & D. H. Zimmerman (Eds.), *Talk and social structure: Studies in ethnomethodology and conversation analysis* (pp. 232–250). Cambridge, UK: Polity Press.

Katz, J. E. & Aakhus, M. (Eds.) (2002). *Perpetual contact: Mobile communication, private talk, public performance*. Cambridge, UK: Cambridge University Press.

Keane, M. (2008, September 29). *Texting overtakes voice in mobile phone usage.* Wired. Retrieved from http://www.wired.com/2008/09/texting-overtak/.

Laufer, P. (1999). *Wireless etiquette: A guide to the changing world of instant communication.* Omnipoint Communications. New York.

Laurier, E. (2001). Why people say where they are doing mobile phone calls. *Environment and Planning D, 19*(4), 485–504.

Laursen, D. & Szymanski, M. H. (2013). Where are you? Location talk in mobile phone conversation. *Mobile Media & Communication, 1*(3), 314–334.

Lindström, A. (1994). Identification and recognition in Swedish telephone conversation openings. *Language in Society, 23*(2), 231–252.

Ling, R., Baron, N. S., Lenhart, A., & Campbell, S. W. (2014). "Girls text really weird": Gender, texting and identity among teens. *Journal of Children and Media, 8*(4), 423–439. doi:10.1080/17482798.2014.931290.

McNeill, P. & Chapman, S. (2005). *Research methods.* Philadelphia, PA: Taylor & Francis.

Pertierra, R., Ugarte, E., Pingol, A., Hernandez, J., & Dacanay, N. L. (2002). *Texting selves: Cellphones and Philippine modernity.* Manila, Philippines: De La Salle University Press.

Plant, S. (2001). On the mobile. The effects of mobile telephones on social and individual life. *Report for Motorola,* p. 30. Retrieved from http://classes.dma.ucla.edu/Winter03/104/docs/splant.pdf.

Puro, J.-P. (2002). Finland: A mobile culture. In J. Katz & M. Aakhus (Eds.), *Perpetual contact* (pp. 19–29).

Rettie, R. (2008). Mobile phones as network capital: Facilitating connections. *Mobilities, 3*(2), 291–311.

Rutter, D. R. (1984). *Looking and seeing. The role of visual communication in social interaction.* Chichester, UK: John Wiley & Sons.

Schegloff, E. A. (1967). *The first five seconds: The order of conversational openings* (Doctoral dissertation). Department of Sociology, University of California, Berkeley, CA.

Schegloff, E. A. (1971). Notes on a conversational practice: Formulating place. In D. Sudnow (Ed.), *Studies in social interaction* (pp. 76–119). New York: Free Press.

Schegloff, E. A. (2002). Beginnings in the telephone. In J. E. Katz & M. Aakhus (Eds.), *Perpetual contact* (pp. 284–300).

Schegloff, E. A. & Sacks, H. (1973). Opening up closings. *Semiotica, VIII*(4), 289–327.

Silverman, D. (Ed.) (1997). *Doing qualitative research: Theory, method, and practice.* London: Sage.

Vincent, J. & Harris, L. (2008). Effective use of mobile communication in E-government: How do we reach the tipping point? *Information, Communication and Society, 11*(3), 395–413.

Weilenmann, A. (2003). "I can't talk now, I'm in a fitting room": Formulating availability and location in mobile-phone conversations. *Environment and Planning A, 35*(9), 1589–1605.

4 Visual Interpersonal Communication in Daily Life

Skype as a Precursor of Perpetual Visual Contact[1]

James E. Katz and Elizabeth Thomas Crocker

When Skype began in 2003, it was hailed as a revolutionary way to connect and communicate. Built upon the peer-to-peer technology of the file-sharing network Kazaa, Skype users could download the program and connect via VoIP in order to hold free phone and video calls over the internet. This allowed users to bypass costly long-distance phone charges and chat with people all over the world about everything from important business contracts to how their local sports team was faring. Skype's creator Niklas Zennström argued that Skype was the phone of the future and many agreed ("How Skype and Kazaa," 2005). But the concept for Skype was not a new one, and in fact, video calls had been tried before. So, why did Skype take off when others didn't? How did free video calls change the way we interact, communicate, and engage with the people and world around us?

One way to consider these questions is from a media ecology perspective. While this term means different things to various scholars, we take a broad perspective wherein technology offers (and limits) possibilities, but humans in relationship to others make choices from among them, often embracing, resisting, and reinterpreting and repurposing them. Their initial choices cascade across social practices and affect the direction of technological options, and these in turn subsequently affect the next round of social practice and technological development. The analogy of a cafeteria is apt: people can choose what they wish to consume from among options, but the options are not unlimited. Likewise, previous choices made earlier in the cafeteria line limit and affect subsequent choices.

It follows that media ecologies affect user choices in both strong and weak ways. In terms of strong ways, the mere physical limits of what can be done by any technology extant at a given time means that certain wishes of the users cannot be fulfilled, no matter how passionately held that desire may be. For example, if in the year 2016, someone in the US and wanted to travel physically in order to be with a person for a face-to-face conversation in Portugal, and accomplish this within, say, 30 seconds, there is no technology available to do this. The US-based person would simply be out of luck. The extant media ecology prevents one in the US from having near instantaneous physical face-to-face conversation with another person in Portugal. On the other hand, there is a contemporary media ecology system—that includes the technological infrastructure, commercial and regulatory regimes, and social practices—which would allow one in the US to have instantaneous face-to-face conversation with somebody in Portugal, providing the US-based person would be willing to accept that this is to be done in a virtual way. Of course, if, in the year 1816, a US-based person wanted to have a physical and immediate face-to-face conversation with someone in Portugal, the US-based person would again be out of luck.

This exceedingly simple example provides an illustration of the grounding of an analysis within a media ecology context from a "strong" perspective. But of course media ecology goes more deeply than this and looks at the methods people decide about using various technologies, and here questions of cost, convenience, social meaning, and degree of relationships (*inter alia*) all affect the usages and configurations of communication technology. This is the deeper and more complex meaning of the way media ecologies "weakly" affect user behavior, as opposed to the "strong" ways that are derived from the physical capabilities and limits of the communication systems technologies extant at any given time.

These strong and weak influences are especially notable in interpersonal communication relationships and have both intended and unintended (and often difficult to observe) consequences, as we seek to outline below.

A Brief History of Video Chatting

The history of video chatting, at least until the 1980s, is mostly a history of human imagination. Since the late 1800s, futuristic worlds would sometimes depict interpersonal video communication. An illustrator for *Punch*, George du Maurier (1834–1896), imagined transcontinental speaking tubes with two-way HDTV that would allow parents in their English mansion's bedroom to chat casually with their children in Ceylon (now Sri Lanka) (Videophone, 2016). Lithographer Albert Robida (1848–1926) illustrated in detail how the idea for the *telephonoscope* would become a central feature of every home. The telephonoscope would project images on a thin crystal screen and provide sound through speakers all transmitted via a telephone cord. The *telephonoscope* could show theater performances, allow virtual shopping, and transmit telephone conversations accompanied by visual images of the person on the other end (Willems, 1999). In 1911, inventor-writer Hugo Gernsback (1884–1967) introduced in *Ralph 124C 41+* the *telephoto*, which not only allowed users to see the person they were speaking to but smell them as well (Westfahl, 1996). Numerous other science fiction writers followed suit and added variations of video calls to their visions of the future.

Despite their fecund imagination, the realization of the dream of these visionaries, due to technological limitations, had to wait until 1936 to see the idea instantiated by the Germans. In that year, the first public telephone-video conference system opened by the Nazi-run *Reichspost* and operated between Berlin and Leipzig. With the outbreak of World War II, development was discontinued, but resumed in several countries in the postwar period (Videophone, 2016).

Yet, these point-to-point conferencing systems do not get at our interests in *interpersonal* video communication, that is, between two people who have control in their local environments over their own systems, which will be the focus of the rest of our discussion. This person-to-person format was demonstrated on a trial basis on numerous occasions, including in 1964 when the American Telephone and Telegraph Company (AT&T) made these historical visions of person-to-person video communication a reality. Making its inaugural call from Illinois to none other than First Lady Ladybird Johnson in Washington, DC, AT&T unveiled the PicturePhone in 1964. Subsequently in that same year, AT&T demonstrated the technology at the New York World's Fair. There the PicturePhone booth was a popular attraction. Spectators were eager to try out the PicturePhone and lined up to speak with users at Disneyland, visible on a small screen. Hugo Gernsback was impressed. He predicted that the PicturePhone would result in, "No more inadequate streets, overcrowded stores, impossible traffic," even though initial market testing suggested users were less convinced (Lipartito, 2013).

As part of the promotional effort, the PicturePhone was installed in some offices of the US's White House during the late Johnson and into the Nixon administrations. According to A. Michael Noll, who supervised an analysis of the program for Bell Labs, the most frequent use of the PicturePhone was in the "self-view" mode (personal communication). Though this finding spoke to the failure of technology as form of interpersonal communication, it also adumbrated the later enthusiastic embrace of the selfie as a global phenomenon (Katz & Crocker, 2015).

Nonetheless, despite these early concerns, Bell Laboratories pursued the technology. The company installed booths in major US cities in 1964 and released units to the public for home use in 1970. Advertisements promised users would "be a star" and it would bring families together. PicturePhone would finally let people adopt technology that science fiction writers and the public had been fantasizing about for almost 100 years.

Yet, after millions of dollars in development, production, and advertising, the PicturePhone was a commercial flop (Lipartito, 2003). In the first 6 months after installation, the PicturePhone booths had only seventy-one patrons. They were charged 16 to 27 dollars per minute, making even short phone calls cost prohibitive (Videophone, 2016). In addition to cost, researchers such as A. Michael Noll (1992) concluded that PicturePhone was too personal, highly invasive for some users, and provided little to no benefit over a regular phone call. Others argue that PicturePhone was clunky, heavy, black and white, and to function required that both parties own one. By 1978, the only PicturePhones that remained were in Bell Labs. Even those didn't last long. Subsequent attempts to revivify the service with new models, costing over $1,500 each, failed. Interpersonal video calls were dead, but only for a while.

Pioneered by web-based internet cameras, video chatting over technology such as Skype has grown to become incredibly popular. By 2013, more than 300 million people used Skype worldwide completing more than 2 trillion minutes of voice and video calls ("Skype Celebrates a Decade," 2013). These statistics reveal just how popular the medium is. In fact, two-way visual conversations are fast becoming not only routine but, in some cases, a predominant way of life as well. To get a better understanding of how young adults utilize Skype, we conducted surveys with students in New England.

Skype Users Today

In March 2014, we invited an undergraduate class of communication research students at Boston University to participate in an omnibus online opinion survey about new communication technology. Foci of the survey included uses of the selfie and Snapchat for interpersonal communication. There were 123 students who began the survey; from this number, 117 usable questionnaires were generated. The respondents' ages ranged from 18 to 24, with a median age of 21. In terms of gender, 19% of the survey respondents were male, and the balance identified themselves as females (no one indicated "other"). We also conducted interviews with twenty-two people utilizing a snowball method. This allowed us to gather in-depth insight into the demographic we surveyed as well as a variety of other backgrounds, such as working parents in New England, American graduate students studying abroad, college students at other universities, and an elderly woman and a teacher living in the southern US. This range of interviewee experiences and demographic backgrounds allowed us to examine whether the survey data were reflected in larger patterns of use and expanded our analysis beyond just New England college students.

All but two of our survey respondents, who were female, had used Skype at least once. In the past month, 65% had Skyped at least once. Of these, 55% said that they thought Skype was more personal than a phone call, but only 17% said they preferred Skype over a phone call. Only six people indicated they sometimes preferred to Skype rather than meet in person. However, 73% agreed or strongly agreed that Skype was more personal than text-based communications such as email and text messages. With the additional input from interviews, we concluded that phone calls were often viewed as easier, simpler, and quicker than a Skype call. Skype also required more attention to the communicative partner, while a phone call allowed people to conduct additional tasks such as cleaning, browsing the internet, or walking. It was this factor, though, that was part of why Skype was more personal—not only do people get to see the person(s) they are speaking with, but it also requires a fair amount of personal attention and focus that other mediums do not. Yet, it is clear that Skype does not replace face-to-face communication entirely.

This same demographic of undergraduates indicated most (84%) used Skype to stay in touch with people who lived in other places. Additionally, 84% agreed or strongly agreed that Skype was a good way to communicate with family, while 81% said it was a good way to communicate with friends. Interestingly, only five people said they liked to Skype with new people and only nineteen said it was a good way to get to know someone. Based upon our qualitative interview data, we argue this is linked to the personal aspect of Skype communications. New acquaintances go through a series of mediated interactions before the relationship is established enough for the personal nature of a Skype conversation. First, people may communicate privately, but via a public profile such as Facebook, then transition to text messaging and chatting with platforms linked to personal emails, and not until that dynamic is established do they meet in person. Skype, more often than not, was explained as a medium for maintaining existing relationships that had already developed into or began as face-to-face interactions. As we will show later, this makes sense, considering some of the novel ways that communicative events play out over Skype.

Skype has been used for many of the predicted and expected uses of video-mediated conversations, such as enhanced phone calls, keeping in touch with family, business meetings, remote teaching, interviews, and the like. These are important to understand as the use of video-mediated conversations increases. However, we were particularly interested in the more creative and novel ways that Skype was integrated into people's lived experiences. These aspects reflect emerging practices that speak to the ways in which video-mediated conversations are unique, rather than simply illuminating existing practices. They may predict ways the medium can evolve in the future. In particular, we look at virtual cohabitation, virtual accompaniment, and new interactants.

Virtual Cohabitation: "Hanging Out" over Skype

Virtual cohabitation references the manner in which some Skype users have begun using the platform as a way to maintain an open window into the life of a friend or loved one. Conversants often referred to this as "hanging out" over Skype. According to interviews, typical Skype conversations usually involved the parties planning a specific time to call, being present in front of the screen during the entire conversation, and actively participating in a conversation until the call ended. In contrast, "hanging out" meant conversants would call and while they often did initially have a conversation, the line was left open as they then proceeded to do other things that may not involve active participation in a conversation or even looking at and engaging with the screen. The Skype call became a window that linked two geographically separate spaces, allowing users to interact similar to the way they might if they were "hanging out" in the same physical space.

> Of our undergraduate survey respondents, 35% said they like to use Skype to hang out with someone and 32% said they would often leave Skype sessions open while doing other things. While this does not encapsulate the entire Skype user base it does suggest a significant portion of Skype users are engaging in this form of interaction. Over half of our survey respondents said that they felt closer to someone after Skyping with them. Given this coupled with our previous point that Skype is primarily used to maintain existing relationships, we argue that it can be a powerful tool for allowing people to share lives in the mundane everyday along with the more exciting eventful moments. In our interviews, we found a few different ways that this manifested and it is worth exploring case examples in order to see how virtual cohabitation is impacting people's communication forms and relationships.

One of the most interesting examples was a couple in a long-distance relationship who used Skype to maintain closeness. She lived in Texas and he in New Mexico, but both frequently travel. Due to work and financial limitations, they were only able to meet up in person about once a month. However, they Skyped daily and often through the night so that they each felt they shared a life together despite the distance. A typical day began by waking up next to their laptop, which was still logged into a Skype call that began the night before with their significant other. She explained,

> It feels normal and it just becomes a habit in your life. It started happening because we would be chatting until very, very late in the night. And I would be like, "I'm tired. I'm going to put my head down." Or he'd be like, "I'm tired and I'm going to put my head down. But I'm just going to leave this open for a while." And so we did that and at one point we fell asleep and accidentally left Skype on all night. And then woke up together. And it was really, really nice. Like, "Good morning!" Which is weird because he was in New Mexico and I was in China… So we did that and it was an accident. And it ended up just kind of being nice to see a face in the morning, you know?

After the initial discovery that waking up together over Skype was pleasant, they began doing it most nights. She said that the interaction provided consistency, which was important for maintaining a long-distance relationship, stating, "I think for him and to me too it does mean a lot to have that regularity. Because it is very regular. It's predictable. It's almost like it's kind of like getting to sleep in the same bed and waking up next to them except not having them physically there. But having their presence there." This last point—that Skyping provided a way to be present without being physically present—was one we found particularly interesting for understanding the pull to create open channels.

Once both parties were awake, they would take their laptops with them as they began their morning routines. "He'll get up, get ready for work, and actually sometimes while I'm still asleep and he's getting ready for work he'll just carry the laptop around the house with him. So he'll bring the laptop in the kitchen and pack his lunch and then he'll bring the laptop in the bathroom and take a shower. And just kind of have me there just on the laptop." They involved one another in the most mundane of daily activities, even bringing the laptop into the bathroom when they had to urinate. Though they did periodically do date nights where they focused on a more purposeful and romantic approach to Skyping, she was clear that the day-to-day activities were not afterthoughts but rather vital to the maintenance of their relationship. "The morning stuff and the falling asleep waking up together stuff is the critical thing for the both of us. It is kind of the most important activity on Skype."

They also engaged in mutual activities over Skype, such as cooking. She explained that a typical cooking night often began with him calling to see what they should cook and figuring out which ingredients they should each pick up from the store. Then when they get home they would cook together. "He'll call me on Skype. And I'll just put the computer facing the sink and the oven and I'll just start cooking and he'll start cooking." She is a more advanced cook than he is, so in the beginning she provided lessons for how to cook basic dishes. Later, as his skills progressed, she was there to support and guide him as he tried to do it independently. "For him cooking is an area of self-improvement that he really feels he needs help with. He feels like I'm good at it, so I'm there to play cheerleader for him while he experiments with doing it on his own." Other mutual activities included drawing together, watching television, and hanging out with a third party such as a roommate. In all of these instances, Skype provided a way to link two geographically separate spaces into one shared space so that they were not each engaging in activities separately but felt they were doing them together. They stopped seeing the computer screen as a marker of their spatial divide but rather a window that could connect.

[Skype] sort of kept us together for the whole first year of college.

Another woman that we interviewed described a romantic relationship she maintained while she was an undergraduate in New York and her boyfriend attended university in Florida. In order to maintain the long-distance relationship, she told us, "We communicated primarily through Skype and texting. And that was very important. It sort of kept us together for the whole first year of college." They did speak on the phone, but she said that phone calls made her more nervous than a Skype conversation. She said, "It's something about hearing someone's voice and hearing their words but not being able to see their facial expression or to read any of those cues," that made phone calls uncomfortable and Skype preferable. However, Skype also allowed the ability to simply leave the program open so that she and her boyfriend could hang out together. The ability to see the person as well as their world around them brought them together despite the distance. She explained, "it gives you a sense that they're there. I mean it's not the same, but it does bring you a lot closer than any other media I've found." At one point during their relationship, she became ill and found Skype to be a helpful way to cope with being bedbound. "I was probably on Skype with him for like five hours. We were doing our own things, you know I was sick in bed and I was just lonely, and it was my first semester at college, so it was really comforting to have that sort of feeling as though someone was there with me, in that moment, even though we were doing different things." The ability to have Skype open meant he could be there for her during her time of need, the way that he would have if they lived closer.

She also made an important point that phone calls emphasize the need to interact during the entirety of the call. If one party is not speaking, then there is just silence. Yet, few people have the ability to have an active phone conversation for hours and hours every day. Skype, however, allows one to still be present and part of the interaction even while not speaking. Long-distance relationships are often hurt by not just the lack of communication, but the lack of shared experiences and day-to-day life. The medium lends itself to allowing users to leave channels open, so that they can do other activities and still be present.

For example, the young woman and her boyfriend often did homework with Skype open on their computers. "I mean, when you're in college, it's a very busy life, so it's hard to… especially if you're dating someone, it's hard to take all those hours in a day and just talk to each other when you just can't be wasting that time, so it's sort of a way to compromise on the romantic aspect of your life and your obligations academically." They would periodically make small comments, ask one another questions, and chat in the manner she would if they lived in the same city and she invited him over to hang out and do homework. The platform allowed them to be present together and share experiences through video mediation.

They would Skype all the time. Literally always Skyping.

Another interviewee relayed the story of her best friend and her ex-boyfriend, who were only able to get together physically every couple of weeks, so they also used Skype to maintain their relationship. "And they would Skype all the time. Literally always Skyping. And when I say literally I do actually mean literally. They would turn Skype on before bed and chat with her partner and then they would just leave it on. They would just leave Skype on all night when they went to bed. And they would have the computers running, Skyping in the dark room!" Her roommate often slept through her alarm, so our interviewee had the job of waking her up for classes. "So I would come wake her up and I would end up waking [the boyfriend] up too on the other line of Skype. And he would go, 'What the hell! Close the blinds!' And it was miles and miles and miles away. But the light in her room wakes him up." This was perhaps the most extreme version of cohabitation via Skype that we found, though it is important to recognize that since it is coming from a third party, it may not reflect how the couple felt about time spent Skyping. However, it is illuminating to consider how other people in their lives felt about the relationship and constant Skype use. The interviewee said of the couple, "I think [the boyfriend] was really clingy and just wanted to be with her. And she loved it for sure. She definitely—it was not one sided. She thought it was the sweetest thing." She felt that this type of relationship was not something she personally would desire, but it made her friend happy so she had supported it.

Other interviews revealed that people would at times also open up Skype to hang out with friends and family to watch a movie or television show together, play a game, or just chat as they did chores. However, it was clear that the use of Skype to hang out regularly and for extended periods was done primarily by people in romantic relationships and it is this we are referring to as virtual cohabitation (though it is feasible that close friends, siblings, and other kinds of relationships could lend themselves to virtual cohabitation as well). This is different from relationships that are maintained by each party visiting a third space such as a video game or simulator. Virtual reality is two or more parties traveling to a new virtual space; this is two or more parties using virtual windows to link existing but geographically separate spaces into one temporary space. Rather than escaping reality to cohabitate in another virtual realm, parties are linking realities to cohabitate in the spaces where they live the everyday. This interaction maintained and even strengthened romantic relationships in a way that grounded them in the intimacy of the mundane.

Virtual Caregiving

However, we did find another form of virtual cohabitation that is perhaps better described as virtual caregiving. Virtual monitoring of children, such as with baby monitors, is quite common. By utilizing Skype, grandparents could be brought in to not only monitor children's activities but also actively engage with them as caregivers. For example, one grandmother living in Italy babysat her 4-month-old grandchild over Skype while the parents were briefly not present. "I was so worried that the kid would wander off to another part of the apartment, and there would be nothing I could do about it. But he was very good, but it took all my wits to try to keep him entertained while his father was onto the flat. I told him stories, asked him questions, and tried to play guessing games. Fortunately nothing happened."

Another interviewee spoke about how her children's grandmother helps out by babysitting from China via Skype. "She watches them in the living room while the daughter is cooking dinner in the kitchen. Then if the grandmother sees something that is of concern, she yells out through Skype. Her daughter turns around and intervenes with whatever is going on with the kids in the living room." This format allows the grandmother to entertain and care for the children with a parent physically present nearby available to intervene if needed.

These examples differ from merely having a scheduled conversation with grandma because the grandmothers are actively caring for the children over Skype and utilize the program to be with the children as they play. In this sense, it is similar to hanging out that couples do, only the adult is required to actively monitor, while the children move about the space. The stationary aspect of the virtual window Skype creates is obviously limited when dealing with small children, who will run into another room without taking the laptop along. However, it still provides an avenue for long-distance grandparenting and we can imagine that many grandparents would be interested in the opportunity to spend extended time virtually caregiving and hanging out with grandchildren who live far away.

Virtual Accompaniment

The second pattern we identified was virtual accompaniment, by which we mean utilizing Skype on a mobile device so that participants can travel virtually with one of the users, experiencing not only their presence but also the experience of that space on the other end of the call. Though everyone we spoke to at least periodically engaged in Skype conversations while seated in front of the computer, a number of interviewees indicated they greatly enjoyed the ability to go with their conversational correspondents as they went out into the world.

One case study example was a father who had been born in Ireland but was currently working and living in Boston, MA. His family members were all still back home. To ensure the grandparents could stay in touch with his young son, they would frequently Skype. Normally, this happened at home in front of a desktop, but he relayed a recent instance where they tried virtual accompaniment. "The most recent Skype conversation I actually had was in the car driving home from a Red Sox game (I was not driving while Skyping by the way!) They [his parents back in Ireland] came through and we tried it to see if it works and we Skyped with them talking to my son in the back of the car." As grandparents, they were excited to not only hear about their relatives' lives overseas but also engage with it virtually. "Seeing scenes from our daily life is very meaningful to them. If it's through Skype as well. 'Oh they are on the street where we go for coffee.' That's more interesting to them in some ways than any tourism stuff. So I think they really enjoy sort of feeling as though they were part of the outing. And not just the pre-planned somewhat artificial setting of sitting at the computer." Seated in their homes in Ireland, his parents were able to travel with their son and grandson through the streets of Boston.

In another example, a 90-year-old woman spoke about why she prefers Skype over other forms of communication. "Skype is a lot more personal than any of the others because you can see the expressions on their faces and things like that. You can see them get up, move around, they can go get something to show you. What they've been working on. Maybe they made something new and they can hold it up. Just that kind of thing you can't do on Facebook or telephone or anything else." For her, the compelling aspect of Skype was not just its ability to provide video-mediated communication but the ability to utilize it as a way to virtually travel to and with the correspondent. Given her age, she was unable to fly or drive to see many of her children and grandchildren, but Skype provided a way to still engage with their lives. For example, she told us about how "Toinette [her daughter] will bring her poodle in for me to see her new haircut or whatever. It's really nice. I can go out in the yard with her. She's got a portable computer she can carry out on the porch and show me her flowers and all that stuff too. It really is almost like being in the room with them and that's what I really like. It is much more personal than any of the others." Virtual accompaniment allows her to be with her daughter and experience her world despite distance and physical disability.

Skype provides a way for conversants separated geographically to tour the same space and travel together. Another interviewee described how she used Skype on a mobile device to give her friend a tour of their new apartment. "So my other friend who was here and I Skyped [her friend] in Sweden and brought her around the new house and like showed her all the rooms, showed her our rooms, showed her the balcony where everyone goes to smoke." This Skype interaction not only brought a distant conversational partner into the space to travel with her friend, but it also allowed her to engage with the people in that space. The interviewee used Skype to bring her friend to her roommates as well, "and sort of like popped in on people and showed Lisa their faces and they waved and said, 'Oh hi! Miss you! This is my room! Can't wait until you're back!' And yeah so she got to see the layout of the house and got to see where everyone was living and what they were doing and their rooms. And she got to see how dirty it was which made her not want to move in." The ability to bring someone from another continent around with you and have them interact with individuals within your space is quite interesting for thinking about how we engage with space, place, and being in the world.

Virtual accompaniment showed up in other interviews as well. While it was rarely a frequent scheduled activity, people spoke about it as an exciting and fun way to utilize the technology. Virtual tours of famous museums, tourist sites, houses, and natural spaces have existed for some time. However, utilizing Skype creates a slightly different dynamic. Most virtual tours are recorded ahead of time so that individuals accessing them do so anonymously and asynchronously. Skype personalizes the experience by creating a synchronous interaction that is typically conducted by people who already have an established relationship. The realities of utilizing mobile devices mean that the camera is often held around face height and jostles along with the steps of the person holding it. This provides an experience that feels much more authentic to the experience of being there and walking the space with the person on the other end of the line. Conversants can request the camera holder turn to reveal a new scene, interact with the environment at the other end, and describe what their experiences are with that space. Thus, we argue that it really is a virtual form of accompaniment where participants feel as though they are actively traveling with the person at the other end and are able to engage with the same spaces and people.

New Interactants in Skype Conversations

Lastly, we found that video-mediated communications allowed new interactants that other forms of communication did not. Text- and audio-based communications do not allow people to interact with participants that cannot speak or type. Video, however, captures other communicative signals that do allow for interacting without text or speech. To this end, some interviewees suggested they used Skype to not only call friends and family but also interact with some interesting parties such as pets, babies, and even spaces. This medium seems to open up interactant possibilities in exciting and interesting ways.

One person we interviewed told us about how a former classmate had dropped out of college to become a lifeguard in Miami. She and her friends in New England often enjoyed Skyping with him, not just to stay in touch but because they also wanted to experience the beach, especially when local weather is unpleasant. "And we are up here in Massachusetts where it is freezing still and it's May and it's still 45 degrees and we had snow in April. So Skyping with him is this whole thing because it's like going to the beach. 'Oh we're going to Skype Carter! He's probably on the beach drinking a margarita right now.'" They at times asked him to turn the camera from his face to the view from his balcony. "When we Skype him yeah he has this beautiful view of the Florida sunset or whatever awesome thing he's look at... And it's gorgeous. So that's an experience for us." Though the former classmate was an important interactant, just as important was the warm beach he lived near. The desire to interact with a space and not just the people within that space is an interesting development of the technology. People can, of course, watch webcams set up in popular spaces, but they cannot control the camera and the feed is available to everyone. Skyping with spaces still utilizes the person who answered the call, who is then able to move the camera as requested. The feed is also personal and, in addition to being personalized, since only the people on the call can see the images, creates a kind of intimacy with the landscape.

However, it was the interactions with living but non-speaking entities that we found particularly interesting. Pets were a common interactant choice since animals can rarely engage on the phone, but video allows users the ability to see the pet and gauge responses to the pet seeing and hearing them. For example, a college student told us how she Skypes with her family back home, not only to speak to them but also to see her family pets. "Sometimes I'll just ask my sister to bring the cat or bring the dog when we Skype. 'Come and show me my pets! I miss them! I haven't seen them in too long.'" Her sister will bring the animals to the screen, so she can see and speak with them. "So I'm not just talking to her. It is not just a phone call for information and catching up and making sure everything is ok at home. It's I want to pet my cat. I miss my dog. Please show them to me!" In fact, her sister sometimes became frustrated at her desire to speak with the animals over her family. "Sometimes my sister gets annoyed, 'Come on! They don't understand. Talk to me! I actually understand you and your words. Stop cooing to the cat!'" Her sister makes an interesting point about the value of speaking to someone who cannot understand you and likely will not respond. Most of our interviewees were ambivalent about whether or not their pets understood it was them on the screen and whether they responded to their calls. Anecdotally, the author attempted to Skype with her cats, but they seemed entirely uninterested. However, another interviewee said that she routinely included family cats Chloe and Charlie in their Skype interactions. "Chloe responds to hearing her name being called in a distinctive high pitched form, 'collapses', rubs herself against my daughters laptop, purrs and even dribbles." Still, even though some pets do respond positively to Skype video calls, it did not seem to be a requirement for the humans engaging to enjoy it.

Another interactant category that cannot fully understand or respond verbally was that of young infants. Once children become older,

Skype appears to be a mutually enjoyable interaction medium for family to stay in touch with grandchildren, nieces and nephews, and so on. However, newborns cannot see well nor can they understand language, so it is doubtful they get much out of a Skype conversation. Like the pets, the person who initiates the interaction receives significantly more gratification from the conversation. Though a few different interviewees mentioned infants, perhaps the most in-depth case study example we can provide also comes from one of the authors who is the mother of an infant.

> Soon after coming home from the hospital, my in-laws insisted we Skype so they could meet the baby. They live in Alabama and we in Massachusetts so it would be a while before they could meet in person. We set up on the couch placing the laptop on the coffee table and the baby in my lap. My in-laws crowded around their desktop in their home office and my mother-in-law squealed with joy at seeing her newest grandchild. My father-in-law, brothers-in-law, nieces, and nephew all took turns saying hello and commenting on how adorable the baby was while my child sat and looked vaguely in the direction of the screen. My mother-in-law was convinced my daughter saw them and was responding and more than once said, "She's looking! The little princess sees us!" However, I am somewhat doubtful that she was really aware of the Skype call at the time beyond noticing some moving blobs and sounds coming from a particular direction. Yet, like people who Skype with non-participatory pets, that did not seem to dissuade my in-laws from enjoying the interaction.

These forms of interacting with non-traditional conversants in face-to-face conditions have been explored by academics such as Deborah Tannen (2004). She notes that humans often utilize non-speaking family members as a particular discursive strategy. They can "ventriloquize," which is when someone speaks for the pet or baby often in a high pitched tone or baby talk. This allows individuals the ability to frame, shift, and express ideas in a manner that softens the impact by speaking through the infant or pet. It can be a highly effective way to buffer criticism, insert humor, gently reprimand, discuss sensitive subjects, or remind those present who constitutes family. The mediating effect of speaking to others through babies and animals can be a powerful buffer that aids conversation and lubricates social situations. However, many of our interviewees and the experience of the author did not include this type of conversation, despite having experienced it in face-to-face interactions with the same pets and babies. This is not to say that it never happens, but, as our interviewee's sister's comments suggest, quite often the human on the other end of the call is left out of the conversation and that includes their ability to ventriloquize. Instead, conversation is still often high-pitched baby talk, but it is directed solely at the new interactant and this may be a particularly interesting line of inquiry for linguistic anthropologists.

Conclusion

Cohabitation, virtual accompaniment, and new interactants suggest fascinating ways that Skype is not only reproducing existing forms of communication but potentially creating new ones. However, it is important that we recognize there are also concerns and limitations regarding Skype use, despite its popularity. In our interviews, 20 people indicated that they also saw Skype conversations as more burdensome than phone calls because of the requirement to be present and active in the conversation. For example, one college student said, "I need to be doing something with my hands. So a lot of the time yeah I'm doing multiple tasks while I'm on the phone or while I'm Skyping. Although with Skype since it is the computer I feel like I'm forced to sit in front of it." With her partner, they have come to an understanding that she simply cannot sit still in front of the computer and is easily distracted. She often cooks or cleans while chatting with him, though sometimes she gets carried away. "Or if I'm gone for five minutes he'll be like, 'Oh she probably forgot that she was cleaning and now she's cleaning and forgot she was in the middle of the Skype.'" However, disappearing during a Skype conversation would be considered rude and much less accepted by people who do not know her as well. Her need to constantly fiddle with things or engage in additional activities like puzzles, cleaning, or texting would also be seen as rude by many Skype users. One solution to this is to Skype without video; however, if only one user turns off their video feed, many interviewees suggested this created an unfair and uncomfortable dynamic. The ability to judge the other person's reactions and interest is enjoyable when it is mutual but seems to be distressing when it is not.

Despite these and other limitations, Skype and programs like it are still widely used and highly popular. While our survey respondents were from a very limited sample group and our snowball method of gathering interview participants certainly does not reflect the usage and attitudes of everyone using Skype, they do reveal some interesting new communicative aspects worth exploring further. It seems clear that technology like Skype and emerging mobile ecologies can be a powerful way to strengthen relationships and interactions. Despite frequent doomsday claims that online interactions and contemporary technology are making us lonelier and less connected, we found quite the opposite. Families, significant others, and friends are increasingly spread apart geographically, but modern technology is giving us the power to stitch those relationships back together. Free and low-cost programs like Skype allow people to travel for jobs, education, and better lifestyle opportunities, but still maintain their relationships in meaningful ways. If technology did create geographic and psychological distancing, then technology is also providing ways to solve it. We can envision a future where hotels and apartments provide large high quality screens and cameras that allow individuals to be with one another virtually, accompany them to new places, and interact with distant spaces and non-speaking beings, with the added convenience of turning it off when we desire privacy and quiet. Such technology makes the world smaller in the sense that it allows us to be in Shanghai while sitting in Paris, but it also makes the world larger in that we can discover so many new people, places, and things through our virtual connected windows. While we will not likely see Gernsback's fantasy of a world without traffic, faulty streets, and crowded stores, the technology does provide a way for people to avoid them and still engage meaningfully with the people and world around them.

Turning back to our opening discussion of the media ecology perspective writ large, we have offered an example of it in an interpersonal visual communication context, especially among those who are (or who want to be) in an emotionally grounded relationship. We noted that although two-way, real-time, conversational interaction was imagined soon after the telegraph was invented, the state of electronics technology was not mature enough to make this possible. But beyond the plausibility of such interaction, early market analyses and experience of visual communication at a distance, such as the PicturePhone provided, indicated that there would be very little interest in such services. However, recent history has proven the prescience of early artistic imagination over later detailed market analysis. In fact, two-way visual conversations are fast becoming not only routine but, in some cases, a predominant way of life in certain ecological niches.

The advent of small, relatively inexpensive digital photographing and video-chatting technologies, coupled with widespread and cheap mobile data coverage, has allowed these mobile technologies to become part of our everyday. Cell phones, wearables, laptops, and tablets are embedded into our lived experiences of place and self. They become not just tools but also extensions of self, changing ideas about presence, participation, and engagement. The self can connect and travel digitally through new mobile geographies that collapse and extend ideas about place and being in the world. All this gives rise to new interactional regimes and senses of self-regard, providing a launching site for yet new innovations in the dance of technologically equipped people with one another.

Note

1 This is a revised version of a paper that was earlier published as Katz and Crocker (2015).

References

Katz, J. E. & Crocker, E. T. (2015). Selfies and photo messaging as visual conversation: Reports from the U.S., U.K., and China. *International Journal of Communication*, *9*, 1861–1872. Retrieved from http://ijoc.org/index.php/ijoc/article/view/3180/1405. Accessed 15 November, 2016.

Katz, J. E. & Crocker, E. T. (2015). Skype in daily life: General patterns, emerging uses, and concerns. In: Carvalheiro, Ricardo & Serrano Tellería, Ana (Eds.). *Mobile and Digital Communication: Approaches to Public and Private* (pp. 5–23). Covilhã, Portugal: LabCom Books.

Lipartito, K. (2003). PicturePhone and the information age: The social meaning of failure. *Technology and Culture*, *44*(1), 50–81.

Noll, A. M. (1992). Anatomy of a failure: PicturePhone revisited. *Telecommunications Policy*, *16*(4), 307–316.

Staff. (2005, June 17). How Skype and Kazaa changed the net. [BBC News]. Retrieved from http://news.bbc.co.uk. Accessed 15 November, 2016.

Steele, E. (2013, August 28). Skype celebrates a decade of meaningful conversations! Retrieved from http://blogs.skype.com. February 2, 2015.

Tannen, D. (2004). Talking the dog: Framing pets as interactional resources in family discourse. *Research on Language and Social Interaction*, *37*(4), 399–420.

Videophone. (2016). Wikipedia entry. Retrieved from https://en.wikipedia.org/wiki/Videophone. May 15, 2016.

Westfahl, G. (1996). Evolution of modern science fiction: The textual history of Hugo Gernsback's "Ralph 124C 41+." *Science Fiction Studies*, *23*(1), 37–82.

Willems, P. (1999). A stereoscopic vision of the future: Albert Robida's Twentieth Century. *Science Fiction Studies*, *26*(3), 354–378.

5 Of Owned, Shared, and Public Access ICT

Constructs of Privacy and Publicness in Marginal Spaces

Cheryll Ruth R. Soriano
and Ruepert Jiel Cao

There has been limited sustained attention paid to the concepts of public and private in the use of information and communication technologies (ICT), especially in the context of marginalized communities in the 'Global South'. Producing intimacies and constructing privacy have been previously understood to be a major driver for the purchase and use of particular ICTs, such as mobile devices (Horst & Miller, 2006; Rangaswamy & Singh, 2009; Casado & Lasen, 2014; Fairfield & Engle, 2015). Yet, more recent studies have also drawn attention toward the use of ICTs for collective purposes (Sreekumar, 2011; Larghi, Aguerre, Calamari, Fontecoba, Mogullansky, Orchuela, Ponce de Leon, 2015, p. 210; Sreekumar & Rivera-Sanchez, 2016) and the routine transgressions of private and public in everyday ICT use (Barnes, 2006; Lange, 2007; West, Lewis, & Currie, 2009). This chapter explores how privacy and publicness in ICT use are negotiated by sociotechnical practices influenced by social, economic, and spatial conditions in marginal contexts. As emphasized in previous studies, there is a need to examine the sociocultural dimensions of ICT use in the political and the economic contexts (Goggin, 2006; Gilbert, 2010; Sreekumar, 2011), and it is imperative to systematically explore local and international cultures of ICT use to comprehend complex and evolving multidimensions of culture (Arora, 2010; Hjorth, 2011). The nature of ICT appropriation and experience, as well as perceptions of privacy in low-income urban communities, represent the interplay of technological and social capital embedded in place. Urban slums offer a rich site for analyzing sociotechnical practice, and in rethinking the concept of private and public spaces in media use, as well as in articulating the fluid boundaries of these spaces.

Notions of Privacy and Publicness

According to Solove (2008), privacy is a multifaceted concept that covers "freedom of thought, control over one's body, solitude in one's home, control over personal information, freedom from surveillance, protection of one's reputation, and protection from searches and interrogations" (p. 12). Post (2000, p. 2088) outlines privacy as a realm for the "creation of knowledge," "dignity," and "freedom," thereby ascribing the concept with aspirational meanings (Fairfield & Engel, 2015). Drummond (2000) describes the private space as a "domestic space" where personal activities occur (p. 2378). The domestic is imagined to be in the context of home and family, and private spaces are determined through possession or ownership (Mitchell, 1995). While "public space" represents sites wherein all social and political activities can occur (Cattell et al., 2008), private space offers a venue where one can perform activities or "exercise his/her freedom" without the intrusion of others (Mitchell, 1995, p. 122). Within private spaces, social norms can be suspended or replaced by rules which community members and visitors are expected to follow (e.g. schools, offices, domestic spaces) (Post, 2000).

According to Flaherty, there are four conditions of privacy: "solitude," "intimacy," "anonymity," and "reserve" (as cited in Hough, 2009, p. 407). Yet, the difficulty in delineating private and public spaces in the constant overlap of these spaces in everyday contemporary life. The continuing movement of private individuals in public spaces and facilities complicates how public spaces are configured (Butler, 2009) and how the public and the private are defined (Sheller & Urry, 2003).

Moreover, there are blurring distinctions between the private and the public spaces, in which activities considered as "intimate or domestic" are performed in "public spaces," due to cramped living conditions in marginalized contexts (Drummond, 2000, p. 2383). For example, Narag (2013) identified the concept of "annex" or the "practice of constructing extended rooms to differentiate residents from owners, sharers (extended family of the owners) and renters (friends paying for extra room)" in low-income communities. The "annexation, a 30 square meter housing unit can accommodate 3 households with 8–12 residents" and rooms are usually separated by curtains for some privacy. Residents are also familiar with "makeshift" rooms, which can be utilized as bedroom by night and a living room by day (Narag, 2013, p. 72). Crowded housing arrangements force household members, especially children, to stay outside of the homes, where they are forced to perform otherwise "private activities" in public, such as taking a bath or brushing the teeth. These suggest that structural and spatial conditions in a locale influence people's experience of private and public.

Public and Private in Media Use

Digital Access Points, Individualism, and Privacy

Much research about the cultural uses of ICT has tended to privilege an individualistic ethos. For instance, the mobile phone first started as an urban phenomenon in affluent countries mostly as a personal, fashionable, and to some extent, even a luxury item. Understandably, a number of studies about the cultural use of mobile devices focused on the phone as a private technology (Puikkonen, Häkkilä, Ballagas, & Mäntyjärvi, 2009; Kurkovsky & Syta, 2010; Balakrishnan & Raj, 2012). Such discussions of media use emphasize the value of individual and private ICT use, as opposed to publicness and collective use (Daliot-Bul, 2007; Butt & Phillips, 2008; García-Montes, Caballero-Munoz, & Perez-Alvarez, 2006). In Japan, for instance, the *"keitai"* (cellphone as a commodity often associated as "extension of self") was found to be personalized with accessories that express the personality of the owner (Daliot-Bul, 2007, p. 955; Ito & Okabe, 2005).

Certain ICTs allow users to consume information and interact with others privately (Balakrishnan & Raj, 2012). Whereas watching a film in a theater, for instance, is a communal experience that has some semblance of publicness, watching videos on a smartphone can be done in private. The owner chooses with whom to share the content. Accessories such as earphones allow one to enjoy the mobile phone experience in privacy. Even consumption and use of certain media content in public raise ethical concerns founded on notions of private or public uses of particular technologies, such as talking loudly over the phone in public spaces, which is considered unethical on trains in Japan (Ito & Okabe, 2005). Users who associate phone ownership with privacy may be empowered by being able to escape into private chats with loved ones, participate in gossip, discuss sex, or access private sites including porn (Horst & Miller, 2006; Pertierra, 2006). Yet, in certain contexts, privacy is thought of in terms of groups of people instead of individuals. McDougall (2002) argued that, sharply contrasting with conceptions of privacy centered on individuals, the Chinese conception of privacy focuses on groups of people (e.g., family). In this sense, privacy in media use may be experienced even when devices are shared within a particular grouping.

Public Access ICTs

The notion of ICTs privately consumed in domestic spaces assumes ownership and the availability of space (Balakrishnan & Raj, 2012). However, individual ownership of ICT is restricted by financial resources (Rangaswamy & Arora, 2015). Public access ICTs such as cybercafés are common in developing economies because many could not afford to buy technology assets (computer and internet) and often depend on various types of public venues that provide access to computers and the internet (Mazimpaka, Mugiraneza, & Thioune, 2015). Even as the number of privately owned mobile devices and personal computers is increasing, there remains a continued presence of cybercafés and telecenters in urban and rural areas in the developing world, especially in shantytowns and slums. Such public access points make technology available and affordable to low-income populations via "smaller portions" (i.e., USD 0.40 for one hour of internet), but the cheaper cost implies that the technology and space for accessing the technology is shared (Rangaswamy & Cutrell, 2012).

However, well articulated in the language of "digital or social inclusion" by governments, this discourse surrounding public ICT use is often focused in the context of "ideological notions of electronic democracy," where ICTs become accessible to the last mile (Lee, 1999, p. 33). This creates a notion of "digital have-nots" emanating from a distinction of private or home-based internet users and those who access ICTs using public access points. This is so even when in much of developing societies, private owners of ICTs constantly move from the use of personal devices and public ICTs actively for various reasons (Lee, 1999, p. 33). Recent studies have also highlighted that beyond financial imperatives, collectivistic cultural logics drive collectivistic ICT use. A study by Sreekumar (2011) found that a subaltern fishing community in Kerala has applied a collectivist ethos in its appropriation of the mobile phone in culturally relevant and ecologically enhancing ways. Rangaswamy and Cutrell's (2012) research also identified the *"adda"* as a sociogeographic presence, wherein the youth of Hafeezpet "discuss, learn, show off, brag, and teach each other about technology collectively" (p. 58). This suggests that youths' uses of mobile phones and the internet in certain contexts often lead to a public gathering, where social groupings among peers with similar interests are formed. In their communal use of devices, entertainment brought these youths together to pass time, helping bridge the gap between socioeconomic backgrounds (Rangaswamy & Cutrell, 2012).

Metro Manila Slums as Site for Analysis

According to the Asian Development Bank (ADB), of the 862 million people globally living in slums in 2013, 60% of them are in Asia (Mathur, 2013). The Philippines is one of the Asian countries with a significant slum population, with 4.3 million people or about 37% of residents in Metro Manila living in slums (Mathur, 2013). These informal settlements can be found across the metropolis amid a background of condominiums and malls. Slum dwellers are among the most vulnerable people due to congested residential areas and poor living standards, such as inadequate water; small, unstable, and insecure living space; and poor sanitation (United Nations Human Settlement Programme [UN-HABITAT], 2003; Ballesteros, 2010). Houses in slums are usually small and are made up of flimsy wooden boards, metal sheets, or poorly finished concrete. Partitions and bedrooms are a rarity as small living spaces normally serve multiple purposes such as living, dining, and sleeping.

Although slum dwellers are generally understood as low-income populations, they differ in the resources that they lack, and slums are also a site of inequality but also of creativity and innovation (Owusu, Agyei-Mensah, & Lund, 2008). Despite the condition in slums urban establishments afford slum dwellers material aspirations, due to their closeness to commercial and industrial establishments and access to major modes of transportation. Also, due to the proximity of slum communities to major city centers, nonprofit organizations, government offices, or educational institutions, some slum dwellers become occasional beneficiaries of social development projects. Some enterprising slum dwellers also engage in the service sector, like barbershops, laundry, housekeeping, factory work, or *tricycle/pedicab* (a mode of local public transportation) driving, and other livelihood opportunities such as *sari-sari* (variety) store, which thrives on *tingi* or sachet economy to cope with harsh economic conditions (Berner, 1997; Portus, 2008).

Traditional conceptions of privacy and publicness are complicated in the context of slums. Practices that are considered intimate in other contexts are carried out in public spaces because of the lack of space (Drummond, 2000). Houses are usually adjacent and cramped in narrow spaces, leaving little room for privacy embodied in the form of a curtain that serves as a divider (Narag, 2013). Smell and sound permeate cardboard-type dividers and water, wash bins, and Wi-Fi are shared. In slums, privacy comes at a rarity, and private moments and domestic activities are generated within these public spaces such as water station talks, street corners, and makeshift bedrooms (Rangaswamy & Arora, 2015). Further, communal spaces are common and continually manufactured to support everyday social activities that support and reinforce collectivistic logics: slum residents conduct weekend *videoke* or *karaoke* sessions in the middle of street alleys, some bathe their kids in public water sources, young boys play basketball along street alleys using makeshift hoops, and residents gather for nighttime drinking in front of variety stores.

Our study is situated in slum communities (*barangays*) in Metro Manila: Barangay 649 of Baseco, Barangay 717 & 718 in Malate, Manila, and Barangay North Daang Hari in Taguig City. The data presented in this chapter are generated from ethnographic interviews with 51 young people (aged 14–24), participant observation in public ICT access points such as *pisonet* and computer shops, participatory mapping exercises and media diaries, and interviews with the owners and managers of public access points conducted between July and December 2015. Questions for youth respondents focused on what modalities they use to access the internet, the social context of use in varied access modalities, the activities that they do online, and perceptions of privacy. During some of the interviews, we invited the users to show their mobile phone units and how they used them. Of these, 20 respondents participated in a 1-week media diary on how they accessed and used the internet using various modalities. As the study progressed, we also conducted participatory mapping exercises to help plot the location of public internet access points in the community and held participant observation in *pisonet* and computer shops to better understand the context of use. Interviews with owners and managers of public access points focused on the nature of access in those spaces, services offered and regulations imposed, and the activities conducted by young people in those spaces.

Cultural Ecology of Media Use in Slums

Low-income users are continually becoming an attractive market for mobile networks in the Philippines, with this specific group featuring in many advertisements of telecommunications networks (Soriano & Lim, 2016). Low-cost and second-hand devices that cater to this market have been made available, whereas local smartphone brands can be purchased for as low as $30 USD. Recently, the launch of Facebook's Internet.org, which provides free access to certain websites such as Facebook, as well as cheaper promotions (i.e., "unlimited internet at P30 [US$0.75] per day"), is expected to be taken up broadly by young people from the middle- to low-income markets, with possibilities that this could significantly influence the dynamics of online access.

However, mobile internet has material requirements such as access to an internet-capable phone and money to buy credit for accessing data plans or Wi-Fi, which several young people in slums are still unable to afford. Further, cheaper units and promotions imply slow connectivity and limited data allowance that limit online activities. In the Philippines, this compels young people to continually rely on public access points such as the "*pisonet*" and "computer shop," which are usually connected to faster and more stable broadband connections. The computer shop (similar to a "cybercafé" but without the café environment) and the *pisonet* facilitate access to the internet at an affordable cost. But there are also key differences between these two access points that influence who access them and what a user can do in each space. Public access ICTs create a different set of relationships in a communicative ecology than does individual mobile or private home access: the internet, through public access, occupies a different location in space and time, and thus creates relationships with a different set of actors.

Many previous studies on ICT use in low-income communities looked at individual technologies, rather than placed in an ecology of multiple technologies simultaneously and interchangeably accessed. A media ecology lens encourages the understanding of how users navigate across ICT access modalities as an "integrated structure," within which each individual platform is used in relation to others (Horst, Herr-Stephenson, & Robinson, 2010; Madianou & Miller, 2012, p. 170). We examine negotiations of privacy and publicness amid this ecology of media use, which contains the relationships people in slums establish with one another through the mediation of different types of ICTs. The succeeding discussions examine constructs of privacy and publicness in the context of use of mobile devices and use of public access ICTs, such as the computer shop and *pisonet*.

Mobile Internet: Privacy and Publicness in Owned, Shared, and Borrowed Devices

Sociocultural and Economic Dimensions of Mobile Communication

The acquisition of the mobile phone unit appears to be generally viewed by our youth respondents as positive, and smartphones are what they aspire to have. As found in previous studies, having a mobile phone is perceived to raise social status, and the better models or brands translate to higher social status (Portus, 2008; Rashid & Elder, 2009). Over 80% of our youth respondents have used a mobile device. Yet, a significant number of young people interviewed do not own internet-capable devices but have experienced using them through shared or borrowed arrangements. Some own locally-assembled units with no internet capability (costing around $15–30 USD) or secondhand units with small screens and that come with some internet access capability such as WAP or 3G. Some have used mobile or smartphones by borrowing parents', sibling's, or partner's handsets, while others have owned a smartphone, but these either had to be sold or pawned, or had broken down. The fast breaking down of smartphones is connected to the quality of units they acquire, many of them secondhand or some low-cost units that end up being prone to malfunctioning. This sharing arrangement for mobile devices was also found in other developing countries. In Rangaswamy and Singh's (2009) study, for example, middle-class Indian families share multiple mobile phones within the household, given that mobile phones are seen as a family tool rather than a personal tool. In South Africa, young people are more familiar with accessing the internet using their shared mobile phones rather than through PCs (Kreutzer, 2009).

One interviewee narrated that his sister passed on a mobile phone to be shared by him, four siblings, and their father, and the six of them take turns using the device for three hours each. The eldest sister, as the official owner of the unit, keeps the phone, and the younger siblings did not have much control over when they can use the device. When the elder sister decided to take the phone back due to concerns of "overuse" and breaking down, they all lost access. In another slum community in Baseco, a group of young people narrated that one relatively wealthy classmate has a Samsung smartphone that can access the internet. She is the only one in the class of 40 students who has such a phone. With limited financial resources to use public internet access facilities regularly, they would take turns to borrow the classmate's phone and Wi-Fi access. Of course, this classmate has become popular to her peers. We also found instances where mobile devices are shared between romantic partners. For example, a young mother, Karen (*alias*, 18), had her device break down a year ago and now relies on her husband's mobile device for checking Facebook, YouTube, and online gaming. She narrates that she can only access the internet when her husband comes home from work. Another respondent, Carla (*alias*, 17), was given a smartphone by her boyfriend as a present, but explained that her boyfriend also uses the device and at times borrows it from her for a week.

Mobile Internet Access in a Sharing Economy

Whether owned, shared, or borrowed, the quality of access to the internet is influenced by the dynamics of a sharing economy popular in slums underscored by available social and financial capital. Most respondents, depending on how much they can save from the day's school allowance or earn from work (some youth we interviewed are compelled to take on various kinds of contractual work at a young age), subscribe to affordable call and SMS promotions that come bundled with free data or free Facebook and Viber. These services can be purchased or obtained by purchasing mobile credit (called *"auto-load"*) or via *"utang"* (i.e., debt) from the nearby variety store at very small increments (from 10 to 30 pesos) depending on which promotion the user wishes to subscribe to. Such transactions are often ruled by social relations, wherein store owners allow friends or friends' family members in good relationship with one another to "borrow" goods or money with promise of future payback. But bundled promotions tend to provide slow internet access speed that severely limit what young people can do in these devices and compel them to use public access modalities such as computer shops or the *pisonet*, where computers are connected to high-speed broadband, even when they have access to mobile devices. For both Wi-Fi and data services, internet access speed, reliability, and cost remain a problem in the Philippines (Gonzales, 2015). Of course, users who can afford the more expensive data and Wi-Fi plans can obtain faster and more reliable internet access with more data capacity.

Not only are shared devices common, but shared Wi-Fi is also a common feature in these communities. Respondents explained that it is normal to request a neighbor's Wi-Fi password. Those who can afford monthly Wi-Fi subscriptions include those who have family members working as overseas contract workers (for constant communication) or with stable local employment. The Wi-Fi password is shared not only to relatives but also to neighbors and friends in nearby houses in good relationship with the Wi-Fi subscriber. In slum communities, the houses are very close to each other, sometimes divided only by a sack material or a thin plywood, which makes sharing Wi-Fi possible. These imply that social relationships serve as capital for obtaining access. In one community, young people narrated how they are able to access the internet using the adjacent university's Wi-Fi connection.

Shared Devices and Notions of Privacy as "Personal Time"

Very few of the respondents who rely on borrowed or shared devices and internet connection had significant concerns about privacy nor security implications. Upon probing, respondents narrated that they do not feel compelled to log out from their social networking site accounts as they share the device, explaining that "there is nothing that I feel I should hide" (Michelle, female, 16, Brgy 717, September 26, 2015). Even romantic partners share and exchange their devices freely with the other, with little concern of securing the content of one's private accounts. Few of our respondents owned e-mail accounts, but even those with e-mail accounts did not appear to have a pressing concern about protecting their privacy. Privacy in the use of devices encompass perceptions of being able to secure one's information, including the extent by which information in accounts or devices are made viewable or accessible only to the owner or to a selected few (Solove, 2008; West, Lewis, & Currie, 2009). The link between security and privacy is so strong that unwanted access to information or device is protected by law (Rainie et al., 2013). Such concerns of security, however, are not apparent for most of our respondents; instead, users expressed greater concern with the limited or inflexible access time and inconvenience of having to borrow and return the devices: "When I was just borrowing my sister's phone unit, of course I can only use it when she comes home. I would also borrow some of my friend's phone. But when I was able to buy my own unit, I can use the device anytime I want, even until the evening when the internet connection is much faster" (male, 19, Brgy 717, Personal communication, translated from Filipino, September 30, 2015). The quote implies that a personal phone is deemed valuable due to the flexibility of access, albeit not mainly on the security that it affords.

Further, despite the apparent lack of importance given toward privacy as security, some of our respondents' accounts validated earlier work on how the affordances of mobile devices facilitate the construction of private time and private space for some users (Ito & Okabe, 2005; Pertierra, 2006; Doron, 2012). For example, some young mothers use the mobile device for accessing Facebook, games, and YouTube while performing household chores and child-nurturing roles such as watching over the baby's sleeping or waiting for the food to cook. The mobility afforded by the mobile device allows these mothers to insert some private time in the midst of constant childrearing. Similarly, some young males shared that accessing the internet represents private leisure from the nagging of parents that they can enjoy in between household chores (e.g., cleaning the house, manning the store). These show how mobile phone use affords users some private time, even when these units are not necessarily privately owned.

The Computer Shop: Imagined Privacy in Communal Spaces

Sociocultural and Economic Dimensions of Computer Shops

The diffusion of new media technologies, particularly in the less affluent countries, has been marked by the proliferation of cyber or internet cafés in the rural and semi-urban areas, as well as in small towns and big cities (Laegran & Stewart, 2003; Liff & Steward, 2003; Larghi, et al., 2015; Sreekumar & Rivera-Sanchez, 2016). In a survey conducted by Yahoo! Philippines and AC Nielsen (2010), internet cafés have become an important access point in the country with 71% of the estimated 20 million internet users saying they have accessed the internet through e-cafés. The demand for the services offered by the cybercafés comes mainly from youth. Cybercafés carry several computers connected to an internet network and would have different additional offerings, ranging from printing and scanning services to voice chat service with headsets.

In the Philippines, cybercafés imply the fancier, enclosed internet access points that can be found in malls or private buildings. In slum neighborhoods, the youth call enclosed internet access points "computer shops," which provide more or less the same facilities as the cybercafé, except that these are located in enclosed spaces without the café environment that includes comfortable chairs, refreshments, or air-conditioning. A computer shop in the slum community would commonly have several (around five to twelve) computer terminals, sometimes separated by makeshift borders made of wood or curtain with plastic movable chairs in each terminal. The computer shop poses an important context of new media use as it is premised on sharing computers and the internet network, as opposed to individual use and ownership (Laegran & Stewart, 2003; Liff & Steward, 2003). This setting also makes them attractive to young people and for networked gaming as it facilitates collaboration and interaction among peers within both the real and virtual space.

Computer Shops and "Manufactured" Privacy

Computer shops have dedicated managers who assign a user to a computer, note down the time and duration of access, and address any connectivity problems experienced by the user or provide additional services needed (e.g., printing, scanning, saving, video chatting, selling of snacks). The mechanisms of control and regulation in computer shops are determined by the cybercafé manager or owner, often via "rules of use" explicitly posted inside the shop. Different computer shops display different "rules of use" ranging from "*Bawal kumain, uminom, manigarilyo*" (No eating/drinking/smoking), "*Bawal ang scandal/porn*" (Porn is not allowed), "*Isang computer, isang tao*" (No sharing of computers), and "*Bawal mag-download*" (No private downloading)—reminders of the publicness of the space that is bound by rules. Some shop managers install a monitoring system to check the computers remotely for those surfing "forbidden sites" such as porn. The reality of access in a computer shop, further highlighted by the mediation of a manager who has access to the computers in the network, implies that access is monitored and regulated, and therefore, not private.

Yet, in many computer shops, owners manufacture some sense of privacy by using curtains or cubicle dividers (see Figure 5.1). This is parallel to what Sreekumar and Rivera-Sanchez's (2016) research study found in cybercafés in other parts in Asia. In the Philippines, makeshift cubicles

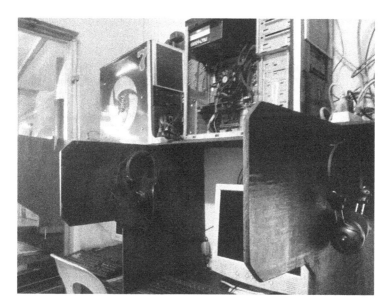

Figure 5.1 Computer shop in Baseco where computer terminals create illusions of privacy.

seem popular for computer shops that offer voice chat facilities such as Skype. These facilities construct an illusion of privacy for the users as they talk on the screen over their headsets in somewhat hushed voices. In one computer shop visit, we sat beside an adult woman who appeared to be chatting with a romantic partner in a split screen. Their conversation, which bordered on the intimate and private at times, was in fact audible to adjacent cubicles and did not escape the gaze of the computer shop manager as well as to others within the cramped space. Yet, the headset and makeshift divider appeared to have constructed a sense of privacy afforded to her by the computer shop. Further, one manager shared that some users are surprised when their attention is called, for example, when caught accessing pornographic sites, not realizing that their screens are accessible to the manager at all times.

In some shops, the computers are positioned so close to one another with no dividers that users share drinks and food and also view others' screens periodically when sharing sites. For groups who come to play games, it is common for a number of young people to stand behind the user, watch the user play, cheer, and even offer tips on how to beat the opponent. There appears to be a sense of community among computer shop gamers. As they coordinate their strategy online, they express their exasperation and satisfaction among the peers seated with them. Some also serve as spectators who travel between screens to watch other people playing. However, it is also in this context of "community gaming" in the computer shop that some of the users raised privacy concerns. As one male interviewee notes:

RANDY (ALIAS): I spent a long time collecting weapons. In gaming, the weapons have important value. But one day someone has stolen my account and I can no longer access it and all the weapons I collected are gone.

INTERVIEWER: How do you think they got access to your weapons?

RANDY (ALIAS): In the computer shop, for sure, because when we play there usually are many people. Someone must have become envious of my account.

(Male, Brgy 717, Personal communication,
September 29, 2015)

Thus, computer shops present a different mode of access, wherein the use of the device is open to the paying public. Computer shops are available to a wider public and this allows a group of people to converge in a physical space and share the experiences and emotions associated with witnessing or doing an activity collectively (e.g., gaming). However, the sense of privacy that wooden dividers or headsets provide can be easily breached by spectators or the owner. Thus, the privacy issues faced by computer shop users are not only digital in nature but also physical.

Pisonet: Complex Constructs of Privacy and Publicness in Spatio-technical Practices

Sociocultural and Economic Dimensions of Pisonet

If the computer shop is an appropriation of the "cybercafé" in poorer communities, the technology of the "*pisonet*" could be argued to have originated from low-income urban and rural communities in the Philippines. The *pisonet*, operated as independent microenterprises found in low-income neighborhoods in the country, allows the lowest entry cost of access. The length of access one peso can allow varies from one *pisonet* to another, although most of them are set at four to seven minutes for one peso ($0.02 USD). The *pisonet* works like a jukebox where internet connection is triggered by slotting in a peso coin. A user can then slot in additional coins to continue access. Connected to the unit's monitor is a timer that tells the user how much time is left for access and beeps to warn the user that only a minute is left (Figure 5.2).

In comparison to computer shop, which commonly allow access for an hour,[1] the *pisonet* allows for much cheaper access entry, making them very attractive to youth who often do not have a stable source of income and rely on their parents, elder siblings, or meager savings from school allowance to access the internet. As an extension of the "*sari-sari* store" and "sachet" culture popular in slum communities in the Philippines, the *pisonet* represents the most "sachet" of sachet internet access modalities.

A striking feature in terms of slum community appropriation of the *pisonet* is that they are mostly situated along the streets and alleys

Figure 5.2 The "*pisonet*."

(Figure 5.3a, b); thus, the screens are easily visible to passersby. The users of the *pisonet* do not sit in comfortable chairs; these usually are stools, plastic chairs, or wooden planks. We also found *pisonet*s where users access the internet while standing, often as a group with multiple users viewing one computer screen. A user can continually use the unit as long as one has more pesos to insert; sometimes users would take turns to slot in peso coins to communally watch a YouTube video. When not in use, the *pisonet* would be covered by a used tarpaulin or sack to prevent it from dust or rain. The *pisonet* is often located along the streets because the owners do not have indoor space, making these units prone to maintenance problems due to heat and rain.

Because access to the *pisonet* is triggered by slotting in of a peso coin, *pisonet*s are generally not managed/monitored. For a *pisonet*, the "manager" is actually a coin-changer, as users would every now and then require more than one peso coins to insert. One manager we met is an old woman who oversees the coin-changing while performing household chores and caring for her grandchildren; another *pisonet* manager is a 45-year-old mother who also owns a variety store and looks after her four children while her husband works for the day in a construction site. Unlike in computer shops where dedicated managers can oversee users' screens and activities in the network, *pisonet* managers rarely see what the users are actually doing in their screens, unless their attention is called. This implies that *pisonet* users are not concerned that a manager is monitoring their use. Further, unlike computer shops with explicit "rules of use," *pisonet*s are managed by micro-entrepreneurs with much less knowledge of security and privacy and our interviews with *pisonet* owners revealed that they relied only on whatever antivirus software was installed when they purchased the units. Unlike some computer shops, which impose site restrictions, young people can technically access any site they want in the *pisonet*, including porn sites, which, based on our interviews, some users have attempted to do.

Publicness as Regulation and Control

However, the spatial positioning of the *pisonet*s along slum alleys serves regulatory purposes. Parental and community regulation of youths' internet access appears most apparent in the *pisonet* context when the user's screen is literally exposed to family members, bystanders, and neighbors. One *pisonet* in Brgy 718 in Leveriza is, by the request of the owner, strategically located opposite to a village CCTV (a project of the local government to catch drug addiction and gangs in slums). The owner narrates that this "controls" young people from accessing "immoral" sites; it also means that these units are "off-limits" to young users after the village-imposed "curfew" at 10 PM.[2] These represent a collectively constructed notion of privacy and ethical use that delimit individual freedom in relation to ICT use.

(a)

(b)

Figure 5.3a and b *Pisonet* in slum neighborhood.

Further, in most of our visits to the *pisonet*, one unit would have several young people browsing the screen at a time, taking turns to slot in one peso coins. Because of this nature of shared access, an owner narrates that the group would usually shout or make noise when a user visits a porn site. Moreover, the positioning of the *pisonet* helps parents easily find their children and control their use, while the village patrol ("*tanod*") who walk along slum alleys at night participate in the regulation. It implies that here, the technology (*pisonets*) also acts as a social regulator that allows parents and village officials in slums to monitor the activities of young people.

At night, after the curfew for young people, elders sometimes converge to use the *pisonet* for streaming movies, television shows, boxing matches, or videoke music collectively, with some of the elders sharing peso coins for uninterrupted access. Young people going to the same school would also use the *pisonet* to work on assignments, and at times, they teach community elders on how to use the computer, access the internet, or search for information such as processing government documents. These examples show that the publicness of the technology also serves a purpose of sustaining a collectivistic culture in the slums.

Pisonet and Imaginaries of "Privacy"

Some young *pisonet* users we interviewed did not see the *pisonet* as particularly restrictive, given its position along slum alleys, but found it limiting in terms of which activities they are unable to do in comparison to a computer shop (e.g., no headsets for voice calling and no USB slot because the machine is fully encased to prevent theft). In fact, some users found the *pisonet* to be one that more closely approximates the experience of having a private mobile phone. In the *pisonet*, they can eat, drink, and even smoke while surfing the net, thereby suspending norms of public access. These activities are often disallowed in computer shops due to regulations imposed by the managers. Treating the *pisonet* as an extension of their private domestic spaces, they shared that, unlike the computer shop, they can access the *pisonet* anytime, sometimes as they wake up in the morning without having brushed their teeth or taken a bath. The nature of access—facilitated by a peso coin and located right along the front of their houses—also allows them to visit the *pisonet* several times a day to check their social media pages or search for information, akin to how one might use social media via a mobile device. Striking here is the apparent contradiction of the *pisonet*'s publicness with the users' construction of it as an extension of a domestic space where formality or restrictive rules can be suspended.

However, the nature of the *pisonet* makes its users prone to exposure of one's private conversations and passwords to bystanders, making them vulnerable to real dangers of identity theft and other security risks.

We used the *pisonet* a few times and while viewing a YouTube video to test the access speed, we ran out of one peso coins before finishing the video. When we managed to change money and insert another peso coin, the computer came back to life as if the video was just put on pause, and it reverted to exactly the same segment of the video where we left off. Indeed, some respondents have experienced instances of account hacking but did not appear to express grave concern. When we asked what they did after the hacking, they said that they simply created a new account to replace the old one. Some users, in a group interview, explained that more savvy users already know that they simply need to turn off the CPU when they are about to run out of peso coins in the middle of Facebook browsing or email, especially as the machine beeps when there is a minute left. They also shared that some users are reminding other users to shut off the CPU after use.

In sum, this nature of access resonates with the reality of slum life, where exposure and publicness is an everyday experience. The point to be made here is that the *pisonet* and the sociospatial arrangements underlying it shape the way users engage with the technology and the way privacy and publicness is experienced and perceived. The *pisonet* technology, including how it is appropriated in slum neighborhoods, constructs social relations of technology that need to be understood within context, for it involves logics of privacy and publicness that deviate from the norm of affluent technological contexts dominant in scholarly literature. The collectivistic culture supported by the *pisonet* allows a community to come together and learn from the use of the technology or extend the realm of their limited domestic spaces, thereby further reinforcing this logic. In turn, the publicness of the *pisonet* exposes these young people to real dangers they may not yet fully grasp.

Discussion and Conclusions: Privacy and Publicness in Situated Access and Use

The emerging environment of proliferating internet access points such as mobile devices, computer shops, and the *pisonet* in Metro Manila slums reflect the nature and dynamics of local conditions and also appear as a site of social ordering, modes of regulation and control, and articulation of the fluid and complex boundaries of privacy and publicness. Here, we see that the situation of ICT access based on local realities shape notions of private and public. The chapter also examines ICT use as an ecology of multiple access modalities, particularly relevant in analyzing the nature of access in slums where various ICTs are utilized interchangeably. An ecology approach, as opposed to looking at single technologies, comes closer to the reality and dynamism of everyday life and technological engagement by young people in the slums.

Notions of public and private are significant in the study of social life. However, discussion of these concepts, especially in the context of media studies, tends to adopt particular (Duffey, 2014) and often "Western" constructs of privacy and publicness (Drummond, 2000). The chapter examined these norms through the lived experiences of youth in slum communities in Metro Manila to understand how space, place, and power interplay in relation to their own frameworks, aspirations, and context of ICT use. ICT use in slums emerge not just as sites of technical access but as spaces of physical, community, and cultural articulation. Privacy is understood and experienced differently in the context of pervasive publicness and a dominant culture of shared resources in the everyday. This perception of privacy is influenced by these users' embeddedness in such sociocultural space. Youth in slums are not much concerned about privacy in terms of being able to use the technology in security or seclusion. Instead, they see privacy in terms of media use as the capability to use devices and access the internet flexibly and with longer time periods. This sharply contrasts against notions of privacy wherein an ICT user must be away from prying eyes or free from external invasion and intervention (Solove, 2008). Further, even in the context of shared devices and public access points, users attempt to manufacture an experience of privacy relevant to them. The capability by which users negotiate privacy in the context of publicness implies that these concepts are not bound solely by ownership (Mitchell, 1995) nor the nature of technology as public or private but instead shaped by culture and negotiations of use.

Our findings also suggest that the nature of public access technologies, their spatial positioning, and regulations imposed either by managers or as a result of local collective practices create ethical boundaries of publicness and privacy in the use of ICTs. It is difficult in the case of internet cafés or *pisonets* to be personalized, given that users do not have much control over these access points that will allow personalization (e.g., how the device would look and functionalities and features). Although these devices may allow them to satisfy their everyday tasks, the devices cannot be configured for privacy purposes. While we emphasize the value of creative individual strategies to construct privacy in everyday publicness, as well as the role of social, economic, and spatial contexts influencing notions of privacy and publicness, of public access technologies in this specific locale impose limits the nature of and condition social action in these spaces. However, we move away from characterizations of impact as mainly influenced by the characteristics of the technology (McLuhan, 1964/2006), but emphasize these characteristics of the technology as they encounter social practice and local culture as embedded in place (Arora, 2010).

Further, based on the experiences discussed in the above sections, we see that the capability to access ICTs, as well as experience and aspiration for privacy is a factor of social, financial, and technological capital (Gilbert, 2010). The capability to access devices and the internet largely depend on a sharing economy and social relationships culturally embedded in the nature of slum life. This is characterized by the very emergence of the *pisonet*, which is very much an appropriation of the "sachet economy" for those who cannot afford access to goods in bigger increments. In these communities, interpersonal and social relationships also influence various forms of "shared access"—from the borrowed phone and shared Wi-Fi to *pisonet* access via debt. Those who can purchase and own a mobile phone and are literate about navigating privacy options exercise more authority or control over the use of devices. Others have to deal with preimposed access limits, shared devices, and publicly accessed *pisonet*s and computer shops that may impose certain limits on the way they can engage in these spaces, or they may realize security risks only when they have become victimized. It is in this context that we need to understand digital inequalities as arising out of nuanced sociospatial and technological inequalities that work to mutually shape access and experience with these technologies.

Understanding the nature of ICT use by youth in urban slums and how private and public operate within this locale enriches the contextual picture of contemporary understanding of media use. In slums, imaginaries of privacy are constructed in public spaces and public ICTs are perceived as extensions of domestic space where norms of publicness can be suspended. Technologies such as mobile devices and mobile internet are experienced simultaneously as private and public. The usual distinctions between the private and public is routinely transgressed and complicated by the organization of ICTs within sociocultural specificities that constantly move dynamically between the public and private, which is thereby important in distinguishing from dominant constructs of media use in contemporary life.

Acknowledgments

This project was made possible by the De La Salle University Challenge Grant. We are also grateful for the research assistance ably provided by Ms Joy Hannah Panaligan.

Notes

1 More recently, however, some computer shops we visited started offering "open time" arrangements that calculate the cost of access per 10 minutes, rather than per hour.
2 There is a curfew imposed in some of these communities where village tanod (watch guards) walk around to prevent street fights, drug use, and screen the "dayo" (village visitors).

References

Arora, P. (2010). *Dot com mantra: Social computing in the Central Himalayas.* Burlington, VT: Ashgate.

Balakrishnan, V. & Raj, R. G. (2012). Exploring the relationship between urbanized Malaysian youth and their mobile phones: A quantitative approach. *Telematics and Informatics, 29*(3), 263–272.

Ballesteros, M. M. (2010). *Linking poverty and the environment: Evidence from slums in Philippine cities.* Makati City, Philippines: Philippine Institute for Development Studies.

Barnes, S. B. (2006). A privacy paradox: Social networking in the United States. *First Monday, 11*(9).

Berner, E. (1997). *Defending a place in the city: Localities and the struggle for urban land in Metro Manila.* Quezon City, Philippines: Ateneo de Manila University Press.

Butler, K. (2009). Blurring public and private sociology: Challenging an artificial division. *Sociological Research Online, 14*(4).

Butt, S., & Phillips, J. G. (2008). Personality and self reported mobile phone use. *Computers in Human Behavior, 24*(2), 346–360.

Casado, E., & Lasen, A. (2014). What is disturbing and why not to disturb. On mobile phones, gender, and privacy within heterosexual intimacy. *Mobile Media & Communication, 2*(3), 249–264.

Cattell, V., Dines, N., Gesler, W., & Curtis, S. (2008). Mingling, observing, and lingering: Everyday public spaces and their implications for well-being and social relations. *Health & Place, 14*(3), 544–561.

Daliot-Bul, M. (2007). Japan's mobile technoculture: The production of a cellular playscape and its cultural implications. *Media, Culture & Society, 29*(6), 954–971.

Doron, A. (2012). Mobile persons: Cell phones, gender and the self in North India. *The Asia Pacific Journal of Anthropology, 13*(5), 414–433.

Drummond, L. (2000). Street scenes: Practices of public and private space in urban Vietnam. *Urban Studies, 37*(12), 2377–2391.

Duffey, M. A. (2014). *Hybrid spaces: Assessing users' perceptions of digitally mediated public space* (Doctoral dissertation). Clemson University, Clemson, SC.

Fairfield, J. & Engel, C. (2015). Privacy as public good. *Duke Law Journal, 65*(3), 385–457.

García-Montes, J. M., Caballero-Munoz, D., & Perez-Alvarez, M. (2006). Changes in the self resulting from the use of mobile phones. *Media, Culture & Society, 28*(1), 67–82.

Gilbert, M. (2010). Theorizing digital and urban inequalities: Critical geographies of 'race', gender and technological capital. *Information, Communication & Society, 13*(7), 1000–1018.

Goggin, G. (2006). *Cell phone culture: Mobile technology in everyday life.* London: Routledge.

Gonzales, Y. (2015, May 19). PH Internet 2nd slowest in Asia, one of the most expensive. Inquirer Technology. Retrieved from http://technology.inquirer.net/42293/ph-internet-2nd-slowest-in-asia-one-of-the-most-expensive.

Hjorth, L. (2011). *Mobile media in the Asia-Pacific: Gender and the art of being mobile.* London and New York: Routledge.

Horst, H. & Miller, D. (2006). *The cellphone: An anthropology of communication.* Oxford, UK: Berg.

Hough, M. G. (2009). Keeping it to ourselves: Technology, privacy, and the loss of reserve. *Technology in Society*, *31*(4), 406–413.

Ito, M. & Okabe D. (2005). Intimate connections. Contextualizing Japanese youth and mobile messaging. In R. Harper, L. Palin, & A. Taylor (Eds.), *The inside text: The social, cultural, and design perspectives on SMS* (pp. 127–145). Dordrecht, Netherlands: Springer.

Kreutzer, T. (2009). Assessing cell phone usage in a South African township school. *International Journal of Education and Development Using ICT*, *5*(5), 43–57.

Kurkovsky, S. & Syta, E. (2010). Digital natives and mobile phones: A survey of practices and attitudes about privacy and security. *Proceedings of the IEEE International Symposium on Technology and Society (ISTAS)* (pp. 441–449). University of Wollongong, Wollongong, Australia.

Laegran, A. S. & Stewart, J. (2003). Nerdy, trendy or healthy? Configuring the internet cafe. *New Media & Society*, *5*(3), 357–377.

Lange, P. G. (2007). Publicly private and privately public: Social networking on YouTube. *Journal of Computer-Mediated Communication*, *13*(1), 361–380.

Larghi, S., Aguerre, C., Calamari, M. L., Fontecoba, A., Moguillansky, M., Orchuela, J., & Ponce de Leon, J. (2015). The appropriation of computer and Internet access by low-income urban youth in Argentina. In Proenza, F. J. (Ed.), *Public Access ICT across Cultures* (pp. 200–231). Cambridge, MA: MIT Press.

Lee, S. (1999). Private uses in public spaces: A study of an internet cafe. *New Media & Society*, *1*(3), 331–350.

Liff, S., & Steward, F. (2003). Shaping e-access in the cybercafe: Networks, boundaries and heterotopian innovation. *New Media & Society*, *5*(3), 313–334.

Madianou, M. & Miller, D. (2012). Polymedia: Towards a new theory of digital media in interpersonal communication. *International Journal of Cultural Studies*, *16*(2), 169–187.

Mathur, O. P. (2013). *Urban poverty in Asia*. Mandaluyong, Philippines: Asian Development Bank.

Mazimpaka, J. D., Mugiraneza, T., & Thioune, R. M. (2015). Impact of public access to ICT skills on job prospects in Rwanda. In F. J. Proenza (Ed.), *Public access ICT across cultures: Diversifying participation in the network society* (pp. 35–58). Cambridge, MA: MIT Press.

McDougall, B. S. (2002). Particulars and universals: Studies on Chinese privacy. In B. S. McDougall & A. Hansson (Eds.), *Chinese concepts of privacy*. Leiden, Boston, and Koln: Brill.

McLuhan, M. (2006). The medium is the message. In M. G. Durham & D. Kellner (Eds.), *Media and cultural studies: Keyworks, revised edition* (pp. 107–116). Malden, MA: Blackwell Publishers (Original work published 1964).

Mitchell, D. (1995). The end of public space? People's park, definitions of the public, and democracy. *Annals of the Association of American Geographers*, *85*(1), 108–133.

Narag, R. (2013). *Mitigating crime in a slum community: Understanding the role of social structures, social processes, and community culture in a neighborhood intervention program* (Doctoral dissertation). Retrieved from ProQuest Dissertations and Theses database. (Publication No. 3559713).

Owusu, G., Agyei-Mensah, S., & Lund, R. (2008). Slums of hope and slums of despair: Mobility and livelihoods in Nima, Accra. *Norsk Geografisk Tidsskrift-Norwegian Journal of Geography*, *62*(3), 180–190.

Pertierra, R (2006). *Transforming technologies, altered selves. Mobile phone and internet use in the Philippines.* Manila, Philippines: DLSU Press.

Portus, L. (2008). How the urban poor acquire and give meaning to the mobile phone. In J. Katz (Ed.), *Handbook of Mobile Communication Studies* (pp. 105–118). Cambridge, MA: MIT Press.

Post, R. (2000). Three concepts of privacy. *The Georgetown Law Journal, 89,* 2087–2098. Retrieved August 30, 2016, from http://digitalcommons.law.yale.edu/fss_papers/185.

Puikkonen, A., Häkkilä, J., Ballagas, R., & Mäntyjärvi, J. (2009, September). Practices in creating videos with mobile phones. *Proceedings of the 11th International Conference on Human-Computer Interaction with Mobile Devices and Services* (p. 3). Bonn, Germany: ACM. doi: 10.1145/1613858.1613862.

Rainie, L., Kiesler, S., Kang, R., Madden, M., Duggan, M., Brown, S., & Dabbish, L. (2013). Anonymity, privacy, and security online. *Pew Research Center.* Retrieved from http://www.pewinternet.org/files/old-media/Files/Reports/2013/PIP_AnonymityOnline_090513.pdf.

Rangaswamy, N., & Arora, P. (2015). The mobile internet in the wild and every day: Digital leisure in the slums of urban India. *International Journal of Cultural Studies,* 1–16, *19*(6), 611–626. doi:10.1177/1367877915576538.

Rangaswamy, N., & Cutrell, E. (2012). Anthropology, development and ICTs: Slums, youth and the mobile internet in urban India. *Information and Communication Technologies and Development 2012, 9*(2), 51–63.

Rangaswamy, N., & Singh, S. (2009). Personalizing the shared mobile phone. In *International Conference on Internationalization, Design and Global Development* (pp. 395–403). Berlin, Heidelberg: Springer.

Rashid, A. T., & Elder, L. (2009). Mobile phones and development: An analysis of IDRC-supported projects. *The Electronic Journal on Information Systems in Developing Countries, 36*(2), 1–16.

Sheller, M., & Urry, J. (2003). Mobile transformations of 'public' and 'private' life. *Theory, Culture & Society, 20*(3), 107–125.

Solove, D. J. (2008). *Understanding privacy.* Cambridge, MA: Harvard University Press.

Soriano, C. R., & Lim, S. S. (2016). Ritual and communal connection in mobile phone communication: Representation of kapwa, bayanihan and "People Power" in the Philippines. In S. S. Lim & C. R. Soriano (Eds.), *Asian perspectives on digital culture: Emerging phenomena, enduring concepts* (pp. 100–118). London and New York: Routledge.

Sreekumar, T. T. (2011). Mobile phones and the cultural ecology of fishing in Kerala, India. *The Information Society, 27,* 172–180.

Sreekumar, T. T. & Rivera-Sanchez, M. (2016). New media, space and marginality: Control and regulation of cybercafe use in small and medium cities in Asia. *Media Watch, 7*(2), 133–149.

United Nations Human Settlements Programme, Global Urban Observatory. (2003). *Slums of the world: The face of urban poverty in the new millennium.* Nairobi, Kenya: United Nations Human Settlements Programme.

West, A., Lewis, J., & Currie, P. (2009). Students' Facebook 'friends': Public and private spheres. *Journal of Youth Studies, 12*(6), 615–627.

Yahoo! Philippines, & AC Nielsen. (2010). Digital Philippines 2010, Yahoo-Nielsen Net Index Highlights. Retrieved August 20, 2016, from http://www.slideshare.net/yuga/yahoonielsen-net-index-2010?from=share_email.

Part III

Delving into the Intimacy Sphere, the Social and the Cultural Space

6 The "Smart" Women

How South Asian Women Negotiate Their Social and Cultural Space through Mobile Technology

Ishita Shruti

Introduction

The growth of information and communication technology has been unprecedented in the last two to three decades. Technology is no longer information or communication technology, but has emerged as a tool to meet our multiple needs. The growth in mobile technology, especially smart phones, has heralded altogether complex space-time context. Some scholars do not shy away to call the present society as "the mobile society" (Wajcman, 2008, p. 636). The mobile phones and, now, smartphones have many advantages over previous communication devices (Kurniwan, 2006). As Wajcman (2008, p. 636) states,

> The capacity of mobile phones to operate regardless of location gives rise to a new pattern of continuous mediated interactions that has become known as constant touch, perpetual contact or connected relationships. This blurring of the boundaries between absence and presence is associated with distinctive and more intense forms of connectedness.

Many scholars (for example, Beck, 1992; Castells, 2010; Giddens, 1992) argued that new modern communications technologies, particularly mobile technologies, have affected our social lives like never before. Academicians and policy makers believe that the ability of the new technologies to travel to previously impervious borders has blurred division of spaces such as public and private spaces (Appadurai, 2006; Sheller & Urry, 2003; Wajcman, 2008).

It has in fact made our lives paradoxical; at any given point of time, we are experiencing contradictory and inconsistent situations (Jarvenpaa & Lang, 2005). It has made our lives easy, as now we can do most of the things with a touch of our fingers, and has also made us completely dependent on these technologies. The present chapter will highlight some of these paradoxes related to new technologies concerning South Asian women. The present research primarily focuses on the sociocultural effect of mobile technologies (Bell, 2006; Goggin, 2006). It argues that the mobile ecosystem is basically a new age cultural ecosystem where mobile phones and smartphones are not just a technical tool but also a cultural site where cultural practices are being produced and reproduced (Bell, 2006). Many scholars have highlighted the gender-based differences in adoption and consumption of new technologies (Hjorth, 2009; Li, 2008). However, studies on female users are very few and do not point out how women are negotiating their sociocultural space in this "information age" (Hjorth, 2009). The chapter attempts to fill that gap in the current scholarships available on women and mobile technologies. The chapter raises some pertinent questions such as: (1) What are the mobile technology consumption behaviors of South Asian women? (2) What do mobile phones/smartphones mean for these women? Is it just a communication and information device? Or, it is also an extension of the "self"? Is it used as a status marker and fashion statement too? (3) Is the access to new technologies blurring the public-private dichotomies for South Asian women (Lee, 1999; Sassen, 2002)? (4) How do South Asian women deal with different paradoxes arising due to incorporation of mobile phones in our everyday lived experiences in a postmodern society? Has the phone become an important aspect of reconstructing identities for South Asian women? Is it giving more "agentic" power to women (Katz & Sugiyama, 2005; Pertierra, 2005)?

The chapter is divided into six sections, including the introduction. The second section explains the methodology adopted in the research. The third section brings out the theoretical and conceptual underpinning around the public-private dichotomy. The fourth section documents the analysis and experiences of present research. This section is further divided into three subsections, each focusing on the questions I raised above. The first subsection deals with appropriation of mobile technology by South Asian women. The second subsection brings out the empirical evidences of blurring binaries of public and private. The third subsection documents how women are now displaying private emotion publicly, and the last subsection deals with questions of postmodernity, women's subjectivity, and agency in a "mobile society."

Methodology

The present research is a digital ethnographic work to deconstruct mobile behavior and practices of South Asian women (Masten & Plowmen, 2003). Since the new mobile technology has made geographical boundaries less relevant, the research is not particularly based on a "locality," city, or country, but on women from South Asia. In the current research, the observer and observant may not be based in the same locality, neighborhood, city, or even the same country (Hesse-Biber, 2011; Murthy, 2008).

The research was started in 2014 when I was intrigued by the obsession of mobile devices among South Asian women. The project, which started in a very organic way, took shape in 2015 when I included WhatsApp and Facebook groups under the observation.

In this research, under mobile technologies, I have considered all mobile devices— mobile phones and tablets and iPads. I am not going to indulge on the hardware aspects of these devices because there is plenty of technical literature available on that. What I will state here is that these devices are different in terms of accessibility and usage. Most of the women in my data set owned personal mobile phones. However, not all of them possess smartphones. The women without smartphones were dependent heavily on tablets and iPads for their online lives. These devices may or may not be a personal device like mobile phones but shared among family members. Pertaining to their different usage and accessibility, I have studied all those women who have some access to mobile devices. For example, most of the women use tablets or iPads for face-to-face online interactions (such as FaceTime or Skype calls) and for entertainment purposes. Mobile phones are also used for other purposes such as calling, messaging, Facebook, and Twitter.

The Subjects

I have studied middle-class women of South Asian origin for this chapter. Though newer researches have pointed out how mobile technology brings transformative experiences in the lives of working-class women as well (Balakrishnan et al., 2010; Thomson & Paul, 2016), for this research, I wanted to bring my subjectivity into the study—an insider's perspective into the analysis of how South Asian women are appropriating mobile technologies in their pursuit of modernity. Hence, I am focusing on middle-class women in my research. The total number of women studied is approximately 200. The majority of them are Indians (85%), followed by Bangladeshis (10%) and some Pakistanis (5%). As explained, I studied their mobile behavior through observing their behavior on my mobile device. Throughout the chapter, I refer my subjects as South Asian women, but I do not intend to generalize all South Asian women here. I understand that there are various layers of subjectivity with the South Asian group, and we need more specific researches to bring out those nuances.

Methods

As Varis (2014, p. 11) understands, "ethnography as an approach in any case is methodologically flexible and adaptive: it does not confine itself to following specific procedures, but rather remains open to issues arising from the field." Further, it is much more difficult to outline techniques and methods when complex digital tools are at play. Therefore, I started an open-ended study of "observing" the online behavior of South Asian women. The study is a combination of methods from traditional ethnography and digital ethnography. For example, I have implied "participant observation" while observing the South Asian women in their physical surroundings, such as private get-togethers and parties, children's school campuses, metro train rides in Delhi, and shopping places in Delhi and Dhaka. However, the large part of observations were done online, in which I was the "invisible observer"; Varis (2014, p. 12) calls it "lurking." Similarly, I had conducted around twenty face-to-face interviews, online chatting sessions, and Skype calls to understand the mobile behavior of the women.

Online Groups

Apart from observing women in my own surroundings (physical and digital), I have also observed practices of women on my Facebook friends list and in various Facebook and WhatsApp groups. I have observed around ten WhatsApp groups and fifteen Facebook groups of various types. The Facebook groups were very diverse, from all-women groups, which promote and discuss India's handicraft, to a localized group like Deshparate in Dhaka, Expat and other foreigners in Dhaka, Dhaka Indians, and Dhaka Malayalis.[1] The WhatsApp groups mainly fall into two categories: long-term groups of friends and families, and short-term groups initiated for a specific purpose. In the long-term groups, the respondents were part of several groups such as families, high school friend groups, college and university friend groups, and work-related friend groups. Short-term groups were mainly event specific or issue based. For example, women would create such groups for specific dinners or parties.

Public/Private Dichotomy in the New Technological World Order

In this section, I delved into the conceptual underpinnings of public-private dichotomy in the present era. The conceptual framework for this chapter broadly focuses on three main concepts: first, the concept of social production of space by Lefebvre (Schmid, 2008); second, the concept of social embeddedness of the new technology (Sassen, 2002); and third, the concept of public-private dichotomy and how the binaries are becoming less relevant in the new world order. The first two concepts form the basis of discussion of the central theme of this chapter—blurring distinctions between public and private.

I bring in Henri Lefebvre's concept of "production of space" (Schmid, 2008 p. 27) and Sassen's (2002, p. 365) notion of "social embeddedness of electronic space" here to unpack the notion of "mobile space." Schmid (2008, p. 28) explains Lefebvre's concept in following terms:

> (Social) space is a (social) product; in order to understand this fundamental thesis it is necessary, first of all, to break with the widespread understanding of space imagined as an independent material

reality existing "in itself." Against such a view, Lefebvre, using the concept of the *production of space*, posits a theory that understands *space* as fundamentally bound up with social reality. It follows that space "in itself" can never serve as an epistemological starting position. Space does not exist "in itself"; it is produced.

Schmid (2008, p. 29) further notes,

> Central to Lefebvre's materialist theory are human beings in their corporeality and sensuousness, with their sensitivity and imagination, their thinking and their ideologies; human beings who enter into relationships with each other through their activity and practice.

So, the social actions of human beings form the basis of production of space. Similarly, electronic spaces[2] are also embedded is social realities (Bell, 2006; Sassen, 2002). Sassen (2002, p. 366) says,

> Digital networks are embedded in both the technical features and standards of the hardware and software, and in actual societal structures and power dynamics... There is no purely digital economy and no completely virtual corporation or community. This means that power, contestation, inequality, hierarchy, inscribe electronic space and shape the production of software.

Castells et al. (2007) further reinforce this succinctly in the *Mobile Communication and Society*. They elaborate in detail how adoption, use, and effect of technology are embedded in sociopolitical and geographical realities and conclude that "technology does not determine society: it *is* society, and can only be understood in social terms as a social practice" (p. 246). Another related concept, which I have used in my analysis of South Asian women, is "domestication" (Haddon, 2001). The concept is widely used in media studies and communication technology studies (Haddon, 2001, 2007). The concept of Haddon (2001, p. 2) says,

> Derived originally from more general studies of the process of consumption, this framework can provide a useful way of bringing together a range of assumptions and perspectives of our relationships with ICTs.

In the case of communication technologies, the framework generally refers to how the technology is appropriated by its users. This appropriation is not just about the use, but also nuances of consumption behavior, as Haddon (2001, p. 3) further notes that

> So attention has been given to what ICTs mean to people, how they experience them and the roles ICTs can come to play in their lives.

To understand both adoption and use we need to appreciate the negotiation and interaction between household members and the politics of the home, which lie behind both conflicts and tensions and the formation of areas of consensus.

In the present research, I would show that "domestication of mobile phones" has gone beyond the physical boundaries of "home" or "domestic/private lives." This brings us to the central theme of the chapter—public-private dichotomy and mobile technology.

Most of the 20th-century works on space and place were centered on positing public and private dichotomy (Sassen, 2002; Sheller & Urry, 2003; Slater, 1998; Wajcman, 2008). Most of the traditional works have considered the distinction between private and public as a rigid one, as Marx (2001, p. 157) points out that "the distinction 'public' and 'private' is often treated as a uni-dimensional, rigidly dichotomous and absolute, fixed and universal concept, whose meaning could be determined by the objective content of the behavior." Perpetuating this dichotomy, Slater (1998, p. 144) opines that "public and private are seen as different realms of experience and value, spatially and temporally separated and epitomized by different sorts of people and roles." Refuting this traditional notion of public and private, Sheller and Urry (2003) succinctly deconstruct the public-private dichotomy in the 21st century. They start by presenting multiple meanings of "publics" and "privates." They point out that (Sheller and Urry, 2003, pp. 107–108)

> There is a tendency in the existing literature to think in terms of "spheres" or "spaces," concepts that are often static and "regional" in character. We criticize such static conceptions and emphasize the increasing fluidity in terms of where (or when) moments of publicity and privacy occur. We show that the characteristic ways in which the public/private distinction has been drawn, and the overwhelming concern with the problem of "erosion" of the public sphere or "blurring of boundaries" between the public and the private, fail to capture the multiple mobile relationships between them, relationships that involve the complex and fluid hybridizing of public-and-private life.

Focusing of multiple meanings of public and private, Sheller and Urry explain five diverse "publics" and "privates," each operating under different forms of exclusion/inclusion boundaries (Sheller & Urry, 2003, p. 110): (1) public and private interests, (2) public and private spheres, (3) public and private lives, (4) public and private spaces, and (5) publicity and privacy. Though all these distinctions are important area of research, I have focused more on public and private spaces as they form the main concept of the present chapter.

As I discuss the digital lives of South Asian women, it is important to further deconstruct the meaning of public and private as I have employed it in the present chapter. I will draw on feminist perspectives to further elaborate on my point. From a feminist point of view, everything outside the realm of "domestic" is public (Rosaldo, 1973; Sheller & Urry, 2003; Wajcman, 2008). This theoretical premise was propagated to show the exclusion of women from the "public," including the work place (Rosaldo, 1973; Slater, 1998; Wajcman, 2008). This remains the core theme of feminist writings. As explained by Pateman (1989, p. 118 in Mulinari & Sandell, 2009, p. 496), "The dichotomy between the private and the public is central to almost two centuries of feminist writing and political struggle; it is, ultimately, what the feminist movement is about." However, things have changed in the postmodern world order, and more and more scholars have looked into how postmodernity or late modernity has facilitated the blurring of boundaries between private and public (Mulinari & Sandell, 2009; Sassen, 2002; Sheller & Urry, 2009; Slater, 1998; Wajcman et al., 2008). In the chapter, I have adopted the feminist notion of "private" and "public," and when I talk about blurring the distinction between public and private space, I mean how the domestication of technology has helped it. But as the chapter progresses, it highlights *how forces of technological advancements have facilitated the "private appropriation of 'public' space" (Sassen, 2002, p. 367) and public appropriation of "private" space*. I will elaborate on "public appropriation of private space" briefly here. In most of the literature on public-private debate in the new technological world order, scholars have mostly highlighted the "private appropriation of public spaces" (Campbell & Park, 2008; Castells et al., 2007; Sassen, 2002). These experts delineate in detail how "personalization of public spaces" is happening across different cultural settings (Campbell & Park, 2008, p. 377). As new communication technology allows people to cross space and time, the private and intimate is no longer restricted to the confines of private and domestic spaces (Leung & Wei, 2000; Moores, 2012). I have found similar phenomenon in this study as well, which I will elaborate on in the next section. The missing link here is that researchers are not talking about "public appropriation of private spaces." Castells et al. (2007) did talk about the role of mobile technology in civil society movements, but what I will point in my analysis section if very different. The chapter will show how South Asian women are participating in various public discourses from the domestic realms. This, to me, is one of the most important impacts of mobile technology in the lives of South Asian women as it gives them a political voice.

Since the chapter focuses on South Asian women, it is worth mentioning the current trend in gender and technology. With the cross-country data, Castells et al. (2007) give empirical examples of the gendered nature of technology adoption. They conclude that, though the male users are higher in number, the gender gap is closing in drastically, globally. However, they do bring in the different cultural contexts in their work and suggests that "gendering of mobile technology" (p. 41) is at different levels in different societies, owing to their cultural differences. Many other studies have shown how different cultural settings affect the adoption and use of mobile technologies (Haddon, 2001; Hjorth, 2009; Lemish & Cohen, 2005). For example, with the advent of mobile telephony, more American women were using it for sociability rather than work purpose (Lemish & Cohen, 2001).

However, there are not enough empirical studies that highlight gender-based usage and adoption (Castells et al., 2007; Hilbert, 2011; Hjorth, 2009; Lemish & Cohen, 2005). Studies on gender and mobile technology are particularly fewer in South Asia. Therefore, the present chapter has tried to fill that gap. I fully understand that many more studies are required to make any broad conclusion about gender and technology. The chapter is a gender analysis of women's mobile usages.

With this theoretical background, the next section analyzes *how South Asian women are appropriating mobile space in their everyday lives.* I argue that a range of social and cultural practices define the mobile space they inhabit (Sassen, 2002; Schmid, 2008; Shuter, 2012).

Before delving into analysis, it is important to clarify that even within scant researches on women and mobile technology, I could not find any comparative literature on these topics, except a few that I will bring in the next section.

Appropriating of Mobile Technology by South Asian Women

G. Bell (2006) published a paper titled "The Age of Thumb: A Cultural Reading of Mobile Technologies from Asia." In 2016, 10 years after the publication of Bell's paper, it's no longer about thumb but the "index finger" because we have moved from keypad phones (such as Blackberry) to touch-based phones where we use our "index finger" to enter into the electronic world. Before the start of this section, I am making a strong statement that for the women in my data set (and the women and men everywhere), the world is revolving around their "index finger." Mobile phones have moved beyond information and communication technology, and it is completely embedded in the everyday lives of South Asian women—from day-to-day mundane activities like waking them up in the morning with alarm, monitoring their exercise routine and diet, cooking tips, to other important activities of their everyday lives like shopping, geographical directions, organizing parties, crafting ideas, fashion input, and the list goes on and on. Mobile devices also work as entertainment tool for some of these (see the case study in the following paragraph). Mobile devices have also become a social and cultural tool for South Asian women (Bell, 2006; Shields, 2002).

The possession of smartphones and presence in social media platforms have become new and important markers of "modernity" for South Asian women (Beck, 1992; Giddens, 1992; Hjorth, 2009; Mulineri & Sandell, 2009). Most of the narratives about the South Asian women in my study are centered on their phones, the "smart" phones. Through new technologies, these women try to recreate their "modern self." In the "information age," the latest model of smartphones, knowing and using new apps and programs, the number of followers on Twitter and/or Instagram, the long list of friends on Facebook, contents of time-line on Twitter, status updates on Facebook, posts getting liked and/or commented on by many people, their profile pictures, and good "selfie" capacity define "who they are" (Bell, 2006) and which class they belong to. Lemish and Cohen (2005) found similar findings in their study in Israel. They found out that for both men and women, owning a mobile phone was a status symbol, but the status markers were different for men and women. For men, owning a new and latest model was a marker for status, whereas Israeli women focused more on the functional aspects of mobile, especially how many calls they were getting.

But one can argue that the presence of social media platforms does not warrant mobile technologies and most of the applications (except WhatsApp and Viber) can be accessed through a computer as well. So, why is this fuss around mobile devices and smartphones then? As shown in the following case, mobile devices have made digital literacy easy for otherwise digitally illiterate women.

IM is a 60-plus women from Bihar, India. She retired as a principal of government high school in 2010. As with most women of that age in South Asia, she did not possess any digital knowledge. Her children gave her the first mobile phone as a birthday present in 2010. Ever since then, she has been using mobile phones. She was not using it for messaging; rather, it remained a "talking tool" for her. Over the years, she started feeling left out as most of the women around her were using some form of mobile technology for other purposes like messaging, social media, and news updates. In December 2014, one day after getting her pension money, she bought a Samsung Galaxy Tab and the digital journey started for her. First, she used it as an entertainment tool, watching Pakistani dramas on YouTube. Slowly, with the help of her children and grandchildren, she entered into the world of social media. Initially operating the "tab" was not so smooth for her. But slowly, she is getting used to the device and mastering it. After entering into social media, she got reconnected to many of her cousins and old friends. She still cannot operate the computer though.

The advancement of mobile technologies has made it easier for digitally illiterate women to appropriate the technology and participate in the electronic revolution of the current era. Also, the mobile devices have given them a unique opportunity to have a control over their communication choices. However, in a study on older women (60 plus in the UK), Kurniawan (2006) found out that mobile devices, though they increased the sense of security among older women in the UK, were not the preferred mode of communication for them. Women in his study preferred landline phones more than mobile for talking to family and friends. This throws light on the fact that women are exercising their agency to choose which device or mode to use and for what purposes. For example, in the above case, IM now owns two devices, a basic mobile set which she uses for talking to her family and friends and a tablet, which is for her entertainment and social networking.

The progress in this sector has also helped in addressing the gender disparity in the access and use of mobile technology. It is difficult to obtain gender segregated data for South Asian countries (India, Bangladesh, Pakistan); therefore, I have taken some crude estimates of the digital divide between men and women in South Asia. These online estimates indicate that there is huge gender gap in terms of mobile users in South Asia. For example, in 2015, among urban users in India, women accounted for just 29% (Emarketer, 2016[3]). Similarly, out of a total 3.2 million Facebook users in Bangladesh, only 22% are woman in 2012,[4] and in Pakistan, this share was around 32% in 2011.[5] Some research and consulting groups have forecasted that the advent of mobile technologies, particularly smartphones, will reduce the gender gap significantly (Emarketer, 2016). The reason for this could be two things: first, easy operating procedures, and second, the mobility aspects of "mobile devices" with data services and mobile Wi-Fi making it possible to access any information from anywhere or start a communication from anywhere. Mobile technologies have facilitated the "space-time compression" in a manner never seen before. For South Asian women with a mobile phone, everything is "now" and "here" and not "then" and "there."

Blurring Public-Private Distinction

As mentioned in the previous section, a space is a socially constructed entity, and feminist scholars believe that spaces are gendered in nature and we can categorize space into two broad but rigid spheres/spaces: private or domestic and public. In this section, I deconstruct the dichotomous relationship between private and public in the "information age"—or as mentioned earlier, "the age of index finger"—particularly the physicality of the space. What I argue here is that the new technology has made the boundaries between physical spaces less relevant. There are two perspectives to this debate. First, the technology has transformed a private space (for example, the home) into a public space. Appropriation of "mobile" space has given tremendous opportunity to South Asian women to participate in public lives, participating in discussions and expressing their opinions in the public sphere without transgressing the physical boundary of a private space (home[6]). Many respondents pointed out that mobile devices have made them better connected to the world outside of the "homes." What makes it more relevant is the spontaneity of this connection. Most of the women always keep their mobile phone near them, so they can instantly participate in any world affairs. I have observed this mostly during some important sporting events involving South Asian nations or, say, the soccer world cup. Some of the women from my data set updated their status on Facebook and Twitter instantly as the event progressed. While conducting online "deep hanging out," it was difficult for me to ascertain whether they were watching the events on television or they were on their mobile devices. It is ironic, in way, that the "mobile device" has reduced the physical mobility of boundary crossing (between private and public) to be less significant.

> I am almost always online, either on my iPhone or on my iPad except when I am doing my some important daily chores and when I go to gym. See my son is in middle school now and I have a maid who does pretty much all the household chores. I have plenty of free time, so I like spending on social media. With the mobile phones (smart phones) it has become so easy. I don't even open my laptop for days. This is given me opportunity participate in the public discussions, etc. without going out of my house. Isn't it great?! The other day you know that Syrian boy who was washed ashore. I was cooking something in my kitchen when I got a ping on my mobile for the Facebook notification. That was so awful, No? I immediately shared it. I shared it because I wanted more and more people to know about it and it also portrays me as a well-informed sensitive woman.
>
> (AC, Indian women migrant in Dhaka, age 40)

In this case, AC was able to display her "well-informed" and "sensitive" self to the world from "domesticated space such as kitchen." The mobile devices have facilitated a real-time interaction between local and global. Now, South Asian middle-class women do not wait to watch CNN, BBC, and Al Jazeera to gain insight into the world affairs. They get everything in their mobile devices. The findings here are contrary to the claim made by earlier research like Rakow and Navarro's (1993, p. 155 in Lemish & Cohen, 2005, p. 512). In the study of mothers in the US, the research notes,

> The cellular telephone, because it lies in that twilight area between public and private, seems to be an extension of the public world

when used by men, an extension of the private world when used by women. That is, men use it to bring the public world into their personal lives. Women tend to use it to take their family lives with them wherever they go.

But we have found here is that it is not just men but women also bringing in the public discourses in the private world.

Second, the social practices of women regarding technology have transformed a public space into a private space. Now, women can get involved in highly personal and private communications in a public space. Since most of the time, families are traveling, the applications for instant free calls have become extremely beneficial for the women[7] (both traveling and non-traveling). Now, they can communicate with their family and friends, colleagues, and/or any other person from anywhere—from the airport lounge to a moving train, from a restaurant or a park, while jogging or driving[8] (Wei & Lo, 2005). Through chats and talks, they create their own private space around them in a well-designated public space. In that space, they travel miles and their physical surroundings become less relevant for them during those transactions.

> FH's husband travels a lot for work. Most of the time he is gone for months. I have observed her talking to her husband when she is at her son's school. At home, she is not very comfortable as her in-laws are there. The space though a public space gives her the "privacy" she needs to talk to her husband. And, most of the time she talks to her husband on FaceTime.[9]
>
> (A Bangladeshi woman based in Dhaka)

In a multi-country study, Jarvenpaa and Lang (2005) echoed similar findings about how mobile users create their own private space and indulge in some very personal and intimate communication in public spaces.

Similarly, Hampton and Gupta (2008, p. 832), in their study on US cities, show how mobile technology is giving rise to "public privatism." They opined that though mobile technology is considered as a personal tool, it has given a greater opportunity for people to participate in public sphere.

Public Display of Private Emotions and Practices

Another aspect, which needs to be highlighted here, is the display of private emotions and practices in a public digital space like Facebook, Twitter, and Instagram through mobile technology. More and more South Asian women are sending well-wishes online to their family members (for example, their husband, children, parents, sibling, and friends) on their important days like birthdays and anniversaries. They share their and their family members' achievements, success, sickness, and anxiety, all on the social media platforms (especially Facebook). The following excerpts from my field notes throw some light on this:

> Through her posts and pictures, which she posted on Facebook I could write a travel diary of her India trip. Everyday she posted about all her activities—when she is checking into different airports, when she landed on a particular airport. Which movies she watched and where all she went for eating out and shopping, her purpose of the trip which was a wedding, different rituals of wedding, her return journey. (Field diary section on RS)

> Yesterday, I went for a women's only dinner to an upmarket eating joints in Dhaka. The dress code was saree.[10] As soon as we reached, AC and FH started taking pictures. We had just started eating our meals when AC asked me "who is this person Ishita." I was taken aback that how does she know a friend from Malawi. I explained about my friend and asked why was she asking about her. She said, "Ah because I have uploaded our pictures on FB and I have also tagged you. So this friend of yours has commented on the picture." By the time I returned home and checked my Facebook, most of the pictures were uploaded and many of my friends had already commented on the pictures.

The display of private emotions and practices has started ever since social media came into picture, but as explained in previous sections, mobile technology has made it possible in real time. It is important here to highlight that some scholars opined that such "exhibitionism" has contributed to empowering women (Koskela, 2004). Even in my research, I found that women make conscious decisions on what to exhibit and what not to exhibit. Deeper observations on South Asian women's mobile space reveal that they share mostly positive and happy emotions and practices. However, some of them also share other negative emotions like death, sickness, and how they are feeling about the different developmental and security issues engulfing the world now. Though private matters are much more exposed and exhibited in the present era, not all is out there. As Koskela (2004, pp. 210–211) states, "There will always be dead angles—both in space and time (–) Angles of privacy, or perhaps angles of shame. Something is exposed but some secrets kept. No matter how much is revealed, there is still something invisible in the visible."

Postmodernism, Mobile Spaces, and South Asian Women: Subjectivity and Agency

Coming back to Leferbve's argument about social production of space, I argue here how mobile spaces are also a gendered entity (Schmid, 2008). Scholars have argued that we cannot talk about mobile technology or any technology in a purely technological manner. Technology is also socially constructed and embedded fully in the present social structures and systems of a given society (Castells et al., 2007; Hjorth, 2009; Lemish & Cohen, 2005; Sassen, 2002; Sheller and Urry, 2003). The present research reveals that, to some extent, advancement of mobile technologies is seen as an important milestone in pursuit of postmodernity among South Asian women (Hjorth, 2009). As argued by Giddens (1992) and Beck (1992), the twin processes of "individualization" and "reflexivity" have remained key to postmodernist society (Mulineri & Sandell, 2009). My analysis shows that access to new technologies has enhanced the agentic power of South Asian women. They hold absolute power over their phones—from how they should be displayed, to which apps and program to use, and in what ways they would use them. They have bigger role is displaying self, which they have aspired to in the mobile space. They are trying to master the art of the "selfie," and it has become the most sought after skill among the "smart" women. Due to mobile devices, they are reconnected to their old friends. Most of the women I studied have at least two to three WhatsApp group of friends—school friend groups, college friend groups, university friend groups, and the list can be longer. On an average, these women were part of eight to ten groups—some very temporary in nature and some long-lasting groups, such as groups of friends and families. The women display a great sense of autonomy while interacting in these groups. So can we conclude that appropriation of mobile space has helped South Asian women to march toward postmodernity? This will be really a naïve conclusion to make, though. While mobile spaces have produced sites of autonomy for South Asian women, it has not led them "to shape their own biographies, choose and construct their own lives without the compulsion/guidance of tradition" (Mulineri & Sandell, 2009, p. 495). My observation here is the autonomy and power achieved through mobile technologies are still at the superficial level. Below this level, South Asian women appear to be "between and betwixt" modernity and tradition. Every day, their display of self is transcending the boundaries of modernity and tradition. For example, PS always makes it a point to upload her picture on *Teej*.[11] When I asked her about this during one of our Facebook messenger chat sessions, she replied, "I am a modern woman. But I also want to show people that I am still connected to our traditional values." However, what is important to note here is that PS is making a conscious decision to observe the festival and display her traditional self to the world. What I want to conclude here is that, though mobile spaces were considered to be less gendered as observed by Lemish and Cohen (2005, p. 520), gender construction even in the postmodern world continues to be based on "performances" and "social practices."

Another point I want to make here is that mobile technologies sometimes create hostile relationships with existing patriarchal norm.

As some of my respondents reveal, in many instances, their posts, pictures, or selfies uploaded on social media or WhatsApp have created frictions in the family. Those uploads were considered inappropriate to the South Asian sensibilities and thus created tension within family. GJ, an Indian by origin, was dating an Australian after her broken marriage. Her boyfriend had uploaded a picture of their vacation on Facebook, which they took while swimming. This practice, which was completely normal in Western sensibilities, stood in stark contrast with Indian traditional sensibilities. GJ had to face extreme reaction from her families back in India. Eventually, she took down that photo from Facebook.

More extreme implications have also been observed such as the following news report (Sunny, 2016):

> Annoyed with his wife for using Facebook and WhatsApp despite repeated warnings, a 36-year-old man shot her dead using his licensed pistol before killing himself with the same weapon in South-west Delhi's Baba Haridas Nagar. According to the police, 36-year-old Jagbir was a private security officer. A native of Gohana in Haryana, he got married to Anita around five years ago. The couple has two children and had recently shifted to a rented accommodation in Baba Haridas Nagar, close to Anita's parents. She allegedly defied Jagbir and purchased a smartphone nearly a fortnight ago. While he wanted to keep her away from smartphones, it was her instant liking towards Facebook and WhatsApp that reportedly left him furious. Investigators said Anita created Facebook and WhatsApp accounts soon after buying the phone, and started spending a lot of time on social media. However, Jagbir viewed her presence on social media with suspicion and told her to delete the accounts. Anita refused to do so and that led to frequent quarrels between them, said DCP (South-West) Surender Kumar. "While leaving for his hometown on Wednesday, Jagbir told Anita to stop using social media. When he returned home on Friday morning, he found her using Facebook and WhatsApp," said Mr. Kumar. This led to a heated exchange between the couple, with Jagbir taking out his licensed pistol and repeatedly shooting Anita at a close range. He then shot himself in the head.

This case once again brings forth the fact that there are different levels of power structure and there are specific social contexts that restrict women's bargaining power with patriarchy (Kandiyoti, 1988). However, we have to move beyond the traditional notions of agency while discussing on the role of mobile phones on women's autonomy and power. The women in my study apply different strategies of negotiations and bargain with patriarchy. Their situation could be best described as what Hoan et al. (2016) observed in the case of Vietnamese foreign brides in Singapore, as "restricted agency." In the case of Vietnamese foreign brides, mobile phones mediated the twin processes of displaying their traditional female self in the domestic sphere and facilitating their individual aspirations at the professional and social context (Hoan et al. 2016).

Conclusion

Deeper exploration of public-private dichotomy in the chapter reveals that South Asian women are making their presence felt in the digital space through mobile phones and devices. The chapter has shown that advancement of technologies has facilitated the blurring of boundaries between private and public. What is important here is that mobile technology has not only created "public privatism," but it also enables public discourses to transcend the boundaries of the home/domestic sphere.

However, the blurring of boundary has not given rise to "placelessness," but has created a "mobile habitus," which enables us to be present in multiple places simultaneously (Moores, 2012). The chapter has shown that mobile technology has produced many paradoxes for South Asian women; it has given them some autonomy and power over their mobile practices, but at the same time, women are, at present, not re-negotiating their status with the patriarchy. Their march toward modernity and postmodernity has not yet actualized. This brings us to the premise that technology per se cannot be liberating for women. Technology is embedded in social context and operates within it. As Lemish and Cohen (2005, p. 512) points out, "gendered nature of the mobile phone is also located within and derived from the interaction between various processes of meaning and actual use of the medium, and not in the nature of the technology itself."

Therefore, we have to be extra cautious when we make big claim about the impact of technology on social structures.

Notes

1 Malayalis are people from state of Kerala, India.
2 I have used digital space, virtual space, mobile, and electronic space interchangeably in this chapter.
3 http://www.emarketer.com/Article/Wide-Gender-Gap-Persists-Internet-Mobile-Usage-India/1014216.
4 http://www.slideshare.net/wearesocialsg/we-are-socials-guide-to-social-digital-and-mobile-in-bangladesh-2nd-edition-nov-2012.
5 http://www.slideshare.net/wearesocialsg/we-are-socials-guide-to-social-digital-and-mobile-in-pakistan-dec-2011.
6 Following the feminist notion, I am considering "home" as a private space.
7 Though women are traveling more than they used to travel before, men still have a higher share.
8 Now, modern cars also enable mobile friendly technology. Through Bluetooth, one can connect to the sound system of the car and can talk freely.

9 FaceTime is a face-to-face calling application inbuilt in Apple devices.
10 Saree is a national outfit in India and Bangladesh.
11 It is festival from state of Bihar, India where wives keep a day-long fast for their husband's longevity and prosperity.

References

Ananth, V. (2016). Only 17% Indians own smartphones: Survey. Livemint (February 24). Retrieved from http://www.livemint.com/Consumer/yT14Ogt SC7dyywWSynWOKN/Only-17-Indians-own-smartphones-survey.html. Downloaded on 13 August 2016.

Appadurai, A. (2006). Disjuncture and difference in the global cultural economy. In M. G. Durham & D. M. Kellner (Eds.), *Media and cultural studies: Key works* (revised addition) (pp. 584–603). US, UK, Australia: Blackwell.

Balakrishnan, K., Tamizoli, P., Abdurrahman, U., & Kanwar, A. (2010). Using mobile phones to promote lifelong learning among rural women in Southern India. *Distance Education 31*(2), 193–209.

Beck, U. (1992). *Risk society: Towards a new modernity*. London: Sage.

Bell, G. (2006). The age of thumb: A cultural reading of mobile technologies from Asia. *Knowledge, Technology & Policy 19*(2), 41–57.

Campbell, S. W. & Park, Y. J. (2008). Social implications of mobile telephony: The rise of personal communication society. *Sociology Compass 2*(2), 371–387.

Castells, M. (2010). *The rise of the network society*. West Sussex, UK: Wiley-Blackwell.

Castells, M., Fernandez-Ardevol, M., Qiu, J. L., & Sey, A. (2007). *Mobile communication and society: A global perspective*. Cambridge, MA: MIT Press.

Emarketer (2016). Wide Gender Gap Persists for Internet, Mobile Usage in India. Retrieved in September 2016 from http://www.emarketer.com/Article/ Wide-Gender-Gap-Persists-Internet-Mobile-Usage-India/1014216.

Giddens, A. (1992). *The Transformation of Intimacy: Sexuality, Love and Eroticism in Modern Societies*. Cambridge: Polity.

Goggin, G. (2006). *Cell phone culture: Mobile technology in everyday life*. London and New York: Routledge.

Haddon, L. (2001). *Domestication and mobile telephony*. Paper presented at the Conference 'Machines that Become Us' Rutgers University, New Jersey, April 18–19, 2001.

Haddon, L. (2007). Roger Silverstone's legacies: Domestication. *New Media & Society 9*(1), 25–32.

Hampton, K. N. & Gupta, N. (2008). Community and social interaction in the wireless city: Wi-Fi use in public and semi-public spaces. *New Media Society 10*(6), 831–850.

Hesse-Biber, S. N. (2011). *The handbook of emergent technologies in social research*. Oxford, UK: Oxford University Press.

Hilbert, M. (2011). Digital gender divide or technologically empowered women in developing countries? A typical case of lies, damned lies, and statistics. *Women's Studies International Forum 34*(6), 479–489.

Hjorth, L. (2009). *Mobile media in Asia Pacific: Gender and the art of being mobile*. London and New York: Routledge.

Hoan, N. T., Chib, A., & Mahalingham, R. (2016). Mobile phones and gender empowerment: Enactment of 'Restricted Agency' *ICTD '16*, June 03–06, 2016, Ann Arbor, MI. Retrieved from https://www.researchgate.net/profile/Arul_Chib/publication/299824834_Mobile_phones_and_Gender_Empowerment_Enactment_of_'Restricted_Agency'/links/5705ec7208ae44d70ee349e4.pdf. Downloaded on September 26, 2016.

Ishii, K. (2006). Implications of mobility: The uses of personal communication media in everyday life. *Journal of Communication* 56(2006), 346–365.

Jarvenpaa, S. L., & Lang, K. R. (2005). Managing the paradoxes of mobile technology. *Information Systems Management*, Fall, 7–23.

Kandiyoti, D. (1988). Bargaining with patriarchy. *Gender and Society* 2(3), 274–290.

Katz, J. E. (2011). *Magic in the air: Mobile communication and the transformation of social life*. New Brunswick (USA) and London (UK): Transaction Publishers.

Katz, J. E., & Sugiyama, S. (2005). Mobile phones as fashion statements: The co-creation of mobile communication's public meaning. *Mobile communications, Vol. 31 of the series Computer Supported Cooperative Work* (pp. 63–82). Retrieved from http://citeseerx.ist.psu.edu/viewdoc/download?doi=10.1.1.126.3888&rep=rep1&type=pdf. Downloaded on 27th April 2016.

Koskela H (2004) Webcams, TV Shows and Mobile phones: Empowering Exhibitionism. *Surveillance & Society CCTV Special* 2(2/3) pp 99–215.

Kurniawan, S. (2006). An exploratory study of how older women use mobile phones. In P. Dourish & A. Friday (Eds.), *Ubicomp 2006, LNCS 4206* (pp. 105–122). Berlin: Springer.

Lee, S. (1999). Private uses in public spaces: A study of an Internet Café. *New Media Society* 1(3), 331–350.

Lemish, D., & Cohen, A. A. (2005). On the gendered nature of mobile phone culture in Israel. *Sex Roles* 52(7/8), 2005. doi:10.1007/s11199-005-3717-7.

Leung L & Wei R. (2000) More than just talk on the move: Uses and gratifications of the cellular phone. *Journalism and Mass Communication Quarterly*; Summer, 77, (2) pp 308–320.

Li, S., Glass, R., & Records, H. (2008). The influence of gender on new technology adoption and use–mobile commerce. *Journal of Internet Commerce* 7(2), 270–289.

Madianou, M., & Miller, D. (2011). Mobile phone parenting: Reconfiguring relationships between Filipina migrant mothers and their left-behind children. *New Media & Society* 13(3), 457–470.

Marx, G. T. (2001). Murky conceptual waters: The public and the private. *Ethics and Information Technology* 3, 157–169.

Masten, D. & Plowman, T. (2003). Digital ethnography: The next wave in understanding the consumer experience. *Design Management Journal* 14(2), 75–81.

Moores, S. (2012). *Media, place & mobility*. New York: Palgrave Macmillan.

Mulinari, D. & Sandell, K. (2009). A feminist re-reading of theories of late modernity: Beck, Giddens and the location of gender. *Critical Sociology* 35(4), 493–507.

Murthy, D. (2008). Digital ethnography: An examination of the use of new technologies for Social Research. *Sociology* 42(5), 837–855.

Nielson. (2012). Smartphones in India: Web browsing is for men, texts are for women. Referred online on September 30 2016 from http://www.nielsen. com/us/en/insights/news/2012/smartphones-in-india-web-browsing-is-for-men-texts-are-for-women.html.

Parrenas, R. (2005). Long distance intimacy: Class, gender and intergenerational relations between mothers and children in Filipina transnational families. *Global Networks* 5(4), 317–336.

Pertierra, R. (2005). Mobile phones, identity and discursive intimacy. *Human Technology* 1(1), 23–44.

Rosaldo, M. Z. (1973). Women, culture and society: A theoretical framework' in. M. Z Rosaldo, & L. Lamphere, (ed.) *Women, Culture and Society*, (pp. 17–42) Stanford Calif: Stanford University Press.

Sassen, S. (2002). Towards a sociology of information technology. *Current Sociology* 50(3), 365–388.

Schmid, C. (2008). Henri lefebvre's theory of the production of space: Towards a three-dimensional dialectic (Translated by Goonewardena B.). In K. Goonewardena, S. Kipfer, R. Milgrom, & C. Schmid (Eds.), *Space, difference, everyday life: Reading Henri Lefebvre,* (pp. 27–45). New York and London: Routledge.

Sheller, M. & Urry, J. (2003). Mobile transformations of 'public' and 'private' life. *Theory Culture Society* 20(3), 107–125.

Shields, R. (2002). A resumé of everyday life. *Space and Culture* 5(1), 4–8.

Shields, R. (2006). Knowing space. *Theory Culture Society* 23(2), 147–149.

Shuter, R. (2012). When Indian women text message: Culture, identity, and emerging interpersonal norms of new media. In P. H. Cheong, J. N. Martin, & L. P. Macfadyen (Eds.), *New media and intercultural communications: Identity, community and politics* (pp. 209–222). New York: Peter Lang Publishing Group.

Slater, D. (1998). Public/private. In C. Jenks (Ed.), *Core sociological dichotomy* (pp. 140–150). London: Sage.

Sunny, S. (2016). Annoyed with wife for using Facebook and WhatsApp, man shoots her dead. [The Hindu]. Retrieved in September 2016 from http://www. thehindu.com/news/cities/Delhi/annoyed-with-wife-for-using-facebook-and-whatsapp-man-shoots-her-dead/article8771259.ece. June 25.

Tandon, S. (2015). How men and women divide their time on smartphones. [Livemint epaper]. Retrieved in October 2016 from http://www.livemint. com/Consumer/TIsU8uiX5kQGMAoTqfI92M/How-men-and-women-divide-their-time-on-smartphones.html. August 12.

Thomson, K. M., & Paul, A. (2016). "I am not sure how much it will be helpful for me": Factors for digital inclusion among middle class women in India. The Library Quarterly: Information, Community, Policy: 86(1) pp. 96–103 (Accessed directly from the author).

Varis, P. (2014). *Digital ethnography.* Tilburg Papers in Cultural Studies, paper no. 104. Retrieved from http://citeseerx.ist.psu.edu/viewdoc/download?doi= 10.1.1.570.8058&rep=rep1&type=pdf. Downloaded on September 28, 2016.

Wajcman, J., Bittman, M., & Brown, J. E. (2008). Families without borders: Mobile phones, connectedness and work-home divisions. *Sociology,* 42(4), 635–652.

Wei, R., & Lo, V. (2005). Staying connected while on the move: Cell phone use and social connectedness. *New Media & Society,* 8(1), 53–72.

7 Inscribing Intimacy
Conceptual Frames for Understanding Mobile Media Affect

Amparo Lasén and Larissa Hjorth

Digital Inscriptions and Intimate Public Entanglements

> This picture with my friend is not a good selfie but I love it because it represents a critical moment for us. We make handicrafts and went to sell them in a market, where we were told that there would be a stand available. We went to Caceres for four days and when we got there, no stand, no nothing, just a space in the sidewalk. And everything you can see there, but our materials, the crafts, everything was lent to us. People there lent us the tables, the stand, the fabrics, an electric generator, lights. After a horrible day, we did it. This picture… it's a bitch that I cannot share it because my friend's family does not know that she was in Caceres, but this picture… I will never delete it.
>
> (Irene, 35, selfies workshop in Madrid in June 2015)

Irene shared this picture at our workshop when we asked the participants to show four selfies (good, bad, old one, and a current profile picture).[1] This is a "good" selfie for her, not for technical or aesthetic reasons, but because it conjures a good memory. She would like to share it online—allowing her friends to witness how a bad situation turned out well—but she can't, because that would get her friend in trouble. Thus, this picture—that she will never delete—is kept to be seen by Irene and to be shared offline with those who do not put her friend's secret at risk (such as the aforementioned workshop).

Maria often shares camera phone images by Facebook and Instagram. But, she also keeps some images on her phone that she *doesn't* share. For Maria, these *unshared* images are too personal and intimate, too vulnerable to compete in the multiple and contesting contexts of social media. Instead, Maria keeps these images on her phone, carrying them around with her everywhere she goes. Sometimes she looks at them, sometimes she feels them as memories by just holding the phone—as if it were an affective repository. A hand of a loved one no longer alive. A flower on a parent's grave. These intimate moments are about a particular digital inscription.

In this chapter, we reflect upon some of the ways in which mobile media contributes to inscribing intimacy as part of new forms of affective practices, including sharing, witnessing, and attunement. Drawing from fieldwork in public and domestic spaces in Melbourne and Madrid, we reflect upon the important role of (shared and nonshared) mobile media images within contemporary culture in the reformulation of the links between public and private with intimacy. In order to do so, we begin with the idea of digital inscriptions that contribute to making visible and durable what use to be fleeting, ephemeral, and hardly noticeable, enlarging the domain of what can be subject to affective sharing and witnessing, and thus contributing to new forms of digital intimate publics. We explore concepts such as affective witnessing, modulations of intimacy, and performing private intimacy.

Affective Witnessing

As the two opening vignettes illustrate, mobile media images can play symbolic and material roles in the imbrication of intimacy with memory. In news media of late, it is often the mobile media images of public disasters or microcelebrities that create types of affective witnessing and digital intimate publics. Mobile media images highlight the role of the network and dissemination in *emplacing* visuality (Pink and Hjorth 2014). However, affective witnessing can occur on the intimate level whereby users don't share the images; instead, over time, the images take on a layering of affective witnessing. For Papailias, affective networks like YouTube create new practices that entangle mourning with witnessing and viceversa (2016). The emotional and affective power of the mobile—as an assemblage of material, symbolic, and immaterial practices—within everyday rituals has been noted by scholars such as Jane Vincent (2010), Leopoldina Fortunati (Vincent and Fortunati 2009), and Amparo Lasén (2004).

When thinking about the textures of digital inscriptions as part of an array of affective witnessing, we are reminded of an example found at a selfie workshop hosted Madrid in 2015, with participants aged 18–25. In previous research projects, we found that after a couple breakup, women deleted the number of their exes. This digital inscription technique operated to "delete" them from their lives; both as a physical and symbolic gesture, it materialized the separation and ending (as well as preventing the temptation of contacting them later). Nowadays, blocking your ex in social media platforms is a current practice, as a gesture marking that they are now out of the circle that shares our digital inscriptions and is allowed to monitor us. This is a digital gesture that ends the mutual accessibility, availability, and transparency that characterized their former full-time intimacy.

The participants in the selfie workshop describe several cases where some of them and some of their friends, mostly women as well, temporarily leave social media platforms, such as Facebook or Instagram, after a breakup, in order to avoid the mutual affective witnessing and disclosure that shaped their couple full-time intimacy. In doing this, they want to prevent the possibility of being in the known of their exes lives and likes and, vice versa, the possibility for them to watch our doings and likes. Then, the temporary break of the social media routine is part of the grieving following the breakup, a digital remediation of the old word "far from the eyes, far from the heart."

The idea that forms of intimacy might be generated in contexts that are at the same time public is not new. As Laurent Berlant observed in last century (well, 1998), intimacy has taken on new geographies and forms of mobility, most notably as a kind of "publicness" (1998, p. 281). In keeping with Michael Warner, Berlant sought to queer traditional and static notions of the public and citizenship by addressing the often tacit and yet increasingly important role of the intimate. In a digital material environment, intimate relations are not simply performed in pairs, bounded groups, or cultural contexts; rather, they also traverse the online and offline. This traversing sees physically public worlds entangled by electronic privacy and an electronic public that is geographically private.

As Hjorth and Michael Arnold have argued (2013), through a revised concept of intimate publics we can understand the competing identities and practices of mobile media that reflect localized and regional histories. They argue for the need to think about intimacy as something that is not just among individuals but also in terms of what Michael Herzfeld calls "cultural intimacy." For Herzfeld, cultural contexts inform the ways in which intimacy plays out in everyday practices. Through a notion of cultural intimacy, we can reconfigure intimate publics as they move in and out of the digital practices. Hjorth and Arnold suggest that intimate publics are being shaped increasingly by the new forms of "mobile intimacy"; that is, the ways in which intimacy and our various forms of mobility (across technological, geographic, psychological, physical, and temporal differences) infuse public and private spaces. These new forms of mobile intimacy, therefore, underpin some of the ways in which life and death are represented—or, as Graham et al. note, "how publics are formed and connected with through different technologies as much as which publics are created and networked" (2013, p. 135).

Within this networked configuration, the changing role of affect needs to be considered. As Sara Ahmed notes in the case of the "cultural politics of emotion" (2004), we need to move beyond Western models of emotion as inside/outside and instead understand its affective capacity that leaves residue on the texture of the body. Ahmed explores the work that the lived emotions do in and around the capitalist nation-state and how emotion works on the surfaces of bodies. For Ahmed, emotions have affective power (2004, p. 60). In her discussion of fear and grief, Ahmed argues that emotions stick to bodies that in turn carry these particular histories and memories. In the case of mobile media, the sticky affect of intimacy creates a particular relationship to memory and practices of witnessing.

Much of the work around memory and affective witnessing has taken the form of images that have gone viral. Memory study scholars such as Anna Reading have highlighted the ways in which public events such as the London 2005 underground bombing played out in particular ways through the affective witnessing dimensions of mobile media, which she calls "mobile witnessing" (2009). This witnessing takes on specific imbrications of the intimate with the public. As Papailias notes in the case of YouTube as "affective network," media create a type of sociality around mourning and witnessing. Through the comments section in YouTube, witnessing texts can be formed as part of what she calls an "intersubjective sphere of mourning" (2016, p. 8). The comments are embodied and create a sense of "bodily intimacy and spatial copresence" through gesturing and linguistic acts such "shuddering, trembling, stomach tightening, crying, and weeping" (2016, p. 8). For Papailias, viral memorials are interwoven with "affective public in the assemblage of mourning" (2016, p. 1).

So too for Reading, mobile media image sharing transforms how we experience, share, and represent events of emotional significance in our lives during disasters. In particular, they highlight the diverse registers of "memory capital" (Reading 2009) as linked to national citizenship and transnational human value chains. However, what happens to the affective and witnessing dimensions when images are shared just for a short lapse of time or only shared with one person or not shared at all? As Reading identifies elsewhere, mobile media can be understood as part of a movement to wearable memories (2009). Remediating analog forms of mobile memorial practices like a photo in necklace, mobile media bring dimensions of the ephemeral into play. While much of the work around camera phone practices has focused upon the images we share, what is kept and *not shared* plays a particular role in the types of affective digital inscriptions.

Digital Inscriptions

So what do we mean when we talk about digital inscriptions? Mobile phone remediations of oral, written, and visual communication produce and keep digital inscriptions as numbers, sounds, images, and texts that are displayed, shared, and stored, and then are susceptible to become wearable memories. They inscribe people's messages, exchanges, connections, movements, ideas, feelings, and physical appearance, while at the same time contributing to inscribe, configure, and track affects, relationships, and subjectivities. By their power of inscription, digital devices make noticeable, to the own users as well as to third parties, users' social networks, connections, and movements as well as the presence of significant others and their affective bonds. They provide information about the cohesion, intensity, reciprocity, and intimacy of social relationships, thanks to different metrics provided by the calls and messages lists, the conversations record, inbox and outbox folders, visit counters, messages and chats logs, or the number of likes or retweets. Recent developments regarding wearables and apps under the terms self-tracking, quantified self and life logging intensify this trend and affordance already characteristic of previous forms of digitalization (Lupton 2016).

After drawings, narratives, and forms of calculation, digitization would be the more recent form of making commensurable a plurality of inscriptions, producing what Bruno Latour calls "immutable mobiles," such as photos, maps, or plans (Latour and Hermant 1996). These entities afford the mobility of relations between different inscriptions that can be shared and compared and the immutability of what is transported. They operate as translations of other entities, following a double movement of reduction and amplifications: reduction of the multiple features of the particular entity represented by the inscription and amplification by the possibilities of being compared, commensurable and combinable with other inscriptions, facilitating their control, management, and transmission.

For instance, a digital self-portrait shared and displayed in a social media platform can be at the same time a reduction of the many features and intensities of the particular body presented and represented in the selfie as a photographic object, as well as the capabilities of that particular body are augmented regarding, for instance, the ability to be present in multiple times and places, the associations made possible with other pictures displayed in the platform, the articulations with other inscriptions afforded by the platform, such as comments, likes, date, localization, etc., as well as the amplifications and reductions due to the different possibilities to be, not just looked at, but grabbed by third parties, from contacts and friends, or other unknown platform users, to monitoring institutions or commercial management of the platform (Senft and Baym 2015).

A double process of inscription takes place in mobile mediations. In one hand, many aspects of our ordinary life, including our bodies and feelings, are inscribed and materialized in our digital devices, becoming noticeable for ourselves and for others, potentially increasing our reflexivity as well as the possibilities of being grabbed and scrutinized by third parties. In the other hand, our self and subjectivity, understood as a complex network of affections, skills, gestures, behaviors, perception, and interactions, are being inscribed and shaped by digital practices and mediations that are part of contemporary subjectivation and embodiment processes. In this case, our self and body become inscribed by digital practices when we learn and acquire different skills, ways of doing, seeing, listening, and interacting, or new disciplines and habits related to the expectations and obligations in interpersonal interactions set by these digital practices and uses. These digital inscriptions take part in our embodiment process in how we learn to be affected by and attached to other people and things, such as digital technologies, apps, and platforms, as the ability to affect and to be affected are intrinsic to both emotions and bodies (Latour 2004).

Digital images, such as self-portraits or selfies, are an example of this double process of inscription (Lasén 2015). Camera phones, web platforms, and mobile apps such as Snapchat or Instagram produce and keep inscriptions of our bodies, at the same time as they contribute to shape, to inscribe, the bodies of those who pose, take, modify, curate, display, and share these pictures—by the skills, gestures, feelings, and perceptions learnt and acquired in the performing of such photographic practices. Considering digital images, sounds and texts as inscriptions, instead of reflections or mere replications of bodies and selves, allow us to account for the participation of mobile mediations in the embodiment and subjectivation processes, with its particular effects on presence and modes of presentation and self-presentation. By being inscribed in smartphones, apps, webcams, and social media platforms, bodies multiply their presence in different spaces and times, as once they enter the space of the "digital super-public," they outlive the time and place in which these photos were originally produced, viewed, or circulated (Senft and Baym 2015, p. 1589).

Bodies become bidimensional in the smooth surface of the screens, reduced then using Latour's terms. But feedback from other bodies facing the screen can contribute to excitations and affective intensities, which take them out of this flat frame, acquiring other dimensions. Digital uses, practices, and consumptions not only relate to the view and the gaze, but the participants' bodies are also grabbed and moved by these mediations. As in the case of the affective witnessing in YouTube analyzed by Papailias quoted above, the bodily intimacy of those commenting on the videos is materialized in "shuddering, trembling, stomach tightening, crying, and weeping." As we should not forget, in digital interactions, our bodies are physically mobilized and affected. Thus, selfies, for instance, not only entail a complex gaze game (being at the same time the photographer, the model, the curator, and the audience of other people's selfies) but gestures, movements, and perceptions related to how our bodies are grabbed in these multiple positions, which prompt tactile interactions and affects such as excitation, pleasure, joy, disquiet, disgust, or repulsion (Senft 2008, p. 46; Paasonen 2011).

The Potential Extension of Everyday Aspects Subject to Affective Witnessing

The power of inscription of digital media generates shifts in two different kinds of aspects of our everyday life and our regime of attention. First, a greater number of ordinary and mundane aspects—such as uneventful interactions, conversations, walks, gestures, impressions, and feelings—that used to be ephemeral and volatile, only inscribed in our floating personal and collective memories, acquire a different kind of materiality and a certain duration or stability when translated into digital inscriptions that can be counted, measured, revised, shared, and compared. Second, ordinary routines, habits, and disciplines regarding everyday activities, patterns of communications, or intimate relationships, which used to be performed in a nonreflexive way, are now digitally inscribed as well, becoming visible, replicable, and measurable, increasing the possibility of being subject to reflexivity, to personal and collective interpretation, and to third parties' scrutiny. Both aspects extend what can be subject to affective witnessing and support intimate bonding and attunement.

Examples of both aspects can be found in what happens when orality translates into written exchanges in email, chats, fora, or messaging apps, that we can read several times, share to get different interpretations, or compare to other conversations—or when orality becomes not only written but visual, in the use of selfies and pictures mixed with text as part of conversations in apps such as WhatsApp and Snapchat, where emerges "your own voice-as-image" (Jurgenson 2014), as these pictures are "part of talking" in words of one of the participants in our selfies research in Madrid (Lasén 2015). Another contemporary example is how our daily walks and runs can become fixed and materialized when inscribed, displayed, and shared in a fitness app, indicating the place, the trajectory, the date, and the time we spent. When what used to be banal aspects of our everyday life (our coffee mug, the content of our meal, the view from our window) are photographed and uploaded to social media, becoming conspicuous, shared and subject to multiple forms of attention, interaction, and affection, this is—in words of Soeren Mork Petersen—when the material aspects of our daily life become mediated as the representation of the everyday, revealing the affective intensity of the everydayness.

It is the affective character of the everyday that moves these cameraphone users to take and upload pictures beyond any particular meaning, sense, or intention, as it is revealed by the difficulties of the participants in Mork-Petersen's research to explain the reasons of their practice (Mork-Petersen 2014). This affective intensity elicited by sharing the banality of the ordinariness and the mundane becomes one of the key aspects of mobile media aesthetics in cameraphones practices

(Koskinen 2007; Hjorth 2008; Mork-Petersen 2009). The banality inscribed in those images gives mobile media practices the authenticity and realism that make them attractive and attaching (Koskinen 2007). Inscribing and sharing banal objects, spaces, feelings, and situations of our daily life become one way of reaching forms of full-time intimacy (Matsuda 2005), where ritual and copresence at a distance are sustained by ambient information, given by the snapshots and other digital inscriptions exchanged, which takes over explicit communications (Ito 2005).

Our research about couples and mobile phones in Madrid provides a last illustration, regarding the materialization of impressions and perceptions that sustain and challenge intimate bonds and expectations. The call and messages register of the phone as well as the instant messaging app log are used to verify the impressions about the asymmetry in the modes of communication, when one of the members is more active in calling and messaging the other, and to support the claims for a more reciprocal interest, measured by the number of calls and messages or by the speed in answering the partner's messages (Casado and Lasen 2014).

Bonds created and sustained in intimate relationships are mobile and fluid, but they let traces in the materialities of bodies and objects. These traces, in the same interactive and relational way, contribute to the production of those materials (Law and Moll 1995). The possibility of tracking those movements and of establishing (at least for a while) the affective flow of interpersonal bonds depends largely on the materialities of bodies and objects, and now of digital devices and their inscriptions as well, which play an important role in the emergence, development, and sustaining of those bonds. Thus, digital inscriptions are another aspect of how "technology is society made durable" (Latour 1990). This is, of the temporal implications of materialities of bodies and objects as conditions for the duration and continuity of social bonds, relationships, practices, and subjectivities.

However, the stabilization of representations, interpretations, affections, modes of doing, and being is always a problem of political order and moral discipline. We cannot understand these processes by focusing attention only on the character of inscription devices themselves; rather, we must investigate the controversies about specific interpretations of digital inscriptions, as well as the disquiets and mixed feelings elicited by them. Moreover, materials are also relational effects; digital inscriptions, in this case, can increase stability, but they do not exist by or in themselves. One of the consequences of the acknowledgment of the relational character of materialities is the recognition of the relational and temporal character of stabilizations as well (Law and Moll 1995).

Thus, enlarging the domain of what is witnessed, noticeable, and susceptible to reflexivity does not necessarily lead to a more stable everyday life, intimate bonds, and social orderings, as it can also increase the possibilities and occasions for disruptions, conflicts and disagreements.

Both aspects emerging with digital inscriptions—the materialization of what was ephemeral and volatile and the increase in the possibilities for reflexivity and monitoring—entail the potential for dissonances, controversies, and mixed feelings, this is, for destabling current situations, norms, expectations, behaviors, and perceptions. The possibilities for reflexivity, knowledge, control, and transmission afforded by digital inscriptions generate different forms of conflicts, disquiets, and mixed feelings for several reasons, such as dissonances between what we say, what we do, and what we believe we should do, increased by the collapse of contexts in social media and by the articulations of online and offline interactions. The ambivalent promise of control and autonomy of mobile phones and their array of apps translates in tensions between a potential for more autonomy, self-control, and individualization, as well as for more heteronomy, as one's self, body, digital devices, and spaces become more available, accessible, and transparent to other individuals, groups, and institutions. Thus, these two shifts, introduced by digital inscriptions are charged with affective potential, increase the ability to affect and being affected.

One of the consequences of the participation of mobile media practices in embodiment processes is that the new habits, disciplines, and skills overflow the previous frames that contained our volatile bodies (Grosz 1994), frames such as the private and public divide or the presence/absence pair, challenged nowadays by the modulations of intimacy afforded by mobile mediations (Licoppe 2004). Both aspects produce shifts in current intimacies that can be grasped by trying to follow the modulation of intimate bonds and interactions through networked spaces and collectives, online and offline, weaving different connections with private and public.

Thus, digital inscriptions can be a privileged site to grasp the instabilities inherent to the public and private divide and its contextual character, as well as the "cruel optimism" (Berlant 2011) of our fantasies supported by public ideological discourses about intimacy and linked to private worlds of love, mutual support, and lack of dissent that starkly contrast with the reality of domesticity as a space of power relationships, negotiations, and conflicts. There is a strong and unspoken ambivalence of the intimate sphere, addressed by Berlant's term of "cruel optimism." Optimism as the affective structure of attachment that enables people to survive and even flourish amid the ordinariness of life-in-crisis is narrowly tied to intimacy, hiding the strong ambivalence of a sphere fraught with the instabilities of sex, money, expectations, exhaustion, and unequal relations (gender, age, etc.), as well as the ambivalences of contradictory desires involved in intimate matters such as love, friendship, sexuality, and pleasures.

The unspoken ambivalence of intimacy and its association with tacit fantasies, tacit rules, and tacit obligations to remain unproblematic elicit strong criticism and feelings when its features become an issue, when one has to face the ambivalences and unfairness of these tacit elements. Digital inscriptions increase the opportunities to materialize and help to verbalize these tacit aspects and ambivalences, helping to problematize intimacy, its expectations, and its norms. In return, as another example of the hostility toward those who point out issues, in intimacy, mobile devices, apps, and social media platforms often become the object of moral panics and the scapegoat to blame for couple and family conflicts.

Modulations of Intimacy: Ephemeral and Archival Digital Inscriptions Management in Mobile Media Practices

There are many scholars who have discussed the shift of the image through camera phones and their proclivity to sharing and the network (Frohlich et al. 2002; Okabe and Ito 2005; Kindberg et al., 2005). The images produced in and through camera phone practices are part of our attempts to make sense of the world as we capture fleeting moments and save and share our lives through social media timelines. The camera phone can be viewed as a lens for and of the intimate. The inscription of the intimate as a changing set of emotions and gestures can be framed in terms of tensions in and around the photograph's relationship to the archive and the fleetingness. In this concluding section, we discuss the role of intimacy within digital inscription practices and how this connects to ephemeral and archival tensions playing out in contemporary camera phone practices.

Intimacy emerges from the "mobile processes of attachment" (Berlant 1998, p. 284) deployed in intimate rituals, routines, and events within the familiar spaces of friendship, family, love, sex, and feeling "at home." Intimacy is always mediated (Hjorth 2009) and mediations are ways of producing attachments, "that set us in motion" (Latour 1999), and attunement between different entities, such as bodies, people, objects, technologies, spaces, and places.

Accessibility, visibility, and transparency are characteristic features of intimacy and intimate relationships: being visible, accessible, and transparent to our intimates are modes of creating trust and recognition necessary to stabilize closeness. At the same time, as the Western modern ideology situates intimacy within the private realm, intimacy should be secret, hidden, and nonaccessible for the strangers who are not our intimates. The conditions and social expectancies about accessibility and transparency are being directly affected by the development of our digital culture and the affordances of digital devices, such as smartphones.

As Lauren Berlant put it, and we stated above with the notion of cultural intimacy, there is nothing more public than privacy, and intimacy is also entangled with the public, from public and mass-media discourses, to religious norms and state policy, for instance in the configuration and regulation of intimacy institutions, such as the couple, the marriage, or the family. Intimate lives absorb and repel rhetorics, laws, ethics, and ideologies of the hegemonic public sphere but also personalize the effects of the public sphere (Berlant, 1998, p. 282). Thus, intimacy is modulated throughout private and public relations and spaces, while this boundary building, sustaining, and challenging is part of these mobile processes of attachment that give rise to intimacy. This boundary work is part of the aesthetics of attachment generated by intimacy relations and practices.

However, this does not mean, as Berlant clarifies, that inevitable forms of feeling come in. Aesthetics, as Rancière puts it, must be understood as that process that separates different domains within the perceptible or what he calls the "sensible." In these terms, divisions in social, cultural, and biological terms are in the first instance aesthetic divisions, which are subsequently politicized—that is, partake in struggles for power. As such, the aesthetic prefigures the domain that we understand as politics and in doing so, it is a political process. Thus, shifts in the regime of attention—in what is perceived, noticed, and affectively witnessed, as those facilitated by digital inscriptions and described in the previous section—belong to contemporary aesthetic and political processes.

In music and voice studies, the term "modulation" refers to the alteration or adaption of one's voice or music making according to the circumstances, the specific context, or situation of the particular listeners, which results in modifications of volume, tone, or attunement. The term modulation is apt to designate how the wide spread of mobile digital inscriptions, which mediate our interpersonal relationships, interactions, modes of presentation, and performances, contribute to shaping different articulations of intimacy with public and private mediated forms of presence and copresence through online and offline spaces, different ways of sharing with different kind of people and groups, modes of accessibility, availability and transparency, as well as forms of affective attunement through digital connections.

Instead of the entanglement of intimacy with privacy, characteristic in modern Western ideology, we can find forms of intimate public with intimate strangers, as well as intimacy being performed in semi-public online spaces, or the growing presence and importance of intimacy in the activities, affects, and connections mobilized in public realms, such as work's intimacies (Gregg 2011) or networked political actions. Intimate publics or the connections between public realms, such as politics and work, and intimacy are not new (Berlant 1998), not did they emerge with mobile media. But current mobile media uses and presence remediate such connections, allowing for particular modulation of intimacy according to its affordances and the practices where they emerge.

Examples of these modulations have received different names in the existing literature about intimacy and mobile mediations, such as mobile intimacy (Hjorth and Arnold 2013), full-time intimacy, or intimate publics. They constitute modulations of intimacy across physical spaces and electronic positions, different modes of presence and absence, as well as public and private. The ability of digital inscriptions to be displayed, replicated, and shared facilitates these forms of public and mobile intimacy and also challenges the negotiation of personal and private territories within intimate relationships, such as family and couple.

Performing Private Intimacy Thanks to Ephemerality

Digital inscriptions increase accessibility, the number of opportunities to share throughout the day, and the modes and contents to access; as well, they make harder the task to hide and keep secret those intimate contents once they become digitally inscribed. Ephemeral ways of sharing digital contents, either afforded by certain apps or enforced by particular ways of managing these inscriptions, can be a form of modulating intimacy that increases privacy in digital exchanges. Nowadays, we can find a modulation of intimacy and privacy linked to ephemeral ways of sharing, in camera phone apps that move beyond the digital archiving model of previous social media. Instead, mobile apps are moving toward the embrace of the ephemeral through Facebook's focus upon "moments," Instagram's "story" function, and apps such as Snapchat or particular uses of Instant Messaging apps such as WhatsApp.

As Gaby David (2015) found in her research with French teenagers using Snapchat, they stress the more private and intimate amusement in personal images, sharing through this app compared to Facebook or Instagram. In our research about selfies in Madrid, we have found something similar regarding selfies shared in WhatsApp messages exchanged with one person or a group of close friends or family. Unlike the self-portraits chosen to be displayed in Facebook or Instagram, these are real-time self-portraits, as those usually shared in Snapchat, considered to be more "authentic" because the posing is less prepared and because there is not a proper procedure of selection among several photos. Authenticity is stressed by not appearing necessarily good-looking and by not striking the usual poses that suit us, but portraying other gestures conveying fun and spontaneity: "sticking my tongue out," "cross-eyed," "playing silly." The participants in the research acknowledge then the contrast between these ephemeral and intimate selfies and the other uploaded to social media.

Often, these are selfies displaying everyday banality, used in visual conversations to say "I am here," "I'm late," or "see my waking-up face." Aesthetics of the photo is its immediacy, coupled with its private and intimate shareability (David 2015). Immediacy is considered as authenticity and realness, which is reinforced by the banality and everydayness. For instance, often changing the profile picture, as a way of accounting for the course of the everyday and achieving full-time intimacy at a distance, helps to increase the ephemerality of the pictures. This practice found in our research differentiates for the users the intimacy and privacy of Snapchat and WhatsApp from other social media platforms used in a more public and professional way, where the stability and durability of the profile picture helps to create a label of yourself.

So these messages and snapshots are understood as more intimate and genuine than the self-curated pictures displayed on Facebook or Instagram. Sharing these pictures is a way of performing trust and materializing feelings of love, friendship, and trust. According to the participants of David's research and our own research about selfies in Madrid, what is important is the attachment, the bond, between the senders and receivers, but not to the particular pictures. "They are not important," not made and taken to be remembered but to share what we are doing at the moment: a picnic, a barbecue, at the swimming pool, shopping, facing the bathroom mirror getting ready to get out, waiting somewhere, or in doctor's waiting room.

Sharing the pictures helps to accomplish intimacy at a distance. This is the case of Jana, one of the participants in the selfie workshop in Madrid, a 35-years-old working mother, who works long hours on weekends and receive pictures of her children throughout the day. These are uneventful pictures of her kids at home or at the park, taken and sent by her husband, that help her to pass the day better, feeling closer and connected to them.

Users differentiate between pictures portraying something to be remembered from pictures that transmit particular feelings and good vibes, but not some specific content to be remembered. As these are only shared with the closest ones, the relevance of the practice does not reside in the lasting content of a memory pictured, but as a signifier of the distinctive character of the recipients, when the immediacy and transiency of these images mark the special intimate status of those who can see them. These practices reveal as well how vulnerable and ephemeral trust can be.

Conclusion: The Attunements and Inscriptions of Non-Sharing

> I carried the picture of him in my phone, much like a hardcopy photo might be kept in a wallet. I had thought a lot about whether I should upload it to Facebook as I often catalogue and archive pictures there. But there was something about sharing the image that seems to devalue the moment and my memory of him.
>
> (Melbourne female, 30 years old, interviewee on non-sharing)

> When my partner was dying of cancer I spent a lot of time sitting by the side of his bed listening to his irregular breathe and thinking about the liminal moment and wanting to remember it. And so

I videoed his breathing on my phone. This is a video I never want anyone else to see. It's too intimate. I keep it on my mobile and so when I want to revisit that liminal moment it is always with me.

(Melbourne female, 42 years old, interviewee on non-sharing)

Much of the literature to date on camera phones has focused upon their role in terms of sharing. Yet, increasingly, people are opting out of the compulsion to "share" for various reasons—control, intimacy, and context to name a few. In an age of cataloguing and archiving, the role of the ephemeral, so pivotal to the genealogy of photography, is playing in surprising ways. Younger generations are opting into Snapchat for its spontaneity and directness, against older generations' desire for the digital archive. To understand the dialogic relationship between sharing and nonsharing, we have draw on the notion of digital inscriptions.

Digital inscriptions of our talks, experiences, thoughts, feelings, and bodies contribute to extending the realm of what can be noticeable, shared, remembered, and witnessed, by inscribing and materializing everyday aspects that previously escaped our attention, because of their fleetingness, their banality, or just because they were below the threshold of our conscious knowledge and reflexivity.

The sharing of these digital inscriptions, such as the camera phone images we have discussed here, sustain forms of mutual attunement and affective witnessing that facilitate the emergence of intimate publics and forms of full-time intimacy with our loved ones. The sticky affect of digitally mediated intimacy blurs the divide between public and private, online and offline, and presence and absence in new ways of copresence, where you do not need to be physically copresent to experience the bodily and affective effects of the mutual attunement to those connected to you by the sharing of digital inscriptions. Not all of these effects are positive, empowering, and comforting. The increased exposure, visibility, and shareability multiply the occasions and opportunities for intimacy, as accessibility and transparency are two of its conditions. However, they also increase people's vulnerability to those with whom we are attuned, as well as to unknown third parties that could have access to this content, now or in the future. The feeling and knowledge of one's own vulnerability can be also increased by the reflexivity afforded by digital inscriptions and their archival in our digital devices, platforms, and apps, which have the potential to make us aware of our tendencies, habits, contradictions, and dissonances.

Thus, we find in our research diverse modes to counter this vulnerability by limiting the exposure of camera phone images, without renouncing to take and keep them—such as ephemeral modes of sharing addressed to particular groups, either by using mobile apps, like Snapchat, which do not function in an archival mode, or by using mobile messaging apps to share images within close groups that are not intended to last and be kept. With these practices, digital affordances are worked to bring back the ephemeral and the fleeting in mediated exchanges. In these cases, ephemerality helps to modulate digital intimacies toward an increased privacy and control by limiting the ability of digital devices and spaces to become affective repositories and archives of digital inscriptions.

Current camera phone practices reveal another way of countering the vulnerability created by the sharing and exposure of digital inscriptions, while keeping, at least for a certain lapse of time, the archival capacity of digital devices. These are personal modes of affective witnessing of pictures kept in the handset to be seen and felt by its owner, but not to be shared with others online. These images become digital forms of wearable memories, as remediations of former wearable objects containing pictures, such as necklaces, wallets, or car picture frame magnets.

In the concluding paragraphs of the chapter, we consider the growing phenomenon of participants choosing not to share camera phone images, against the backdrop of the past decade of rise in camera phone practices from first to second generation, whereby camera phone apps allow for quick taking, editing, and sharing across multiple networks with their own types of affective publics and politics of sharing and disclosure. However, what has started to emerge more recently is a movement toward a nonsharing of some particularly personal and intimate digital inscriptions, as part of a pushing back against the proclivity to over-share.

For researchers, this presents new challenges as to how to study nonshared images. Often, participants who don't share certain images via a network also don't necessary want to show and discuss them with researchers. Yet, increasingly, there are participants in fieldwork who deploy mobile media for "wearable memories" (Reading 2009) that form particular relations to the digital inscriptions on and through the body. Obviously, ethnographic approaches that focus upon nuanced narratives of practices would be one method that would allow for more understanding into this growing phenomenon of ephemeral camera phone practices. Indeed, the stories that could be told via personal affective witnessing of camera phone as memory moment maker could play out in ways that don't just shape notions of intimacy but also its shaping of publics around enclosure and disclosure.

There is much research to be done on nonsharing and what it says about new forms of enclosure, disclosure, witnessing, and inscription. For researchers, the task of analyzing the nonshared image is much harder and requires more nuanced and in-depth fieldwork into these emerging tactics, working against the technological default to share and overshare. Indeed, as shifts against the archive can be noted by practices around ephemeral media like Snapchat, the relationship between the image, inscription, memory, and the archive needs to be given more and more thought.

Note

1 These workshops are part of the research project funded by the Spanish National Plan of R&D of the Ministry of Economy and Competitiveness: CSO2012-37027 *Innovaciones metodológicas para prácticas emergentes. Controversias y desasosiegos en torno a lo público/privado* (IMPE) (Methodological innovation for emergent practices. Controversies and disquiets around the public/private divide) Team members are Antonio García, Elena Casado, Héctor Puente, Laura Cassain, and Juan Carlos Revilla. The workshops were organized in Madrid between December 2014 and May 2015, with people of different age groups (18–25, 25–30, 30–35) who were selected because they take selfies and use them in social media and because they were interested in taking part in a research about their selfie practices. Different activities were performed, such as selfie taking, sharing selfies they have chosen following our request (good one, bad one, current one, and one of the firsts they took), and discussing them in the group, and the elaboration in groups of a set of rules about what make a good and a bad selfie, and what-to-do and not-to-do with them.

References

Ahmed, S. (2004). *The cultural politics of emotions*. Edinburgh, Scotland: Edinburgh University Press.

Berlant, L. (1998). Intimacy. A special issue. *Critical Inquiry*, 24(2), 281–288.

Berlant, L. (2011). *Cruel optimism*. Durham, UK: Duke University Press.

Casado, E., & Lasén, A. (2014). What is disturbing and why not to disturb. On mobile phones, gender and privacy within heterosexual intimacy. *Mobile Media and Communication*, 2(3), 249–264.

David, G. (2015). All what we send is selfie. Images in the age of immediate reproduction. In J. R. Carvalheiro & A. Serrano (Eds.), *Mobile and digital communication: Approaches to public and private* (pp. 77–98). Covilha, Portugal: LabCom Books.

Frohlich, D., Kuchinsky, A., Pering, C., Don, A., & Ariss, S. (2002). Requirements for photoware. Proceedings of the 2002 ACM conference on Computer Supported Cooperative Work. ACM Press: 166–175

Graham, C., Gibbs, M., & Aceti, L. (2013). Introduction to the special issue on the death, afterlife, and immortality of bodies and data. *The Information Society*, 29(3), 133–141.

Gregg, M. (2011). *Work's intimacies*. Cambridge, UK: Polity Press.

Grosz, E. (1994). *Volatile bodies. Towards a corporeal feminism*. Bloomington, IL: Indiana University Press.

Herzfeld, M. (2005). *Cultural intimacy*. New York: Routledge.

Hjorth, L. (2008). Being real in the mobile reel: A case study on convergent mobile media as new media and sense of place. *Convergence: The International Journal of Research into New Media Technologies*, 14(1), 91–104.

Hjorth, L. (2009). Imaging communities. Gendered mobile media in the Asia Pacific. *The Asia-Pacific Journal*, 7(9, 3). Retrieved from http://apjjf.org/-Larissa-Hjorth/3064/article.html. Accessed September 8, 2016.

Hjorth, L., & Arnold, M. (2013). *Online at Asia Pacific*. New York: Routledge.

Ito, M. (2005). *Intimate visual co-presence*. Unpublished Paper Presented at the Pervasive Image Capture and Sharing Workshop, Ubiquitous Computing

Conference. Retreived from http://www.itofisher.com/mito/archives/ito.
ubicomp05.pdf. Accessed September 7, 2016.

Jurgenson, N. (2014). The frame makes the photograph. Retrieved from http://
blog.snapchat.com. Accessed September 7, 2016.

Kindberg, T., Spasojevic, M., Fleck, R., & Sellen, A. (2005). The ubiquitous
camera: An in-depth study of camera phone use. *IEEE Pervasive Computing,*
April–June, 42–50.

Koskinen, I. (2007). *Mobile multimedia in action.* New Brunswick, NJ: Transaction Publishers.

Lasén, A. (2004). Affective technologies-emotions and mobile phones. *Receiver,*
11. 1–8.

Lasén, A. (2015). Digital self-portraits, exposure and the modulation of intimacy. In J. R. Carvalheiro & A. Serrano (Eds.), *Mobile and digital commu-*
nication: Approaches to public and private (pp. 61–70). Covilha, Portugal:
LabCom Books.

Latour, B. (1990). Technology is society made durable. *The Sociological Re-*
view, S1, 103–131.

Latour. (1999). Factures/Fractures. From the Concept of Network to the Concept of Attachment. *RES: Anthropology and Aesthetics, 36,* 20–31.

Latour, B. (2004). How to talk about the body? The normative dimension of
science studies. Body & Society, 2004, 10 (2–3): 205–229.

Latour, B., & Hermant, E. (1996). Ces Réseaux que la Raison Ignore:
Laboratoires, Bibliothèques, Collections. In C. Jacob & M. Baratin (Eds.),
Le Pouvoir des Bibliothèques. La Mémoire des Livres dans la Culture
Occidentale (pp. 23–46). Paris: Albin Michel.

Law, J., & Moll, A. M. (1995). Notes on materiality and sociality. *The Socio-*
logical Review, 43, 274–294.

Licoppe, C. (2004). 'Connected' presence: The emergence of a new repertoire
for managing social relationships in changing communication technoscape.
Environment and Planning D. Society and Space, 22(1), 135–156.

Lupton, D. (2016). *The quantified self: A sociology of self-tracking.* Cambridge,
UK: Polity Press.

Matsuda, M. (2005). Discourses of *Keitai* in Japan. In M. Ito, D. Okabe, &
M. Matsuda (Eds.) *Personal, portable, pedestrian: Mobile phones in Japanese*
life. Cambridge, MA: MIT Press.

Mørk Petersen S. (2009). Common banality: The affective character of photo
sharing, everyday life and produsage cultures (Unpublished doctoral thesis).
ITU Copenhagen.

Mork-Petersen, S. (2014). Una banalidad ordinaria. El carácter afectivo de com-
partir fotos en línea. In A. Lasen & E. Casado (Ed.) *Mediaciones tecnológi-*
cas: cuerpos, afectos, subjetividades (pp. 101–112). Madrid, Spain: CIS.

Okabe, D. and Ito, M. (2005). 'Intimate Visual Co-Presence'. Paper presented at
Ubicomp, Takanawa Prince Hotel, Tokyo, Japan, 11–14 September, accessed
28 June 2006. http://www.itofisher.com/mito/.

Paasonen, S. (2011). *Carnal resonance affect and online pornography.* Cambridge,
MA: MIT Press.

Papailias, P. (2016). Witnessing in the age of the database: Viral memorials, affective publics, and the assemblage of mourning. *Memory Studies,* January 6,
2016, doi:10.1177/1750698015622058.

Pink, S. and Hjorth, L. (2014). New Visualities and the Digital Wayfarer: Reconceptualizing camera phone photography, Mobile Media & Communication 2(1): 40–57.

Rancière, J. (2004). *The politics of aesthetics: The distribution of the sensible.* New York: Continuum.

Reading, A. (2009). Mobile witnessing: Ethics and the camera phone in the 'War on Terror'. *Globalizations*, 6(1), 61–76.

Senft, T. (2008). *Camgirls: Celebrity and community in the age of social networks.* New York: Peter Lang.

Senft, T., & Baym, N. (2015). What does the selfie say? Investigating a global phenomenon. *International Journal of Communication*, 9, 1588–1606.

Vincent, J. (2010). Me and my mobile phone. In L. Fortunati et al. (Eds.), *Interacting with broadband society. Participation in broadband society.* Berlin: Peter Lang.

Vincent, J. & Fortunati, L. (Ed.). (2009). *Electronic emotion. The mediation of emotion via information and communication technologies.* Bern, Switzerland: Peter Lang.

Whittaker, S., Bergman, O., & Clough, P. (2010). Easy on that trigger dad: A study of long term family photo retrieval. *Personal and Ubiquitous Computing, 14*(1), 31–43.

8 The Afterlife of Intimacy
Selfies, Loss, and Intimate Publics

Larissa Hjorth

In the sinking of the South Korean MV Sewol boat on April 16, 2014 (known as "Sewol"), mobile phones functioned across multiple forms of haunting—individual, collective, social, and cultural. Many of the 250 high school children that died filmed selfies during the disaster. These selfies became repositories for damning footage of procedures gone wrong. Photography has always had a complicated relationship with power and representation, especially when those photographed are absent or dead (Barthes 1981; Sontag 1977). But now, the relationship between the memory, image ownership, and dissemination is changing.

With some of the movies taken by children as young as 8 years old, camera phone footage showed terrifying scenes of people panicking. These selfie movies were not about narcissism as obsessive self-love but about the numbness and misrecognition that trauma can bring with it (Wendt 2014). They become about what Paul Frosh calls the "gestural image"—that is, a combination of photographic theory and kinesthetic sociality (2015). In the case of the Sewol selfies, they *visualized* and *embodied collective trauma*.

Here, the camera phone footage was not just a witness for court prosecutors and trauma-laden images for the families of the deceased, but the footage also functioned as highly affective memorials that quickly spread and consolidated global public outcry. The rawness of camera phones, as mementos for lives unfairly taken, became fuel in the palpable grief felt worldwide. Parents across the world felt the unspeakable pain of watching a child's last image to the world.

In this chapter, we want to argue that the selfie can be understood as a tool *for* and *of* digital intimate publics. In particular, I want to focus upon the selfie as a site for misrecognition as well as a vehicle for understanding trauma and grief. Much work of late has been conducted into the various meaning of the selfie as a vehicle for politics, sociality, and cultural practice (Senft & Baym 2015). In particular, the selfie inflects the cultural milieu in which it is taken—in this case, the selfie (or "selca") has one of the longest histories in South Korea, emerging in the 2000s (Lee 2005, 2009). This digital genealogy also informs how the specific notions of cultural intimacy play out in and through the public.

I will draw from the traumatic events of the South Korean ferry disaster of 2014 to discuss the role selfies play in reflecting cultural intimacies and intimate publics. In this disaster (called "Sewol"), we see the power of the selfie to not only remind us that media has always been *social*, but also that mobile media is challenging how the social is constituted by the political and the personal. Social media isn't just a dissemination or publicity tool. It is part of the multiple seams that bind and unbind the *personal* to the *political*, the *intimate* to the *public*. While intimacy has always been mediated—if not by media, then by language, gestures, and memory—we can see particular manifestations of continuities and discontinuities in and around mobile media practices. First, this chapter will consider a working definition of digital intimate publics.

Digital Intimate Publics

Mobile media amplify inner subjectivities as they do conform to existing sociocultural rituals and practices. As one of the most intimate devices in everyday life, mobile phones are vehicles for haunting upon multiple material, symbolic, and immaterial dimensions. They are vessels *for* and *of* our intimacies and emotions, shaping and being shaped by affective bonds. As I have argued elsewhere, mobile media are also increasingly vessels for *intimate publics* and *mobile intimacy* (Hjorth & Arnold 2013). The mobile engages particular forms of intimacies across digital and nondigital spaces, as well as expanding the temporal and geographic possibilities and continuities. Here, we can understand mobile intimacy as an overlay between the electronic with the social, the emotional with copresent. Intimacy is a multilayered and contextual concept.

As noted by others (Berlant 1998; Warner 2002; Hjorth & Arnold 2013; Dobson 2015), the idea that forms of intimacy might be generated in contexts that are at the same time public is not new. As Laurent Berlant observed in the last century, intimacy has taken on new geographies and forms of mobility, most notably as a kind of "publicness" (1998, p. 281). In keeping with Michael Warner (2002), Berlant sought to queer traditional and static notions of the public and citizenship by addressing the often tacit and yet increasingly important role of the intimate. In a digital material environment, intimate relations are not simply performed in pairs, bounded groups, or cultural contexts; rather, they also traverse the online and offline. This traversing sees physically public worlds entangled by electronic privacy and an electronic public that is geographically private. As Mimi Sheller puts it, "there are new modes of public-in-private and private-in-public that disrupt commonly held spatial models of these as two separate 'spheres'" (2004, p. 39).

Advancing this further in work with Michael Arnold, we have proposed a concept of intimate publics, through which we can understand the competing histories, identities, and practices within the Asia-Pacific region. Here, we argued the need to think about intimacy as something that is not just among individuals but also in terms of what Michael Herzfeld calls "cultural intimacy." For Herzfeld, cultural contexts inform the ways in which intimacy plays out in everyday practices. Herzfeld notes that the "intimate seeps into the public spheres that have themselves been magnified by the technologies of mass mediation" (p. 44). Here, cultural intimacy takes three forms: historical, institutional, and geographical. Through a notion of cultural intimacy, we can reconfigure intimate publics as they move in and out of the digital practices.

In the case of the Sewol disaster and its hundreds of selfies-as-eulogies, it also signified a relational bond—a *cultural intimacy* and *digital intimate public*—specific to Korean culture. Here, the Korean concept of *Jeong* is significant as one of the most "endearing and evocative" words of which there is no English equivalent. As Luke Kim notes, "Koreans consider *jeong* an essential element in human life, promoting the depth and richness of personal relations... In times of social upheaval... *jeong* is the only binding and stabilizing force in human relationships. Without *jeong*, life would be emotionally barren and person would feel isolated and disconnect from others" (1996, p. 14).

Arnold and I suggested that intimate publics are being shaped increasingly by the new forms of "mobile intimacy"; that is, the ways in which intimacy and our various forms of mobility (across technological, geographic, psychological, physical, and temporal differences) infuse public and private spaces. These new forms of mobile intimacy, therefore, underpin some of the ways in which life and death are represented—or, as Graham et al. note, "how publics are formed and connected with through different technologies as much as which publics are created and networked" (2013, p. 135).

In keeping with Berlant's queering of definitions of the public, I would like to expand upon the current array of Anglophonic examples of the selfie to consider non-Anglophonic ways in which South Korea—as one of the oldest users of selfies—has taken on subgenres such as the Sewol selfie-as-eulogy to dimensions through a South Korean example. Here, we see not only ways in which we might understand the selfie as a complex vehicle for digital intimate publics and cultural intimacies but also how we might think through the "life" of data as we move increasingly into a space haunted by specters both digital and nondigital.

Picture This: The Affect of Camera Phone Agency

Contemporary media has been characterized as playful (Sicart 2015). In many public urban contexts around the world, camera phones function as an intrinsic part of this playful fabric. The visual culture and physical spaces of public places have been quickly transformed over the past decade by camera phone apps (Hjorth & Hendry 2015). Events and street art are determined by their "Instagammable" qualities. From taking a picture of a coffee as part of an everyday ritual to the sharing of a joyful moment between friends, camera phone apps like Instagram operate to capture, share, and represent the mundane, intimate, ephemeral, tacit, and phatic (Villi & Stocchetti 2011). These images not only play with how place is experienced and mapped but also how these cartographies are overlaid by copresence across geographic, temporal, social, and spatial distances.

Camera phone practices shape, and are shaped by, various modes for conceptualizing place. As such, camera phone cultures provide particular ways in which to understand the role of cartography and copresence as an overlay between media, visual culture, and geography (Frohlich et al. 2002; Kindberg et al. 2005; Van House et al. 2005, 2011; van Dijck 2008; Rubinstein and Sluis 2008; Whittaker, Bergman, & Clough 2010; Palmer 2012; Zylinska 2015). Camera phones are key players in the idea of representing place (e.g., maps) as performative. Camera phone practices provide playful, ambient, and reflective ways to remap places and spaces across copresent platforms, contexts, and subjectivities. Genres such as the selfie have become an omnipresent barometer for contemporary, networked global culture (Walker Rettberg 2014; Senft & Baym 2015), which represent new configurations between photography, digital culture, and what can be called "kinesthetic sociability" (Frosh 2015). At the crossroads between the aesthetic and the social, camera phone practices can provide insight into contemporary digital media.

While camera phone images are shaped by the affordance of mobile technologies, they also play into broader photographic tropes and genres (Palmer 2012; Zylinska 2015). However, for Chris Chesher, the iPhone "universe of reference" disrupts the genealogy of mass amateur photography that was formed through the rise of the Kodak camera (2012). Moreover, the creative capacities of mobile media are transforming how photography overlays the social with the aesthetic in ways that remediate as they do define new visual phenomenon (van Dijck 2007). Jose van Dijck, in her detailed study of digital photography, highlighted the relationship between memory and remediation (2007).

Yet, on the other hand, through their networked and yet intimate capability, camera phones also depart in terms of their ability to transgress temporal and spatial distances and differences (Van House 2011; Villi & Stocchetti 2011). This transgression sees camera phone pictures as part of the acceleration of accumulative global images. A political crisis or uprising across one side of the world can be viewed and experienced almost instantaneously on the other side of the world (David 2010). Networked images have the potential to impact, effect, and affect in a manner unimagined by analog photography practice (Frohlich et al. 2002; Kindberg et al. 2005; Van House et al. 2005; Whittaker et al. 2010).

The role of camera phones to highlight and challenge "performances of power" and citizen agency are magnified during times of disasters and celebrations (Frosh 2001). Expanding upon Kodak's advertising rhetoric of making moments "memorable" events by photographing them (Gye 2007; Palmer 2012), camera phones not only memorialize and accelerate the amount of events shared between intimates but also to anonymous publics. For Paul Frosh, digital networked photography is not just a medium of visual communication but also has the ability to render the performance of power visible (2001). Reflecting upon the role of digital photography in the aftermath of Princess Diana's death, Frosh "explores the ways in which photographic performance at the public/private boundary dramatizes power relations through forms of social transparency, voyeurism and memoralization" (2001, p. 43).

These changing processes in modes of transparency and memorialization are integral to the rise of camera phone apps. Arguments about democratizing media and user-created content (UCC) have been integral to the camera phone genealogy (Burgess 2007), helped in part by the likes of Nokia, who claim to have put more cameras in the hands of everyday users than the whole history of photography. According to some studies, 90% of the world's population who have taken a photo have done so *only* with their camera phone (Palmer 2014). In the abundance of millions of images taken, shared, and forgotten daily, we could argue that now we photograph, like Kafka, in order to close our eyes and forget. Indeed, the continuities and discontinuities around visual culture in an age of the camera phone remind us that new media is always remediated and haunted by older analog technologies. Take, for example, the retro aesthetics of Instagram, which suggest a remediation and nostalgia for analog-looking images—what Nathan Jurgenson calls a yearning "nostalgia for the present" (2011).

Yet, in disasters we are reminded of the powerful social, cultural, and political role of the camera phone as a lens into contemporary visual culture. A recurring theme in photographic literature on photography has been the role of power and representation, especially when the subjects are absent or dead (Sontag 1977; Barthes 1981). Camera phones both extend and expand upon that tradition in remediated and new ways. This situation is particularly apparent when thinking about camera phones and their representative and nonrepresentational dimension. With networked media, it is now more possible to appropriate context and content. Camera phone practices are part of the emergence of online cataloging (boyd & Ellison 2007; Livingstone 2008) as part of the "quantified self" movement or, what Lee Humphreys dubs more accurately, the "qualified self" (forthcoming). As Nancy Van House notes, through digital networked photography, "personal photographs may be becoming more public and transitory, less private and durable, more effective as objects of communication than of memory" (2011, p. 133).

Camera phone practices are also playing a key role in the changing memorialization processes. As Connor Graham, Martin Gibbs, and Lanfranco

Aceti argue, new media are affording people's lives today to be "extended, prolonged, and ultimately transformed through the new circulations, repetitions, and recontextualizations on the Internet and other platforms" (2013, p. 133). Digital data allow new ways in which to construct one's life, death, and afterlife. This is amplified in the work of Jason Stanyek and Benjamin Piekut (2010), who explore the ghosts of the posthumous performances and performativity. While online data afford new pathways for representing and experiencing life, death, and afterlife, much of the literature has focused upon online memorials (de Vries and Rutherford 2004) and grieving processes (Veale 2003).

Increasingly, the mobile phone is not just a witness, repository, and disseminator of events; it also amplifies a type of affect in the way in which events are experienced. Here, we are using Sara Ahmed's notion of affect as a cultural and political practice. For Ahmed, affect is something that "sticks"—emotionally and psychologically. As Ahmed notes in the case of the "cultural politics of emotion" (2005), we need to move beyond Western traditional models of emotion that see emotion coming from inside to outside. Instead, Ahmed focuses upon the skin as a repository for affective textures. Ahmed explores the work that the lived emotions do in and around the capitalist nation-state and how emotion works on the surfaces of bodies. For Ahmed, emotions have affective power (2005, p. 60). In her discussion of fear and grief, Ahmed argues that emotions stick to bodies, which in turn carry these particular histories and memories.

This relationship between emotion, grief, and affect is most apparent in the Sewol disaster, whereby selfies operated as self-designated eulogies for the high school children who were tragically killed. These selfie images spoke to a new type of what Roland Barthes would call punctum (1981)—that is, the emotional affect of these images on spectators. Here, we witness a mobile punctum, whereby immediacy, ubiquity, and intimacy are entangled within the sticky aesthetics of the affect.

Memorialized, Intimate Publics: A Case Study of Camera Phones during a Disaster

As soon as the ferry capsized on April 16, 2014, multiple mobile phones were on hand, capturing the sheer terror of the events unfolding. After the ship sunk, killing over 300 passengers (246 school children) by either drowning or hyperthermia, it was the mobile media footage that friends and family cradled in their disbelief as the traumatic reality unfolded. YouTube began to fill with hundreds of UCC videos, consolidating public grief, anger and outcry. Most traumatic were the mobile media fragments of children leaving messages to their parents that they loved them as the reality of the situation started to dawn on them.

Through these highly distressing instant message (IM) and video messages, a process of shock, trauma, memorialization, and grief had begun.

In many cases, the now deceased used camera phones to not only expose the chaos of the situation but to also provide a copresence and continuing bond between themselves and their loved ones. Many used their mobile phones to film a tribute to their loved ones, while others filmed the disaster in a narrative that suggested they would survive. While a few of these stories were documented and disseminated in global press after being translated from Hangul into English, dozens of stories of mobile media memorialization processes remained untranslated and were shared just across vernacular, Korean sites.

While the remixing of the mobile footage of the deceased afforded different ways in which people could participate in the memorialization process globally, it also signified a particular type of relational bond specific to Korean culture. Here, the concept of *Jeong,* as mentioned earlier, is significant as one of the most "endearing and evocative" words, of which there is no English equivalent (Kim 1996). This is not to essentialize experience but rather to understand the specific cultural milieu from which the grief was formed.

While a similar notion of *jeong* can be found in Chinese and Japanese culture (e.g., *jyo*), it has a far less significant and poignant meaning (Kim 1996). The feeling of *jeong* is palpable in and through the tragic events and memorialization of the disaster. *Jeong* binds the various camera phone memorialization with the loved ones left behind.

The mobile footage taken during the disaster still leaves a raw affect, in that it captures the pain, confusion, and terror of the victims as they face their death. The role of mobile media to capture this liminal stage is a testament to its intimate and ubiquitous role and unquestionably, this area of mobile media memorialization before death will continue to grow and become a key area for analysis in the future. Given the newness of this phenomenon, in this section we will detail some of the events and mobile media fragments captured from the disaster to consider the changing role of mobile media in and through moments of life, death, and afterlife.

One of the most tragic is from the high school girl Park Ye-seul, who filmed the disaster at 9:40 am (the disaster was first reported at 8:40 am).[1] Ye-seul and her friends documented the disaster as it happened through selfie videos. In the video, we see typical selfie performativity (i.e., peace symbol with fingers by smiling girls) juxtaposed with other passengers crying with terror.

The video conversation, which can be found on YouTube, consists of a conversation between Ye-seul and her fellow passengers, as well as her copresent parents. She talks of how scared she and other passengers are while begging, "Please rescue us." They talk about the increasing tilt of the boat. Then, there is an official announcement "Please double check your life jacket whether it was tighten well or not. Please check and tighten it again." Ye-seul says to her videoing phone (as if her parents are inside it),

"Oh we're going to diving into the water," followed by "Mum, I am so sorry. Sorry Dad! It's bullshit!! We will be okay! See you alive."

Ye-seul's father recovered his daughter's smartphone after the disaster. He dried it out and replaced the SIM card. In the phone were videos she had filmed before she died. For this father, his daughter's phone was not just a vessel for channeling a reenactment of his daughter's last moments alive, but in doing so it afforded him the ability to move back in time and space to be "present" with her during her last moments. Here, the power of the phone and its affective affordances cannot be underestimated.

Ye-seul's selfies are far from a vehicle for narcissism. They are, as noted earlier, about a numbness and misrecognition of the event (Wendt 2014). They become part of the process of memorialization for her family and friends, spectres of *jeong*, while the deceased was still alive. Here, we see the power of the mobile phone as one of the most intimate devices to capture the fleeting moments of the deceased before they pass away. For loved ones, mobile media becomes a crucial embodied part of that passage from life to death and afterlife. The role of the mobile phone as continuing bonds between the living and the dead was evidenced in one scenario between a deceased son and his father on Kakao IM. Here, the mobile phone became like a portal between Earth and heaven. It is not uncommon for mourning relatives and friends to send messages to the deceased in order to continue the bonds and *jeong*.

The mobile phone could be viewed as a remediation of older memorialization devices, such as the photo album and letter writing. Holding onto treasured objects and inducing afterlife communication via letter writing are activities recognized now as a part of facilitating the grieving process (Klass, Silverman & Nickman 1996). While photography has always had a complicated relationship with power, representation, and death (Sontag 1977; Barthes 1981; Deger 2008), the social life of the mobile media is changing the relationship between the memory, image ownership, and dissemination. What happens to Barthes's notion of punctum, used to talk about analogue photography, in the context of digital and mobile photography? Mobile media photography provides a vehicle for continuing these activities, while at the same time, it uniquely allows for these activities to extend across temporal and spatial boundaries (Brubaker, Hayes & Dourish 2013). Far from narcissist vehicles, selfies are not only used to connect in moments of trauma and grief but also play a key role in mobilizing the Korean population into a collective action against first, the boat company and second, the government.

Conclusion: Localizing Selfie Agency

Writing two years after the Sewol disaster, one can feel the haunting of a country still in mourning for all those young, unlived lives (Choi 2014; Kim & Jeon 2014; Mullen 2014). The mobile media specters are haunted with residual punctum. As the grief goes through a variety of shades and depths, we see a country struggling with the reality of the disaster and the tragic loss of lives unlived (Amore & Scarciotta 2011; Af Segerstad et al. 2014). During and after the disaster, mobile phones have functioned in such a pivotal way, to not only generate complex ways in which we might understand the entanglements between copresence and deadness, but also the ways in which loss and grief can be channeled and memorialized in new and remediated ways.

Mobile media become haunted vessels for, and of, grief. They become interlocutors between liveness and deadness across multiple forms of presence, copresence, and telepresence (Bennett & Bennett 2000). As our lives become increasingly entangled within digital traces, the possibility for afterlife haunting takes on new terrains (Lingel 2013; Gibson 2014). Much of mobile media literature, through the work of STS (science and technology studies) sociologist Christian Licoppe and anthropologist Mizuko Ito (Ito 2003; Ito & Okabe 2005), has discussed the importance of understanding mobile media intimacy in terms of copresence—that is, electronic proximity when physically apart. However, this copresence can be further extended in the case of deadness or afterlife.

Much like the young high school children killed in this chapter's case study, the ability of mobile media images to create a type of punctum affect is clear. The slightly blurring images of many mobile media during the disaster have created a new tapestry between the spectrum and punctum. The selfie images taken by the high school children not only became highly politicized but they also resonated such posthumous "punctum." For Roland Barthes, it is the punctum that not only "pricks our skin" but also *bruises* us with an affective texture that haunts. This is amplified in the case of visual mobile media—and especially selfies—whereby digital data is entangled within the lives, death, and afterlives in new ways. Moreover, we see how punctum combines with the Korean-specific notion of *jeong* to create a particular, unique Korean experience of the tragedy.

Writing this during the second-year anniversary, it is clear that the grief still remains palpable and has transformed in citizen agency. After the suicide of the boat company owner, Koreans are have turned their focus onto the government. The selfies eulogies of the high school children spur on Koreans in their mobilization. It will be interesting to see how the stories of mobile media memorialization operate as sites for family and loved ones to continue their connection and *jeong* between life and afterlife. Some of the selfies have been lost in the dark web, with only a few remaining to haunt online. One thing remains clear, mobile media is playing an increasingly pivotal role in the continuing bonds between loved ones and the deceased, as well as providing various forms of intimate publics across global and local media.

Acknowledgment

This chapter discusses themes explored in greater detail in the forthcoming book by Katie Cumiskey and Larissa Hjorth entitled *Haunting Hands* (2016).

Note

1 https://www.youtube.com/watch?v=dVEfPP8zLLc.

References

Af Segerstad, Y. H., & Kasperowski, D. (2014). A community for grieving: Affordances of social media for support of bereaved parents. *New Review of Hypermedia and Multimedia.* doi:10.1080/13614568.2014.983557.

Ahmed, S. (2005). *The cultural politics of emotion.* London: Routledge.

ALT. (2014). Please get involved of yellow ribbon campaign for victims of Sewol Ferry Tragedy, [weblog post]. April 21, 2014. Retrieved from http://m.blog. naver.com/alterlt/208493346. Viewed April 22, 2014.

Amore, S. D, & Scarciotta, L. (2011). Los(t)s in transitions: How diverse families are grieving and struggling to achieve a new identity. *Journal of Family Psychotherapy* 22(1), 46–55.

Barthes, R. (1981).*Camera lucida.* New York: Farrar, Straus and Giroux.

BBC. (2014). Korea ferry: News conference. Retrieved from http://www.bbc. com/news/world-asia-27062348. Viewed April 18, 2014.

Bennett, G., & Bennett, K. M. (2000). The presence of the dead: An empirical study. *Mortality,* 5(2), 139–157. doi:10.1080/13576270050076795.

Bollmer, G. D. (2012). Demanding connectivity: The performance of 'true' identity and the politics of social media. *Journalism Media and Cultural Studies Journal,* 1, 1–13. Retrieved on 20 October 2016 from http://www.cardiff. ac.uk/jomec/jomecjournal/1june2012/bollmer connectivity.pdf.

boyd, d. m., & Ellison, (2007). Social network sites: Definition, history, and scholarship. *Journal of Computer-Mediated Communication* 13(1), 210–230, doi:10.1111/j.1083–6101.2007.00393.x.

Brubaker, J. R., Hayes, G. R., & Dourish, P. (2013). Beyond the grave: Facebook as a site for the expansion of death and mourning. *The Information Society: An International Journal,* 29(3), 152–163. doi:10.1080/01972243.2013.777300.

Burgess, J. (2007). *Vernacular creativity* (Ph.D. thesis). Queensland University of Technology.

Chesher, C. (2012). Between image and information: The iPhone camera in the history of photography. In L. Hjorth, J. Burgess, & I. Richardson (Eds.), *Studying mobile media: Cultural technologies, mobile communication, and the iPhone* (pp. 98–117). New York: Routledge.

Choi, I. Y. (2014). Breaking news: Funeral parade in honour of the deccased filled the online memorial alter, *Yonhap News.* Retrieved from http://www. yonhapnews.co.kr/bulletin/2014/04/24/0200000000AKR20140424151500017. HTML. Viewed April 25, 2014.

Choi, I. S., & Kwak, S. H. (2014). "I really want to live…the temperature of my brain is 100 degree", another disclosed video was found, *Oh My News*. http://www.ohmynews.com/NWS_Web/View/at_pg.aspx?CNTN_CD=A000 2014660. Viewed July 18, 2014.

Church, S. H. (2013). Digital gravescapes: Digital memorializing on Facebook. *The Information Society: An International Journal, 29*(3), 184–189. doi:10.1 080/01972243.2013.777309.

CNN Staff. (2014). 'Please hurry'—Transcript of sinking Ferry's desperate calls released. *CNN News*. Retrieved from http://edition.cnn.com/2014/04/18/world/asia/south-korea-ferry-transcript/index.html. Viewed April 21, 2014.

David, G. (2010). Camera phone images, videos and live streaming: A contemporary visual trend. *Visual Studies, 25*(1), 89–98. doi:10.1080/14725861003607017.

Deger, J. (2006). *Shimmering screens*. Minneapolis, MN: Minnesota University Press.

Deger, J. (2008). Imprinting on the heart. *Visual Anthropology, 21*(4), 292–309.

de Vries, B., & Rutherford, J. (2004). Memorializing loved ones on the World Wide Web. *Omega: Journal of Death and Dying, 49*(1), 5–26.

Dobson, A. S. (2015). *Postfeminist digital cultures: Femininity, social media, and self-representation*. New York: Palgrave Macmillan.

Frohlich, D., Kuchinsky, A., Pering, C., Don, A., & Ariss, S. (2002). Requirements for photoware. *CSCW '02: Proceedings of the 2002 ACM conference on Computer Supported Cooperative Work*, 166–75. New York: ACM Press.

Frosh, P. (2001). The public eye and the citizen voyeur: Photography as a performance of power. *Social Semiotics, 11*(1), 43–59. doi:10.1080/10350330123316.

Frosh, P. (2015). Selfies: The gestural image: The selfie, photography theory, and kinesthetic sociability. *International Journal of Communication, 9*(2015).

Gibbs, M., Kohn, T., Nansen, B., & Arnold, M. (2015a). (DP140101871) *Digital Commemoration* ARC Discovery. Retrieved from https://researchdata.ands.org.au/discovery-projects-grant-id-dp140101871/517844.

Gibbs, M., Meese, J., Arnold, M., Nansen, B., & Carter, M. (2015b). Funeral and Instagram: Death, social Media, and platform vernacular. *Information, Communication & Society, 18*(3), 255–268. doi:10.1080/1369118X.2014.987152.

Gibson, M. (2014). Digital objects of the dead: Negotiating electronic remains. In L. Van Brussel & N. Carpentier (Eds.), *The social construction of death: Interdisciplinary perspectives* (pp. 221–238). Basingstoke, UK: Palgrave Macmillan.

Graham, C., Arnold, M., Kohn, T., & Gibbs, M. R. (2015). Gravesites and websites: A comparison of memorialisation. *Visual Studies, 30*(1), 37–53. doi:10.1080/1472586X.2015.996395.

Graham, C., Gibbs, M., & Aceti, L. (2013). Introduction to the special issue on the death, afterlife, and immortality of bodies and data. *The Information Society, 29*(3): 133–141. doi:10.1080/ 01972243.2013.777296.

Gye, L. (2007). Picture this: The impact of mobile camera phones on personal photographic practices, *Continuum, 21*(2), 279–288.

Hansen, B. et al. 2014. *Selfies at funeral*. Association of Internet Researchers Conference, October, South Korea.

Hjorth, L., & Arnold, M. (2013). *Online@AsiaPacific*. London: Routledge.

Hjorth, L., & Hendry, N. (2015). A snapshot of social media: Camera phone practices. *Social Media + Society*, April–June, *1*(1), 2056305115580478.

Humphreys, L. (2018). *The "qualified self"*. Cambridge, MA: MIT Press.

Ito, M. (2003). Mobiles and the appropriation of place. *Receiver, 8*. Retrieved from http://www.academia.edu/2717464/Mobiles_and_the_appropriation_of_place. Accessed February 11, 2017.

Ito, M., & Okabe, D. (2005). *Intimate visual co-presence*. Paper presented at Ubicomp, Takanawa Prince Hotel, Tokyo, Japan, September, 11–14. Retrieved from http://www.itofisher.com/mito/. Accessed June 28, 2006.

Jones, S. (2004). 404 not found: The Internet and the afterlife. *Omega: Journal of Death and Dying, 49*(1), 83–88.

JTBC News. (2014). Came the Kakao Talk messages when the Ferry was sinking. Online video. Retrieved from http://news.jtbc.joins.com/article/article. aspx?news_id=NB10465003. Viewed April 16.

Jurgenson, N. (2011). The faux-vintage photo. *The Society Pages*. Retrieved from http://thesocietypages.org/cyborgology/2011/05/14/the-faux-vintage-photo-full-essay-parts-i-ii-and-iii/. Accessed February 11, 2017.

Kim, M. S. (2014). "Please see you soon" they said but...their conversation was finally stopped in group chatting room, *Kuki News (Kookmin Ilbo)*. Retrieved from http://news.kukinews.com/article/view.asp?page=1&gCode= soc&arcid=0008254 300&cp=nv. Viewed April 21, 2014.

Kim, S. H., & Jeon, S. Y. (2014), Ferry captain sentenced to 36 years in prison. *The Chosun Ilbo*. Retrieved from http://english.chosun.com/site/data/html_dir/2014/11/12/2014111201226.html. Viewed November 12, 2014.

Kindberg, T., Spasojevic, M., Fleck, R., Sellen, A. (2005). The ubiquitous camera: An in-depth study of camera phone use. *IEEE Pervasive Computing, 4*(2), 42–50.

Klass, D., Silverman, P. R., & Nickman, S. L. (1996). *Continuing bonds: New understandings of grief*. New York: Routledge.

Klugman, C. M. (2006). Dead men talking: Evidence of post death contact and continuing bonds. *Omega: Journal of Death & Dying, 53*(3), 249–262.

Lee, D. H. (2005). Women's creation of camera phone culture. *Fibreculture Journal*. Retrieved from http://six.fibreculturejournal.org/fcj-038-womens-creation-of-camera-phone-culture/.

Lee, D. H. (2009). Mobile snapshots and private/public boundaries. *Knowledge, Technology, Policy, 22* (3): 161–171.

Lee, H. H., & Song, J. H. (2014). "I feel really scary. I want to live", disclosed video of victims of Dan Won high school was found. *Oh my news*. Retrieved from http://www.ohmynews.com/NWS_Web/view/at_pg.aspx?CNTN_CD= A0002014649. Viewed July 18, 2014.

Lim, M. S. (2014a). Mum this might be the last chance to tell you, I love you mum. *Korea JoongAng Daily*. Retrieved from http://article.joins.com/news/article/article.asp?total_id=14469894. Viewed April 17, 2014.

Lim, S. Y. (2014b). Does the yellow ribbon have copyright? *DKB News (Dong A Ilbo)*. http://news.donga.com/DKBNEWS/3/all/20140422/6295 8038/3. Viewed April 22, 2014.

Lingel, J. (2013). The digital remains: Social media and practices of online grief. *The Information Society: An International Journal, 29*(3), 190–195. doi:10.1080/01972243.2013.777311.

Mullen, J. (2014). Ferry disaster: Yellow ribbons become symbol of hope, solidarity. *CNN News*. Retrieved from http://edition.cnn.com/2014/04/24/world/asia/south-korea-yellow-ribbons/. Viewed April 24, 2014.

Nansen, B., Arnold, M., Gibbs, M., & Kohn, T. (2014). The restless dead in the digital cemetery. In C. M. Moreman & A. D. Lewis (Eds.), *Digital death: Mortality and beyond in the online age* (pp. 111–124). Santa Barbara, CA: ABC-CLIO.

Neimeyer, R. A, Klass, D., & Dennis, M. R. (2014). A social constructionist account of grief: Loss and the narration of meaning. *Death Studies*, *38*(8), 485–498. doi:10.1080/07481187.2014.913454.

Ohmynews.com. (2014). "I really want to live…the temperature of my brain is 100 degree", another disclosed video was found. Viewed July 18, 2014.

Palmer, P. (2012). iPhone photography: Mediating visions of social space. In L. Hjorth, J. Burgess, & I. Richardson (Eds.), *Studying mobile media: Cultural technologies, mobile communication, and the iPhone* (pp. 85–97). New York: Routledge.

Palmer, D. S. V. (2014). Mobile media photography. In G. Goggin & L. Hjorth (Eds.), *The Routledge companion to mobile media* (pp. 245–255). New York: Routledge.

Rettberg, J. W. (2014). *Seeing ourselves through technology*. London: Palgrave.

Rosenblatt, P. C. (1995). Ethics of qualitative interviewing with grieving families. *Death Studies*, *19*(1), 139–155.

Rosenblatt, P. C. (1996). Grief does not end. In D. Klass, P. R. Silverman, & S. L Nickman (Eds.), *Continuing bonds* (pp. 45–58). Washington, DC: Taylor & Francis.

Rosenblatt, P. C. (2000). *Parent grief*. Philadelphia, PA: Brunner.

Rosenblatt, P. C. (2008). Grief across cultures. In M. S. Stroebe, R. O. Hansson, H. Schut, & W. Stroebe (Eds.), *Handbook of bereavement research and practice* (pp. 207–222). Washington, DC: APA.

Senft, T., & Baym, N. (2015). What does the selfie say? Investigating a global phenomenon. *International Journal of Communication*, *9*(2015), Feature, 1588–1606.

Sicart, M. (2015). *Play matters*. Cambridge, MA: MIT Press.

Sontag, S. (1977). *On photography*. New York: Farrar, Straus and Giroux.

Stanyek, J., & Piekut, B. (2010). Deadness technologies of the intermundane. *TDR: The Drama Review—A Journal of Performance Studies*, *54*(1), 14–38.

Van House, N. (2011). Personal photography, digital technologies and the uses of the visual. *Visual Studies*, *26*(2), 125–134, doi:10.1080/1472586X. 2011.571888.

Veale, K. J. (2003). A virtual adaptation of a physical cemetery for diverse researchers using information science methods. *Computers in Genealogy*, *8*(4), 16–38.

Veale, K. (2004). Online memorialisation: The Web as a collective memorial landscape for remembering the dead. *Fibreculture*, 3. Retrieved from http://three.fibreculturejournal.org/fcj-014-online-memorialisation- the-web-as-a-collective-memorial-landscape-for- remembering-the-dead/. Accessed February 10, 2017.

van Dijck, J. (2007). *Mediated memories in the digital age*. Stanford, CA: Stanford Uni Press.

Villi, M., & Stocchetti, M. (2011). Visual mobile communication, mediated presence and the politics of space. *Visual Studies*, 26(2), 102–112, doi:10.1080/1472586X.2011.571885.

Warner, M. (2002). Publics and counterpublics. *Public Culture*, 14(1) 49–90. Retrieved from https://muse.jhu.edu/login?auth=0&type=summary&url=/journals/public_culture/v014/14.1warner.html. Accessed February 10, 2017.

Walter, T. (1996). *The revival of death*. London: Routledge.

Walter, T., Hourizi, R., Moncur, W., & Pitsillides, S. (2011). Does the Internet change how we die and mourn? Overview and analysis. *Omega: Journal of Death and Dying*, 64(4), 275–302.

Wendt, B. (2014). *The allure of the selfie*. Amsterdam, Netherlands: Institute of Networked Cultures.

Whittaker, S., Bergman, O., & Clough, P. (2010). Easy on that trigger dad: A study of long term family photo retrieval. *Personal and Ubiquitous Computing*, 14(1), 31–43.

YouTube. (2014). The undisclosed last video filmed by a student, 17 July, online video. Retrieved from https://www.youtube.com/watch?v=FAbdIywTB7M. Viewed July 18, 2015.

Zylinska, J. (Ed.). (2015). *Photomediations*. Open Humanities Press.

Zylinska, J., & Kember, S. (2012). *Life after new media*. Cambridge, MA: MIT Press.

Part IV

The Performance of the Self, the Mobile Content and the Copyright

9 A Comparative Study between Japanese, US, Taiwanese, and Chinese Social Networking Site Users

Self-Disclosure and Network Homogeneity

Kenichi Ishii

Self-disclosure is key to understanding personal relationships both online and in face-to-face interactions, as sharing personal information develops relationships. Previous studies have demonstrated that Asians are less likely than Americans to disclose personal information: Americans disclose more in their conversations than either the Japanese (Gudhykunst & Nishida, 1984) or the Chinese (Chen, 1995). Cultural psychological research has found the "self" to be more dependent on those with whom one has personal relations in Asia, while in the US, the self is more independent (Markus & Kitayama, 1991). Recently, cultural differences between the US and Japan have been explained by the concept of relational mobility, which is the amount of opportunities people have in a given society or social context to select new relationship partners when necessary (Yuki et al., 2007, Yuki & Schug, 2012). In societies where relational mobility is higher (e.g., the US), self-disclosure levels are higher (Schug, Yuki, & Maddux, 2010). In societies where relational mobility is lower, interpersonal relationships are stable and chances to find new relationship partners are low (e.g., Japan). In such societies, people are less willing to disclose information about themselves (Schug, Yuki, & Maddux, 2010). In the Information Age, however, it is more important to understand disclosure of personal information on the Internet, because privacy is more at risk online than in face-to-face interactions. Despite the increased risk, many users still disclose their personal information online. Parks and Floyd (2006) revealed how self-disclosure is promoted more by online than face-to-face communications. This is a dilemma for users whose intention to develop personal networks conflicts with privacy risks.

Facebook, the most popular social networking site (SNS) globally, requires users to disclose their real name (www.facebook.com/help/) based on the *one identity* principle, because Facebook founder Mark Zuckerberg believes that "radical transparency will overtake modern life" (Kirkpatrick, 2011, p. 200). However, the one identity principle does not hold true in Japan: 65.3% of Japanese agreed that the "true self is not necessarily the only one" (Matsuda, Dobashi, & Tsuji, 2014). In this sense, the Facebook platform reflects the individualistic culture of the US and does not fit in Japanese culture. Actually, local SNSs have been popular in Japan; Mixi, a Japanese SNS, was most embraced until around 2008. As of 2016, LINE, an application for instant communication that is mainly used for closed communication among friends and family, is more popular than Facebook among Japanese people.

In 1998, a content analysis study of personal web pages written in Japanese, English, and Chinese, which were randomly selected via the Yahoo! search engine, also demonstrated a remarkable cultural difference in the disclosure of personal information on the Internet (Ishii et al., 2000). This study found that Japanese websites showed the lowest level of self-disclosure of high-risk personal information (*personally identifiable information*), such as name and phone number, and a relatively high level of self-disclosure of low-risk items, such as their favorite celebrities and PCs (Table 9.1). Table 9.1 shows that Japanese users tend to avoid privacy risks even in the early stages of online communication. To further understand the unique self-disclosure patterns in Japan, it is useful to review the communication culture among the country's young people. In the mid-1990s, many Japanese high school students chatted with their virtual friends on pagers (*beru-tomo*, "pager friends") (Tomita et al., 1997), never meeting or knowing one another's names despite frequently exchanging short messages about their daily news and feelings. According to Nakamura (1997), 17% of high school students had beru-tomo in 1996. Switching from pagers to increasingly popular mobile phones, they continued to exchange anonymous emails with *meru-tomo* ("email friends") (Tsuji & Mikami, 2001).

These virtual relationships (beru- and meru-tomo) followed self-disclosure patterns similar to those on websites: the Japanese do not disclose objective (name, address, etc.) personal information in such messages, instead sharing only subjective (emotional state) personal information. Tomita (2006) coined the term "intimate stranger" to refer to a social relationship emerging between Japanese young people through open networks on a variety of media, where anonymity is a condition of intimacy. An association between intimacy and anonymity in friendship became possible with new telecommunication services in the 1980s, such as pagers and dial-up telephone messaging (Tomita, 2006). One of the key factors in understanding low disclosure is the degree of trust in the Internet. Interestingly, the degree of user trust in the Internet varies greatly across countries. Many previous survey results have revealed that Japanese people do not trust the Internet, as compared with other countries (Ishii, 2016). For example, Figure 9.1 compares the percentage of respondents among 11 countries who stated that "most or all"

Table 9.1 Comparison of self-disclosure on personal home pages across three language websites retrieved through Yahoo!

Personal information	Japanese (%)	English (%)	Chinese (%)
N	293	170	164
Name (first and last names)	45.1	58.2	57.9
Gender	18.1	24.1	43.3
Age	41.3	30.6	54.3
Job	46.8	45.3	53.0
Status	4.8	21.8	0.6
Education	20.8	37.1	49.4
Home postal address	1.4	17.6	5.5
Telephone number	0.3	14.1	8.5
Marital status	10.9	14.1	13.4
Children	8.9	11.8	9.8
Race	0.0	8.2	0.6
Religion	0.7	4.1	0.6
Hair/eye color	1.0	1.8	3.0
Body type	9.6	1.8	15.9
Personal history	10.6	17.6	14.6
Hobbies	44.4	36.5	53.0
Favorite celebrities/sport players	17.1	12.4	17.1
Personality	8.2	4.7	14.0
PC	24.6	4.1	4.3
Family	18.4	23.5	10.4
Boy/girlfriend	1.4	8.2	6.7
Other friends	22.2	15.3	20.7
Pets	7.8	4.7	4.9
Neighbors	1.4	3.5	0.6
Company/school	18.1	27.6	18.9
Community	13.3	15.9	9.1
Diary	23.5	8.3	3.7
Essay	67.1	36.9	21.5

Note: The results in this table have been obtained from a reanalysis of the data by the author.

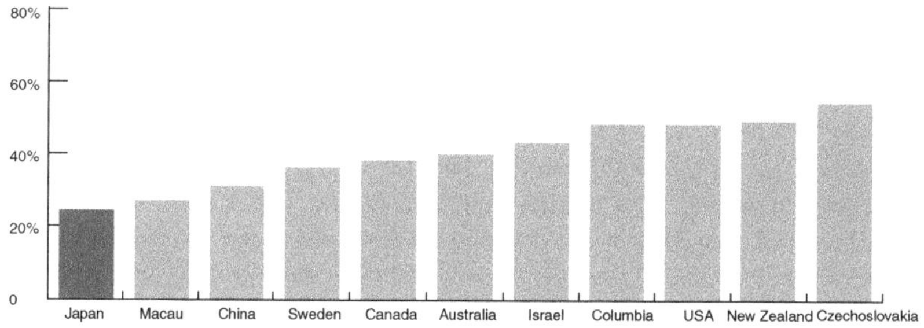

Figure 9.1 Percentage of respondents who trust Internet information.
Source: Communications Research Laboratory (2004).

of the information they find online is reliable and accurate (Communications Research Laboratory, 2004). The figure reveals that Japanese people have the lowest degree of trust in Internet information among the 11 surveyed countries.

To fully comprehend the unique mobile Internet use among Japanese people, one needs to understand the historical background of Japanese mobile technologies. Since the 1990s, Japan has enjoyed advanced mobile Internet such as "i-mode" and 3G/4G (third and fourth generation) mobile networks (Ishii, 2015). In Japan, thanks to the advanced mobile technologies, mobile phones have been more popular than PCs to connect to the Internet (Ishii and Wu, 2006). As will be discussed later (Table 9.3), more people use mobile phones to access SNS in Japan. However, a recent report shows that the smartphone ratio is relatively low in Japan (54.0%), as compared with China (74.0%), Taiwan (67.0%), and the US (58.0%; AUN Consulting, 2016). One historical reason for the low penetration rate of smartphones and high rate of feature phones in Japan is the adoption of a unique Japanese mobile protocol "i-mode" for featured phones (Ishii, 2004, 2015). In contrast with handset technologies, Japan has the second highest (95.52%) 3G/4G availability ratio in the world, as compared to Taiwan (93.87%), the US (91.69%), and China (75.47%) (Global State of Mobile Networks – OpenSignal, 2016). Since following the early success of i-mode and other mobile Internet services, major Japanese mobile phone carriers started 3G (third-generation) mobile phone services earlier than in other countries.

Also of note in Japanese Internet behavior is the greater use of Twitter (microblogs) and blogs. In fact, the second most used language on Twitter is Japanese, according to the API (Application Program Interface) aggregation company Gnip (Yap, 2016); in 2007, 37% of blogs were written in Japanese, edging out English, according to statistics from Technorati (Salzberg, 2007). Considering the Japanese comprise only 2% of the world's population, Twitter and blogs are unusually popular in Japan.

Why are Twitter and blogs so popular among the Japanese? According to the results of a tweet analysis, Japanese Twitter users have a smaller number of followers and a higher rate of mutual relations (follower–follow relations), as compared with English Twitter users (Ishii, 2011b). Based on a comparison between Twitter messages (tweets) of Japanese and American college students, Acar and Ayaka (2013) found that the former tweeted more self-related thoughts than the latter (Japanese = 39%, Americans = 31%); moreover, there were more friend- and family-related tweets in the American (13%) than the Japanese (6%) sample. In summary, Japanese users post messages more about personal feelings and interests without disclosing their personal information because users are not required to disclose their personal information. In this sense,

Twitter and blogs fit in the Japanese communication style of the "intimate stranger." It is thus important to examine privacy-related behaviors to explain the unique characteristics of Japanese Internet users.

Previous Studies

We have reviewed privacy-related behaviors on the Internet, focusing on Japanese users. In Japan, only a few studies have examined privacy-related behavior on SNS from a comparative perspective. Based on a survey conducted in Japan and the US, Thomson, Yuki, and Ito (2015) showed privacy concern on SNS was higher in Japan than in the US and this difference was significantly mediated by relational mobility and general trust. Ishii (2014b) compared Facebook users in Japan, the US, and Taiwan and found cultural differences: compared to users in the US and Taiwan, Japanese users have only one-third the number of friends on Facebook and show a higher level of homogeneity in their friendship network and have more offline friends. The results of a multi-level analysis indicate that only Japanese users show a positive and significant correlation between the homogeneity, the number of Facebook friends, and the disclosure of personal information. These results suggest the friending process via Facebook varies between these three countries. However, national differences are mixed with cultural differences and age differences in this study (Ishii, 2014b), as the average age of the respondents was very different across the three countries, ranging from 32 years in Taiwan, 38 years in Japan, to 44.2 years in the US. Another problem of this study is that high-risk personal information (personally identifiable information) and low-risk personal information items are not distinguished in the analysis for self-disclosure. In the present study, these problems are overcome and the effect of relational mobility is examined to account for cultural differences in self-disclosure levels.

A number of studies have examined what factors determine online self-disclosure behaviors from a psychological perspective. Zlatolas et al. (2015) found self-disclosure is significantly related with privacy value/privacy concerns, privacy awareness, privacy social norms, privacy policy, and privacy control. In addition, Loiacono (2015) revealed that personality traits and perceived risks and benefits had a strong impact on the decision to self-disclose on SNS. Compared with Americans and Koreans, the Japanese demonstrated the lowest level of self-disclosure in conversations (Yum & Hara, 2005), revealing that self-disclosure was positively associated with relationship quality; however, the association between self-disclosure and trust varied greatly across cultures. Whereas all of these studies used a psychological scale to measure self-disclosure levels on the Internet, Al-Saggaf and Nielsen (2014) examined users' profiles to measure actual disclosure behaviors, discovering that lonely women were more likely to disclose more personal information in their Facebook profile.

Purpose of Study

This study focuses on the disclosure of personal information on SNS in Japan and three other countries: the US, Taiwan, and China. Many previous studies have examined the factors associated with such self-disclosure, but few have focused on the cultural differences. Although Thomson et al. (2015) used relational mobility to explain cultural differences in privacy concerns on SNS, there are many other potentially important variables to be examined.

This study thus poses the following research question about cultural difference:

RQ1: How different is disclosure of personal information on SNS across cultures?

In this study, two types of personal information are distinguished. The first is personally identifiable information: high-risk privacy-related information—for instance, name, date of birth, photograph, phone number, email address—that can be used to identify, contact, or locate an individual (Personally Identifiable Information, 2016). The second is personal attributes information: relatively low-risk information, such as gender, marital status, and body type. The content analysis results in Table 9.1 suggest that the Japanese tend to avoid disclosing personally identifiable information, and thus the following hypothesis is proposed:

H1-1: The Japanese are less likely to disclose personal information on SNS, especially personally identifiable information.

This study also seeks to identify which factors account for disclosure levels:

RQ2: What variables account for the disclosure level of personal information on SNS in these four countries?

Perceived risks and benefits are expected to affect how users disclose their personal information. As many previous studies show that women are more likely to perceive privacy risks, the following hypothesis is thus proposed:

H2-1: Men are more likely than women to disclose personal information on SNS.

It is expected that frequent SNS users benefit more from disclosing personal information, since doing so makes it easier to exchange messages with many friends. Thus, the following hypothesis is proposed:

H2-2: The frequency of using and posting messages on SNS is positively correlated with disclosure levels.

Likewise, users with more SNS friends benefit more from disclosing more personal information. Thus, the following hypothesis is also proposed:

H2–3: The number of SNS friends is positively correlated with disclosure levels.

Young people in many countries often exchange messages using mobile phones within closed communication networks (Katz & Aakhus, 2002). Furthermore, stronger homogeneous ties may encourage the disclosure of personal information because users feel a stronger intimacy. The following hypothesis is therefore proposed:

H2–4: The homogeneity of SNS friends is positively correlated with disclosure levels.

As previously mentioned, large cultural differences exist in self-disclosure. We hypothesize that relational mobility mediates such differences in self-disclosure:

H2–5: Relational mobility is positively correlated with disclosure levels.
H2–6: Relational mobility mediates correlations between disclosure levels and country effect (Taiwan, China, and Japan).

Additionally, this study explores how mobile devices have effected the use of SNS.

RQ3: How have mobile devices effected SNS use?

Mobile telephony has contributed to a shift toward a new "personal communication society" (Campbell & Park, 2008). Mobile devices, which people carry on their person, have changed Internet use, enabling users to keep in constant contact online (Katz & Aakhus, 2002). Previous studies showed that use of a mobile phone is positively correlated with the frequent communication with close friends in many countries (Boase & Kobayashi, 2007; Ishii, 2006, 2009; Kobayashi & Ikeda, 2007; Miyata, Boase, Wellman, & Ikeda, 2005). The following hypothesis is thus proposed:

H3–1: Mobile device users use SNS more actively.

In Japan, mobile phones are mainly used to exchange emails and maintain homogeneous ties with close friends (Miyata et al., 2005; Ishii, 2006, 2009; Kobayashi & Ikeda, 2007). Thus, it is hypothesized that

PC and mobile phone users differ in their levels of friend homogeneity and personal information disclosure:

H3–2: Friend homogeneity levels are different depending on the devices people use to access SNS.
H3–3: Disclosure levels are different depending on the devices people use to access SNS.

Method

To achieve the aforementioned research purposes, and given the convenience and efficiency of collecting data online from SNS users who are all Internet users, an online questionnaire survey was conducted in 2013 by online survey companies in Japan, Taiwan, the US, and China: (1) in Japan, the survey adopted a quota sampling method and attracted a pool of 800 respondents, from which 500 were selected according to gender and four age categories (18–27, 28–37, 38–47, and 48–57), each including 125 respondents; (2) in Taiwan, a survey of SNS users aged over 18 was conducted, yielding a total of 750 responses; (3) in the US, a Survey Monkey Audience Panel for those aged over 18 was used and received a total of 849 responses; and (4) in China, SNS users were surveyed and a total of 769 responses were obtained. However, some of the responses were omitted from the following analysis. First, although the purpose of this study is to compare users of Facebook, the most popular SNS in the world, it was not used by all the respondents from each country; therefore, only those respondents who used Facebook as their primary SNS were selected. However, since Facebook is not available in China due to government control of the Internet, users of three relatively similar SNS that allow one to create a personal home page were selected: Renren, Kaixin, and Q-Space. Second, the age of respondents varied greatly across these four countries, due to the difference in quota sampling; therefore, only respondents aged below 40 were selected. Consequently, the number of responses was as follows: (1) 258 in Japan, with an average age of 29.7; (2) 590 in Taiwan, with an average age of 29.4; (3) 300 in the US, with an average age of 30.9; and (4) 208 in China, with an average age of 30.5.

Measures

The questionnaire asked respondents about the frequency with which they used and posted messages on Facebook or other SNS each week, as well as what information they disclosed to general users. Table 9.1 shows 14 items of personal information disclosed. Based on these items,

we define the disclosure of two types of personal information: personally identifiable and personal attributes information. Although age and
birthday are not independently personally identifiable information, they
become so when combined, and thus the personally identifiable information scale is the sum of binary responses to name (real name), name
of employer/school, both age and birthday, email address, and phone
number. The Cronbach's alpha index is over .600 for Japan, the US, and
China (Table 9.2), but is somewhat low for Taiwan (.536). In contrast,
it is generally not possible to identify individuals from other relatively
lower-risk personal attributes information. The personal attributes information scale is defined as the sum of all items other than those cate-
gorized as personally identifiable information. The Cronbach's alpha
index is over .600 for all four countries. The Pearson correlation between the two scales is .566.

Table 9.2 Disclosure of personal information on Facebook and other SNS

	Japan (%)	USA (%)	Taiwan (%)	China (%)	Chi-square
N	258	300	590	208	
Personally identifiable information					
Name (real name)	79.1	79.0	60.7	33.7	46.0***
Photograph of face	43.8	67.3	63.6	44.2	40.0***
Current employer/school	24.8	30.0	46.9	29.3	49.8***
Email	4.7	16.7	27.6	46.6	69.2***
Telephone number	2.3	7.0	6.3	13.9	27.2***
*1 Age (or year born)	61.6	32.7	47.8	73.1	53.2***
*1 Birthday	57.0	31.3	60.0	61.5	69.3***
[Both age and birthday]	49.2	22.7	39.3	52.4	60.3***
Personally identifiable information scale (average)	2.04	2.23	2.44	2.20	F = 4.66**
Cronbach's alpha	.679	.730	.536	.664	
Personal attributes information					
The state (prefecture or province) where they live	70.5	56.7	72.2	77.9	26.0***
Gender	73.3	63.7	85.6	91.3	59.2***
Marital status (married/unmarried)	32.2	35.0	44.7	56.3	16.0***
Hobbies or interests	32.9	25.0	32.7	66.3	20.3***
Ideas or values	7.4	14.7	15.1	40.9	26.4***
Body type (height, weight, etc.)	1.6	5.0	6.6	26.4	24.3***
Relationship to friends	7.8	13.3	30.2	29.3	74.2***
Personal attributes information scale (average)	2.25	2.13	2.87	3.88	F = 50.8***
Cronbach's alpha	.652	.799	.660	.693	

Note: *1 These two items are combined into "both age and birthday" for the personally identifiable information scale. *p < .05, **p < .01, ***p < .001.

The respondents were also asked about their number of SNS friends, which were classified into *offline* and *online* friends. Respondents stated the number of friends they knew before friending on SNS, which provided the number of offline friends. This figure was then taken from the total number of SNS friends to calculate the number of friends with whom they became acquainted through SNS, which provided the number of online friends.

The homogeneity of SNS friends was measured using the five response categories of "very untrue," "somewhat untrue," "neither true nor untrue," "somewhat true," and "very true" for the following questions: "How many of your SNS friends are in the same age group, whose age differs by three years or less?"; "How many of your SNS friends are of the same gender?"; "How many of your SNS friends are of the same generation?"; "How many of your SNS friends do you often see offline?"; "How many of your SNS friends live in the same region as you?"; and "How many of your SNS friends live in the same country?" The Cronbach's alpha index was .727.

Relational mobility is defined as the degree to which individuals in a given society have the opportunity to form new and terminate old relationships (Schug, Yuki, Maddux, 2010). To test whether this variable mediated the effect of country, the relational mobility scale was rated by 12 statements (Yuki et al., 2007) in Japan, China, and Taiwan; due to the number of questions, however, this scale was not included in the US.

In addition, respondents were asked on which device (desktop PC, laptop, mobile phone, or tablet) they most often accessed their primary SNS. Finally, demographic factors, such as age and gender, were also measured.

Results

Descriptive Results

Devices used to access SNS vary widely across countries (Table 9.3). Japanese respondents are more likely to use mobile phones, while those from the US, China, and Taiwan are more likely to use laptop/desktop PCs. However, it should be noted that the respondents are not representative of the general population.

Table 9.3 Devices used to access SNS

Device	Japan (%)	USA (%)	Taiwan (%)	China (%)
N	500	618	693	32
PC	52.4	65.2	72.3	75.0
Mobile phone	44.0	26.4	25.1	15.6
Tablet PC	3.6	8.4	2.6	9.4
Total	100.0	100.0	100.0	100.0

Table 9.2 indicates the percentages of those who disclose each item of personal information. Generally, the Japanese are less likely to disclose personal information on SNS, but are surprisingly most likely to disclose their name. Most unexpectedly, the Taiwanese disclose their real name least often, which is probably because most Taiwanese users have an English name that they use on Facebook, such as Jimmy Lin. The 14 items are classified into two types, from which two scales were calculated: high risk (personally identifiable information) and low risk (personal attributes information). Table 9.3 also indicates the average for these two scales, which show the Japanese with the lowest level for personally identifiable information, while ranking third for personal attributes information. This result is consistent with H1–1.

Table 9.4 shows the averages of the main variable. Of the four countries, Japanese users have the smallest number of offline and online SNS friends, the highest level of friend homogeneity, and access SNS most often. Table 9.5 indicates the Pearson correlations for the disclosure of the two types of personal information. The number of offline friends is positively and significantly correlated with the disclosure of personally identifiable information for the Japanese, Taiwanese, and Chinese, while the same is true with the number of online friends for all countries. SNS friend homogeneity is also positively and significantly correlated with the disclosure of personally identifiable information for the Japanese, Taiwanese, and Chinese. Relational mobility, however, is only significantly correlated with the disclosure of personal attributes information for the Taiwanese. Except for the US, the frequency of using and posting messages on SNS is positively correlated with the disclosure of both personally identifiable and personal attributes information (albeit not significant).

Effects of Mobile Device

To examine how mobile devices affect SNS use, a statistical test (F test) is conducted between desktop/laptop PC, mobile phone, and tablet

Table 9.4 Averages of main variables

Country	N	N of offline friends	N of online friends	SNS friend homogeneity	Frequency of SNS use	Frequency of posting on SNS
Japan	258	69.79	21.41	18.31	78.34	20.53
USA	300	239.82	99.15	18.23	69.15	20.28
Taiwan	590	144.63	101.55	17.49	64.84	14.44
China	208	92.30	149.20	18.00	47.45	20.83
F value		54.66	3.69	4.32	29.61	5.80
		***	*	**	***	**

Note: $^*p < .05$, $^{**}p < .01$, $^{***}p < .001$.

Table 9.5 Pearson correlations with disclosure of personal information

	N of offline friends	N of online friends	SNS friend homogeneity	Frequency of using SNS	Frequency of posting on SNS	Relational mobility
Personally identifiable information						
Japan (N = 237)	.377***	.189**	.221***	.213***	.133*	−.034
USA (N = 300)	.059	.212***	.022	.040	.003	
Taiwan (N = 590)	.184***	.165***	.114**	.112**	.108**	.037
China (N = 208)	.222**	.138*	.154*	.144*	.226**	−.133
Personal attributes information						
Japan (N = 237)	.129*	.105	.213***	.176**	.130*	−.003
USA (N = 300)	−.118*	.224***	.025	.027	.052	
Taiwan (N = 590)	−.023	.110**	.036	.090*	.162***	.103*
China (N = 208)	.095	.042	.118	.149*	.129	.105

Note. $*p < .05$, $**p < .01$, $***p < .001$.

PC users. Table 9.6 shows there is a large difference in the frequency of SNS use between these groups. Mobile device users use SNS more frequently, and the difference is statistically significant, except for China. In contrast, the disclosure level of personal information is not significantly different for devices among the Japanese, Americans, and Chinese, but it

Table 9.6 Self-disclosure level, frequency of SNS use, and homogeneity by device

Device	Japan (N = 258)	USA (N = 300)	Taiwan (N = 590)	China (N = 208)
Self-disclosure level				
Desktop/Laptop PC	4.00	3.94	5.15	6.81
Mobile phone	4.39	4.02	6.03	7.50
Tablet PC	3.63	4.17	6.29	9.67
F value	0.78	0.04	5.94**	1.02
Frequency of SNS use				
Desktop/Laptop PC	68.4	65.1	62.4	46.5
Mobile phone	86.5	74.0	73.1	50.9
Tablet PC	79.8	76.9	54.3	56.7
F value	3.38*	4.37*	8.10***	0.48
Friend homogeneity				
Desktop/Laptop PC	17.2	18.2	17.3	18.0
Mobile phone	19.2	18.2	18.0	17.5
Tablet PC	18.6	19.0	17.1	19.2
F value	5.86**	0.52	2.01	0.73

Note. $**p < .01$.

is statistically significant for the Taiwanese. In Taiwan, mobile phone and tablet users show higher disclosure scores than laptop/desktop PC users. It is interesting to note that only Japanese users exhibit a significant difference in friend homogeneity between these groups. This result suggests that mobile devices promote friend homogeneity and interaction on SNS among Japanese users, as addressed in previous studies (Ishii, 2006, 2009, 2014a; Ito, Okabe, & Matsuda, 2006).

Factors Determining Disclosure Levels

To examine the factors determining the disclosure level of personal information, a regression model was estimated. The two disclosure scales were regressed on the number of offline and online friends, frequency of use and posting messages, homogeneity of friends, mobile device use (mobile phones and tablets), gender (male = 1, female = 2), and age (Table 9.7). The results indicate that very different variables account for disclosure scores across countries: in Japan, homogeneity is positively and significantly correlated with both disclosure levels, while in the US, the number of online friends are positively and significantly correlated with both disclosure levels; in Taiwan, the number of online and offline friends, mobile device, and gender are significantly correlated with the disclosure of personally identifiable information, while only mobile device and gender are correlated with the disclosure of personal attributes information. Thus, H2–3 and H2–4 are partially supported. With regard to H2–2, this hypothesis is also partially supported, because the frequency of posting messages is only positively correlated with the disclosure of personally identifiable information in China. Finally, women are less likely to disclose personal information in all countries, although the parameter is not significant in many cases, which indicates that H2–1 is partially supported. As mobile device use is associated with the frequency of SNS use for three countries including Japan, the US, and Taiwan, self-disclosure is associated with the frequency of SNS use for the Taiwanese, and friend homogeneity is associated with the frequency of SNS use for the Japanese, H3–1, H3–2, and H3–3 are thus partially supported.

Mediation Effects via Relational Mobility

A previous study concluded that cultural differences in self-disclosure between the US and Japan are mediated by relational mobility (Schug, Yuki, & Maddux, 2010). Because relational mobility was not measured in the US in this study, it is only tested as a mediator for the correlation between country and disclosure of personal information in Japan, China, and Taiwan. Two structural equation models (SEMs) were estimated using Amos 23, and standardized parameters are shown in

Table 9.7 Regression models predicting disclosure of personal information (standardized coefficients)

	Japan		USA		Taiwan		China	
Personally identifiable information								
Number of offline friends	0.309	4.901***	0.066	1.123	0.145	3.357***	0.407	2.297*
Number of online friends	0.067	1.081	0.226	3.817***	0.133	3.301***	-0.254	-1.456
Frequency of use	0.087	1.379	0.017	0.266	0.020	0.466	-0.040	-0.500
Frequency of posting	0.075	1.208	-0.033	-0.533	0.059	1.431	0.174	2.193*
Homogeneity	0.188	3.125**	0.016	0.272	0.072	1.716	0.098	1.484
Mobile device	0.004	0.060	0.004	0.060	0.116	2.900**	-0.014	-0.214
Gender	-0.094	-1.610	-0.041	-0.700	-0.179	-4.481***	-0.205	-3.199**
Age	0.093	1.583	-0.103	-1.737	-0.032	-0.713	-0.213	-3.122**
Personal attributes information								
Number of offline friends	0.067	1.014	-0.105	-1.803	-0.031	-0.707	0.279	1.453
Number of online friends	0.043	0.659	0.206	3.496***	0.077	1.864	-0.210	-1.113
Frequency of use	0.090	1.363	-0.003	-0.047	0.054	1.231	0.104	1.208
Frequency of posting	0.091	1.391	0.014	0.221	0.120	2.825	0.042	0.487
Homogeneity	0.235	3.719***	0.033	0.573	0.054	1.275	0.087	1.207
Mobile device	0.034	0.544	0.040	0.687	0.105	2.590**	0.013	0.190
Gender	-0.104	-1.690	-0.057	-0.971	-0.151	-3.706***	-0.125	-1.801
Age	0.165	2.674**	-0.081	-1.369	0.063	1.370	0.022	0.304

Note. $*p < .05$, $**p < .01$, $***p < .001$.

Figures 9.2 and 9.3. The results indicate that relational mobility significantly mediates the difference between Japan and other countries for the disclosure of personal attributes information only. The indirect effect of country on disclosure of personal attributes information (standardized parameter) is 0.010 for Taiwan and 0.006 for China, with 90% confidence intervals of .010–.041 and .005–.025, respectively, based on the bias-corrected percentile method. Since the lower limits are over 0, this bootstrapping method thus shows that the mediation effect is significant. Hence, H2–6 and H2–7 are partially supported.

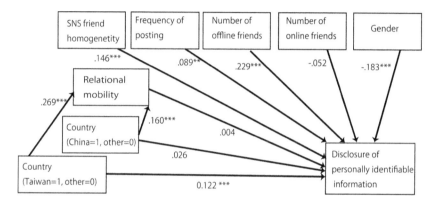

Figure 9.2 Mediation effect on disclosure of personally identifiable information via relational mobility for country difference between Japan, China, and Taiwan.

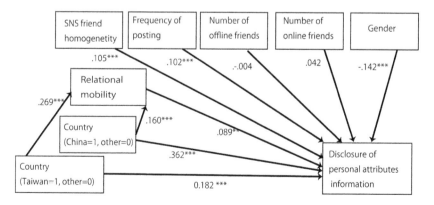

Figure 9.3 Mediation effect on personal attributes information via relational mobility for country difference between Japan, China, and Taiwan.

Conclusions

A common determinant of self-disclosure for all four countries is gender: women are less likely to disclose their personal information on SNS. However, most of the results indicate that different factors determine disclosure of personal information across countries. In Japan, homogeneity of Facebook friends is positively correlated with self-disclosure for both personally identifiable and personal attributes information. In Japan and China, disclosure of high-risk (personally identifiable) information is correlated with the number of offline friends. In the US, it is correlated with the number of online friends, while in Taiwan it is correlated with the number of both offline and online friends. These results suggest that the SNS friending process is different between the four countries. In Japan, Facebook friends are based more on existing offline friends, resulting in higher homogeneity and a smaller number of purely online friends. Moreover, regression results suggest that disclosure of personally identifiable information occurs more with offline friends in Japan. In contrast, in the US and Taiwan, the disclosure of personal information occurs more with online friends (Ishii, 2014b).

Results indicate that mobile devices play a role in promoting communication via SNS in all of the countries except China. Mobile phone users use SNS more frequently than desktop/laptop PC users. As shown in previous studies that reported mobile phone use is positively correlated with frequent communication with close friends in many countries (Katz & Aakhous, 2002), the results suggest that SNS use is closely linked with personal communication. These results suggest that mobile telephony has contributed to a shift toward a new "personal communication society" (Campbell & Park, 2008).

A unique Japanese pattern, conceptualized as "intimate strangers" (Tomita, 2006), is also apparent when comparing Facebook users in Japan, the US, and Taiwan: the Japanese are less likely to disclose personally identifiable information, such as employer/school name, number, and email address. A similar pattern was also found on Japanese personal web pages in the 1990s (Ishii, 2004). Such results regarding cultural characteristics can account for the high popularity of Twitter and blogs among the Japanese, where users are not required to disclose personally identifiable information. In other words, Japanese people tend to avoid disclosing personal information for online friends, except for those with whom they have offline connections.

Many previous studies used psychological scales to measure self-disclosure levels on the Internet. However, to address the privacy risks on SNS from a practical perspective, it is more effective and useful to use behavioral measures when assessing the level of disclosing personal information. Moreover, psychological scales based on Likert-type questions are not appropriate for cross-cultural comparisons, as the language differences make scale equivalency uncertain. Hence, this study adopted behavioral measures for self-disclosure, and the results indicate two types of personal information (personally identifiable and personal attributes) that are associated differently with the other variables.

This study found that the country difference in personal attributes information between Japan, China, and Taiwan is mediated by relational mobility. However, this mediation effect is not as large as the direct country effect, meaning a large amount of the country differences remain to be explained by other factors.

Finally, this comparative study has some limitations. Even though we compared Facebook users between Japan, the US, and Taiwan, the situation in each country varies significantly. While Facebook is ranked number one in Taiwan and the US, the most, or equally, popular platforms in Japan are LINE (a chat application) and Twitter. As LINE is a closed network communication platform (Ishii, 2017), Japanese users choose between LINE and Facebook according to their purposes: for example, many college students create Facebook pages to publicly disclose their personal information when job hunting (Ishii, 2011a), but use LINE to privately communicate with close friends. The situation is even more complicated in China: selecting three alternative SNS may have affected the results, while stronger regulations for SNS might affect disclosure patterns among Chinese users. For example, Chinese users must use their real name (along with their identification card number) to register for SNS. Due to such differences, it is difficult to apply a single theory to all countries. Other limitations of this study include the following: first, as the study was based on a correlational design, it was not possible to measure the causality between the variables; second, although this study focused on the behavioral characteristics of online self-disclosure, a greater variety of psychological variables should be evaluated, including the motivation for using SNS.

Acknowledgment

The author would like to thank the KDDI Foundation for supporting this study in 2012/2013.

References

Acar, A., & Ayaka, D. (2013). Culture and social media usage: Analysis of Japanese Twitter users. *International Journal of Electronic Commerce Studies*, 4(1), 21–12. doi:10.7903/ijecs.989.

Al-Saggaf, Y., & Nielsen, S. (2014). Self-disclosure on Facebook among female users and its relationship to feelings of loneliness. *Computers in Human Behavior*, 36, 460–468. 10.1016/j.chb.2014.04.014.

AUN Consulting. (2016). Press Release (March, 18, 2016). Retrieved from https://www.auncon.co.jp/corporate/2016/0318.html. Accessed on February 10, 2017.

Boase, J., & Kobayashi, T. (2008). Kei-Tying teens: Using mobile phone e-mail to bond, bridge, and break with social ties—a study of Japanese adolescents. *International Journal of Human-Computer Studies, 66,* 930–943.

Campbell, S.W., & Park, Y, J. (2008). Social implications of mobile telephony: The rise of personal communication society. *Sociology Compass, 2*(2), 371–387.

Communications Research Laboratory (Tsusin sougou kenkyuusyo). (2004). Internet use trends report 2003. Retrieved from http://www.medialabo.info/wip/report2003j/chapter13-j.pdf. Accessed on February 10, 2017.

Global State of Mobile Networks – OpenSignal. (2016). Retrieved from http://opensignal.com/reports/2016/08/global-state-of-the-mobile-network/3G. Accessed on February 10, 2017.

Gudhykunst,W.B. & Nishida, T. (1984). Individual and cultural influences on uncertainty reduction, *Communication Monographs, 51,* 23–36.

Ishii, K. (2004). Internet use via mobile phone in Japan. *Telecommunications Policy, 28*(1), 43–58.

Ishii, K. (2006). Implications of mobility: The uses of personal communication media in everyday life. *Journal of Communication, 56*(2), 346–365.

Ishii, K. (2009). Mobile Internet use in Japan: Social consequences of technology convergence. *Media Asia, 36*(4), 201–209.

Ishii, K. (2011a). The "strong-tied" SNS and "weak-tied" SNS: A comparison regarding the disclosure of personal information and personal relationships. *Journal of Information and Communication Research, 29*(3), 25–36.

Ishii, K. (2011b). Understanding Japanese users on microblog Twitter. *Department of Social Systems and Management Discussion Paper Series,* No. 1277, 1–7.

Ishii, K (2014a). *Mobairu wa ta no media to dou chigaunoka?* [How mobile is different from other media?]. In M. Matsuda, S. Dobashi, & I. Tsuji (Eds.), Keitai no 2000 nendai: seijyukusuru mobairu syakai (*Keitai in the 2000s: Maturation of Japanese mobile society*) (pp. 43–64). Tokyo: University of Tokyo Press.

Ishii, K. (2014b). Facebook riyosha no nichibeitai hikaku: kojin joho no kaijito nettowaku no dousitusei wo chyusin ni [A comparative study of Facebook users between Japan, US, and Taiwan: Focusing on disclosure of personal information and network homogeneity]. *Journal of Information and Communication Research, 109,* 39–50.

Ishii, K. (2015). Mobile internet use in Japan: Text-message dependency and social relationships. In Z. Yan (Ed.), *Encyclopedia of Mobile Phone Behavior* (Volumes 1, 2, & 3) (pp. 61–70). Hershey, PA: IGI Global.

Ishii, K. (2016). Intanetto riyo to bunka: kokusaihikaku deta ni yoru bunseki [Internet use and culture: An empirical test based on international comparative survey data]. *Journal of Media, Information and Communication, 1,* 1–15.

Ishii, K. (2017). Online communication with strong ties and subjective well-being in Japan. *Computers in Human Behavior, 66,* 129–137.

Ishii, K., Hashimoto, Y., Mikami, S., Tsuji, D., & Mori, Y. (2000). Naiyou bunseki ni yoru homupeji no kokusaihikaku [Content analysis of personal home-pages in Japan, U.S.A. and China]. *The Research Bulletin of the Institute of Socio-Information and Communication Studies, 14,* 1–82.

Ishii, K., Tsuji, D., Hashimoto, Y., Mori, Y., and Mikami, S. (2000). Naiyoubunseki ni yoru homupeji no kokusai hikaku: jikokaiji jikohyousyutu wo chusin ni (Cross-cultural comparison of homepages based on content analysis: focusing on self-disclosure and self-presentation), *The research bulletin of the Institute of Socio-Information and Communication Studies*, 14 pp. 1–82

Ishii, K., & Wu, C. (2006). A comparative study of media cultures among Taiwanese and Japanese youth. *Telematics and Informatics, 23*(2), 95–116.

Ito, M., Okabe, D., & Matsuda, M. (2006). *Personal, portable, pedestrian: Mobile phones in Japanese life.* Cambridge, MA: MIT Press.

Katz, J., & Aakhus, M. (2002). *Perpetual contact: Mobile communication, private talk, public performance.* New York: Cambridge University Press.

Kirkpatrick, D. (2011). *The Facebook effect: The inside story of the company that is connecting the world.* New York, NY: Simon & Schuster.

Kobayashi, T., & Ikeda, K. (2007). Jyakunensou no syakaika kateni okeru keitai meru no riyo no kouka: pasonaru nettowaku no dousitusei ishitusei to kanyousei ni chumokusite [The effect of mobile phone e-mailing in socialization in adolescence: Focusing on the homogeneity and heterogeneity of personal networks and tolerance]. *The Japanese Journal of Social Psychology, 23*(1): 82–94.

Loiacono, E. T. (2015). Self-disclosure behavior on social networking web sites. *International Journal of Electronic Commerce, 19*(2), 66–94.

Markus, H. R., & Kitayama, S. (1991). Culture and the self: Implications for cognition, emotion, and motivation. *Psychological Review, 98*(2), 224–253.

Matsuda, M., Dobashi, S. & Tsuji, I. (Eds.). (2014). *Keitai no 2000 nendai: seijyukusuru mobairu syakai* [Keitai in the 2000s: Maturation of Japanese mobile society]. Tokyo: University of Tokyo Press.

Miyata, K., Boase, J., Wellman, B., & Ikeda, K. (2006). Mobile-izing Japanese: Connecting to the Internet by PC and webphone in Yamanashi. In M. Ito, D. Okabe, & M. Matsuda (Eds.), *Personal, portable, pedestrian: Mobile phones in Japanese life* (pp. 143–164). Cambridge, MA: MIT Press.

Nakamura, I. (1997). Idotai tsusin media ga wakamo no ningen kankei oyobi seikatsu kodo ni ataeru eikyo: pokketo beru PHS risyou ni kansuru paneru chosa no kokoromi [Effects of mobile communication media on personal relationships: Panel survey on the pager and PHS telephone]. JSICR Annual Report 1996, pp. 27–40.

Parks, M. R., & Floyd, K. (2006). Making friends in cyberspace. *Journal of Communication, 46*(1), 80–97. doi:10.1111/j.1460–2466.1996.tb01462.x.

Personal Identifiable Information. (n.d.). In Wikipedia. Retrieved from https://en.wikipedia.org/wiki/Personally_identifiable_information. Accessed on February 10, 2017.

Salzberg, C. (2007). Japan: Number 1 language of bloggers worldwide. Retrieved from https://globalvoices.org/2007/04/16/japan-number-1-language-of-bloggers-worldwide/. Accessed on February 10, 2017.

Schug, J., Yuki, M., & Maddux, W. (2010). Relational mobility explains between- and within-culture difference in self-disclosure to close friends. *Psychological Science, 21*(10), 1471–1478.

Thomson, R., Yuki, M., & Ito, N. (2015). A socio-ecological approach to national differences in online privacy concern: The role of relational mobility and trust. *Computers in Human Behavior, 51*(Part A), 285–292.

Tomita, H. (2006). Keitai and the intimate stranger. In M. Ito, D. Okabe, & M. Matsuda (Eds.), *Personal, portable, pedestrian: Mobile phones in Japanese life* (pp. 183–201). Cambridge, MA: MIT Press.

Tomita, H., Fujimoto, K., Okada, N., Matsuda, M., & Takahiro, N. (1997). *Pokeberu/Keitai Shugi! (Pager/Mobilism!)*. Tokushima: Just System.

Tsuji, D., & Mikami, S. (2001). Daigakusei ni okeru keitai meru riyou to yujin kankei [A preliminary student survey on the email uses by mobile phones]. Paper presented at JSICR, June 2001, Tokyo.

Yap, J. (2016). Top 10 languages of tweets: English tops the chart, followed by Japanese. Retrieved from https://vulcanpost.com/7760/the-top-10-languages-of-tweets/. Accessed on February 10, 2017.

Yuki, M. & Schug, J. (2012). Relational mobility: A socioecological approach to personal relationships. http://hdl.handle.net/2115/52726.

Yuki, M., Schug, J. Horikawa, H., Takemura, K., Sato, K., Yokota, K., & Kamaya, K. (2007). Development of a scale to measure perceptions of relational mobility in society. Center for Experimental Research in Social Sciences Working Paper Series, No. 15. pp. 1–14. Retrieved from http://lynx.let.hokudai.ac.jp/cerss/workingpaper/2007.html. Accessed on February 10, 2017.

Yum, Y.-o. and Hara, K. (2005). Computer-Mediated Relationship Development: A Cross-Cultural Comparison. Journal of Computer-Mediated Communication, 11: 133–152. doi:10.1111/j.1083-6101.2006.tb00307.x

Zlatolas, L. N., Welzer, T., Heričko, M., & Hölbl, M. (2015). Privacy antecedents for SNS self-disclosure: The case of Facebook. *Computers in Human Behavior, 45*, 58–167. doi:10.1016/j.chb.2014.12.012.

10 Doing Things with Content

The Impact of Mobile Application Interface in the Uses and Characterization of Media

Juan Miguel Aguado, Inmaculada J. Martínez and Laura Cañete Sanz

Introduction

Just two years after App Store and Google's Android Market launch, the editors of *Wired*, Chris Anderson and Michael Wolff, anticipated in a polemic article a change in the use of the Internet, which they expected to quickly evolve toward a browser-less, semiclosed, platform-based environment with applications as the main interface. The article was titled "The Web is Dead. Long Live to the Internet" (Anderson and Wolff, 2010). Six years later, the Web is not dead, but the use of mobile applications as a prevalent Internet middleware has rocketed. Mobile now represents 65% of all digital media time, with mobile apps dominating that usage (ComScore, 2016; KPCB, 2016).

Mobile has become a prevalent access platform to media content, transforming both the flows and consumption routines of audiences. In the UK, 60 out of the total 80 h of average monthly digital media content consumption are on mobile devices (OFCOM, 2016). Mobile applications, rather than mobile browsers, appear to be the catalyzers of the digital growth: in 2015 in the US, mobile browser use involved only a 10% of the total mobile Internet use, while the remaining 90% was mobile applications driven Internet use (Khalaf, 2015); in the UK, 81% of the mobile Internet time is spent on apps, while 19% is on mobile browsers (E-Marketer, 2016); and in Spain, leading the EU smartphone penetration, 88% of the population using their small screens spend 89% of their mobile time on apps, with near 4 million apps installed daily (The App Date, 2015).

Digital content, together with communications, stars the average application-mediated mobile Internet use: almost 75% of the time using mobile apps involves digital-content-related activities (Khalaf, 2015). In specific cases like news, that trend shows industry-changing proportions: in 2014, already the 10 most important newspapers in Europe and the US received more traffic from mobile devices than from desktop

(De Prato, Sanz, and Simon, 2014). Two years later, most national UK newspapers have twice as many readers on mobile as they do on desktop, and in the case of the *Mirror*, mobile users provide four times the traffic that desktop users contribute (NRS, 2016). The strategic dimension of media content in the mobile environment is only comparable to the impact that mobile technology and its emerging players have in the content industries, still trying to cope with a painful adaptation to the digital world (De Prato, Sanz, and Simon, 2014).

Functional optimization is one of the reasons behind the success of mobile applications as an interface to the Internet (Scolari, Aguado, and Feijóo, 2012). But, the success of mobile apps is also related to the recent evolution of the Information and Communication Technologies (ICT) market around platform models. According to Fransman (2014), mobile-first digital platforms like Apple/iOS or Google/Android accomplish two strategic objectives via the consolidation of the mobile application ecosystem.

In the first place, with application and content stores (such as Apple's App Store and iTunes or Google's Google Play), platforms take on the prevailing distribution channel, which, in addition, allows them embedding value-added services like advertising platforms, cloud synchronization and storage services, digital payment and billing systems, and metrics (Aguado and Martínez, 2014). In fact, this situates platforms in the very core of a tailored multisided market that increases legacy players' dependence (De Prato, Sanz and Simon, 2014).

In the second place, thanks to the application-driven ecosystem, ICT platforms are able to produce an emerging innovation environment (Fransman, 2014) based in some of the principles of evolution: population growth, variation, and selection. By providing stimuli to developers (70% of app revenues, SDKs and developing tools, discoverability management, value added services, etc.), ICT platforms produce a rapidly growing population of mobile applications with an increasing variety.

At the same time, ICT platforms foster users' selection capacity via their category management systems and also by spreading deferred or limited cost models, like advertising based apps, *lite* versions, or *freemium* apps, which allow users to try an application (totally or partially) before assuming its final cost. These revenue models subsidize the users' opportunity cost for the learning curve of the mobile application interface (Fransman, 2014). In so doing, they help users to efficiently resolve the uncertainty about the cost/benefit balance, an undoubtedly relevant issue in the concurrence of content industries and innovative services. By all this, ICT platforms habilitate a selection process through which only a very small part of the total population of apps gets to be effectively installed and used. That selected population, though, becomes the main interface for accessing mobile content and related services (Khalaf, 2015).

In that context, mobile applications are no longer finished products. They are rather evolving access and management services that, through consecutive versions and updates, transform their functional capacities and, hence, their very nature as content interfaces. Leaving aside the debate about the death of the Web, the key idea underlying Anderson and Wolff's article seems still valid: a change in the prevailing interface involves a change in the very logic of the Internet pragmatics.

Mobile applications are also the dominant interface of current relational technologies (Aguado and Martínez, 2010). Communication is still the prevalent cultural meaning and the prior functional attribution of smartphones and other mobile devices (OFCOM, 2016): seven out of the ten most downloaded apps are communication applications (e.g., instant messaging or social networking apps) (Richter, 2016) and so are nine out of the ten most used apps in the world (half of them belonging to Facebook: WhatsApp, Instagram, Messenger, Facebook, Youtube) (Surveymonkey Intelligence, 2016). Mobile technology has taken over socialization processes (Ling, 2008; Campbell, Ling, and Bayer, 2014), and the extensive use of messaging and social networking apps is only one face of the trend.

Everything within mobile—including content and media—is entangled with identity performance and interpersonal dynamics (Aguado and Martínez, 2014; Van Dyjck, 2013). This new pervasiveness of the self, fostered by ubiquitous rituals of exposure through mobile technologies (Walker Rettberg, 2014), raises concerns not only about the transformation of identity management practices but also about the redefinition of privacy and the balance between public and private (Serrano Tellería, 2015). In this paper, we are particularly interested in two convergent aspects of that transformation: on one side, how the identity-centered drift is transforming application interfaces and mobile media content conception and, on the other side, how identity performances and (re)presentations adapt to these technological affordances. The process concerns the redefinition of technology-mediated and cultural-consumption-related social pragmatics, and it raises specific aspects of the public/private dilemma in the form of functional and symbolic appropriations.

Exploring the Functional Evolution of Mobile Content Applications

Mobile Applications as Content Interfaces

Mobile applications are software pieces designed to be installed and run in mobile devices. They conform to the limitations of this kind of hardware, but they also take advantage of it, as in location-enhanced services or accelerometer-based video game interfaces (Allen, 2003). Since they are designed to fulfill concrete functions, like displaying located weather forecasts or comparing prices in nearby stores, mobile applications are characterized by their functional economy and the importance of the interface design (Humphreys, Von Pape, and Karnovski, 2013). This has to be intuitive and natural in order to adequately respond to mobility's prerequisites of immediateness, ubiquity, and convenience (Joyce and Lilley, 2014).

Content—digital or mobile—is here understood as any kind of textual unit (written, iconic, audiovisual, hypermedia, etc.) that makes sense for the user or receiver. This traditionally refers to the product of creative industries and news media. Nevertheless, with the development of the so-called Social Web and the rise of a communication-driven mobile environment, social interactions among users are also to be taken as forms of digital content that, in fact, comprehend and contribute to redefining traditional content (Jenkins, Ford, and Green, 2013).

Coherently, mobile content applications are those mobile applications that refer their instrumental nature to content-related actions in mobility. According to the kind of functions they allow, the range of actions upon digital content in mobility can be ascribed to four main categories:

a   Creation/edition (producing textual units and modifying their structure, appearance, or extension)
b   Management (storing, organizing, classifying, and connecting textual units)
c   Performance (presenting, displaying, or making accessible a textual unit in order to be understood and/or enjoyed)
d   Communication (including textual units in dialogue threads that can themselves be taken as meaningful textual units)

Conventional software tools have been dealing with these different instrumental spheres for decades, often approaching them as functionally disaggregated environments. In the recent past, we could usually find powerful but narrow focused software tools, like text or image editors (creation), music or video players (performance), interaction tools like chat/message clients (communication), or OS-embedded file management tools (management). As hardware and networks evolved, some of these tools increasingly included functional aspect of the other spheres. Typically, social networking sites, but also email clients and alike, increasingly included forms of attached or embedded content. As long as the Internet evolved from a content-access-and-display centered structure towards a social-interaction centered communication network, the coordination amongst the four spheres of content-related functions became relevant. Mobile and digital media are now considered according to their spreadability (Jenkins, Ford, and Green, 2013) and the digital mobile environment is increasingly characterized by the merging of content, computing, and communication (Aguado and Martínez, 2014).

Assuming this, we intend to situate Anderson and Wolff's point in the specific context of the recent mobile content evolution; that is:

a   A change in content usage/access interface involves a change in the ways content is consumed and in its very conception.
b   Understanding how such change is pushing toward a greater malleability of digital content and toward a deeper integration of cultural content into social interaction dynamics.

To do so, this research aims at analytically founding a functional typology of mobile content applications involving a model to explain their functional evolution. Upon the preliminary findings of this model's application, we shall subsequently discuss whether the functional evolution of mobile content applications in recent years occurs in the direction of merging the characters of tools and media, continent and content.

Toward a Typology of Mobile Content Applications

Understanding the changing diversity of mobile applications demands a previous classification work in order to differentiate sorts and families. This is even more relevant to the case of content and media-related mobile applications, in which the merge of different formats and genres and different functions and services makes it a challenge.

Many of the existing classifications on mobile content applications resort to category management criteria (as in other marketing product management implementations) or to genre and purpose criteria (starting from the canonical triad advertising-persuasion, information-knowledge, and entertainment-amusement) (Scolari, Aguado, and Feijóo, 2012). Though these criteria may prove useful in facilitating the management of content access and discoverability in crowded environments like current mobile platforms, they are not congruent enough to be used in analytical purposes (Scolari, Aguado, and Feijóo, 2013). A functional differentiation approach may provide instead a more useful insight for efficient taxonomical purposes (Aguado and Martínez, 2014).

Based upon the functional categories outlined before (performance, creation, management, and communication), the authors have developed in previous works (Aguado and Martínez, 2014; Scolari, Aguado, and Feijóo, 2013) a positional model for the classification of mobile content applications in terms of functional composition/evolution. For measurement reasons, in this research we are focusing on platform applications (also called native applications), consequently leaving aside mobile web apps and other kind of mobile applications. The proposed model (Figure 10.1) is articulated in two orthogonal dimensions of mobile content applications:

The opposition between content narratives (where functions address the capability to see, to enjoy, or to access content) and tool (addressed to make or to rearrange content). For instance, the BBC iPlayer app would belong to content category, while Photoshop or Microsoft Word app would be ascribed to the category of tools.

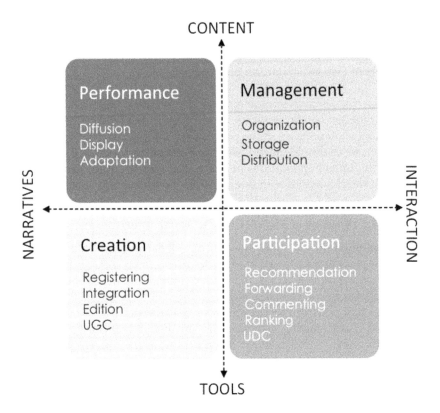

Figure 10.1 Functional typology of mobile content.
Source: Adaptation from Aguado and Martínez (2013) and Scolari, Aguado, and Feijóo (2013).

The opposition between discursive forms focused on storytelling (narratives), on one hand, and on conversational forms (interaction), on the other. For example, apps like Netflix or iMovie would be identified here as narrative addressed apps, while conversational tools like Twitter or Snapchat would rather fit the category of interaction-oriented apps.

At this point, the reader may have noticed that the boundaries of the proposed categories are not clear: YouTube may be an narrative-oriented app, but it also includes relevant forms of conversation; and though considered a typical conversational app, Facebook increasingly involves different forms of access to content. That is precisely why the model is proposed as an evolutionary space in which position marks the overlapping functional attributions of mobile content applications and how these change through time.

In the proposed model, the two orthogonal axes define a conceptual space where the prevailing functions (and hence the interface) of mobile content applications can be included into four main groups:

a   Performance area includes applications whose functions are focused on content performance, where narrative construction has a relevant dimension. Here, the ability to do things with content or its dialogic dimension show it to have a collateral nature. Those applications that have adapted to the mobile environment content from other existing media (television, music, books, etc.) are to be located in this space. Applications such as HBO GO, BBC iPlayer, or The New York Times are examples of this category.

b   Creation area includes applications functionally focused on the construction of different forms of narrative texts (written, iconic, video, etc.). They are the mobile transcript of the well-known editing software (word processors, photo or video editors) that allow creating and integrating different contents. Unlike their desktop counterparts, applications in mobile environment have a simplified, predefined, and modular disposition. For example, photo editors have replaced the complexity of integrated tools (color management, focus, brightness, etc.) with predefined filters. This favors the extension of the business model (by selling different filter types, for example) and the integration of other functions (exchange addressed social interactions, essentially).

c   Management area comprises mobile applications addressed to the organization, storage, and distribution of different kinds of content (mainstream media content and/or user created content). In the desktop environment, most of these functions were included in the operating system interface (file explorers). In the mobile environment, however, it is necessary to separately design specific tools. Different functions such as media libraries management, playlist creation, and content aggregation may be included within this area. Specifically, many functions related to content management are naturally integrated with e-commerce and digital content distribution channels. Main platform based distribution channels (iTunes, App Store, or Google Play) include management functions in order to implement data intelligence about user behavior as a part of their advertising monetization strategies and recommendation systems (Feijóo and Gómez Barroso, 2013).

d   Participation area includes mobile applications focused on communication and interpersonal interaction (messaging and social networks). These spaces for dialogue increasingly integrate content into everyday social interactions (Papacharissi, 2012), turning users into effective content distributors (Noguera et al., 2013).

A proposal for the Functional Analysis of Mobile Content Applications

The outlined model allows identifying the functional orientation of mobile content applications' interfaces in relation to the described areas (content, narratives, tools, and interactions). The values processed to define the functional orientation of a given application in the model are taken from an adapted content analysis procedure upon the functional descriptions available in Apple's iOS App Store. Update history in the App Store contains schematic descriptions of the versions of an application throughout time, highlighting innovations or functional contributions, with codes and dates for each version. The update history goes back to older versions published approximately two years before the latest one. Each version includes a detailed list with all the changes included. It is important here to stress that this is a form of technical discourse, a description that developers do to users, explaining product improvements and characteristics. It is, thus, a discursive practice produced in terms of a recognizable experience of use (Aguado, Martínez, and Cañete, 2015).

Table 10.1 presents, as example, the items of Flipboard, 2.0 version—a content aggregator with social network features counting with over 50 million registered users.

In order to perform content analysis, the items of the updates have been taken as units of analysis, providing their conciseness and sequentiality. Those items not specifically related to content functionalities have been discarded (for example, generic functionality assertions such as "bug fixing" or "performance enhancements"). Those items specifically related to content have been codified in three levels (between 0 and 1), ranking their meaning adscription to each of the following aspects: reproduction or displaying content (Content), performing actions on content, such as editing or rearranging (Tool), content organization (Management), and communication among users (Interaction). In this way, we are able to describe not only the functional articulation of a given mobile content app, but its evolution throughout the different identified versions in a

Table 10.1 Flipboard 2.0 items

Application: FLIPBOARD. 2.0 version March 27, 2013. Developer: Flipboard
1 You can now collect and save content into your own magazines. Tap the new "+" button to get started.   2 Your magazines are public, but can be made private (viewable only to you).   3 Use the new bookmarklet to add items to your magazines from your browser.   4 Get Flipboard notifications when people like, comment or subscribe to your magazines.   5 Easily email or share magazines to Facebook, Twitter, G+, etc.   6 Faster page-loading and faster flipping performance.

Source: AppStore (2015).

given period of time and in reference to the four proposed functional categories (performance, creation, management, and participation).

Data obtained can be expressed in a radar chart that allows to see the evolution of the different functional dimensions analyzed, that is, by studying the trend of an application located in a specific function and its evolution toward a functional multidimensionality and how it evolves in each area (Figures 10.3 to 10.7). A validation test was carried out on a qualitatively significant sample of four applications along the proposed functional areas (NYT for Performance, Garage Band for Creation, Flipboard in Management, and Twitter in Participation). Results obtained were consistent for different encoders.

After the validation test, the model was applied to a convenience sample of 12 applications (Table 10.2) selected among the five most downloaded free applications in each category, according to Apple App Store's metrics. Some significant applications, such as Facebook, have been necessarily excluded from the sample because of the lack of information about functional innovation in their updates. Whenever possible, different kinds of applications have been selected within the same category: news media or games in Performance area; editing tools for different kinds of content in Creation area; content managers, aggregators, and data managers in the Management category; and different kinds of social networks for Participation area.

The application history available in the App Store for the sample of the selected applications was extracted and processed, taking a two-year period from March 2013 to March 2015, resulting in 646 valid functional items distributed along 153 versions. These involve around 28 new functional items and seven new versions per application and year. This alone illustrates the argument about mobile applications as evolving interfaces.

Testing the Model

The results obtained show a general trend toward multifunctional integration in different mobile applications, with percentages close to 30% of the assigned values dealing with improvements in those functional fields related to Content (27.5%), improvements or modifications in the instrumental functionalities of the apps (Tools) (29.2%), and functions

Table 10.2 Sample selection of mobile applications sorted by categories

Performance	Creation	Management	Communication
The New York Times	PicsArt	Flipboard	Twitter
Clash of Clans	GarageBand	Runtastic	Google+
YouTube	Clipper	Sing Karaoke	Pinterest

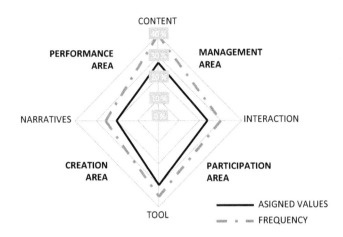

Figure 10.2 Global results for assigned values and frequence (%).

dealing with forms of interaction (24.6%). Generally, the functional areas more intensively developed in the period under analysis belong to the categories of Management and Participation (Figure 10.2). Furthermore, comparing the assigned values for each category with the frequency (number of times that a category rates in different items analyzed) and according to the proximity of these two kinds of values (in Figure 10.2, where the lines of the chart appear significantly closer), we can observe some acceleration in the increasing relevance of those functional aspects within management and participation areas.

However, this observable trend is not identically valid to all the kinds of applications considered in the sample. In those apps within the Performance category, there appear to be differences as to the intensity and direction of their functional evolution. In the case of news media apps (The New York Times), functional evolution on content access is prevalent (45.2%), showing a constrained but steady propensity to multifunctionality in the social interactions and management fields (Figure 10.3).

The differences with mobile video games, such as Clash of Clans, are evident. In this case, accumulated values are concentrated in content-related functional categories (29.4%) and participation (30.1%) with a sustained increase in consecutive versions (Figure 10.4). Clearly enough, narratives and editing capacities are secondary functional areas, whereas social interactions and visual content (graphs and structure) consolidate as prevailing functional areas.

The YouTube mobile application deserves specific attention because of its functional versatility. Its functional evolution happens mainly in the areas of Content (33.3%), Narratives (30.6%), and Tool (22.2%), leaving only 13.9% to interaction-related functions. While being a kind of video based social network, YouTube's mobile app version seems to have evolved in the analyzed period rather toward a content management and

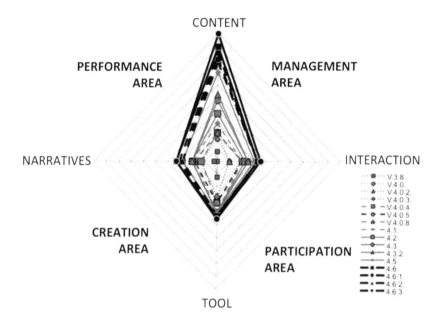

Figure 10.3 Results for The New York Times mobile application.

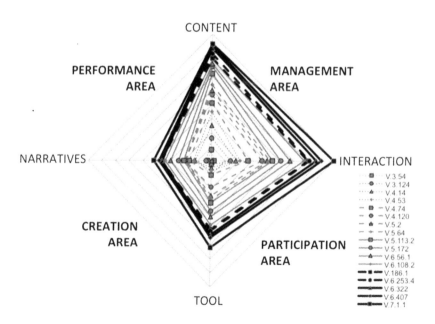

Figure 10.4 Results for Clash of Clans mobile application.

edition tool. Its natural integration into a powerful social network such as Facebook may contribute to explain that functional rearrangement.

The evolution of those applications within the functional area of Management is especially interesting, since it condenses the main aspects of the overall evolutionary trend in the sample. The case of Flipboard is highly illustrative to this respect. Flipboard was born as a content aggregator with social functions (namely, the integration of Twitter and Facebook accounts into the content aggregation flow). In the period under study, Flipboard significantly developed its functional features related to editing capacities (Tool; 28.2%), including aspects like creating personal magazines, new ways to integrate and manage content curation, and following users and magazines indistinctively. Interaction-related functions (30.3%) have substantially evolved, while content (21.8%) remains a focal—but somehow steady—point. As a result, Management and Participation areas drive the evolution of the app, turning Flipboard into something closer to a content-focused social network, rather than a socially oriented content aggregator (Figure 10.5). To a lesser extent, the same driving role in the merge of Management- and Participation-related functions is reproduced in the two other management applications studied (Runtastic and Sing Karaoke).

Similar to Performance applications, those apps located in the functional area of Creation show a slower evolution towards functional

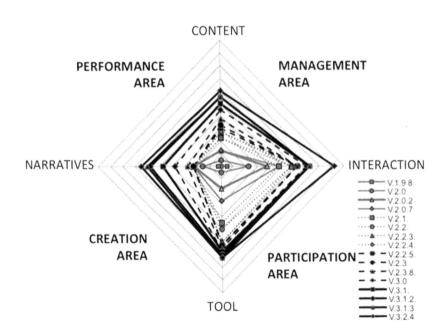

Figure 10.5 Results for Flipboard mobile application.

integration. These applications—traditionally identified as editing tools—concentrate their main evolution in the functional area that defines them. Applications such as PicsArt (graphic edition), GarageBand (audio and music edition), or Clipper (Video edition) are examples of this kind of slow and focused evolution. Here, interaction-related aspects, like sharing works and ranking filters or clips (11.5% in PicsArt; 3% in Garage Band), are interestingly underdeveloped. The resulting picture (Figure 10.6) is almost symmetrical to that of Performance area (Figure 10.3), perhaps because their interface structuration is addressed to discrete and isolated items: content units in the case of adapted legacy media (like The New York Times) and functional arrangements (filters, clips, sets of effects, etc.) in the case of editing tools.

If applications in the functional area of Management evolve in the direction of socially oriented, content-focused interfaces, mobile social networks (i.e., apps within the area of Participation) seem to progressively become content-oriented, interaction-focused applications. In other words, while in the first case, functional integration shifts from content to interaction, and in the latter, the observable trend is the opposite: a shift from interaction to content. The functional evolution of mobile social networks in the sample is characterized by the diversification and enrichment of those capabilities related to communication (new forms of interaction and monitoring) and by the growing inclusion of content access in the interaction-related functionalities. Thus, values assigned to participation

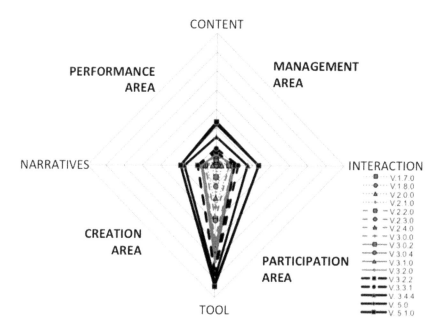

Figure 10.6 Results chart for PicsArt application.

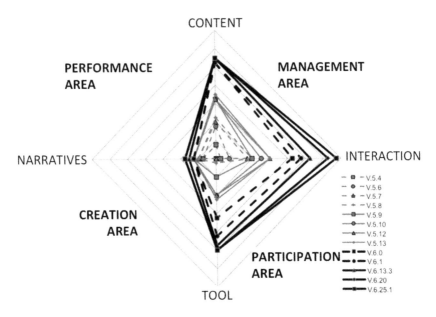

Figure 10.7 Results chart for Twitter application.

functions (30.2% Twitter, 28.5% Google+, or 29.2% Pinterest) and content functions (27.1% Twitter, 29.9% Google+, or 41.7% Pinterest) stand over those dealing with tool functionalities (editing content) (26.2% Twitter, 19.7% Google+, or 20.8% Pinterest). Twitter results accurately illustrate these trends (Figure 10.7), showing some symmetry with those of socially oriented mobile games (Figure 10.4).

These outcomes allow concluding—though on a basic descriptive level—that there is an observable evolution toward functional integration in the case of mobile content applications and that such evolution is marked by the increasing prevalence of social- and management-related functions around content. In other words, the uses of content in the mobile environment involve *doing things* with content, rather than only accessing or enjoying media content.

What Users do with Content?

Exploring Identity-Related Uses of Content Sharing in Mobile Social Networks

Social Networks as Identity Presentation Scenarios

According to the results previously discussed, social network sites and mobile apps constitute a relevant scenario for the integration of digital media content into social interaction dynamics. Not only have social networks sites become increasingly mobile first (if not mobile only) in the last few years, but also they have become one of the main windows for media and news access among young users (Noguera et al., 2013; Gottfried and Shearer, 2016).

The role of media in how individuals construct and understand their selves in modern societies has been widely approached as a matter of symbolic appropriation (Thompson, 1995). An increasing part of these processes has turned to take place in the digital world—and specifically in the context of new digital forms of interaction, such as mobile-first social networks—where the features and symbolic rituals of legacy media and many-to-many interaction tools overlap (Van Dyjck, 2013). As Enli and Thumin (2012: 87) put it, "social network sites such as Facebook have institutionalized and mediatized personal processes of socializing and display of identity, which traditionally have belonged to the private and non-mediated spheres." Goffman's view about the strategic nature of interaction rituals (Goffman, 1967) finds in these technologies of social saturation (Gergen, 2009) a breeding ground to bring light over the new forms of impression management (Papacharisi, 2012).

Media and digital content in mobile social networks are not mere sources of entertainment or information through new different channels. The stories, videos, and news shared on Facebook, Twitter, or Snapchat are also part of the ways users present themselves in conditions of relative context and audience uncertainty. A strategy-oriented approach to the ways individuals (re)present themselves by means of content-related expressive actions may contribute to understanding the functional drift in mobile application interfaces toward interactional and editing features.

As suggested in the title of this section, we intend to explore what users do with media content as a symbolic and strategic resource in the context of their management of social interactions. In this respect, we assume Hogan's (2010) dichotomy between self-(re)presentation (as self-exhibition, self-statement, or self-expression) and performances of the self (as more complex processes involving recognizable rituals and conversational environments) (Papacharizi, 2012). Resorting to Goffman's (1967) conceptual frame, Hogan's dichotomy involves a "distinction between the sorts of online spaces where actors behave with each other ('performance' spaces, or behaviour regions) and 'exhibition' spaces where individuals submit artefacts to show to each other." To our aims, that distinction presupposes and deals differently with shared content, either as an artifact (an addressed signal) or as a language (a situated behavior).

With this in mind, we have carried out an ethnographic analysis of non-user-generated content shared in mobile first social networks during a lapse of four random days between March and April 2016. We have focused our analysis on younger users (18–20) because they are the most mobile-social-network-centered media consumers, according to Pew Research Center report (Gottfried and Shearer, 2016). The sample included 95 informants who produced 974 field records of the content shared. That is 10.25 content items shared per informant, with an average rate of 2.6 content items shared per informant and day. Field records included answers about social network used for sharing, type of content shared, nature of addressees and purposes of sharing, regard of the shared content to the ongoing online conversation, and the source of shared content. Informants were invited to briefly discuss the role of the content shared in their interaction with others. Though the interviews and records were conducted in Spain, the sample and results might be illustrative for culturally consistent European developed countries.

Social Uses of Media Recommendation and Publishing Rituals

Facebook and Twitter clearly dominate the social network landscape in the studied sample, with a minimum presence of activities in other networks such as Instagram or Snapchat. As in many other cases for young people in developed countries, the two prevalent mobile first social networks are deeply intertwined in the informants' everyday life, becoming a core driver of their social interactions, in which performances and representations of identity take place (Enli and Thumin, 2012; Papacharissi, 2012; Walker Rettberg, 2014).

There is, however, a relatively low level of dialogue implication in relation to content sharing practices: more than two-thirds of the informants do not share content as a part of an ongoing conversation. They rather post it as it comes to them, for a wide variety of reasons, but rarely integrating content as a part of a dialogue. Content sharing, thus, seems to have more to do with "showing something" than with "saying something." In this sense, for the informants in the sample, the shared content is predominantly part of a self-presentation strategy: "I identify with that video, and I want my contacts to know I feel like that" (Woman, 18); "I want people to know what my opinion is on that matter and why I think this way" (Woman, 19).

Even in those cases in which content is given a questioning purpose—as, for instance, in a provocative statement—this seems to happen rather as an attention-gathering practice: "I share it mainly as a way to protest and vindicate, but I don't really mean something concrete, cause it's a rather stale issue already, you know?" (Man, 20). In this sense, the dialoguing attitude is relatively absent, mostly substituted by forms of phatic communicative behavior (Miller, 2008), in which the meaning functions attributed to content sharing focus on the very creation of a link. The use of content as a mark of belonging operates as well in a similar mood ("I share it with my contacts because I think there might be someone that may like photography as well, and then find this interesting") (Woman, 19).

Along with that prevalence of the phatic function, the role of content is attached to a certain sense of opportunity and randomness: rather than sharing the content they *would want* to share, users tend to share the content they *have at hand.* Users mostly share what they find interesting while exploring the very same social network in which they share, which suggests a kind of self-centered reading of media content in social networks at the expense of dialogic or informational practices. Recent research results showing users being more willing to share an article than read it (Gabielkov et al., 2016) seem to match that same conception of content as a self-presentation symbolic resource. This principle of opportunity that speaks of at-hand digital content reusability and re-signification matches, as well, the compulsion to spreadability by design addressed by Jenkins, Ford, and Green (2013).

The kind of content shared relates to three dominant categories (out of 13 used): news and stories, quotations, and videos. Other categories, such as pictures, memes, and audio clips, remain far less shared forms of content. Thematic categories are less concentrated: humor, political or social issues, sports, and curiosities outstand in the sample. The prevalence of news and stories seems to be consistent with some kind of editorializing attitude as a self-presentation or even self-affirmation strategy. This kind of appropriation of the public discourse as a matter of private self-delimitation—the very use of media content as an identity marker—appears to work as a counterbalance to the inflation of the exposure to others: using media content as an identifier at the same time exposes and hides.

Social networks constitute their own range of interaction spaces, and as such, they are clearly differentiated as identity performance scenarios: Facebook is more linked to known contacts (friends, family) and to everyday life episodes and interests, while Twitter is perceived as a more anonymous environment in which the presentation of the self may be more emphatic: "I don't share this kind of things in Facebook. I think Facebook is a more familiar social network, you have to think better what you post there" (Woman, 20); "Twitter is much freer, out of the elders' sight [...] I can freely make my point and open new debates" (Man, 19).

Despite the level of conversational and contextual uncertainty, the potential reactions of addressees are clearly present in users' minds when sharing content on social networks. In fact, the very identification of addressees as groups determines the conception of the social network as an interaction frame. There are different types of addressees in the horizon of a shared content: the user, known people present in users' everyday life (family, friends, peers), bigger groups functionally differentiated around shared interests or hobbies, and wider anonymous audiences. Motivation and purposes vary according to whether shared content addresses one or another of these categories and so do identity presentation strategies. In Table 10.3, we summarize the main purposes showed by informants in content sharing for each category of address-ees. Obviously, these are qualitative estimations, and some of the stated purposes may find their place in different categories. However, the table is illustrative enough to determine the importance of self-representation and self-definition over more complex behavioral attitudes.

Table 10.3 Main purposes for content sharing in social networks according to different kinds of addressees

Addressees	Oneself	Close/Known Persons	Interest Groups	Anonymous
Content Sharing Purposes	Self-statement "That's just for me, because I like it" (M, 20)	Self-presentation "Just for them to know I'm there" (M, 18)	Self-presentation "I want them to know I identify with that and why I do" (M, 18)	Self-presentation "Because this is how I think" (M, 20)
	Access to past interests "In order to know the things I used to like" (W, 19)	Marks of belonging "We use to like these kind of cute things" (W, 18)	Marks of belonging "There's some kind of competition to see who gets the funniest video" (M, 20)	Raising awareness "I am looking for more people aware of what sexism means to our society" (W, 19)
		Raising awareness "I want them to think about this, because this is important" (W, 19)	Contributing to others "Because I think it may be useful to people interested in this kind of courses" (W, 18)	Identification "I think that, since I had fun with that, others may have as well" (W, 19)
			Identification "I felt moved and I shared it" (W, 19)	

In broad terms, interviewed users seek a connection between the positive reactions to shared content and their inherent (but limited) performance in the social network (as curators, as being portrayed by the shared content, etc.). These positive reactions are mostly related to identity presentation strategies, such as complicity, agreement, or identification. The importance given to presentation strategies appears to be more intense as audiences become potentially wider and more anonymous. In these cases, content is given a radically significant role as an identity mark. This kind of "message in a bottle"—that shows to be more about saying "Hey, I'm here, that's me" than about saying something at all—shows again a prevailing phatic function that blurs the dialogic potential of shared content as a message.

According to the results outlined, there is an observable concordance between increasingly social network oriented content consumption practices and the strategic articulation of digital media content into social network interactions in terms of identity presentation. Content seems to play a relevant role in presenting and representing one's identity to others, rather than in more elaborated performances of the self. These, according to Papacharissi (2012), take place in conversational levels in which media content do not seem to play a role as a meaningful form of expression. From that perspective, the performance of the self in social networks seems to be separated from presentation and suspended until eventual interactions around statements posted or content shared take place: "I like when my contacts share what I have shared and when they post comments" (Man, 20); despite this, expectations about concrete interactions triggered by content shared are not high: "I really don't know how they may feel. I don't even care. It's just me posting what I like" (Man, 19).

The process of building and presenting one's identity prefigures an important driver in digital content consumption rituals. There are also reasons to understand that the pervasiveness and ubiquity that came along with mobile technology have contributed to emphasizing the phatic nature of social interactions (Miller, 2008; Aguado and Martínez, 2010). Whatever the case, the importance of media content as a strategic resource for the presentation of the self in mobile social networks feeds the need to be able to eventually manage, transform, and share digital content, mostly on the go, as it comes at one's hand. So that managing and editing content is no more just a matter of being informed or entertained, but a social skill necessary to communicate to others. It is not a matter of private consumption, but a public capacity.

Conclusions

In this paper, we have outlined two convergent research lines that seek to offer some answers about the increasing symbolic and functional interdependence between media and social networks in the context of the so-called mobile media revolution (De Prato, Sanz, and Simon, 2013).

In pursuing these answers, we intend to go beyond the common arguments about new distribution channels and audience-fashionable behaviors. We are aware of the complexity of summarizing and connecting different methodological approaches and conceptual frameworks. However, we believe these approaches may bring some light about the consolidation of new media consumption scenarios that have to do with socializing as much as with knowing things around or having fun with others.

The approaches outlined in this paper are part of an ongoing research line that seeks to identify existing correspondences between the functional evolution of mobile content applications and the social rituals involved in new media content consumption. These aspects involve the symbolic appropriation of public and private discourses and the constitution of polyvalent scenarios where private and public categories are strategically redefined. As part of an ongoing research, these approaches are subjected to further development and refinement, especially in what concerns the size and diversity of the sample and the inclusion of a third qualitative fieldwork with developers. The current results, however, seem to us consistent enough and illustrative for a general conclusion about these correspondences.

The driving idea emerged after developing a proposal of taxonomy of mobile content applications (Scolari, Aguado, and Feijóo, 2012; Aguado and Martínez, 2014) that subsequently founded a methodological approach. The method for the functional evaluation of mobile content application distinguishes four main functional categories for possible actions around content: Performance, Creation, Management, and Participation. Taking the version history record of a selected sample of mobile content applications, the proposed method allows researchers to identify its functional evolution through a period of time and to valuate the relative weight of each of the four considered functional areas in the content interface (Aguado, Martínez, and Cañete, 2015).

The sample selected validates the descriptive potential of the proposed approach and offers a preliminary insight about the increasing weight of functions related to Management and Participation areas in the most relevant kinds of mobile content applications. The resulting picture underlines as well the strategic importance of content in social network and management applications, which are progressively embracing the content performance features that once distinguished legacy media. On the opposite side of the picture, legacy media mobile platforms seem to be failing in integrating social interaction and content management functionalities into their mobile interfaces. The general landscape depicts a process of progressive in-app functional integration with a central role for social interaction and content-editing features. Those interface proposals structured around services and fluid objects (conversations) seem to better manage that functional integration than those others conceiving the mobile interface in a shop-like, discrete, product-delivery fashion (Aguado, Martínez, and Cañete, 2015).

That evolution puts into play a different, more active, and socially grounded conception of media content, transcending its role as an object of consumption and turning it into a symbolic resource in the very boundary between private and public pragmatics. Content is no longer just something that can be read, watched, or listened to in order to be informed or amused; it is becoming something upon which we carry on symbolic communicative actions (share, link, comment, rate, edit, etc.), and thus something that is functionally integrated into social interaction dynamics (it can be forwarded, linked, commented, parodied, etc.). In that very sense, in the mobile, social-interaction-oriented environment, media news and stories become discursively appropriated by users as symbolic resources.

The functional shift of mobile content toward communication and social interaction demands thus to explore the uses and meanings attributed to content-related symbolic actions in the mobile social environment. We have approached that task through an ethnographic analysis of the 974 field records provided by 95 young informants on their content sharing practices in mobile social networks. It is in these social networks where these Z generation users (18–20 years old) access the vast majority of the media content they consume (Gottfried and Shearer, 2016), merging in one single flow of social interactions the enjoyment of media content (public discourses) and the presentation and performance of the self in their everyday digital (private discourses).

The results sustain a differentiation between communicative practices around the presentation of the self and those others, behaviorally more complex, related to the performance of the self (Hogan, 2010). Communicative practices involving content sharing are predominantly phatic (Miller, 2008), attached to self-presentation strategies, rather than to conversational rituals. They tend show forms of self-introduction, self-exhibition, or self-definition, addressed to establish a communicative link that may or may not be developed in further conversational rituals. Shared media content operates in the observed sample as a mark of identity, often pointing to interests, concerns, or views that strategically depict aspects of identity.

That phatic, self-presentation-oriented communicative strategy appears to be especially relevant in contexts of uncertainty and audience anonymity. Not by chance, uncertainty and anonymity are also a relevant variable in the users' definition of the different social networks as interaction landscapes (that is, fields for plausible interaction scenarios); unlike in the traditional sphere—at least in the times of the mass society—anonymity comes to be here associated with privacy. The nature and thematic adscription of the media content shared reinforces the conclusion that, while sharing media content is not part of conversational rituals, expressing one's identity has become definitely an important part of young users' media content consumption rituals. Public discourses and private discourses are symbolic resources for strategic appropriation.

Further research in regard to these results may take into account young users reading practices and meaning construction pragmatics on shared media content. It may also be interesting to delve into the economic implications of the merge between self-expression and media consumption for digital players and media industries in terms of product design, business model definition, and personal information exploitation.

Acknowledgments

The results and discussions in these pages are part of two coordinated research projects: "Mobile Communication and Personal Data: Impact in Media Industries, the Advertising System and Users' Perceptions," funded by the Spanish Ministry of Economy and Competitiveness (CSO2013-47394-R) and "MOB AD: The Impact of Mobile Technology in Strategic and Advertising Communications," funded by the Regional Agency for Science and Technology, Seneca Foundation (19451/PI/14).

References

Aguado, J. M., & Martínez, I. J. (2010). Liquid digital selves: Mobile media implicit cultures, social relations and identity management. *Encyclopaideia: Journal of Phenomenology and Education, 15*(1), 63–88.

Aguado, J. M., & Martínez, I. J. (2014). The relationship is the medium: Understanding media in a mobile age. In J. Katz (Ed.), *Living inside mobile social information* (pp. 77–108). Boston, MA: Boston University Press.

Aguado, J. M., Martínez, I. J., & Cañete, L. (2015). Tendencias evolutivas del contenido digital en aplicaciones móviles. *El Profesional de la Información, 24*(6), 782–790.

Allen, J. P. (2003). The evolution of new mobile applications: A sociotechnical perspective. *International Journal of Electronic Commerce, 8*(1), 23–36. doi:10.1111/j.1751-9020.2007.00080.x.

Anderson, C., & Wolff, M. (2010). The web is dead, long life to the Internet, *Wired*. Retrieved from http://www.wired.com/2010/08/ff_webrip/. Accessed July 3, 2016.

Campbell, S.W., Ling, R., & Bayer, J. (2014). The structural transformation of mobile communication: Implications for self and society. In M. B. Oliver & A. Raney (Eds.), *Media and social life* (pp. 176–188). New York: Routledge.

ComScore. (2016). 2016 US Cross-Platform Future in Focus. Retrieved from http://www.comscore.com/Insights/Presentations-and-Whitepapers/2016/ 2016-US-Cross-Platform-Future-in-Focus.

De Prato, G., Sanz, E., & Simon, J. P. (2014). *Digital media worlds. The new economy of media*. New York: Palgrave-Macmillan.

E-Marketer. (2016). How UK users engage with mobile. Retrieved from http:// www.emarketer.com/Article/How-Users-UK-Engage-with-Mobile-Apps/ 1013504.

Enli, G. G., & Thumin, N. (2012). Socializing and self-representation online: Exploring Facebook. *Observatorio (OBS*) Journal*, 6(1), 87–105. Retrieved from http://obs.obercom.pt/index.php/obs/article/viewFile/489/487. Accessed May 2, 2016.

Feijóo, C., & Gómez-Barroso, J. L. (2013). Hacia una economía de la información personal. In J. M. Aguado, C. Feijóo, & I. J. Martínez (Eds.), *La comunicación móvil: hacia un nuevo ecosistema digital* (pp. 305–322). Barcelona: Gedisa.

Fransman, M. (2014). "Models of innovation in global ICT firms: The emerging global innovation ecosystems". *EC-JRC Science and Policy Reports*. European Commission. Retrieved from https://ec.europa.eu/jrc/sites/default/files/jrc90726.pdf.

Gabielkov, M., Ramachandran, A., Chaintreau, A., & Legout, A. (2016). Social clicks: What and who gets read on Twitter?. *ACM SIGMETRICS/IFIP Performance 2016*, June 2016, Antibes Juan-les-Pins, France.

Gergen, K. J. (2009). *Relational being: beyond self and community*, New York: Oxford University Press.

Goffman, E. (1967). *Interaction ritual*. New York: Doubleday Anchor Books.

Gottfried, J., & Shearer, E. (2016). *News use across social media platforms 2016*. Pew Research Center: Journalism and Media. Retrieved from http://www.journalism.org/2016/05/26/news-use-across-social-media-platforms-2016/. Accessed June 11, 2016.

Hogan, B. (2010). The presentation of the self in the age of social media: Distinguishing performances and exhibitions online. *Bulletin of Science, Technology & Society*, 30(6), 377-386. doi:10.1177/0270467610385893.

Humphreys, L., Von Pape, Th., & Karnowski, V. (2013). Evolving mobile media: uses and conceptualizations of the mobile Internet. *Journal of Computer-Mediated Communication*, 18(4), 491–507. 10.1111/jcc4.12019.

Jenkins, H., Ford, S., & Green, J. (2013). *Spreadable media: creating value and meaning in a networked culture*. New York: New York University Press. 10.1111/jpcu.12110.

Joyce, G., & Lilley, M. (2014). Towards the development of usability heuristics for native smartphone mobile applications. In A. Marcus (Ed.), *Design, user experience, and usability. Theories, methods, and tools for designing the user experience, lecture notes in computer science* (pp. 465–474). *Third International Conference, DUXU 2014, Held as Part of HCI International 2014, Heraklion, Crete, Greece, June 22–27, 2014, Proceedings, Part I.* Springer International Publishing. 10.1007/978-3-319-07668-3-45.

Khalaf, S. (2015). Seven years into the mobile revolution: Content is king... again. *Flurry Analytics*. Retrieved from http://flurrymobile.tumblr.com/post/127638842745/seven-years-into-the-mobile-revolution-content-is. Accessed February 1, 2016.

KPCB. (2016) Internet Trends Report 2016. Retrieved from http://www.kpcb.com/internet-trends. Accessed June 21, 2016.

Ling, R. (2008). *New tech, new ties: How mobile communication is reshaping social cohesion*. Cambridge, MA: MIT Press.

Miller, V. (2008) New media, networking and phatic culture. *Convergence: The International Journal of Research into New Media Technologies*, 14(4), 387–400.

Noguera, J. M., Bourdaa, M., Villi, M., Nyiro, N., & de Blasio, E. (2013). The role of the media industry when participation is a product. In N. Carpentier, K. Schroder, & L. Hallett (Eds.), *Transformations. Late modernity's shifting audience positions* (pp. 172–190). New York: Routledge.

NRS (National Readership Survey). (2016). NRS PADD: Mobile & Tablet data. June 2016, Retrieved from http://www.nrs.co.uk/downloads/mobile-data/pdf/nrs_padd_mobile_standard_tables_jul_15_jun_16.pdf. Accessed July, 6, 2016.

OFCOM (2016). *The communications market report.* Retrieved from http://www.ofcom.org.uk/opendata. Accessed June 28, 2016.

Papacharissi, Z. (2012). Without you, I'm nothing: Performances of the self on Twitter. *International Journal of Communication, 6*(18), 1989–2006.

Richter, F. (2016). The most popular apps in the world. In *Statista blog.* Retrieved from https://www.statista.com/chart/5055/top-10-apps-in-the-world/. Accessed July 3, 2016.

Scolari, C., Aguado, J. M., & Feijóo, C. (2012). Mobile media: Towards a definition and taxonomy of contents and applications. *International Journal of Interactive Mobile Technologies, 6*(2). Retrieved from http://online-journals.org/i-jim/article/view/1880. Accessed January 22, 2016.

Scolari, C., Aguado, J. M., & Feijóo, C. (2013). Una ecología del medio móvil: Contenidos y aplicaciones. In J. M. Aguado, C. Feijóo, & I. J. Martínez (Eds.), *La comunicación móvil: hacia un nuevo ecosistema digital* (pp. 127–154), Barcelona: Gedisa.

Serrano Tellería, A. (2015). The role of the profile and the digital identity on the mobile content. In J. M. Aguado, C. Feijóo, & I. J. Martínez (Eds.), *Emerging perspectives on the mobile content evolution* (pp. 263–283). Philadelphia: IGI Global.

Surveymonkey Intelligence. (2016). *The 60 most popular apps of 2016.* Retrieved from https://www.surveymonkey.com/business/intelligence/most-popular-apps-2016/. Accessed July 28, 2016.

The App Date. (2015). *Sexto Informe sobre el estado de las apps en España.* Retrieved from http://www.theappdate.es/static/media/uploads/app_date_v2.compressed.pdf. Accessed July 28, 2016.

Thompson, J. B. (1995). *The media and modernity: a social theory of the media.* Cambridge, UK: Polity Press.

Van Dyjck, J. (2013). *The culture of connectivity: A critical history of social media.* Oxford, UK: Oxford University Press.

Walker Rettberg, J. (2014). *Seing ourselves through technology: How we use selfies, blogs and wearable devices to see and shape ourselves.* London: Palgrave McMillan.

11 Copyright and User-Generated Contents for Mobile Devices

News, Entertainment, and Multimedia

Javier Díaz Noci

Introduction

Involvement of audiences in the production process is an increasing reality in any field of cultural production, from fan fiction and transmedia productions to news comments. The mobile environment, an increasing reality, enhances this tendency. As for 2014, the number of mobile device users in the European Union countries reached more than one half of the whole population, since 51% of the European people were using notebooks, cell phones, or tablet computers, according to the figures by Eurostat (2015). The proportion of users aged 16 to 74, following that same source, was even greater in some countries, such as Sweden, Denmark, and the United Kingdom, reaching 75% of that population.[1] Everyone with a mobile device, a smartphone, or a tablet is a consumer and a potential author who can simply upload pictures from literally everywhere, when there is Internet connection available. The fact that those creations are perishable or ephemeral— another question to be considered, since social networks are huge repositories to which the user assigns unlimited licenses on the storage of their works—does not give them a smaller protection under the copyright umbrella. Done for profit or as the divertimento of amateurs, any work with a minimum originality right is protectable by intellectual property laws.

Contributions by authors, individual or corporate, professional or amateur, not to mention user-generated contents, have adopted many shapes and have introduced new levels of complexity to legal protection of intellectual works. Through purely personal authorship or using collaborative strategies with other users, through derivative works or through collaborative works, audiences are claiming a role as authors themselves. Active audiences have joined journalists, photographers, and media companies as part of the information flow and are part of the business as well.

This chapter intends to pinpoint some aspects related to intellectual property (more properly speaking: copyright or, attending to the Civil Law tradition as well, authors' rights) in an increasingly changing digital world, whose continuous mutations introduce new legal challenges. We will mention mainly two: user-generated contents and mobile communication.

The launching of the so-called social networks turned the Internet into the Web 2.0; contents were not just displayed but shared, and the interaction among people and the contents shared by active users has been since the essence of the World Wide Web. Social networks have been—since at least 2004, when Facebook was created, and 2006, when Twitter and YouTube (later to be acquired by Google) were launched—a major tool for content dissemination. From a legal point of view, this has implications for copyright.

The great question that the emergence and acceleration of user-generated contents (de Beer, Mogyoros and Stidwill, 2014: 83) and some other factors, such as the widespread use of mobile devices, not unusually transnationally, have posed is new problems to the regulation and protection of the intellectual work and of its authors. Due to this, copyright law 'has become a more visible, if quite puzzling, part of the lives of hundreds of millions of people' (Samuelson, 2010: 778).

What is the balance given to all the producers—and also reproducers—in a worldwide digital environment, facing different legal traditions while harmonization is claimed and implemented at a national level? We will try to find out which are the needs posed by the popularization of the mobile devices that makes everyone of us not just a consumer, but a potential producer of intellectual works of equally potential economical value. Production and consumption need to be regulated, since law has to give positive answers to social needs, and the widespread use of social digital tools, mainly using smartphones or tablets, means a complete change on the traditional order of information and cultural creation.

The problem is far from being solved. Supranational entities, such as the European Union, are reluctant to legislate user-generated contents, not even in the shy way that Canada did in 2012. Active users are in no man's (or woman's) land when they decide to create contents upon previous works. Even when commercial profits are far from their intention, copyright law does not cover all subsequent results. In this respect, law is behind technology. In this paper, we intend thus to examine some of the main legal implications of this new reality. We will examine, using news industry as the main case, first, the nature of the intellectual work and to which extent copyright protects access to knowledge, creativity, and investment. Second, we will examine how active users and their cultural products need to be covered by copyright law—and they are not. Third, and focusing on mobile contents most especially, we will examine with some detail the question of territoriality and portability of contents, at least in the European Union, in a moment in which a need for deep reforms on intellectual property law are explicitly mentioned as a way to build, if possible, the so-called 'Digital Single Market'. Precisely, this will be our final remark: to what extent copyright law, which is in force from the beginning of the eighteenth century, adapting itself to the requirements of every new technology and medium, is still a valuable tool to face the challenges of the digital market.

Enhancing Innovation and Protecting Investment

One of the goals of intellectual property is clearly to promote creativity, and in many scholars' point of view, this is related to 'the nurturing of a creative professional class', as Robert Merges explained in 2009, adding: '[This is] a view I defend against the implicit charge of elitism, which is latent in much of the current scholarship emphasizing the "democratic" nature of the Internet' (Gibson et al., 2009), a point of view supported by other scholars, like Deborah Halbert (2009: 927). As Steven Hatcher has explained, from a legal point of view, it is important that 'the misconception of the necessary connection between UGC and public goods is dispelled', since in many occasion the production of user-generated content (UGC) is meant to private interests more than to a public motivation (Hetcher, 2008: 874, 875). This is not, however, an easy effort, due to the complexity of authorship and the typology of intellectual works.

Individual and Corporate Authors

Who is to be considered the author of a work, concretely in the digital environment, is the first question we are about to deal with. Alongside with the importance of the individual, skilled author, copyright law also protects the interests of corporate entities. The situation has been crudely and precisely defined by Pamela Samuelson:

> Complaints have been legion that copyright industry groups and corporate copyright owners have sough and too often obtained extremely strong and overly long copyright protections that interfere with downstream creative endeavors and legitimate consumer expectations.
>
> (Samuelson, 2013: 740)

In both legal traditions, Common Law (identified with the so-called 'copyright system', considered to be more 'entrepreneurial') and Civil Law (identified with the 'authors' rights' system and considered to be more inclined to protect people), this protection of the corporate entities is achieved through the qualification of some work as 'collective', for instance a newspaper or a webpage. This has led to some scholars, for instance Lionel Bently and B. Sherman, to even distinguish between *authorial works* and *entrepreneurial works* (Bently and Sherman, 2014: 32). Although this is not the terminology used by copyright acts, the distinction is extremely relevant. The collective work is the one that puts together the creation of many authors to be included in a greater, unitary work, which is in turn created under the investment and coordination of a company.

Moreover, in the Civil Law legal tradition, the audiovisual work is not necessarily considered a 'joint work', which gathers the individual creation of some concrete people recognized as authors; the director, the script writer, and the composer of the original score are the authors of a film in the authors' rights countries. Instead, in the Common Law tradition, it is considered a work created due to the initiative of the producer, to whom the original rights on the whole product are assigned.

Since the enacting of the so-called *Loi Hadopi* in France, in 2009, similar solutions, even if based in different legal rationale, are in use in the Civil Law countries. According to that reform of the French *Intellectual Property Code*, the economic or exploitation rights on the collective work, namely on newspapers (and on their online editions) and on the individual works that compose it, are considered to be assigned in origin to the corporate person through labor contract, a solution that gets both legal systems closer to each other.

It is true that the Civil Law tradition still preserves the core importance given to moral rights, waivable or even unrecognized in the case of the news produced for the collective work in the Common Law countries, but since they are kept within the sphere of the personal and with little, if any, economic implication, this is not a proper and complete way to balance the tension between the interests of the individual and the collective author.

The tension and the necessity of balancing the right of access to culture, the right of the people to earn a living creating intellectual works, and the right on individual and corporations to get some money out of the investment in expensive and complex production structures has been in the background of copyright law since the first act, the British one in 1710 (the so-called Statute of Anne 8 Ann. c. 19 or 21, or more concretely *An Act for the Encouragement of Learning, by Vesting the Copies of Printed Books in the Authors or Purchasers of such Copies, during the Times therein mentioned*). Much theory has been generated since then. For instance, the distinction among privative and collective goods seems not to be appropriate in every case. The public interest can be, to some extent, guaranteed through protecting private interests, at least in a liberal capitalist model. This is what has been defined, when proposing an intellectual property policy making for the next future, by Meir Perez Pugatch, who distinguishes the 'social and general welfare' and the 'industrial policy dimension'. So, there is a shift from the individual to the organizational aspect of copyright protection (Perez Pugatch, 2011: 71–72). For instance, the public can know the news because a free market is provided, in which public and private media compete to offer a better product. Even when the user-generated (or derived) content is protected, as was enacted in Canada in 2012, it is guaranteeing that the economic interest of the copyright holder is preserved. User-generated content, when it is not fully authored by the user, must be of non-commercial use, otherwise the law tackles the legality of the derivative work, unless the permissions are asked to and given by the copyright holder. Behind this conception is the idea, explained by William Posner and Richard Landes (Landes and Posner, 1989) or Shapiro and Varian (1998), that producing cultural or intellectual goods requires a high investment. The production of an informational good requires expensive fixed costs, while the marginal cost is uncertain.

The Digital Divide and the Intellectual Work

The digital divide and the irruption and popularization of the Internet have introduced some possible changes to this assumption. Costs are of different nature, since the physical structure is not so necessary as it was in other times. Distribution of physical issues of the work is no longer necessary. The musical industry is a clear example of this. The electronic management of rights upon the works, the possibility of packaging information in many ways, and deep changes in the consumption of cultural goods are an everyday reality for, most especially, young people. Moreover, the digital technology has amplified the characteristics of 'non rivalry' and 'non exclusion' of the informational goods (Benhaumou and Farchy, 2014: 55). The digital technology makes copies easier. This is not necessarily bad in economic terms: to copy a work, while respecting the attribution rights, can enhance its value in the market; this is called the *exposure or sampling effect*. This does not mean necessarily to cause appropriability, adding a new tension among innovators and mere emulators. Tolerating, if not encouraging, the production of derivative works, can be an incentive for economy as well. In spite of the different legal roots, copyright laws are applied within national boundaries, but highly influenced by supranational institutions like the European Union or the World Intellectual Property Organization (WIPO), and respond to an increasing convergence and globalized scenario.

Strategies on Copyright Law

New actors have appeared in this legal landscape. News aggregators like Google News have caused some legal reforms in several countries of Europe and in Brazil. Users have an increasingly important role in the intellectual production and some advanced economies, like Canada, have explicitly recognized the importance of enhancing users' intellectual production, with several restrictions: collaborative work is fairly ignored, since the lawmakers need to balance the right of the copyright holders, both individual and companies, while promoting the original and the derivative works produced by the users. Other legal areas like the European Union, although giving some importance to the user-generated content, have decided to delay this discussion, attending probably the interest of the great copyright holders—the companies. Press publishers have actively lobbied and finally managed to get the so-called publishers' right included in the *Proposal for a Directive of the European Parliament and of the Council on Copyright in the Digital Single Market*, launched on September 14, 2016. This is configured as a related right explicitly designed to help press publishers 'obtaining a fair share of the value they generate [and] aiming at facilitating online licensing of their publications, the recoupment of their investment and the enforcement of their rights', but it is unclear how the rights of the individual authors who contribute to the collective work, being those authors professional practitioners of journalism or amateur user-generators, would be guaranteed.

As recently as in 2004, the International Labor Office showed its concern about the situation of media workers, a sector 'marked by innovation, communication and creativity'. The report verified that 'the workforce in the creative industries has grown faster than in other sectors', but at the same time 'the emergence of ICTs has fostered an environment where violation of intellectual property may flourish', thus 'employers and creative workers share a strong interest in the role of copyright and neighboring rights' (International Labour Office, 2004: 24–25). In 2014, another meeting took place in Geneva about the employment relationships in the media industry. The report, signed by Andrew Bibby, observed a 'shift to atypical and freelance working' due to a 'decline in traditional jobs'. This has led to the description of these workers as 'atypical' in many countries, for example Spain, so that the fact that in one time was exceptional now is the common norm (Sánchez de Lara Sorzano, 2014: 149). The ILO's report recommended solutions based on, for instance, the collective bargaining and competition law (see Alén-Savikko, 2016). It will be a matter for discussion in the next years to what extent this situation collides with the proposed guidelines for the future of copyright law drafted by the European Union in the aforementioned proposal.

User-Generated Content: The Prosumer as an Author

The recent importance (the term itself is no much older than 1999) given to users who at the same time produce, and not only consume, intellectual contents, is a fact whose consequences are still to be foreseen in all their dimensions. In principle, at least for the law to protect them, it is supposed that they act in *bona fide* (Hetcher, 2008: 865). Some studies reveal a quite widespread discourse on the existence of democratic potential linked to citizen participation, specially in journalism

(Berger et al., 2013, *apud* Masip, 2014), in such an euphoric way that needs to be redefined in three ways, according to Pere Masip: a disappointment toward media that offer different participation tools but without pretending to modify the preexistent publishing model; a disappointment toward the economic motivations of most of the participation initiatives; and a disappointment toward the passivity of the users themselves (Masip, 2014: 260). However, it may be, it is clear that participation is a very sensible topic in social sciences, including law and communication, and it has introduced a change in the paradigm since it obliges us to put a focus on audience research (Livingston, 2013).

Collaborative and Joint Works

Regarding the regulation, there is a need to combine the right of 'motivated' consumers (Masip et al., 2015), citizens, and authors. All those terms 'are used to promote stakeholder interests in the media and communications sector, not always to the benefit of citizens', in Sonia Livingston and Peter Lunt's opinion (Livingston and Lunt, 2007). Still, as Cohen says, 'copyright doctrine is characterized by the absence of the user'. (Cohen, 2005: 368). The question of defining copyright ownership of UGC is of extreme importance, since, as Steven Hetcher remembers, copyrightable works must be owned by someone. In his opinion, the classical doctrine of originality is not fully applicable to UGC, at least not in term of 'artistic merits', as stated in *Bleistein* v. *Donaldson Lithographing Co* (188 U.S. 239, 251–52 (1903)). The joint work ('a work prepared by two or more authors with the intention that their contributions be merged into inseparable or interdependent parts of a unitary whole', 17 U.S.C_§ 101 (2000) *DMCA*) is not applicable in all the cases, for instance when users send comments to a previously published post or news, because individual contributions are hardly separable, or at least conceivable, without belonging to a chain of other comments, as is not to be separately exploited.

As a recurrent background, the urgent necessity of the media industry to find ways to reduce the effect of the crisis 'to create a more financially viable approach', using the words that Thomas C. Rubin, chief counsel for intellectual property strategy at Microsoft, addressed to Patrick Maines, president of the American Media Institute (*apud* Gibson et al., 2009). The diagnosis provided by Robert Picard is accurate: 'The value creation challenges today are caused by technological, economic, and social changes are that are reducing the roles played by journalists and news enterprises in modern society and providing alternative mechanisms for the public to obtain, create, and distribute news and information' (Picard, 2009: 1). James Gibson, professor of the University of Richmond, said it plainly: 'New distribution technologies often have a negative effect on established business models, but that's not necessarily a bad thing' (Gibson et al., 2009).

This question has been examined with some detail by Jop Esneijer, Ottilie Nieuwenhuis, Carolien Mijs, Corné Versloot, Natali Helberger, Bart van der Sloot, and Tarlach McGonagle in their *Making User Created News Work*, an excellent legal approach to the problems and solutions of user-generated contents. The process of authorship attribution of works created by active users leads to the description of the resultant item as a 'collaborative work' of different nature: a work that uses previous contributions, in which every one of them is distinguishable and individually exploited, or 'combined contributions, where the work is the result of such close cooperation between authors that the individual contributions cannot be separated, all authors enjoy the rights on the work in joint ownership, which must be exercised with the consent of every author, including the amateur'. It is up to the corporate entity that produces the collective work in which this kind of collaborative or joint works are produced to ensure the exploitations rights of the users' contributions to create new works (Esneijer et al. 2012: 43).

Access is one thing; interaction and participation are another (Carpentier, 2015: 9–10). Sharing is another recurrent concept when dealing with users' participation. This is related to both (re)distribution of contents, which is usually—when it involves profits—harassed by media, obsessed with piracy, and to production of fully original contents by users. In this case, they have to decide to which extent and how do they decide or not to distribute, communicate and transfer the derivative rights of the work to the people. Finally, it is related to the possibility of using other people's work to make use, when possible, of the transformative rights: 'Whether they are acceptable uses permitted by the respective jurisdiction or an unlawful infringement of the creator's exclusive rights ... whenever someone who is not the copyright holder (or a licensee) exercises the exclusive right' (Lillà Montagnani, 2009: 61). At the same time, as for instance the Organisation for Economic Co-operation and Development (OECD) stresses, the fact that digital technologies make it easier to possibly infringe copyright law must not discourage the innovative business models, in which the users' participation is extremely welcome (OECD, 2004).

Media, regardless of all their reluctance, show some interest in controlling user-generated content as 'newsworthy material'. The BBC was one of the early creators of platforms for the users. 'Have Your Say' was launched in 2005 to 'share with BBC News' and to send news or material for stories that might be elaborated later in the newsroom by professional journalists and that may be considered a joint work. The permission is not exclusive, but the user grants the BBC 'the right to change or edit the materials in your contribution for operational and editorial reasons [and] also share your contribution with trusted third parties, for instance with other users of BBC Online Services or, in the case of news-related material, the BBC may share your contribution with its overseas partners (for instance reputable foreign news broadcasters)'. Some other media have joined in this respect, for instance CNN in 2006 ('iReport'; user's content is specifically ruled) or *El País* in Spain in 2008 ('Yo, periodista'; this service is no longer available).

Sharing Pictures and Video through Social Networks

Two of the most widespread, and controversial, forms of user-generated contents are photograph and video. They are also the most individual-authored contents as well. 'Because of the nature of photography', explain Emma Carroll and Jessica Coates, 'and the manner in which third parties use images, the growth of Creative Commons licensed content on Flickr has had (or at least it is feared it will have) a strong effect on the pro-am photographer community, and particularly the market for stock-photographs, which has traditionally been the main and often only source of income for many photographers' (Carroll and Coates, 2011: 182).

One of the most meaningful cases, although it has never reached the courts, was the publication of a picture by user María Claudia Montano, uploaded by the author to Flickr under a Creative Commons Attribution, Noncommercial, No derivative license, which only allows the reproduction of it without alterations and for nonprofitable uses. The picture was reproduced and modified by the Colombian newspaper *El País*. The first answer by the ombudsman of the daily newspaper caused an earthquake on the Internet: 'Why did you upload the picture to a place where it can be easily downloadable [sic]? One cannot tell from the site that the picture is not available for others to use' (*apud* Carroll and Coates, 2013: 18). Some days after that, however, the director and commercial manager of the newspaper, María Elvira Domínguez Lloreda, addressed a letter to Montano recognizing the offense (even a lack of authorship attribution) and apologizing for it. To the purposes of this chapter, it is important to insist that the Creative Common licenses could include a demand of recognition of attribution, which is, actually, redundant in the Civil Law legal tradition, since it is an unwaivable moral right. The assumption, exemplified by the first behavior of *El País*, that those rights can be waived when dealing with material found on the Internet, is quite clear about the kind of attitudes that must be already overcome. It is still noticeable how, according to Carroll and Coates, 'specifically states that the license requires attribution in the manner specified by the author or licensor', including the name or pseudonym of the author, the title of the work, and 'any uniform resource identification', e.g., a link to the original work (Carroll and Coates, 2013: 192–193). This can be a question to be considered when dealing with mobile communications, since the quickness and facility of uploading materials, e.g., photographs taken from the same device used to perform the action of making a work available, can lead to sign them with pseudonyms or nicknames, while the trace of digital identities are attached to both the file itself (following the same example, digital photographs use metadata, which states the serial number of the device) and to the IP number of the machine used to upload that material—obviously related to a physical person who has purchased the device. To what extent this can affect moral rights of paternity—everyone has the right to decide whether his or her work should be signed to his or her own name, anonymously or using a pseudonym—is a question to be considered and further investigated as well (van Eijk et al., 2012; Helberger et al., 2013). The possibility of tracking IPs and digital identities poses new questions on old assumed assumption, like the foundations of copyright – and of *droit d'auteur* system, more based on the identity of the individual.

One of the most influential cases on determining the responsibility of the service provider is *Viacom v. YouTube and Google*, filed by the District Court for the Southern District of New York. Viacom alleged that YouTube and its owner, Google Inc., 'has harnessed technology to wilfully infringe copyright on a huge scale, depriving writers, composers and performers of the rewards they are owed for effort and innovation, reducing the incentive of America's creative industries, and profiting from the illegal conduct of others as well. Using the leverage of the Internet, YouTube appropriates the value of creative content on a massive scale for YouTube's benefit', because YouTube does not only store other people's content, but 'knowingly reproduces and publicly performs the copyrighted works uploaded to its site' enabling 'massive infringement by its users' (*Viacom International, Inc.* v. YouTube, *Inc.*, No. 07 Civ. 2103). *Viacom v. YouTube* and *UMG Recordings* v. *MySpace* established that a copyright holder can prevent the dissemination of contents to these companies, but the situation is worrying for content producers: 'A user may upload a music video to YouTube or a news article may be wholly copied into a personal blog. Copyright owners are unable to protect their works effectively by suing uploaders because the quantity of UGC is so large', estimates Michael S. Sawyer (Sawyer, 2009: 431).

It is a common assumption that 'user activity inevitably infringes' (Halbert, 2009: 931). Induction to infringement and contributory and vicarious infringement are the causes, according to the plaintiff's version of the behavior by YouTube. Instead, this company, the largest digital video repository of the Internet, alleged that it was a permitted behavior under the *Digital Millennium Copyright Act*. It was alleged that YouTube was liable to the accusations because of 'volitional acts'. The court did not find any intentional behavior in YouTube's everyday proceedings. Similar litigation has happened in relation to other digital platforms, like MySpace, Veoh, Grouper, and Bolt, which 'also have the potential to extend to more participatory intermediaries, such as blogs and wikis' (O'Brien, 2008: 228). In 2009, as Lili Levi reminds, Facebook tried to impose an univocal clause in its terms of use to secure 'an irrevocable license in perpetuity to user-generated contents', but had to revoke it because of the many protest of the users, and then returned to a limited time of enjoying the exclusive rights upon the UGC.

Several other cases, like *Lenz* v. *Universal Music Group*, shed some light on when a content previously uploaded should be removed by the IPS. The case law has not been enough for some companies, so in 2007 CBS, Dailymotion, Disney, Fox, NBC Universal, Microsoft, Veoh, and Viacom produced a document entitled *Principles for User Generated Content Services*, in which the company established how to proceed. The main principles are as follows: '(1) eliminate infringing content on user-generated services, (2) encourage uploading of wholly original and authorized user-generated audio and video content, (3) accommodate fair use, and (4) protect legitimate interests of user privacy'. Among the concrete measures proposed, 'incorporate searching mechanisms that would allow copyright owners registered with the service to search for infringing content, and implement a notice, takedown, and counter notice procedure, similar to that required by Section 512 and other policies that accommodate fair use' (*apud* Biederman and Andrews, 2008: 17–8).

Robert Picard has explained well, in our opinion, the problems and challenges of this new situation:

> If value is to be created, journalists cannot continue to report merely in the traditional ways or merely re-report the news that has appeared elsewhere. They must add something novel that creates value. They will have to start providing information and knowledge that is not readily available elsewhere, in forms that are not available elsewhere, or in forms that are more useable by and relevant to their audiences. Finding the right formula of practice, functions, skills, and business model will not be easy, but the search must be undertaken. It is not just a matter of embracing uses of new technologies. Journalists today are often urged to change practice to embrace crowd sourcing, to search specialty websites, social networks, blogs and micro-blogs for story ideas, and to embrace in collaborative journalism with their audiences. Although all of these provide useful new ways to find information, access knowledge, and engage with readers, listeners, and viewers, however, the amount of value that they add and its monetization is highly debatable. The primary reason is that those who are most highly interested in that information and knowledge are able to harvest it themselves using increasingly common tools.
>
> (Picard, 2009: 6)

Flexibility in courts' interpretations has been proposed by many scholars (for instance, Wong, 2009). A robust license system, much more developed and concrete that the simple Creative Commons license, whose goals seem to protect non-professional creations above all, is needed (Woods, 2009). One good example seems to be the BBC Archives Licence (BAL), created in 2003, based on Creative Commons, which gives a free use on content with five limitations: on-commercial use, a territorial model (they are licenses to be applied only in the United Kingdom), attribution must be respected, they cannot be used for endorsement purposes, and subsequent derivative works must be licensed under similar terms.

Territoriality of Rights, Territoriality of Markets

One of the main questions when dealing with the increasing transnationalization of intellectual property is how copyright holders operate in global and, at the same time, fragmented national markets, which licenses use to assign rights to the user inside the borders of a concrete state. Related to this is the question of geo-blocking. This is a question of special interest in the European Union, where legal and market fragmentation is evident and where users face difficulties to access content beyond borders. This is a question that the copyright holders have faced using the rules of unfair competition, rather than copyright law. When they use intellectual property law, it is upon the rules applied to the distribution of physical copies of the work and the exhaustion principle, which is difficult to apply online.

Instead of thinking of it as a personal right, so that people who move across the different countries of the European Union could access the contents they have paid for according to their freedom of movement (which is called 'multiterritorial access'), copyright law rather protects the interests of copyright holders through geo-blocking those contents, and so it is not surprising how this could encourage piracy. Since geo-blocking measures are intended to protect territorial licensing systems, users are forced to find other solutions when they are abroad. The scholars have proposed solutions based on portability, though this is not fully satisfactory in the announced European Digital Single Market— which, at the time of writing, is just a strategy to be developed in the future years. According to, for instance, Giuseppe Mazziotti and Felice Simonelli, there are some 'unsettled issues', i.e. the so-called 'temporary presence' of the user in another state different from that in which he or she has subscribed the service. Moreover, 'the consequence of this legislative proposal' (*Towards a Modern, More European Copyright Framework*, a communication from the European Union to the Parliament and the Council, December 9, 2015) 'will mostly depend on whether the regulation will be applied strictly or loosely' (Mazziotti and Simonelli, 2016: 2) to travelers and tourists or to European citizens who stay in another country for some time, working for instance. It will depend on the stakeholders' interests, most probably, the real scope of the implementation of a directive on the topic, if it is finally produced. The European

Union stated clearly enough through the *Reda Report* in 2015 that it is against the end of copyright territoriality. Even though geo-blocking could be still necessary to 'protect sustainability of content production and the various forms of adaptation and versioning of creative content to local and culturally diverse audiences (Mazziotti, 2015: 14), it must be done with respect to the users' rights as well.

Another aspect to be carefully considered is that in a space like the European Union, culturally and linguistically fragmented and plural, to enhance authors' and users' creativity is a necessary incentive to produce adapted versions (for instance, translations or subtitles for audiovisual productions) that can be done by users. On a non-commercial, fair-dealing basis, derivative works could be acceptable, since they increment the value of original works in that fragmented market. In the process of adapting the existent business models to the online environment (see, for instance, *How the New Business Models in the Digital Age Have Evolved*, 2015, from micropayment to pay-per-use, subscriptions and membership, embedded advertising, crowdfunding, direct selling or pay-what-you-want models), cultural industries should consider, as was done in Canada in 2012 with occasion of the reform of the *Copyright Act*, enhancing possible innovation coming from users. Anyway, the European Union is reluctant to enact in any way the users' rights.

Conclusion: Is intellectual Property Still a Good Legal Solution to a Full-Digital Market?

Many 'major players' of the information economy, for instance newspaper publishers, are tirelessly lobbying to receive compensation for the secondary exploitation of the works they have primarily published. Alan Rusbridger, then editor of *The Guardian*, linked the cultural industry with the economy of attention, when he said that 'newspapers are increasingly about views rather than news', so he renamed newspapers as *viewpapers*, in which traffic is important (Rusbridger, 2005: 16). The target is on the new enemy: aggregators like Google News. Legal reform has been the way preferred in Europe, for instance in Germany and Spain, to make Google News pay for supposedly reproducing the news (instead, Google argues that they actually provide access to those news through links). Meanwhile, the solution proposed from the United States has been the (problematic) resurrection of a doctrine preempted statutorily, the so-called 'hot news misappropriation doctrine', created by the US courts in 1918 to protect, for a period of time, usually 24 hours, the interest of news agencies, preventing the reproduction of news by competitors. Scholars are divided in this respect: some consider this doctrine obsolete and inapplicable, while many others would prefer to ask for its extension to the federal courts and some advocate to enact it in the American *Copyright Act*, to stop what they define as 'free-riders'.

The problem is not the gratuity of contents (Benhamou and Farchy, 2014: 69), but to ensure the transfer of profitability in the value chain. The proposed solutions are diverse. Blanket licenses are one of those solutions, like the ones used in radio broadcasting, 'eat as much as you can in exchange for a fixed fee as opposed to a scheme requiring payment for each individual content' (Strowel, 2009: 76). Another solution could be to use Creative Commons licenses, which cover very general terms (on a wider theory of commons applied to intellectual property, see Mitchell, 2005).

Compensation through taxes is a solution interdicted by the European Court of Justice, which in 2016 decided that only final users of the private copies, and not all the citizens, should pay a compensation to authors and copyright holders (see EUJC, press release 60/16). Technical implementations like the Digital Rights Management (DRM) system are also possible and controversial. A collective management system, partially used by copyright holders (for instance, newspaper publishers to ensure compensation for press-clipping activities) but never decidedly assumed by individual authors, is another possible way.

Even a paying public domain (for the historical foundations of it, see Grosheide, 2006; on its nature, Deazley, 2006) has been proposed, a system in which the term of duration of copyright law's protection would be shortened, depending on the nature of the work, and even short terms that could be automatically renewed. William Patry proposed a shorter copyright term, since most copyrighted works enjoy a 'relatively short commercial live' but instead long protection terms 'inhibit the creation of new works based upon expression from earlier works', which is of extreme importance for derivative works created by users (Patry, 2011: 189–201). Instead, in the United States, the term of duration has been extended by the so-called *Sonny Bono* (or *Mickey Mouse) Act*, precisely to protect the interests of huge corporations such as Disney.

Some other reform directions have been suggested for copyright law. Lawrence Lessig is one of the main and probably best known of those reformers. There are some others. In 2010, a group led by Jessica Litman and Pamela Samuelson proposed a set of 25 possible reforms for the United States (Litman and Samuelson, 2010). Compensation (for instance, through compulsory licenses or collective licensing), instead of exclusivity, is another recommendation by William Patry, just the opposite of what is the norm in media companies' practices. Jason Mazzone, on the other hand, proposed a more flexible use of fair use and contractual and technical measures to prevent unlawful uses of works on the public domain, which makes the creation of derivative works more difficult. This is not the common practice of the media industry, which, through digitization of all their contents, copyrightable or not, blocks any actual possibility of performing legal derivative rights of those works, although presumably giving free access to them on the Internet—with no compensation to the authors. The claim of the European newspaper publishers' lobby is in favor of a 'publisher [exclusive] right', which appears in the *Proposal for a Directive… on Copyright in the Digital Single Market*, September 2016. What is happening is that, as Pamuela Samuelson states, 'the Internet and the World Wide Web have destabilized many copyright industry sectors as the economics of creating, publishing and disseminating information-rich works have dramatically changed' (Samuelson, 2010: 770), so that 'more consumer-friendly ways to access content at a reasonable price should be designed' (Strowel, 2009: 76).

We face a dichotomous situation here: to favor the access to public knowledge or to protect investment through favoring virtual monopolies. The scenario seems to be quite binary: 'Business as usual [that] shows a trend towards information being treated as property' or 'a world where one of the primary desires is to set information free and information becomes a self-standing entity' (de Beer, Mogyoros, and Stidwill, 2014: 88). To define the priorities is essential for policy making (Waelde, 2006). Amending the economic intellectual property rights is difficult; the reproduction right, actually the first one in copyright's history and related to the production and dissemination of physical copies that are no longer needed to the transmission of the intellectual work, essentially an immaterial property (Westkamp, 2006: 272), is an obstacle. The massive digitization of works puts them to the public access, but when it is performed by private hands, there is a risk of turning temporary rights (allegedly, all authors' rights, except the moral ones in the Civil Law area, are temporary) into perpetual rights. This is the case of the historical archives of newspaper, which offer altogether orphan works, works in the public domain, and works whose transformation rights have not been transferred to the companies. This is the case of Google Books as well, a private company digitizing private and public archives.

Combined with the increasingly transnational nature of the economic transactions and the territoriality of copyright provisions, the fragmentation, both legal and commercial, is extreme in areas like the European Union. The *Communication from the Commission to the European Parliament, the Council, the European Economic and Social Committee and the Committee of the Regions*, entitled *Towards a Modern, More European Copyright Framework*, insists in that copyright 'rewards creativity and investment in creative content' and in saying so, the EU is clearly adopting a doctrinal approach among many others (see Bently and Sherman, 2014: 379). This is an ideological decision that has been criticized by, for instance, Yoshiyuki Tamura, who insists on his turn on the 'problem of striking a just and adequate balance between the interests of right holders and users, more urgent and serious than ever before' (Tamura, 2009: 68). Recognizing the territoriality of copyright and the difficulties in effectively implementing portable content makes things more difficult. More concretely, the audiovisual sector, financed 'to a large extent, based on territorial licensing combined with territorial exclusivity granted to individual distributors or service providers' could be against the legitimate interest of users. The exceptions (and limitations) system, equally fragmented, is another obstacle to be solved in the future. In this respect, the main legal traditions collide as well: the Common Law approach prefers an open system, based on fair use (or fair dealing, according to the British terminology), to be decided case by case by the courts using a four-step test. The Civil Law tradition, instead, prefers a closed list of exceptions, so it has been accused of being far less flexible than the Anglo-Saxon system. Instead, at least in the United States, fair use is trying to be replaced by a resurrection of the hot news doctrine, at least to face the problem of news aggregators.

At least the European Commission acknowledges, on page 12 of the *Communication*, that 'the full harmonization of copyright in the EU, in the form of a single copyright code and a single copyright title, would require substantial changes in the way our rules work today'. It is neither the smallest of the obstacles to be removed nor the latest goal to be achieved for a 'fair remuneration of authors and performers', using mechanisms like 'the regulation of certain contractual practices, unwaivable remuneration rights, collective bargaining and collective management of rights', understanding that all those mechanisms should be at the service of the companies and of the authors.

The bases for future discussion on the copyright system in the digital world are, in the European Union, both the *Proposal for a Directive... on Copyright in the Digital Single Market* and the *Proposal for a Regulation... on the exercise of Copyright and other Related Rights applicable to certain Online Transmissions of Broadcasting Organisations and Retransmission of Television and Radio Programmes*, made public in September 2016. The second one recognizes that 'in order to make their services available across borders, broadcasting organizations need to have the required rights for the relevant territories and this increases the complexity of the rights' clearance'. To find solutions would be anything but easy, as the same *Proposal* acknowledges, since 'consumers are generally in favor of a broad extension of the country of origin principle to cover all online services', while 'by contrast, commercial broadcasters, right holders and CMOs express strong reservations on extending the application of the country of origin principle. They consider that any such extension would restrict their ability to license rights on a territorial basis'. When it comes to be applied not only to broadcasting but also to on-demand services, it is stated in the first of the two proposals mentioned before that they 'have the potential to play a decisive role in the dissemination of European works across the European Union', but at the same time, it is obvious that 'agreements on the online exploitation of such works may face difficulties related to the licensing of rights'. Having said that, it is obvious that the weakness of some authors' collectives hinders this goal (which has been defined by Jason Mazzone as *copyfraud*, see Mazzone, 2011), not to mention the role and presence of active users in this situation.

Note

1 At the time of writing this chapter, United Kingdom still was a state member of the European Union.

References

Alén-Savikko, A. (2016). Copyright-proof network-based video recording services? An analysis of the Finnish solution. *Javnost – The Public, 23*(2), 204–219.

Benhamou, F.; Farchy, J. (2014). *Droit d'auteur et copyright*. Paris: Éditions La Découverte.

Bently, L., & Sherman, B. (2014). *Intellectual property law*. Oxford: Oxford University Press.

Berger, M., van Hoof, A., Meijer, I. C., & Sanders, J. (2013). Constructing participatory journalism as a scholarly object. *Digital Journalism, 1*(1), 117–134.

Carpentier, N. (2015). Differentiating between access, interaction and participation, *Conjuctions, 2*(2), 7–28.

Carroll, E., & Coates, J. (2011). The school girl, the billboard, and virgin: The virgin mobile case and the use of creative commons licensed photographs by commercial entities. In M. Perry and B. Fitzgerald (Eds.) *Knowledge policy for the 21st century. A legal perspective* (pp. 181–204). Annandale: The Federation Press.

Cohen, J. E. (2005). The Place of the User in Copyright Law. *Fordham Law Review, 74*, 347–374.

Deazley, R. (2006). Copyright's public domain. In M. Perez Pugatch (Ed.), *The intellectual property debate. Perspectives from law, economics and political economy* (pp. 21–34). Cheltenham, UK and Northampton, MA: Edward Elgar.

de Beer, J., Mogyoros, A., & Stidwill, S. (2014). Present thinking about the future of intellectual property: A literature review. *ScriptEd, 11*(1), 69–117.

Demnard-Tellier, I. (dir.) (1996). *Le multimédia et le droit. Internet, off line, on line*. Paris: Hermès.

Esneijer, J., Nieuwenhuis, O., Mijs, C., Versloot, C., Helberger, N., van der Sloot, B., & McGonagle, T. (2012). *Making user created news work*. TNO 2012 R11277. Amsterdam: IViR.

Eurostat. (2015). *Digital economy and society statistics – household and invididuals*. Brussels: European Union. Retrieved from http://ec.europa.eu/eurostat/statistics-explained/index.php/Digital_economy_and_society_statistics_-_households_and_individuals. Accessed November 15, 2016.

Gibson, J., Ginsburg, J. C., Hughes, J., Lichtman, D., Liebowitz, S., Menell, P., Merges, R. P., Picker, R. C., & Smolla, R. A. (2009). *Virtual panel discussion. ACAP and the online challenges facing newspapers. Featuring members of the advisory council of the media institute's national cyber education project. Reactions to a speech by Thomas C. Rubin, Chief Counsel for Intellectual*

Property Strategy, Microsoft Corporation. Arlington, VA: The Media Institute. Retrieved from http://www.mediainstitute.org/IPI/2009(021909_VPD.php. Accessed November 15, 2016.

Grosheide, W. F. (2006). In search of the public domain during the history of copyright law. In M. Perez Pugatch (Ed.), *The intellectual property debate. perspectives from law, economics and political economy* (pp. 1–20). Cheltenham, UK and Northampton, MA: Edward Elgar.

Halbert, D. (2009). Mass culture and the culture of the masses: A manifesto for user-generated rights. *Vanderbilt Journal of Entertainment and Technology Law, 11*(4), 921–961.

Helberger, N., Loos, M. B. M., Guibault, L., Mak, C., & Pessers, L. (2013). Digital content contracts for consumers. *Journal of Consumer Policy, 36* (1), 37–57.

Hetcher, S. (2008). User-generated content and the future of copyright: Part one – investiture of copyright. *Vanderbilt Journal of Entertainment and Technology Journal, 10*(4), 863–892.

International Labour Office (2004). *Note on the Proceedings. Tripartite Meeting on the Future of Work and Quality in the Information Society: The Media, Culture, Graphical Sector. Geneva, 18–22 October 2004*. Geneva: International Labour Office.

Landes, W. M., & Posner, R. A. (1989). An economic analysis of copyright law. *Journal of Legal Studies, 18*, 325–363.

Lillà Montagnani, M. (2009). A new interface between copyright law and technology: How user-generated content will shape the furute of online distribution. *Cardozo Arts and Entertainment, 26*, 719–773.

Litman, J., & Samuelson, P. (2010). The copyright principles project: Directions for reform. *Berkeley Technology Law Journal, 25*(3), 1175–1245.

Livingston, S. (2013). The participation paradigm in audience research. *The Communication Review, 16*, 21–30.

Livingston, S., & Lunt, P. (2007). Representing citizens and consumers in media and communications regulation. *Annals AAPSS, 611,* 51–65.

Masip, P. (2014). Audiencias activas, democracia y algoritmos. *Notas ThinkEPI, 8*, 260–263.

Masip, P., Guallar, J., Peralta, M., Ruiz, C., & Suau, J. (2015). Active audiences and journalism: Involved citizens or motivated consumers? *Brazilian Journalism Research, 1*(1), 234–255.

Mazziotti, G. (2015). *Is geo-blocking a real cause for concern in Europe? EUI Working Papers, Law 2015/43*. Firenze: European University Institute.

Mazziotti, G., & Simonelli, F. (2016). *Regulation on 'cross-border portability' of online content services: Roaming for netflix or the end of copyright territoriality? CEPS commentary series*. Brussels: Centre for European Policy Studies. Retrieved from https://www.ceps.eu/publications/regulation-%E2%80%98cross-border-portability%E2%80%99-online-content-services-roaming-netflix-or-end. Accessed November 15, 2016.

Mazzone, J. (2011). *Copyfraud and other abuses of intellectual property*. Stanford: Stanford University Press.

Mitchell, H. C. (2005). *The Intellectual Commons: Toward an Ecology of Intellectual Property*. Langham: Lexington Books.

O'Brien, D. (2008). Copyright challenges for user generated intermediaries: Viacom v YouTube. In B. Fitzgerald, F. Gao, D. O'Brien, and S. X. Shi

(Eds.), *Copyright law, digital content and the Internet in the Asia-Pacific* (pp. 219–233). Sydney: Sydney University Press.

Organisation for Economic Co-operation and Development (OECD). (2004). *Recommendation of the council on broadband development, C(2003)259/FINAL*. Paris: OECD.

Patry, W. (2011). *How to fix copyright*. Oxford and New York: Oxford University Press.

Perez Pugatch, M. (2011). Intellectual property policy making in the 21st century. *The WIPO Journal: Analysis of Intellectual Property Issues, 3*(1), 71–80.

Picard, R. G. (2009). *Why journalists deserve low pay?* Presentation by Robert G. Picard to the Reuters Institute for the Study of Journalism, RISJ Seminar Series, University of Oxford, May 6, 2009. Oxford: Reuters Institute. Retrieved from http://www.robertpicard.net/PDFFiles/whyjournalistsdeservelowpay.pdf. Accessed November 15, 2016.

Rusbridger, A. (2005). *What are newspapers for?* Hugo Yound Lecture. Sheffield: University of Sheffield. Retrieved from http://image.guardian.co.uk/sys-files/Guardian/documents/2005/03/15/lecturespeech.pdf. Accessed November 15, 2016.

Samuelson, P. (2013). Is copyright reform possible? *Harvard Law Review, 126,* 740–779.

Sánchez de Lara Sorzano, C. (2014). *Freelance y colaboradores: Relación laboral*. Valladolid; Pamplona: Lex Nova; Thomson Reuters.

Sawyer, M. S. (2009). Filters, Fair Use & Feedback: User-Generated Content Principles and the DMCA. *Berkeley Technology Law Journal, 24*(1), 363–404.

Shapiro, C., & Varian, H. R. (1998). *Information rules*. Cambridge, MA: Harvard Business School Press.

Strowel, A. (2009). Internet piracy as wake-up call for copyright law makers – is the "graduated response' a good reply? *WIPO Journal, 1,* 75–85.

Tamura, Y. (2009). Rethinking copyright institution for the digital age. *The WIPO Journal: Analysis of Intellectual Property Issues, 1,* 61–74.

van Eijk, N., Helberger, N., Kool, L., van der Plas, A., & van der Sloot, B. (2012). Online tracking: questioning the power of informed consent. *Info, 14*(5), 57–73.

Waelde, C. (2006). The priorities, the values, the public. In M. Perez Pugatch (Ed.), *The intellectual property debate. Perspectives from law, economics and political economy* (pp. 226–245). Cheltenham, UK and Northampton, MA: Edward Elgar.

Westkamp, G. (2006). Author's rights and Internet regulation: The end of the public domain or constitutional re-conceptualization? In M. Perez Pugatch (Ed.), *The intellectual property debate. Perspectives from law, economics and political economy* (pp. 268–289). Cheltenham, UK and Northampton, MA: Edward Elgar.

Wong, M. W. S. (2009). 'Transformative' user-generated content in copyright law: Infringing derivative works or fair use? *Vanderbilt Journal of Entertainment and Technology Law, 11*(4), 1075–1139.

Woods, T. M. (2009). Working Towards Spontaneous Copyright Licensing: A Simple Solution for a Complex Problem. *Vanderbilt Journal of Entertainment and Technology Law, 11*(4), 1141–1168.

Part V

The New Generations
on the Mobile Ecosystem

12 Educating for Privacy in the Digital and Mobile Ecosystems

Toward a Proposed Syllabus

Ana Serrano Tellería, Maria Luísa Branco and Sandra Carina Guimarães

Being a Citizen in the Digital Age

At the end of the 20th century, the concept of citizenship expanded and diversified as a result of economic and cultural globalization and the resulting crisis of the nation state as a body of power, model for coexistence, and representative of the common good (Turner, 2002). The diversification of citizenship has been reflected in the proliferation and mobility of forms of loyalty/identification and affiliation (Ross, 2007; Marshall, 2009), and the concept has mostly become interpreted in the wider sense of "people who live in society with other people in many different situations and circumstances" (Council of Europe, 2000, p. 9). Although the main reference point for citizenship continues to be the nation state, current concepts of citizenship emphasize the importance of citizens participating in different ways to build and pursue the common good in a context of interpersonal relations and mutual obligations that go far beyond the previous model (Bloemraad, 2015). The emphasis placed on the participative side of citizenship indicates the importance of designing democratic political life that goes far further than the simple act of voting, as well as the need to remove social and economic obstacles to more effective participation (Fraser, 2007; Nussbaum, 2014; Bloemraad, 2015).

The development of the many different aspects of the digital world and its omnipresence in today's societies has also largely helped change the concepts of exercising citizenship to shift toward greater involvement in the social sphere and a diversification of forms of intervention. Keen (2012) highlights the social question as the heart of the World Wide Web and is backed up by Ling (2004) and Groening (2010) as regards the effects of mobile devices, specifically mobile phones, on the increase in social capital, as devices that encourage interaction and permanent contact. Nonetheless, as Groening (2010) warns, the social interactions provided by these new means are not accompanied by the weight of social obligation, since their virtual nature encourages (at the same time, yet paradoxically) separation and isolation. They may even produce weaker social cohesion (Ling, 2004; Arroyo-Almaraz & Gómez-Díaz, 2015). The quality and impact of citizenship participation through the use of internet is also debatable, falling in most cases under the category of weak activism (Zapatero, Brandle, & San-Román, 2015).

Alongside this, other authors highlight the effects of mobile communications on stimulating autonomy (Castells, 2008) and many other aspects of freedom by increasing the options available (Katz, 2008). Bennet, Weels, and Rank (2009) propose a distinction between paradigms of citizenship originated by digital expansion. For them, the proliferation of digital devices therefore competes with the emergence of a new type of citizen, the actualizing citizen, who joins the more traditional type of dutiful citizen. These two types of citizen are characterized by different concerns, diverging styles, and various forms of acting in the public sphere. They cannot be considered sealed, which means that, in practice, the exercise of citizenship may combine aspects from both types. The former appears to be more appropriate to describe the way younger generations, born and raised in a globalized world and familiar with the internet and interactive media, think of and exercise their citizenship.

Actualizing citizenship consists of a citizenship that is not limited to political aspects per se and increasingly includes the social sphere in different contexts, among which are those made possible by new digital media such as social networks (according to Patrocínio, 2008, being digital—and mobile—even creates a new culture of citizenship). In fact, younger generations are more focused on concerns that include human rights, the quality of the environment, and lifestyles, and they share some distrust about democratic processes and the role of governments. The forms of participation they favor are also not the traditional ones, with a focus here too on the importance of using social networks. Although characterized by tenuous relationships, they are a favored and expressive medium and multiply the opportunities to take and be involved in social action. Bessant (2014) advances the term Digital Spring (inspired by the phenomenon of Arab Spring) to underline the democratic potential of digital space to develop civic cultures and enhance participation among young students. As Couldry et al. (2014) sustain, there is evidence, however, that this participation will be more effective if supplemented by offline practices.

Educating for Citizenship in the Digital and Mobile Age: The Importance of Educating for Privacy

In two projects carried out by the Council of Europe, the *Education for democratic citizenship project* (Council of Europe, 2000, 2002) and more recently the *Competences for democratic culture project*

(Council of Europe, 2016), educating for citizenship is viewed as a demanding process that involves the different aspects of the human person and should tend to move toward/culminate in common, consented public action. The main goal of this education consists of enabling individuals to carry out action as active and responsible subjects throughout their lives, while, at the same time, promoting a free, fair, and tolerant society in which the values and principles of freedom, pluralism, human rights, and the rule of law are effectively defended. According to the Portuguese Basic Law on the Education System (Law no. 46/86 of 14 October, renumbered and republished as Law no. 85/2009 of 27 August), education for citizenship is designed within a framework of integrated education and should stimulate both personal fulfillment and community development. This conception remains in recent Portuguese legislation (Decrew-Law no. 139/2012 of 5 July; DGE, 2013).

Bearing in mind these recommendations, the main goal of education for democratic citizenship appears to consist of learning about the democratic experience, which translates into *coexistence* with different people. This includes developing the following skills: (1) valuing the experience of interdependence (mutuality and reciprocity); (2) valuing individual differences and resulting conflict (as essential elements in the search for and construction of a collective identity). Education/learning citizenship therefore deals with three areas:

1   Ethics, corresponding to recognizing and reflecting on the ethical principles of freedom, justice, and solidarity (which are the foundations of democracy itself);
2   Praxis, corresponding to developing social and personal practices that are consistent with those principles;
3   Information/knowledge, which corresponds to recognizing and reflecting on social structures and political institutions that make it possible to safeguard and activate those practices and constantly improve them.

The use of online and digital media, and the use of networks in particular, has substantially changed how citizenship is exercised. Today, we can talk about a digital citizenship that is characterized by a more interactive, horizontal style based on the creative use of media. At the same time, this enables jointly created content and the evaluation/certification of its credibility. From this point of view, civic learning requires the acquisition of digital literacy so that individuals can work together as citizens in order to influence policy and decisions relating to life and the common good. This skill is extremely topical in light of the terrorist threat facing Europe and the rest of the world. After the attacks in France and Denmark at the beginning of 2015, the European Union's education ministers drew up a declaration at an informal meeting that highlights the importance of empowering children and young people to think and critically evaluate information available on the internet and social media (Informal Meeting of European Education Ministers, 2015).

Rheingold (2012) distinguishes between five components of digital literacy: attention; the capability of detecting trash; participation; collaboration; and the clever use of networks. The goal of developing digital literacy should be to empower subjects, reflected in more responsible, conscious participation based on greater trust in networks and participation skills themselves.

Considering empowerment as the ability to, in the case of digital citizenship, actively and responsibly participate in social and political life through new interactive media, implementing it inevitably involves learning to participate on the internet. According to the Rheingold (2012), this learning assumes the need to be aware of our digital footprint, which is why he warns: "Think before you post, because your digital actions are findable, reproducible, and available to people you don't know, and will remain available to all indefinitely" (p. 249). Learning to participate on the net encourages more intelligent, confident use. Regarding this field, the same author highlights the four properties of any social network (persistence, replicability, scalability, and searchability) to remind us of the importance of being aware of what we share and with whom we share it (i.e., behind networks there are invisible audiences and unclear intersections between the public and the private). Confident, safe participation and the development of collaboration with others involves awareness of the amplifying role of human actions on networks. The development of digital citizenship, designed within the wider context of education for democratic citizenship, therefore includes cognitive, affective, and ethical and axiological and practical factors (knowledge about processes, choices made using criteria and conscious, effective action toward the common good).

In today's European education systems, education for citizenship has a more cross-cutting nature and is viewed in terms of the general goals of different national syllabuses and cross-syllabus topics. In most countries, it is also offered as a freestanding discipline or is included in several disciplines or in a specific area of teaching and education (Eurydice, 2005). In Portugal, it is given as cross-cutting training and can also be provided as additional syllabus items with a flexible timetable, as part of school credit or by implementing projects. The features of education for citizenship mentioned include education for the media, the goal of which is "the adoption of behaviours and attitudes appropriate for the critical use and safety of the internet and social networks" (Direção-Geral da Educação, 2013, p. 4).

As highlighted above, use is not just one more citizenship skill but, as a result of its current configuration, especially among younger generations, it can be considered a basic skill for accessing critical, responsible citizenship. Educating for citizenship in this setting also involves an awareness of what can and should be made public and what should not be shown on the network: i.e., it involves educating for responsible participation, which must include greater reflection and clarification on the difficult boundary between what is public and what is private.

The Redefinition of the Mobile Media Ecosystem and the Private Sphere

The distinction between public and private in the digital and mobile context involves making an incursion into the mobile medium ecosystem and its impact on redefining the private sphere. Mobile devices and their media environment have produced a series of fluid parameters for configuring online virtual communication, mostly altering space and time dimensions. In this sense, the research fields involved have indicated a variety of concepts that underline a major area of tension to deal with: the state of "perpetual contact" (Katz & Aakhus, 2002) and the "liquid environment" (Serrano Tellería, 2014, 2015a, b, c, d, e, 2016; Serrano Tellería & Oliveira, 2015). From the creation of profiles and digital identities to the emergence and maintenance of different kinds of networks on and offline, both consciously and unconsciously, academics have delved into aspects and/or dimensions of identity, big data, social media, digital literacy, and interface design that reflect core questions about how we deal with and understand this ecosystem.

Media is everywhere and we live immersed "in" it (*Media Life*, Deuze, 2012). It can be seen in how interface design works to dilute the boundaries between humans and machines (HCI), incorporating these mobile devices into our daily life by fulfilling our motivations and, at the same time, generating interactions to produce them (Serrano Tellería, 2014, 2015a,b,c,d,e, 2016; Serrano Tellería and Oliveira, 2015). Therefore, "invisible audiences" (Rheingold, 2012; boyd, 2014) play a determining role and a lack of awareness about their existence is one of the consequences of the "architecture of intimacy" (Turkle, 2011) or "disclosure" (Marichal, 2012) or "exposure" (Serrano Tellería, 2014, 2015c) designed for social media (The Desire for More, Facebook; Grosser, 2014) and the mobile user interface (Serrano Tellería, 2014, 2015c). There is an increasing awareness about the development of a specific code of ethics for design and for an interface that alerts and protects the user (Serrano Tellería, 2017).

The freedom to construct our personal identities online is no longer the freedom of anonymity; instead, it is the freedom associated with self-determination and autonomy insofar as users can manage it, as well as uncontrolled searching of huge amounts of data. The online experience is similar to Proust's account book, but with us as coauthors (Foridi, 2014; Fidalgo et al., 2013; Serrano Tellería and Oliveira, 2015). As stated by Preston (2014): "Privacy, precisely because it ensures we're never fully known to others or to ourselves, provides a shelter for imaginative freedom, curiosity and self-reflection. So to defend the private self is to defend the very possibility of creative and meaningful life."

Those features are intertwined with Bauman's metaphor of modern life, i.e. liquid life: fluidity, transience, reticula and the dissolution of defined borders and boundaries (Bauman, 2005; Aguado, Feijóo, & Martínez, 2013; Serrano Tellería & Oliveira, 2015; Serrano Tellería, 2015a, 2016) in a society where a "curious reversal" has redefined the private sphere characterized by the right to confidentiality as a sphere that has fallen prey to the right to publicity (Bauman, 2008).

For Responsible Participation by Children and Young People in the Digital World

The internet, e-mail, Google, social media (Facebook, Instagram, etc.), and the growing importance of text messages, among so many other tools, have opened up new horizons and opportunities for children and young people to expose themselves. But while the Web is learned about interactively and intuitively, there are new risks and problems that can harm freedom and integrity of the self and others, as research in this area has shown, and many are linked to managing privacy. Therefore, learning how to participate appropriately is also learning how to manage privacy and therefore interact through digital and mobile devices properly.

Research on children and young people's participation online began by focusing on the dangers and concerns experienced, which varied between positive and negative technological determinism (appropriation of technologies as something beneficial or not beneficial). At the moment, however, there is a change in perspective in academia, which is reflected in the following hypotheses: (a) the digital environment is no more or less dangerous than other environments inhabited by young people offline; (b) the problems posed by digital technology are not exclusive but are instead extensions of social interaction and the problems of extensive media consumption in several environments, and should be considered holistically rather than alone; (c) appropriate responses should not specialize in training for the safe use of the internet but should focus on more general education for life, social interaction, and emotional intelligence skills and education for the media (boyd, 2014; Finkelhor, 2014). Therefore, to foster significant and responsible participation of children and youth through digital and mobile technologies and achieve digital citizenship requires more than digital literacy competences *strictu sensu*.

Around 10 years ago, research began on the use and appropriation of the internet by children and young people and how they adopt and explore new, emerging technologies on different devices. The research done by danah boyd (2014) in the US is one such case. According to this research, the use that young people make of the internet, technology, and social networks is seen by the groups themselves as a continuation of their relationships with peers and friends and, at the same time, as an opportunity to access the adult world and the public sphere, which are often closed off to them. Teenagers visit social networks to experiment and to learn, observing their peers or adults. They seek privacy in relation to those who hold authority over them and who wish to monitor them, but that does not affect their desire to participate in public by regularly sharing content on social networks without fully understanding the risks and problems that arise.

Davis and James (2013), in a study conducted with younger children in the US, aged between 10 and 14 ("tweens"), concluded that they still regard Facebook and other similar sites as predominantly peer spaces. They already valued privacy and have developed strategies to protect their privacy from strangers and especially from people they know (friends, parents, siblings, acquaintances) when they go online. Although all participants talked about using strategies to protect privacy online, it was noticed that sometimes they do not use any strategies at all.

The idea that more opportunities to access the digital world do not necessarily lead to greater risks is one of the most interesting conclusions reached by EU Kids Online, which emphasizes the importance of digital education to learn how to manage participation online. *EU Kids Online* was a study led by Sonia Livingstone in 2010, which dealt with internet use and access on several devices in 25 European countries. In 2014, the *Net Children Go Mobile* study was published. The study was managed by Giovanna Mascheroni and Andrea Cumman (2014) and reproduced parts of the previous study in 7 European countries (Belgium, Denmark, Ireland, Italy, Romania, Portugal, and the United Kingdom), focusing on the changes produced by greater access to mobile devices. The *Children's online risks and opportunities: Comparative findings from EU Kids Online and Net Children Go Mobile* report (Livingstone et al., 2014) shows us some trends in the use made by children and young people (aged between 9 and 16).

The percentage of children aged between 9 and 16 who have a profile on a social network grew between the two studies, from 61% to 68%. Two-thirds of these have at least 100 contacts and changed their settings from public to private, a result that seems to show greater awareness of risks and the strategies to deal with them, while also revealing that there is a long way still to go. The results that confirm that more children are able to use the internet more safely are encouraging, and efforts should be made to broaden this safe use to everyone.

In most of the countries studied, there was an increase in the number of children who reported feeling bothered online; the percentage was higher among girls and increased with age. In the area of disturbing incidents, there was a decrease in sexting and a slight increase in exposure to sexual messages, above all among girls. Cyberbullying grew among girls and in younger age groups and appeared to be part of a trend of the phenomenon of bullying getting worse in general, with a larger proportion of it happening online. These trends seem to justify an education for privacy in order to manage interpersonal relationships properly in digital and mobile environments.

The results of the *EU Kids Online* report in Portugal (Ponte, 2012) show it to be one of the countries with the lowest occurrence of risks in internet use, below the European average (13%): only 7% of children and young people said they had encountered them. This trend continued in 2014, with 10% of Portuguese children stating that they had felt bothered online, compared with 17% (the average for all the countries studied). This may have something to do with its usage rate, which is lower than the European average, although this is together with widespread possession of mobile devices. Nonetheless, according to Ponte (2012), it is one of the countries where more children and young people (49%) reported feeling that they used the internet too much (higher than the European average of 30%) and that appropriate mechanisms and strategies were needed to maximize potential and minimize the adoption of potential risk behavior (Monteiro & Gomes, 2009).

Despite the progress seen in some areas, the studies mentioned show a need to invest in developing full digital literacy among children and young people, going beyond mere technical skills and ensuring that they are able to adopt appropriate behavior when using such skills. The fact that children and young people continue to show risk behaviors suggests that education on this topic needs to be increased and more effective ways to inform them, train them, and make them aware need to be identified, encouraging the adoption of new initiatives and methods for education/training by schools and parents/guardians. The spread of mobile devices has brought with it, in some cases, a further ingraining of risk behaviors and has helped create an even more tenuous boundary between public and private spaces, focusing in particular on the need to design education programs for privacy in the digital space that let young people participate online responsibly, while safeguarding their own rights and identity and the rights and identities of others.

The Public and Private Project

The *Public and Private in Mobile Communications* project, led by LabCom, UBI, from 2013 to 2015, was designed with the goal of understanding how the frequent use of mobile devices (smartphones/tablets) has contributed to changing and redefining the boundaries between public and private spheres. Although the focus of the study was not citizenship participation, we believe that the conclusions help us envisage a way to optimize participation in the digital and mobile space, in order to help younger people protect their integrity and respect the others.

The study included three focus groups, each one formed of six teen-agers aged between 15 and 17 (one group of female teenagers, one of male teenagers, and one mixed group). They were students at a state school in the north-central region of Portugal and were chosen accord-ing to a criterion of convenience (possession of a smartphone).

The focus groups were processed using thematic analysis, a method for qualitative analysis that has the advantage of providing a rich and detailed account of data, frequently surpassing the descriptive level and reaching the interpretative one. It involves identifying patterns or themes in answers relevant to the research questions (Braun & Clark, 2006).

Focus groups were recorded and transcribed verbatim for analysis and coding. The project team was divided into two groups; each one deve-loped a set of initial codes and matched them with data extracts. This identification was made by combining deductive processes (research goals, literature review) with inductive processes (resulting from inter-preting the data). After all the data were coded and collated, different codes achieved by the groups were compared and sorted into themes. Some themes included subthemes because of their complexity. A list of eight final themes was achieved.

Results

We shall now present and briefly discuss the results related to the themes of *privacy in the digital space* and *surveillance*, since we consider them to be the most relevant to the topic of education for privacy under dis-cussion in this chapter.

The first theme is complex and considers several subthemes that corre-spond to its different features: *invasion of privacy; violation of privacy; privacy control strategies; loss of control.*

Invasion of Privacy

As regards the first subtheme, the female teenagers in particular high-lighted how easily a piece of information, for example an image received on a mobile phone or a conversation, could be seen or heard by some-body next to them, whether friends or strangers, for example on public transport. They also mentioned, with displeasure, parental control.

Teenagers in the mixed group also discussed parents' interference and demonstrated particular discomfort about them posting photographs from childhood. This invasion is felt even more intensely because there are more and more people they know on Facebook. Two teenagers ex-plicitly mentioned using or having used passcodes on mobile phones to stop their mothers from keeping watch over them. They mentioned them listening to conversations and reading others' messages as common prac-tices within the group itself (the laughter that went with these statements leads us to believe that it is a relatively normal practice and is not considered a true transgression). The teenagers in the male group were less sensitive about this aspect and reiterated that invasion of privacy had a great deal to do with the person's attitude and what they let happen.

Violation of Privacy

The three groups of teenagers demonstrated awareness of this aspect, with one of the participants in the female group stating that she was concerned about publishing only boring things. Another female teenager reported that her Facebook password was stolen by someone who entertained himself or herself by doing things to her account. There is an awareness that a lot of care should be taken over what is posted.

One of the participants in the mixed group was particularly aware of digital footprints: "what goes into the internet doesn't leave it." Serious privacy violations that cause damage were clearly condemned by some group participants, who showed sympathy for the victims of it. Others, however, highlighted that these situations were the result of somebody exposing himself or herself unduly, suggesting that the individuals themselves are responsible. When questioned on the theft and dissemination of intimate photographs, members of the male group also mentioned that those who expose themselves unduly were responsible and mentioned cases involving public figures.

Privacy Control Strategies

This feature was especially emphasized by the groups of teenagers, who reported being concerned about asking friends if they could post photographs of them on the internet and, when they did not do this, they would post photographs only if they knew the people involved did not mind and looked good in the photograph. They were also concerned about not identifying people in the photographs they published and restricting information given on social networks and went as far as not putting full names or using nicknames to identify one another. This concern, nevertheless, was not shared by all members of the groups and there were some who believed that "however much care you take, something bad can always happen."

Not all of them demonstrated care in not identifying the places where photographs were taken. If they were taken in unfamiliar places, identification was not a problem. One participant mentioned that when she took photographs at home, she only took photographs of people and not surroundings.

How images taken were made available on Instagram and Facebook also followed some criteria and was subject to a selection process. The preference was for images to be processed on the computer and at home so that an assessment could be made as to which images would be posted. The safety strategies mentioned when using mobile phones were codes and PINs. They also mentioned selecting the people with whom they share information. One teenager mentioned that when conversations were really important, she preferred to have them face-to-face and not use a mobile phone.

In the mixed group of teenagers, the issue of changing privacy criteria was highlighted by some participants. Regarding photographs, they published those photographs of friends in which people looked good, since normally nobody would mind. Two members mentioned asking for permission beforehand, when the photograph was taken and while they were all together. They also mentioned the advantage of text messages, since they are less noticeable, and changing privacy definitions to "friends", although "friends" could just be people they know by sight (between 300 and 4000 people in this group). The information found on profiles was what they consider basic information; they sometimes used fake names, which they believed would prevent certain types of behavior (harassment, for example).

In the male group of teenagers, one of the participants in particular defended the idea that the number of friends should be limited and composed of people they really know and interest them. This position was somewhat contradicted when he said that he had 130 friends on Facebook and that some he knew only by sight. Two members said that they rarely actively added people, only accepting friend requests, and rejected friend requests from people they did not know. Several participants in this group reported having changed their Facebook privacy settings several times since they had created their accounts.

Loss of Control

In the three groups of teenagers, it was found that they did not read privacy terms and conditions. It was common for them to watch, install, and play while accepting everything without reading it. In the mixed group, some participants mentioned using the fact that friends had installed an application as a factor for deciding to download it. This group in particular demonstrated that they were aware that not reading the privacy terms and conditions could incur risks. In both the mixed group and the female teenager group, there was awareness that the length of the text and the small font encouraged this type of behavior and corresponded to manipulation. Despite awareness of the importance of using access codes and PINs, only some of the participants said that they used them (female teenager group), while others stopped using them because it was too much work (mixed teenager group).

The participants in the different groups were not very sensitive to the topic of surveillance. The members of the male group recognized that there was supervision but did not attach much importance to this issue. As one of the participants said: "Facebook has an algorithm for understanding likes and suggesting advertising related to those likes. Ummm. ... what's that... it doesn't stop me!" Most members of the mixed group said that they did not feel watched or supervised in the digital space. Only two said that they did and one of them mentioned the example of online shopping websites: "A little. When we're on those online shopping websites. We go to look at some things and then the next day we get emails about other products we've been looking at."

Discussion

Among the results presented above, the idea that the use of mobile devices simultaneously increases public exposure stands out. In this context, violation of privacy is seen essentially as the responsibility of the individual involved and his/her behavior in the digital space, which may be interpreted as being associated with a false feeling of control over privacy. There is awareness about the characteristics of social media mentioned by Rheingold (2012) and boyd (2014), but also some nonchalance, which is reflected specifically in downloading applications without reading privacy policies. This is, however, common behavior in other age groups and is linked to how complex and ambiguous the policies are (Serrano Tellería & Oliveira, 2013).

The results presented also suggest knowledge and implementation of some privacy strategies that are, nonetheless, weak. Limiting who can view a profile to just friends is a common strategy, but is ultimately insufficient because of the breadth of the concept of friends, which includes people known only by sight. This corroborates the conclusion found in the literature that teenagers view social networks as an extension of their social relationships (Davis & James, 2013; boyd, 2014). The implementation of weak strategies to safeguard privacy corroborates the play on words used by Eszter Hargittai (mentioned by boyd, 2014), who calls teenagers digital naïves rather than digital natives.

Together, these results coincide with several studies mentioned previously, in which the risks of using social media are less the result of knowledge about technology and more the effect of the behavior followed in the digital environment (Monteiro & Gomes, 2009; Livingstone et al., 2012; Mascheroni & Cumman, 2014; boyd, 2014; Collier, 2014; Finkelhor, 2014). This conclusion suggests a need to implement policies to raise awareness about the risks of digital media, through a concerted effort by all stakeholders involved, particularly education institutions and staff but also the industry as the creator of content and the internet's technological characteristics.

Toward a Proposed Syllabus for Educating for Privacy

Based on the literature review carried out and the conclusions of the teenage focus groups, we can now present a proposed syllabus for educating for privacy in secondary-school teaching covering 13–17 year olds. Although the studies suggest the need to begin education on the responsible use of digital, mobile, and online media at younger and younger ages, it is true that access to the internet intensifies in all European countries from age 13/14 upwards (Mascheroni & Cuman, 2014), which justifies our choice of this target audience.

This proposal is part of a broader education for new citizenship, understood as a demanding process that involves several personal features and should tend toward common, consented public action, assuming that education for the media "is a pedagogical process that seeks to empower citizens to be more critical and proactive in their experience of current day 'communicational ecology'" (Ministry of Education, 2014). To exercise responsible digital citizenship involves being aware of new media characteristics and reflecting on the new boundaries between public and private spheres they generate.

As mentioned before, education for citizenship is given as cross-cutting training in different European countries, including Portugal. Within the context of current legislation, it is still possible for it to be offered as part of a syllabus with a flexible workload, as school credit, or by carrying out specific projects.

The syllabus guidelines, presented below, can be applied using any of these forms and may be incorporated into specific subjects offered by schools or be part of a specific project. They comprise the identification of a range of themes and sequential subthemes that are considered to be essential to this type of education and goals, intertwining privacy approaches in the mobile and online environment and the exercise of an ethical and responsible citizenship that includes not only cognitive skills but also ethical, axiological, and social skills, i.e., knowledge, values, attitudes, and actions. Some method strategies, mostly framed by so-called active methods, are also suggested. They involve a dynamic relationship with knowledge (Simões, 2015) and with application translated into personal growth (Table 12.1).

Conclusion

The development of digital, mobile, and online technology has substantially changed relationships between the public and the private. Today, we live immersed in a "liquid atmosphere" in which the outlines and boundaries between "me" and "others" seem to be ever more diluted. New technologies emerge as opportunities for exponentiation to infinity, social interactions, and also intervention in the public space and

Table 12.1 Proposed syllabus for education for privacy

Themes	Content	Goals	Method strategies
Digital citizenship	How a digital footprint is formed: profile and digital identity; Concept of digital citizenship; Properties and functions of "new media"; Role of human action in "new media."	Promoting knowledge of oneself and one's physical and social setting, particularly the way this is expressed in the digital, mobile, and online world; Characterizing forms of expression in the digital, mobile, and online world; Reflecting on the "role of the digital citizen" and the need to govern and take responsibility for one's actions on "new media"; Identifying how "new media" can influence our image of the world and how we can intervene in order to influence them; Communicating emotional states, opinions, criticisms, etc.; Increasing awareness about the importance of individual behavior within the group and underlying choices (for those that produce and those that receive); Promoting interaction with others, establishing constructive relationships.	Personal reflection on the self and how to express oneself in the digital, mobile, and online world; Analysis of the information expressed on "new media"; Exhibition of content: concept of digital citizenship, properties, and functions of "new media"; invisible audiences, digital footprint; Topics for discussion: – "how do I express myself in the digital world…" – "the value(s) I want to encourage in my life…" – "what impact does my behavior and the behavior of my group have on people's lives".

| Public/private in the digital and mobile space | Building and managing profiles and digital identity on several applications, devices, and platforms that include different media and "new media"; Main risks and strategies for defending privacy; Digital footprint. | Understanding the concepts of public/private in the digital and mobile space; Being aware of the ambiguity and complexity of privacy policies and the technology involved (location, push notifications, synchronization between email accounts, applications, social networks, and stored data; sharing files; building profiles and digital identities and their relationship with video games; differences between operating systems, mostly iOS and Android, and how the relationships between different applications and personal data work; Recognizing the reality that content on the net is permanent; Understanding that personal data has an economic value in the context of capitalist surveillance; Managing content, audiences and contexts; Identifying different points of view; Understanding and putting oneself in the place of others. | Exposure of content, strategies for defending privacy; Case analysis; Topics for discussion: –"there is no boundary between public and private in the digital and mobile space"; –"only the people I choose have access to the information that I express in the digital, mobile and online world." |

(Continued)

Themes	Content	Goals	Method strategies
For responsible use of new media and active participation in open government;	Personalization of content and notifications; Information architecture—big data, open data, open government; Decision-making in a digital, mobile, and online environment.	Managing content, audiences, and contexts; Reflecting on use of "new media"; Stimulating research and information selection skills; Identifying the possibilities of responsible, active citizen participation in digital media and participation through open government; Valuing the role of participation in building the common good; Anticipating the consequences of our actions in the digital, mobile, and online field in the short, medium, and long term; Valuing the need to produce an extensive range of alternatives to the problem before making a decision; Encouraging a feeling of responsibility in preventing and resolving a problem;	Debating personal experience; Exposure of content (e.g. common good); Problem resolution; Analyzing news; Practical exercises (e.g., creating a public petition; giving opinions on the exercise of public power; denouncing situations of injustice). Topics for discussion: –"Knowing is not always synonymous with doing…" –"before doing things we have to anticipate the consequences…" –"how can I manage my consumption of new media in a balanced way?" –"the way I express myself in the digital, mobile and online world may compromise my personal and social life plan…"

| | | Practicing the decision-making process, making the different steps and connections between them intentional. | —"it is important to cooperate and be involved in projects that help improve citizens' lives, the expression of their interests and the defense of their rights." |
| Cyberbullying | Definition of cyberbullying; Characteristics of those involved; Consequences of cyberbullying. | Understanding the phenomenon of cyberbullying; Knowing how to identify situations of cyberbullying; Recognizing the importance of reporting cases of cyberbullying; Recognizing and considering the opinions and feelings of others; Anticipating the consequences of our actions in different fields in the short, medium, and long term; Encouraging cooperation with others to pursue common goals. | Exposing content; Problem resolution; Case analysis; Roleplaying; Topics for discussion: —"being made fun of is important for personal development..." "cyberbullying at school. How we can help." |

decisions that affect the common good, creating a new army of citizenship. This unprecedented expansion of social contacts, data circulation, and activity in the digital, mobile, and online environment requires an understanding of how to safeguard privacy as management of public exposure, which involves awareness of risks, accountability, and creativity.

Findings from the *Public and Private* project, together with previous research, suggest that teenagers are aware of the social horizons opened by the use of social media and the inherent risks, applying some strategies to minimize them. However, some of the strategies are weak strategies, and there is also a certain noticeable negligence in the management of digital environments. This can be explained by the fact that for younger generations, who have grown up fascinated with the potential created by the expansion of the digital, mobile, and online world, risk behaviors are part of the "naturalization" of this experience. Social networks seem to be viewed mainly as a continuation of their relationships and less as an arena to express and share public concerns.

In this scenario, developing education for privacy programs, aligned with citizenship guidelines, in order to create more responsible participation, seems imperative. This education must be based on awareness that the use of applications, platforms, and new media are part of how individuals' online and offline identities are built and expressed. In fact, although young people generally have a good level of digital literacy together with knowledge of the risks of actions in digital, mobile, and online environments, reflections on digital footprints, invisible audiences, and the liquid environment need to be investigated more deeply in order to safeguard privacy and responsible participation.

The proposed syllabus should be understood as a path to follow, signposting the main concerns collected based on the literature review and the results of the focus groups carried out as part of the *Public and Private* project. These concerns are framed within a wider context of education for citizenship and active participation. The syllabus favors contact with and reflection on real situations, establishing a connection with students' experiences and seeking to generate an active attitude and full development.

Future studies should seek to deepen the way young people manage privacy in digital, mobile, and online environments, in order to refine and propose a more detailed syllabus and evaluate its effectiveness.

References

Aguado, J. M., Feijóo, C., & Martínez, I. J. (cords.). (2013). *La comunicación móvil. Hacia un nuevo ecosistema digital*. Barcelona: Gedisa.

Arroyo-Almaraz, I., & Gómez-Díaz, R. (2015). The undesired effects of digital communication on moral response. *Comunicar, 44*(22), 149–158.

Bauman, Z. (2005). *Liquid life*. Cambridge: Polity.

Bauman, Z. (2008). *Em busca da política.* Rio de Janeiro: Zahar; (1999) *In search of politics.* Stanford: Stanford University Press.

Bennet, W., Wells, C., & Rank, A. (2009). Young citizens and civic learning: Two paradigms of citizenship in the digital age. *Citizenship Studies, 13*(2), 105–120.

Bessant, J. (2014). Digital Spring? New media and new politics on the campus. *Discourse: Studies in the Cultural Politics of Education, 35*(2), 249–265.

Bloemraad, I. (2015). Theorizing and analyzing citizenship in multicultural societies, *Sociological Quarterly, 56*(4), 591–606.

boyd, d. (2014). *It's complicated. The social lifes of networked teens.* Yale New Haven and London: University Press.

Braun, V., & Clarke, V. (2006). Using thematic analysis in psychology. *Qualitative Research in Psychology, 3,* 77–101.

Castells, M. (2008). Afterword. In C. Katz (Ed.), *Handbook of mobile communication studies* (pp. 447–451). Cambridge, MA: MIT Press.

Collier, A. (2014). *Risk implications of kids going mobile: Research.* Retrieved from http://www.connectsafely.org/risk-implications-kids-going-mobile-research/. Accessed on November 30, 2015.

Couldry, N., Stephansen, H., Fotopolou, A., MacDonald, R., Clark, W. & Dickens, L. (2014). Digital citizenship? Narrative exchanges and the changing terms of civic culture. *Citizenship Studies, 18*(6–7), 615–629. doi: 10.1080/13621025.2013.865903.

Council of Europe. (2000). *Project "Education for democratic citizenship" Basic concepts and core competences for education for democratic citizenship.* (Doc. DGIV/EDU/CIT (2000) 23). Strasbourg: Council of Europe.

Council of Europe. (2002). Recommendation Rec (2002)12 of the Committee of Ministers to membres states on education for democratic citizenship.

Council of Europe. (2016). *Competences for democratic culture.* Strasbourg: Council of Europe.

Davis, K. & James, C. (2013). Tweens' conceptions of privacy online: implications for educators. *Learning, Media and Technology, 38*(1), 4–25.

Decrew-Law 139/2012 of 5 July (Curriculum review for primary and secondary school level).

Deuze, M. (2012). *Media life.* Cambridge, UK: Polity Press.

Direção-Geral da Educação (2013). Educação para a cidadania – linhas orientadoras. Retrieved from http: //www.dge.mec.pt/educacao-para-cidadania-linhas-orientadoras. Accessed on December 2, 2013.

Eurydice. (2005). *A educação para a cidadania nas escolas da Europa.* Brussels and Lisbon: Eurydice.

Fidalgo, A., Serrano Tellería, A., Carvalheiro, J. R., Canavilhas, J., & Correia, J. C. (2013). Human being as a communication portal: The construction of the profile on mobile Phones. *Revista Latina de Comunicación Social, 68.* Retrieved from: http://www.revistalatinacs.org/068/paper/989_Covilha/23_Telleriaen.html.

Finkelhor, D. (2014). Commentary: cause for alarm? Youth and internet risk research – a commentary on Livingstone and Smith (2014). *Journal of Child Psychology and Psychiatry, 55,* 655–68.

Foridi, L. (2014). The Facebook-ification of everything! Sex, authenticity and reality for the status update era. *Salon.* Retrieved from http://www.salon.

com/2014/08/31/the_facebook_ification_of_everything_sex_authenticity_
and_reality_for_the_status_update_era/?utm_source=twitter&utm_
medium=socialflow. August 31.

Fraser, N. (2007). Reconhecimento sem ética? *Lua Nova, 70,* 101–138.

Groening, S. (2010). From a box in the theater of the world' to the 'world s
your living room': cellular phones, television and mobile privatization. *New
Media & Society, 12,* 1331–1347.

Grosser, B. (2014). What do metrics want? How quantification prescribes social interaction on Facebook. *Computational Culture: A Journal of Software
Studies.* Retrieved from: http://computationalculture.net/article/what-do-
metrics-want. November 9.

Informal Meeting of European Education Ministers (2015, 17 March). *Declaration on promoting citizenship and the common values of freedom, tol-
erance and non-discrimination through education.* Paris: Author. European
Council.

Jenkins, H. (2006). *Convergence culture: Where old and new media collide.*
New York: New York University Press.

Katz, J. E. (2008). Mainstreamed mobiles in daily life: Perspectives and
prospects. In C. Katz (Ed.), *Handbook of mobile communication studies*
(pp. 1–11). Cambridge: MIT Press.

Katz, J. E., & Aakhus, M. (Eds.) (2002). *Perpetual contact. Mobile communication, private talk, public performance.* Cambridge: Cambridge University Press.

Keen, A. (2012). *Vertigem digital: Por que as redes sociais estão nos dividindo,
diminuindo e desorientando.* Zahar: Rio de Janeiro.

Ling, R. (2004). *The mobile connection: The cell phone's impact on society.*
San Francisco: Elsevier.

Livingstone, S., Mascheroni, G., Ólafsson, K., & Haddon, L. with the networks of EU Kids Online and Net Children Go Mobile (2014). *Children's
online risks and opportunities: Comparative findings from EU Kids Online
and Net Children Go Mobile.* Retrieved from http://eprints.lse.ac.uk/60513/.
Accessed on December 10, 2015.

Livingstone, S., Ólafsson, K., O'Neill, B., & Donoso, V. (2012). *Towards a
better internet for children: findings and recommendations from EU Kids
Online to inform the CEO coalition.* EU Kids Online, London: The London
School of Economics and Political Science. Retrieved from http://eprints.lse.
ac.uk/44213. Accessed on December 10, 2015.

Marichal, J. (2012). *Facebook democracy. The architecture of disclosure and
the threat to public life.* United Kingdom: Ashgate.

Marshall, H. (2009). Educating the European citizen in the global age: Engaging with the post-national and identifying a research agenda. *J. Curriculum
Studies, 41*(2), 247–267.

Mascheroni, G., & Cumman, A. (2014). *Net children go mobile: Risks and
opportunities.* Milano: Educatt.

Ministery of Education and Science. (2014). *Referencial de educação para os
media.* DGE/MEC. Libson.

Monteiro, A., & Gomes, M. J. (2009). Comportamentos de risco na internet
por parte de jovens portugueses: um estudo exploratório. In B. D. Silva,
L. S. Almeida, A. Barca, & M. Peralbo (Eds.), *Actas do X Congresso Interna-
cional Galego-Português de Psicopedagogia* (pp. 5599–5613). Braga: CIED.

Nussbaum, M. (2014). *Educação e justiça social*. Mangualde: Edições Pedago.

Patrocínio, T. (2008). Para uma genealogia da cidadania digital. *Educação, Formação & Tecnologias*, 1(1), 47–65.

Ponte, C. (2012). Digitally empowered? Portuguese children and the national policies for internet inclusion. *Estudos em Comunicação*, 11, 53–70.

Portuguese Basic Law on the Education System (Law nº 46/86 of 14 October, renumbered and republished as Law nº 85/2009 of 27 August).

Preston, A. (2014). The death of privacy. *The guardian*. Retrieved from http://www.theguardian.com/world/2014/aug/03/internet-death-privacy-google-facebook-alex-preston?CMP=twt_gu.

Rheingold, H. (2012). *Net smart. How to thrive online*. Cambridge and London: The MIT Press.

Ross, A. (2007). Multiple identities and education for active citizenship. *British Journal of Educational Studies*, 55(3), 286–303.

Serrano Tellería, A. (2014). Interface design on mobile phones: The delimitation of the public and private spheres. In: F. Paiva, & C. Moura (Orgs.) *Designa: interface international conference on design research*, (pp. 87–108). Portugal: LabCom, Beira Interior University. Retrieved from http://www.livroslabcom.ubi.pt/book/111.

Serrano Tellería, A. (2015a). The role of the profile and the digital identity on the mobile content. In: J. M. Aguado, C. Feijóo, & I. J. Martínez, (Eds.), *Emerging perspectives on the mobile content evolution*. IGI Global, Idea Group Inc, EEUU. Retrieved from http://www.igi-global.com/chapter/the-role-of-the-profile-and-the-digital-identity-on-the-mobile-content/138000.

Serrano Tellería, A. (2015b). Liquid spheres or constellations: Reflections towards mobile devices. In: J. R. Carvalheiro & A. Serrano Tellería (Eds.), *Mobile and digital communication: Approaches to public and private* (pp. 173–198). Covilhã, Portugal: LabCom Books, University of Beira Interior. Retrieved from http://www.livroslabcom.ubi.pt/book/141. Video *International Conference 'Public and Private in Mobile Communications'* https://www.youtube.com/watch?v=q39TPaq8tBo.

Serrano Tellería, A. (2015c). Emotion and mobile devices. In: F. Paiva & C. Moura (Ogrs.) *Designa: Desire*, International Conference on Design Research. Portugal: LabCom. IFP, Beira Interior University. Retrieved from http://www.labcom-ifp.ubi.pt/book/253.

Serrano Tellería, A. (2015d). Twitter e a privacidade: a partilha de estratégias e ferramentas. In: *IX Congresso SOPCOM: Associação Portuguesa de Ciências da Comunicação: Comunicação e Transformações Sociais*. University of Coimbra, Portugal. http://sopcom2015.com/. November 12–14, 2015

Serrano Tellería, A. (2015e). Reddit e a privacidade: uma análise das interacções e conversas. In: *IX Congresso SOPCOM: Associação Portuguesa de Ciências da Comunicação: Comunicação e Transformações Sociais*. University of Coimbra, Portugal. http://sopcom2015.com/. November 12–14, 2015.

Serrano Tellería, A. (2016). Liquid communication in mobile devices: Affordances and risks. In: B. Baggio (Ed.). *Analyzing digital discourse and human behavior in modern virtual environments*. EEUU: IGI Global. Idea Group Inc. Retrieved from http://www.igi-global.com/chapter/liquid-communication-in-mobile-devices/145920.

Serrano Tellería, A. (2017). Innovations in mobile interface design: Affordances and risks. In: *EPI, el profesional de la información.* v. 26, n. 2 (March–April). Special number 'Ethics, research and communication' (Ética, investigación y comunicación). ISSN 1386-6710. Retrieved from https://recyt.fecyt.es/index.php/EPI/issue/view/2999/showToc.

Serrano Tellería, A., & Oliveira, M. (2015). Liquid spheres on smartphones: The personal information policies. *International Journal of Interactive Mobile Technologies, 9*(1). Retrieved from http://online-journals.org/index.php/i-jim/article/view/4065.

Serrano Tellería, A., & Pereira, P. (2015). Instagram e a visibilidade das imagens dos utilizadores. In: J. R. Carvalheiro. *Público e privado nas comunicações móveis,* (pp. 297–316). Coimbra, Portugal: Minerva Coimbra.

Serrano Tellería, A., Portovedo, S., & Albuquerque, A. I. (2015). Negociações da privacidade nos dispositivos móveis. In: J. R. Carvalheiro. *Público e privado nas comunicações móveis,* (pp. 119–158). Coimbra, Portugal: Minerva Coimbra.

Simões, F. (2015). Métodos ativos e aprendizagem autorregulada. In M. L. Branco & J. A. Domingues (Eds.), *Currículo e cidadania* (pp. 117–134). Rio de Janeiro: Publicações Dialogarts.

Turkle, S. (2008). Always-on/always-on-you. The tethered self. In J. E. Katz (Ed.), *Handbook of mobile communications studies* (pp. 121–138). Cambridge, MA: MIT Press.

Turkle, S. (2011). *Alone together: Why we expect more from technology and less from each other?* New York: Basic Books.

Turner, B. S. (2002). Cosmopolitam virtue, globalization and patriotism. *Theory Culture Society, 19*(1–2), 45–63.

Zapatero, M., Brandle, G., & San-Román, J. (2015). Hacia la construcción de una ciudadanía digital. *Prisma Social, 15,* 643–684.

13 Sociability, Smartphones, and Tablets

Leslie Haddon

Jeanette: *Communication between friends (has changed). Just that example of sitting on the sofa with the iPads altogether... the number of times I've said:* 'Why don't you talk to your friend who's come round? Why don't you talk about your day?' *(....) I always used to talk to my friends. You'd go up to your bedroom, you'd chat about what you learned at school, about him, about her. And now with the boys they're playing these things. With the girls they're probably texting each other about things rather than talking.*

—(Mother of a 12-year-old)

Daniel: *Well, when I got my BlackBerry it made me more social because of BBM—that was a really big thing. With BlackBerry it made you know what was going on. Because when I didn't have a BlackBerry people would say:* 'There's this happening, there's this happening.' *And I'll be:* 'Oh, where did you hear this? Oh, BBM.' *I was:* 'Oh, I don't have BBM'. *(...) Before, when I didn't have the BlackBerry, people said that:* 'I live 60% of my life on BlackBerry.' *I was:* 'You can't really live that much of your life on a phone!' *But then as I got into the phone I started to realize what they were saying, and my parents started seeing that I'm spending too much time on the phone.*

—(15-year-old boy)

Clearly, Jeanette and Daniel have different views on how smartphones and tablets have affected children's sociability. For Jeanette, these technologies are undermining social interaction among a new generation of children. In contrast, for Daniel, such technologies are socially liberating, enabling him to be much more informed about his peers. That said, Daniel's last comments suggest he would understand Jeanette's viewpoint, that parents might see this change in a different light.

Yet, given Jeanette thinks that the girls she refers to are communicating—being social via texting—why does she think children are now being less sociable? Meanwhile, Daniel has not actually said that his parents are wrong to believe that he is spending too much time on the smartphone. As we shall see later, other children also have their apprehensions about the temptation of these technologies.

The chapter explores two overlapping themes that will help to make sense of the above quotes and more generally throw light on the differences and similarities between parents and children's perspectives:

- To what extent are technologies like smartphones and tablets changing children's interactions compared to an older generation of children who used their precursors, mobile phones for a variety of purposes and PCs and laptops to access the internet? Do the newer devices raise different concerns among parents?
- What do parents and children consider to be appropriate norms about face-to-face and mediated sociability? How do they both evaluate the children's interactions through such devices as smartphones and tablets, especially in terms of how the devices affect children's sociability?

Sociability, sometimes referred to as sociality, is not a precise theoretical concept but an umbrella term used in everyday language, along with various synonyms like 'being social' and related concepts like 'social skills,' to capture the nature of our interactions, our communications, and our relationships. There is, therefore, scope for ambiguity about how to apply these labels. Yet, in different ways, the theme of sociability has been discussed across a number of subliteratures on information and communication technologies (ICTs). Hence, this chapter first reviews how sociability is discussed across three literatures—the one on the internet, the one on the mobile phone (especially in relation to teenagers), and the one on parental concerns about children's experience of ICTs. It then draws on empirical evidence from the *Net Children Go Mobile* project about parents' and children's perceptions of smartphones and tablets.

Literature Reviews

The Internet's Consequences for Sociability

When the internet first became widely available in the mid-1990s, there was initially some enthusiasm about meeting people in new virtual communities (Castells, 2001). Thus, there was a certain degree of surprise in the academic community when some of the earliest studies suggested that the internet led to adults becoming less sociable (Kraut et al., 1998[1]; Nie, 2001). At the time, two arguments were proposed to explain this. One argument, sometimes referred to as 'time displacement,' was that time spent online meant that there was less time to spend offline interacting with friends and family. The other line of argument recognized that sometimes people were interacting on the internet, but questioned the quality of interaction online and by implication, the quality of mediated relations constructed through the online world. Some deemed the medium to be impoverished compared to face-to-face interaction, by virtue of the fact that non-verbal cues were missing. Therefore, such frameworks have more recently been referred to as 'cues filtered out' theories (Baym, 2015).

However, the picture even at that time was far more complicated. Other contemporary quantitative studies found that either the internet led to more sociability or that it made no difference (for a review see Katz and Rice, 2002). Meanwhile, the cues filtered out approaches assumed interaction was purely online, but since most of those with whom we interact online are already known offline, in general, people do not solely rely on online channels for maintaining relationships. Hence, there were later discussions of the internet 'supplementing' or 'complementing' offline ties (e.g. Peng and Zhu, 2011). The cues filtered out arguments were also challenged in research that showed how textual interactions could be quite rich, such as one study focusing on the communications of Trinidadian diaspora with friends and family back home (Miller and Slater, 2000). More recently, there have been discussions of the various strategies people use, such as adding emoticons, to enhance textual media like email, to inject them with sociability (Baym, 2015). That said, communication online still has its academic critics, concerned that it only creates shallow relationships (e.g. Turkle, 2011).

Since the early discussions of sociability online, there have been two developments. First, the internet continued to evolve, and while there had always been communication online, many think that this is now a more significant component of 'Web 2.0,' especially because of social media. Therefore, empirical research has, in recent years, focused on social networking sites, including studies that have stressed how these have become important sites where specifically youth socialize, especially given constraints on their ability to 'hang out' together offline (boyd, 2014). Second, the research interest changed. Sociability in itself was never an academic concept, whereas social capital—the idea that individually or collectively we can benefit from developing trust through a sense of reciprocity—had a more scholarly track record in the writings, especially of Bourdieu (1985), Coleman (1988), and Putnam (2000), and in general research on this topic had been growing from the mid-1990s (Wilken, 2012). What followed was a shift in argument, from asking what effect the internet had on sociability to asking what effect it had on social capital. Did the internet enhance social capital, decrease it, or make no difference? The older arguments were transposed to this new framework, new refinements emerged such as whether social networks were more significant for bridging or bonding capital, and later studies asked about the types of activities on social networking sites that promoted these different types of social capital (e.g. Ellison, Steinfield, & Lampe, 2011). It is not the intention in this chapter to follow up debates on social capital, but rather to draw attention to how questions about sociability on the internet at a certain period went out of academic fashion.

Mobile Phones and Sociability

Although, for the most part, mobile phone researchers did not use the word 'sociability' in the same ways as early internet studies, the notion was arguably implicit in analyses of how this technology changed the nature of interaction. This was captured in the early literature in terms of the 'perpetual contact' that mobiles enabled (Katz & Aakhus, 2002). 'Hyper-coordination' referred to how teens, especially, presented themselves to peers through the ways in which they used the phone, where they used it, and even by how they carried it (Ling and Yttri, 2002). Meanwhile, 'connected presence' referred to the reassuring feeling that others were always potentially available to us because of the mobile phone (Licoppe, 2004).

In the first mobile phone studies, specifically of children, the focus was often not on children in general but on teenagers as relatively early adopters of mobile phones and especially as pioneers of texting (Ling, 2004). Such studies noted the types of 'lightweight interaction' (Ito, 2005) we shall see in the chapter's later empirical material that helped maintain relationships with peers and enhance awareness of peers' activities. Moreover, that sociability was mediated through what various studies noted was a very personal and intimate device, more so than say a PC, as young people carried their social worlds around with them (Vincent, 2003).

In general, that mobile phone literature was less concerned about the quality of mediated relationships compared to contemporary internet studies, although there were negative sides to new developments in sociability. Frequent mobile phone contact with close peers could create 'bounded solidarity' (i.e., reinforcing cliques—Ling, 2008), possibly to the detriment of maintaining other relationships and making new ties (Campbell, 2015), while constantly being available to peers and being expected to reply to them could produce a feeling of being entrapped (Hall and Baym, 2012). In general, though, the sense that comes across is that these young people are very enthusiastic about mobile phones and that the researchers themselves saw this in a positive light (for a review, see Ling and Haddon, 2008).

Parental Concerns about ICTs and Children's Sociability

There is a long history of concerns about ICTs and children, both in the academic literature and in more general societal discourses (for a review, see Critcher, 2008). These form the backdrop to parental worries about their children's experiences of technologies, which in turn influence 'parental mediation'—i.e., how parents try to influence their children's experience of ICTs (Haddon, 2015).

Parental concerns are quite diverse, including worries about the influence of the content children experience through media (e.g., pornography, representations of violence). But they often have echoes of the time-displacement theses, that children are spending 'too much' time with television (Winn, 1977) and later home computers (Turkle, 1984) at the cost of other activities. Here, we find cross-cultural variation in the fears about what is displaced: for example, while taking time away from education studies is mentioned by Western families, it was paramount in a study of parents' attitudes in rural India (Pathak-Shelat & DeShano, 2014). But sometimes what is displaced is broader, including time for exercising, creative play, and, of interest in this chapter, socializing with peers and developing social skills. Clearly, while many internet researchers may have moved on to focusing on social capital, parents still talk in terms of their children's sociability.

The strongest parental concern is about children becoming 'addicted' to technology, and again, there is cultural variation, as gaming addiction received particular media attention in China and Korea, where parents were more sensitized to the danger of excessive use (Lim and Soon, 2010; Haddon, 2016). In Western studies, parents' worries are often expressed through the food metaphor, whereby parents seek a 'balanced diet' of activities in their children's lives (Livingstone, 2002), wanting a balance in their children's lives that too much time with ICTs could upset. The particular significance of this concern in the academic literature is that this may be happening at a crucial stage in children's development, including when they are developing social skills (Turkle, 1984).

The Net Children Go Mobile Project

Having considered the various relevant literatures, we now turn to the empirical study reported in this chapter. *Net Children Go Mobile* was a multicountry European project lasting from 2011–2014 that was funded by the European Commission's *Safer Internet Programme*. The project's aim was to look at possible online risks faced by children as smartphones and tablets provided a new channel for accessing the internet. The motivation for this was a longer term concern about risks related to internet use in general, which had originally led to the *EU Kids Online* project (2006–2014). Many of the *Net Children Go Mobile* members were from *EU Kids Online*, and so, in effect, these became sister projects, sharing much of the same structure (e.g., quantitative and qualitative studies, common questions, and common modes of analysis across countries).

Mascheroni and Ólafsson (2014) reported the quantitative findings from *Net Children Go Mobile* while Haddon and Vincent (2014) discussed the European qualitative research covering Belgium, Denmark,

Germany, Ireland, Italy, Portugal, Romania, Spain, and the UK. In addition, there was a specifically UK qualitative report, which is why there are more UK quotations in this chapter (Haddon & Vincent, 2015). Since there was limited research on smartphone use by children, the qualitative research reported here had to cover more general questions about adoption, use, and consequences before dealing with the risk agenda and it is some of this material that forms the basis for the analysis below.

The main fieldwork was carried out from January to September 2014 and was conducted in two phases: interviews and focus groups with children were generally completed by the end of April 2014. The focus groups with adults (parents, teachers, youth workers) continued in certain countries until September 2014. There were 55 focus groups with children (N = 219) and 107 interviews (N = 108) across the nine countries.[2]

Parents' Views

> Nick: *I think there's more consciousness of it in mainstream press (now), about children being exposed to too much of one thing and also about quality time with parents. Not having time to actually engage with them and just letting them do things where they just go off... which sounds a bit hypocritical, given that I just used to come home from school and go off on my bike, but that was a world in itself. But I guess it was physical and it was social. It involved other children so there was friction, there were social lessons to be learned whereas I feel just being on an iPad is a bit lonely. Whilst it's OK for a while, if you're doing that for your whole entertainment...*
>
> (Father of a 10-year-old)

In many ways, this father provides in one quote many of the themes identified in the literature review. Nick refers not to academic research per se but to media discourses about time displacement ('*too much of one thing*'). He values the importance of the time children spend interacting or socializing with parents ('*quality time*'), while acknowledging that when he was a child, this did not actually happen so much, since he prioritized time with peers. While not using the word 'sociability' he nevertheless valorizes '*social*' behavior and learning '*social lessons.*' In the last line, he picks up on concern about the solitary use of technology (the iPad), using the unbalanced diet metaphor once again ('*your whole entertainment*').

Jill (mother of children aged 13, 12, and 9) indicated a similar worry about children being antisocial when she described how her visiting 14-year-old niece would have the screen of her smartphone close to her face all the time: '*She doesn't interact with the others, with my other children. I feel a bit out of control, with what she's doing on it all the* time. *And I'd rather she be like the other two (older children).*' In fact, the niece was socially interacting, in that much of her use of the screen related to social network sites. The 'problem' for Jill was that her niece was not communicating with those peers (in this case, cousins) immediately around her. To add another layer of meaning, part of that concern may also reflect the fact that the niece was visiting them and this is a special situation where the parent felt it was appropriate to prioritize face-to-face interaction with the other children. In other words, rather than considering parents' general statements about children, we need to take into account how the specific context in which this behavior occurs may also make a difference to adult evaluations of children's actions.

This comes across even more clearly in the first quote right at the start of this chapter, when Jeanette complained that her children did not interact face-to-face with friends who had made the effort to visit them. This particular quote also referred to both issues from the old sociability debates—the boys gaming, displacing time for communicating, and the girls texting, but such mediated communication is devalued compared to the face-to-face communication.

While Nick and Jeanette provided particular succinct articulations of concerns identified in the literature, they were not isolated. If not actually complaining about this vision of children being together but not communicating aloud, some parents were at least uncomfortable with what was, to them, an unfamiliar form of socializing, like Jan (mother of a 12-year-old): '*Yes, all meeting up with each other. But they'll meet up with each other in Minecraft, which is, I think, a bit spooky really. They can be sitting there not talking to each other, but communicating.*' Others expressed an even stronger reaction than just a malaise about this generation of children, as when Jill (mother of a 15-year-old) commented: '*I hate it with a vengeance but I kind of know there's not a lot I can do.*'

This very last response about '*not a lot I can do*' also picked up on the particular difficulties of intervening in children's use of intimate devices, a quality the smartphone inherited from the mobile phone. The *Net Children Go Mobile* study found that, although some parents demanded it, the right to check what was on the mobile was often resisted and resented, especially by older teenagers (described in more detail in Haddon, 2015). Other parents thought such intervention was a lost cause:

SARAH: *I'm not even allowed to touch it.*
LISA: *Yes, they would go completely ballistic, if I tried to.*
SARAH: *No, she won't even let me hold it, when she's showing me a photograph. I have to… 'I need to hold it because I need to…' …She can't let go of it. In case, I somehow, see something.*

(Mothers of children 14–16 years old)

If the above quotes provide the examples best exemplifying themes already identified in the literature, we can now start turning to more nuanced responses. One of these was to see any changes in socializing as evolving from previous behavior, such that they did not reflect a sudden break from the past.

STAN: *I just wonder whether it's just, this is just an extension of the texting world, so they all group through texting. And now they just happen to have a different method of communicating, which is a little bit easier to use. And a bit more instant. But it's... I think this generation's sort of grown up all the way through it. It's not like it's a new adoption for them.*

(Father of several children ranging from 11–16 years old)

The smartphone (and the tablet) may be 'new' ICTs, but Stan refers here to continuities from children's use of the basic mobile phone that have been available to young people for much longer. In fact, this generation had *'grown up all the way through it.'* The language stresses the underlying incremental nature of change in his eyes: *'little bit easier to use,' 'a bit more instant.'* In fact, some parents took a more relativistic perspective, as when Ellis' mother Mary reflected back in time to when she and her brother were themselves children, noting similarities to the current day in order to put into perspective some of the concerns about children and the latest ICTs (in this case, in a discussion of Ellis' smartphone).

MARY: *I'm not worried about the amount of usage time by Ellis. He's getting much more out of it so I'm not worried that modern times are any different from the '80s... since the Sinclair ZX whatever it was called. My brother's a computer programmer. He was constantly on his computer back in the '80s. I don't think anything technologically is really robbing our children of any childhood differently from the '80s.*

(Mother of a 12-year-old)

Referring to an even earlier period, 50 years ago, in the focus group of those working with children, Rachel questioned Nigel's view about the extent to which this new generation is radically different. Here, she refers to the history of moral panics, noting how people were concerned about older technologies that we now take more for granted.

NIGEL: *The social interaction with youngsters now is that they are very much always Facebooking, Twittering, all that stuff. Society has changed!*
RACHEL: *I think that's showing your age.*

MARY: *I am with Nigel, though. I think what are we...? We're sociable creatures. We should interact...*

RACHEL: *But 50 years ago that's what people were saying about the television or the radio. Isn't it part of development and we have to go with it. Rather than saying 'no' to it, saying: 'How do we get around this? How do we make it acceptable?*

(Youth workers)

In arguing how we should make it *'acceptable,'* Rachel is acknowledging the social concerns that regular apply to children's experience of new technologies and, in effect, raising the question of how we should question or rethink these issues.

In fact, parents were positive about children's use of ICTs, including smartphones, where they led to socializing that might not have taken place otherwise. Deirdre, Helen, and Rula (Mothers of 13–14-year-old boys) started by talking about their children participating in closed on-line gaming groups on laptops, but later, when discussing FaceTime, they implied that a range of devices, including tablets, had enabled their boys to meet up online with friends from abroad at times when they might normally not be doing much at all.

DEIRDRE: *So, (my son and I) talk about stuff. Like the Minecraft on lap-top you could access worldwide far more easily than on Xbox... but you have to be invited onto a certain server. So my son is playing with his friends in the States, with Carl. But only their friends. It's their server, they've set that bit up. So, he's invited Tom (Rula's son) to play on that server and Bill (Helen's son) to play on the app server. So only them. Of course, they're not talking online, because they can't through that... they can only 'see' it if they're tied to each other. But they (also) FaceTime each other on the other devices.*

HELEN: *At ten to eight on a Sunday morning! They're there and they're talking to each other!*

DEIRDRE: *Yes, they're talking to each other, FaceTiming. So it's a differ-ent social set up. Because they can actually... there is 'face to face' contact, ...it's just that it happens to be through ICT, which is just mind boggling for us. Why can't you just be around a table?*

(Mothers of 13-year-olds)

While a slight sadness creeps in that the children as not interacting like the parents did when they were young (*'around a table'*), the three parents were nevertheless impressed that their children have made the ef-fort to do something jointly through these ICTs and that it even involves communication early on a Sunday morning. It was a far different social arrangement compared to what the parents are used to (*'mindboggling'*), but it was acceptable.

Some parents acknowledged that being social was also becoming manifest in new forms because of a range of ICTs. For example, later in the chapter, we will see how the children reported that they checked their peers' social network updates more frequently now, because it was easy to do through smartphones. This behavior was sometimes acknowledged by parents to be 'social' in the sense that it made children more aware of what their peers were doing. Mothers in the focus group of parents of 14–16-year-olds appreciated how smartphones had enabled their children to keep track of each other more, with Lisa noting that when she asked her daughter: 'Who's around this week?' or 'Did you talk to anyone today?' *She can reel off where everybody is! They know exactly where each other is. And I said:* 'Did you speak to anyone?' *And she went:* 'No'. *But they know!*

Lastly, parents can think critically about their own nostalgia for their childhood, expressed in some of the earlier quotes.

JEANETTE: *I think the (smartphone's) definitely made a difference in all the ways I've said. I just think it's probably mostly they're not forced to do the things we used to have to do, I'd have been playing out in the street.*

INTERVIEWER: *Were you forced to play out in the street?*

JEANETTE: *I say 'forced' because there wasn't anything good on telly after a certain time. We couldn't just play wherever we wanted to, so Sunday afternoons were classic, weren't they, there was nothing on telly. You just go out, you go out and play, you go out and call on your friends.*

(Mother of a 12-year-old)

Whereas Nick had been among the parents valuing outdoor activities with peers, here we see that in Jeanette's childhood '*playing out on the street*' had not been the priority (being undermined by tempting technologies). For this parent, going out to play with friends had, a generation earlier, been merely a default because there was nothing better to do, specifically when there was nothing (interesting) on television! In other words, even twenty years ago, ICTs could sometimes offer attractive alternatives to socializing—there was certainly a place for them in Jeanette's life as a child.

In this respect, one can argue that one of the significant changes that may have occurred for the current generation of children is that there are more online (and even television) activities on offer and more portable devices like smartphones and tablets to access these new options. In other words, there are more positive alternatives available competing with 'going out' and more alternative spaces and moments for mediated communication to supplement face-to-face socializing.

In sum, this section first illustrated how some concerns reflected in the general literatures on sociability and parenting have found their way into parents' discussions of smartphones and portable technologies like tablets. More specifically, we again find the long-standing concern about ICTs leading children to be more antisocial is now also voiced in relation to these portable devices. Arguably, there have been some developments in the broader technological landscape children inhabit that can exacerbate these concerns. Mediated communication options have been increasing, for example with the arrival of social networking sites, and smartphones and tablets in part add to this trend. It may well be that because there is more to do on smartphones compared to older mobile phones that some behavior, such as sitting side by side with peers while on the device, has also simply become more visible.

Yet, to put these concerns into perspective, although mobile internet access changes children's options somewhat, as part of the changing internet in general, some parents recognize how this is not leading in itself to children behaving in totally new ways. Sometimes parents point to various continuities or parallels with the experience of children in different eras. Even if some parents have qualms about mediated communication, other parents can see ways in which smartphones can actually enhance their children's social behavior. Parents can sometimes reflect critically on any nostalgia about their own childhood, qualifying the valorization of going out to play with friends, because even when they were themselves young, technologies like television sometimes offered attractive alternatives to socializing. In this respect, the other change in these technologically savvy children's lives, more generally, is that nowadays there may be 'better' (or at least 'other') things to do online and once again smartphones and tablets may add to this trend of having alternatives to hand.

Children's Views

In an initial exercise at the start of the interviews with the children, the participants listed positive and negative aspects of the devices. By far the most common thing these young people commented on was how smartphones had affected their communications.[3]

As with their European counterparts, many of the UK children interviewed felt that now they communicated more because of the smartphone.[4] Assuming there is some truth in their observations, one key reason for the change that they noted was the smartphone's sheer convenience. As Joshua noted: *Probably because it's just more readily available, not having to go up to your room, wait 20 minutes for the laptop to turn on.* Others added that the smartphone had led to more communication among peers in general (compared to the days of texting), in part because the WhatsApp messaging system was free and in part because of its greater affordances, allowing group messaging.

ANUJ: *In the morning when I wake up I find there's been text on the group already, because it's free. …Because if you had normal text people only message you if they need to message you. And you can't really create groups on text message so I think that's why you might message more. So if you want to tell, let's just say, about your birthday party, or something, you could instead of sending it individually, and paying a lot on the text message, on the group you could send it one time for free and everyone would know about it on the group.*

(12, boy)

Yet others pointed to the way the smartphone gave new mobile access specifically to social networking sites. For example, Abdur (12, boy) noted that when *Facebook* was accessed solely through his computer, he used to check it once or twice a day. Now that he could access it through an app on his smartphone, he checked it *'constantly: oh yes, who's doing this, who'd doing that?'* In fact, given that some of the interviewees adopted the smartphone in the same period as they joined social networking sites, it was really the combination of the two innovations that had made a difference in their lives.

ALAN: *I talk a lot more to people in general because the ability is there in my hands, it's much easier to… Previously if I didn't have Facebook I wouldn't be talking to this person, but because I have Facebook and they have Facebook and I have my phone and it's quite easy to communicate with them.*

(15, boy)

No wonder that the *Net Children Go Mobile* survey showed that 59% of children in the UK thought that the smartphone had enabled them to feel more connected with their friends (Livingstone et al., 2014; the average across the European countries was 81%, Mascheroni & Ólafsson, 2014). In contrast to some parental worries about smartphones making children antisocial, clearly many children themselves felt the technology was enhancing their sociability. Parent Lisa had earlier commented that her child, like others, had a greater awareness of peer activities because of the technology. In the second quotation right at the start of the chapter, Daniel had confirmed this with the observation that it *'made you know what was going on.'* Some the European interviews added further insights into the specificities of that sociability, as when Ionela (girl, 10, Romania) described how: '*I started befriending them more because of WhatsApp, going into groups and finding more things about them.*'

Stefania (girl, 13, Italy) noted how online communication supplemented offline contact in her account: *'This year I started to practise athletics, and I met this girl who is the best friend of a (girl) friend of mine. So I met her, but through the smartphone, messaging ... we became closer friends thanks to the opportunity to keep in touch without ... meeting face to face, just through messages.'* Meanwhile Hannah (girl, 12, Ireland) added that with the smartphone: *'I feel more connected with people, as I have freedom to talk to them whenever I can.'* In sum, the smartphone facilities appear to enhance the number of channels for strengthening relations and create a sense of peers being even more available.

However, children could also be critical of these developments. One problem was that there was now too much sociability. One downside of more communicative possibilities was the sheer traffic this generated. In the initial exercise at the start of interviews, we saw how those in focus groups had written down a list of positive and negative things about the smartphone. In the UK interviews, Pranev (12, boy) explained why one of his negatives was 'Notifications during the night': *'If one of my friends stays up later than all the others and I get that one notification and then my screen will turn on and wake up and the light will come on. And usually my brightness is right up so it will wake me up and then have a disturbed sleep so... That is a common problem.'* In fact, Abdur, in the same focus group, then added that he generally pointed the screen downwards precisely to avoid that problem. This led Wilson to join in:

WILSON: *I got rid of (WhatsApp) ...because normally I used to lay there and then suddenly, because I'm in loads of groups... and then they're all talking to each other at ten o'clock at night. I used to have this really annoying text message sounding, it's like a laser, it goes pew-pew-pew... then I just kept hearing it go de-de-de, de-de-de because everyone's speaking to each other. It's so late, why?*

(12, boy)

Moreover, it was not just the late timing of this flood of messages but sometimes their trivial content (in the eyes of young people themselves, not just the parents) that drew some criticism. For example, Alan (15, boy) noted: *'You get things like people instagramming their food which I don't see the point in to be honest. Because it's just food. It's nice but there's no need to share it with the world!'* Or from the European interviews:

GAIA: *There's much more communication now, because ... SMS had a certain cost, so you sent one, without writing two thousand things. Instead, now one writes thousands of messages, with thousands of emoticons, thousands of nonsense, really useless things, thousands of exclamation marks, and stuff!*

(15, girl, Italy)

Clearly for some young people the 'lightweight communication' identified in the mobile phone literature can be too lightweight, especially when any intimacy is lost through the fact that the message was broadcast.

The other side of the coin of peers being more available because of more channels on the smartphone was that the children themselves were more available to others and often felt obliged to be so—as noted in academic discussions of 'entrapment.' Jens (15, boy, Belgium) lamented: '*What bothers me is that you're always busy, and that you have no rest!*' In fact, in the *Net Children Go Mobile* survey, 72% of the European sample felt they had to be always available to family and friends since having a smartphone (Mascheroni & Ólafsson, 2014).

This extra sociability also had its pitfalls. Given the increase in communication, as smartphones add various forms of internet messaging to texting, some young people felt that it was even more likely that these devices could increase the chances of replying too quickly, without forethought.

ALAN: *If you see that message and it fires you up a little bit... then you're probably going to reply to it and not think through what you're going to say. And that then leads to problems and issues with other people.*

(15, boy)

Finally, a number of comments made by children indicated that they were, like the parents, aware that the smartphone could be just too tempting and take away from the face-to-face interaction that they also valued.

VICTORIA: *We arrange to meet on a Saturday at six in the afternoon and each one of us has our mobile and there are times when maybe we don't talk for ten minutes. And that is what we've met up for, to do that!*

(15, girl, Spain)

This could lead to complaints about peers constantly looking at the smartphone and not attending to other things that are around them, or that it affected their social skills.

ELSA: *I think it stops face-to-face communication, which you need. Because social interaction is becoming so. ... it's disappearing I think. Some people I talk to can just be so. ... lack social interaction because they're so used to being just on their phones.*

(15, girl)

To summarize, the children argued that smartphones especially have led to greater communication with peers for a number of reasons: the increase in communication channels, convenience of using devices at hand, the affordances of the technology (group messages), and the fact that some messaging is now free. This has, in their eyes, led to greater sociability, including, and in conjunction with social media, creating a broader awareness of what peers were doing, a theme originally explored in the mobile phone literature. However, there are a number of negative aspects to this, including the problem of too much and untimely communication, trivial content, demands on their own availability, the potential for replying too quickly to messages, and taking time from face-to-face interaction with peers.

Conclusions

We now return to the two sets of questions identified in the introduction about the changes in interaction arising from smartphones and tablets and implications for mediated sociability. If the children are right that there is more interaction because of smartphones especially, then interaction with these devices may simply be more visible to contemporary parents because it is more frequent than mobile phone use had been. In Jeanette's example at the start, we have the striking example of children visibly sitting together but not communicating face-to-face. For many parents, including older parents who were already past their teens when texting became popular, this felt so different from own childhood and could clearly produce strong reactions ('*spooky*,' '*mind boggling*,' '*hate with a vengeance*'). However, other parents were more sanguine about continuities with the past. We also saw that parents' nostalgia about their own childhood days of playing out with friends might sometimes be misleading. It did not necessarily do justice to the fact that if there had been better alternatives on TV, this might have been prioritized over socializing!

Turning to the children's perspective, smartphones especially made a difference compared to texting on older mobile phones (by virtue of free messaging and the one-to-many communication) and compared to previous forms of internet access (because of the convenience of having portable devices to hand). The children also noted their greater use of these devices because of getting updates from social media. The children's perception is that this had created more interaction with the device and more communications. But, as seen in their comments, children could also view this as a very mixed blessing.

As regards the consequences of smartphones and tablets for sociability, a number of parents thought that the use of these devices, even if it involved mediated communication with distant other, should not be prioritized over face-to-face interaction with peers, especially in more special moments like visiting friends. Although these particular parents did focus on the quality of this mediated sociability as discussed in the academic literature, they certainly thought it to be inappropriate at times. We also saw the concern about the time displacement that was noted in academic internet discussions: entertainment on devices like tablets was sometimes seen as having the potential to displace interaction altogether, making children lonely. That said parents sometimes had a more complex view than in the academic debates, appreciating how interacting through devices can lead to new forms of socializing that would otherwise not have taken place and that there were different dimensions of sociability that could be enhanced through these devices, such as having a greater awareness of what peers were doing.

While being generally more positive than parents about the mediated social communications, children could also critically assess changes brought about by smartphones and tablets. Overall, the children shared the parents' assessment that there were more mediated interactions because of smartphones especially and some even went so far as to say this helped to make them more sociable. Yet, the parents might be surprised to know that some children agreed with them that, on certain occasions, such as when making the effort to go out together, face-to-face interaction should take priority, even if that does not always happen in practice. The children were also aware of various downsides of increased communications through these devices that were not mentioned by the parents in this study. In various ways, the enhanced potential for communications could lead to too much 'noise' that could be disruptive or tedious.

Finally, it is worth noting that few studies of ICTs cover both parents' and children's perspectives. In order to understand parents' reactions and interventions, it is important to appreciate what parents want for their children, their concerns, and their own childhood experiences that act as a benchmark, even while parents may reflect critically upon these experiences. Some parents' observations reflect academic debates, but so do their reservations about how much has really changed. Meanwhile, giving children the chance to express their views shows both where their evaluations differ from and agree with those of parents, providing insights that parents might not have thought about and showing how children have more ability to question the consequences of new technologies than their parents might credit them.

Notes

1 The follow-up study with this group modified its position, but still thought that the internet might make introverts less sociable (Kraut et al., 2002).

2 In some of the focus groups and interviews we only had the age range that had guided the choice of the sample (e.g. 11–13 years old). When this happens in the quotes and average figure is given (e.g. 12).

3 This was also relevant because the whole research project was aimed at exploring online risks. On the whole, children did not prioritize these risks when listing negative aspects and when they were willing to discuss online risks, in their view, the smartphone and tablets had not increased risks. They were simply more devices through which risks could be experienced.

4 One confounding factor is that when these children compared their current lives to a few years ago, they might be becoming more sociable with peers partly because of becoming simply more mature themselves.

References

Baym, N. (2015). *Personal communications in a digital age* (2nd ed.). Cambridge, UK: Polity.

Bourdieu, P. (1985). The forms of capital. In J. Richardson (Ed.), *Handbook of theory and research for the sociology of education* (pp. 241–58). New York: Greenwood Books.

boyd, d. (2014). *It's complicated: The social lives of networked teens*. New Haven, CT: Yale University Press.

Campbell, S. W. (2015). Mobile communication and network privatism: A literature review of the implications for diverse, weak, and new ties. *Review of Communication Research*, 3(1), 1–21.

Castells, M. (2001). *The internet galaxy. Reflections on the internet, business and society*. Oxford: Oxford University Press.

Coleman, J. (1988). Social capital in the creation of human capital. *American Journal of Sociology*, 94, 95–120.

Critcher, C. (2008). Historical aspects of public debates about children and media. In K. Drotner & S. Livingstone (Eds.), *The international handbook of children, media and culture* (pp. 91–104). London: Sage.

Ellison, N., Steinfield, C., & Lampe, C. (2011). Connection strategies: Social capital implications of Facebook-enabled communication practices. *New Media and Society*, 13(6), 873–892.

Haddon, L. (2015). Children's critical evaluation of parental mediation. *Cyberpsychology: Journal of Psychosocial Research on Cyberspace*, 9(1) Article 2.

Haddon, L. (2016). Domestication and the media. In P. Rössler (Ed.), *The international encyclopedia of media effects*. Hoboken, New Jersey: Wiley-Blackwell.

Haddon, L., & Vincent, J. (Eds.) (2014). *European children's and their carers' understanding of use, risks and safety issues relating to convergent mobile media*. Report D4.1. Milano, Italy: Unicatt. http://eprints.lse.ac.uk/60147/. Accessed on February 8, 2017.

Haddon, L., & Vincent, J. (2015). *UK children's experience of smartphones and tablets: Perspectives from children, parents and teachers*. Net Children Go Mobile. London: The London School of Economics and Political Science. http://eprints.lse.ac.uk/62126/. Accessed on February 8, 2017.

Hall, J.A., & Baym, N.K. (2012). Calling and texting (too much): Mobile maintenance expectations, (over) dependence, entrapment, and friendship satisfaction. *New Media & Society, 14*(2), 316–331.

Ito, M. (2005). 'Mobile phones, Japanese youth and the replacement of social contact. In R. Ling & P. Pedersen (Eds.), *Mobile communications: Renegotiation of the social sphere*. (pp. 131–148). London: Springer.

Katz, J. E., & Aakhus, M. (2002). *Perpetual contact: Mobile communication, private talk, public performance.* Cambridge, MA: Cambridge University Press.

Katz, J. & Rice, R. (2002). *Social consequences of internet use: Access, involvement and interaction.* Boston, MA: MIT press.

Kraut, R., Kiesler, S., Boneva, B., Cummings, J., Helgeson, V., & Crawford, A. (2002). Internet paradox revisited. *Journal of Social Issues, 58*(1), 49–74.

Kraut, R., Patterson, M., Lundmark, V., Keisler, S., Mukhopadhyay, T., & Scherlis, W. (1998). Internet paradox. A social technology that reduces social involvement and psychological well-being? *American Psychologist, 53*(9), 1017–1031.

Licoppe, C. (2004). "Connected" presence: the emergence of a new repertoire for managing social relationships in a changing communication technoscape. *Environment and Planning D: Society and Space, 22*(1), 135–156.

Lim, S. S., & Soon, C. (2010). 'The influence of social and cultural factors on mother's domestication of household ICTs: Experiences of Chinese and Korean women'. *Telematics and Informatics, 27*, 205–216.

Ling, R. (2004). *The mobile connection. The cell phone's impact on society.* San Francisco, CA: Morgan Kaufmann.

Ling, R. (2008). *New tech, new ties. How mobile communication is shaping social cohesion.* Cambridge, MA: MIT press.

Ling, R., & Haddon, L. (2008). Children, youth and the mobile phone. In K. Dortner & S. Livingstone (Eds.), *International handbook of children, media and culture* (pp. 137–51). London: Sage.

Ling, R., & Yttri, B. (2002). 'Hyper-coordination via mobile phones in Norway'. In J. Katz and M. Aakhus (Eds.), *Perpetual contact: Mobile communication, private talk, public performance* (pp. 139–169). Cambridge, UK: Cambridge University Press.

Livingstone, S. (2002). *Young people and new media.* London: Sage.

Livingstone, S., Haddon, L., Vincent, J., Mascheroni, G., & Ólafsson, K. (2014). *Net Children Go Mobile: The UK Report. A comparative report with findings from the UK 2010 survey by EU Kids Online.* London: London School of Economics and Political Science. Available at http://eprints.lse.ac.uk/57598/. Accessed on February 8, 2017.

Mascheroni, G., & Ólafsson, K. (2014). *Net children go mobile: Risks and opportunities* (2nd ed.). Milan, Italy: Educatt. Available at http://eprints.lse.ac.uk/56986/. Accessed on February 8, 2017.

Miller, D., & Slater, D. (2000). *The internet. An ethnographic approach.* Oxford: Berg.

Nie, N. (2001). Sociability, interpersonal relations and the internet. Reconciling conflicting findings. *American Behavioral Scientist, 45*(3), 420–435.

Pathak-Shelat, M., & DeShano, C. (2014). Digital youth cultures in small town and rural Gujarat, India. *New Media & Society, 16*(6), 983–1001.

Peng. T.-Q., & Zhu, J. (2011). 'A game of win–win or win–lose? Revisiting the internet's influence on sociability and use of traditional media. *New Media and Society, 13*(4), 568–586.

Putnam, R. (2000). *Bowling alone: The crumbling and revival of American community.* New York: Simon and Schuster.

Turkle, S. (1984). *The second self: Computers and the human spirit*. London: Granada.

Turkle, S. (2011). *Alone together: Why we expect more from technology and less from each other*. New York: Basic Books.

Vincent, J. (2003). Emotion and mobile phones. In K. Nyiri (Ed.), *Communications in the 21st century mobile democracy: Essays on society, self and politics* (pp. 215–224). Vienna, Austria: Passagen Verlag.

Wilken, R. (2012). 'Bonds and bridges: mobile phone use and social capital debates'. In R. Ling & S. Cambell (Eds.), *Mobile communication: Bringing us together and tearing us apart* (pp. 127–150). New Brunswick, NJ: Transaction Publishers.

Winn, M. (1977). *The plug-in drug*. Harmondsworth, UK: Penguin.

14 The Mobile Generation and Instagram Photography

Lev Manovich

This chapter offers the analysis of contemporary popular photography created and shared by millions of young mobile Instagram users. In contrast to older media sharing services such as Flickr, Instagram was designed as mobile-only network and app. From its start in 2010, it grew to over 500 million users six years later. In my analysis, I focus on particular Instagram aesthetics and sensibility that I call *Instagramism*.

I use this term as an analogy to modern art movements such as futurism, cubism, surrealism, etc. Like these earlier –isms, Instagramism offers its own vision of the world and its visual language. But unlike Modernist art movements, Instragramism is shaped by hundreds of thousands (if not millions) of authors connected by, and participating in, Instagram and other social networks. They influence each other and share advice on using mobile photo apps to create, edit, and sequence photos to be shared on Instagram. I will discuss these and other aspects of Instagramism that are an important part of the larger phenomenon of networked mobile photographic culture (see the analysis in "Rules of the Photographers' Universe" by Alise Tifentale, 2017).

A note about the two terms that frequently appear in this chapter: "aesthetics" and "class." The words "aesthetics" or "aesthetic" are used prominently by Instagrammers and authors of advice posts and videos. For example, the search on YouTube for "Instagram aesthetic feed" returns 7,200 videos, while the search for the phrase "Instagram aesthetic" on Google returns 144,000 results (both searches performed on November 22, 2016).

When I talk about "Instagram class," I am not referring to a class in economic sense or to a hierarchy of groups in society based on wealth, education, prestige, or other factors. Instead, I use *class* to refer to millions of young people in many countries who use Instagram in systematic ways to create visually sophisticated feeds (as I will explain below). Often, they edit the photos in third-party apps such as VSCO, in addition to the basic Instagram app.

Karl Marx's concept of "means of production" is useful here because Instagrammers can be said to own the means of "cultural production." This means, however, not only simply owing mobile phones and apps but more importantly having *skills* in using these apps, understanding Instagram's rules and strategies for creating popular feeds, and being able to apply well these strategies in practice. Importantly, Instagrammers do not have to always sell their skills to "capitalists"—instead, they mostly use their skills themselves to have meaningful and emotionally satisfying experiences, to meet like-minded people and have human relations, or to acquire social prestige.

Using these skills also creates "cultural capital" (Pierre Bourdieu), measured by numbers of followers or respect in the community. This cultural capital can be translated into economic capital if an Instagrammer starts working with advertisers and marketers to promote products in her/his feed or if followers purchase goods or services via the linked blog or website.

Since content creation skills and understanding of the digital platforms and styles of expression and communication are what matter here, Instagrammers can also be thought of as "knowledge workers" in a "knowledge society" (Peter Drucker coined the term "knowledge worker" in 1957, writing that "the most valuable asset of a twenty-first-century institution, whether business or non-business, will be its knowledge workers and their productivity." See Drucker, 1959). However, I would like to propose instead different terms: "aesthetic workers" and "aesthetic society" (i.e., the society of consumer goods and services). In this society, production and presentation of beautiful images, experiences, styles, and user interaction designs is central for its *economic and social* functioning. Rather than being a property of art, aesthetic is the key property of commercial goods and services.

Consequently, *aesthetic society* values space designers, user experience designers, architects, photographers, models, stylists, and other design and media professionals, as well as regular people who are skilled in using Instagram, other social networks and blog platforms, and media editing, creation, and analytics tools. "Using" in this context refers to creating successful content, promoting this content, communicating with followers, and achieving desired goals.

Three Types of Instagram Photographs: Casual, Professional, Designed

The analysis in this chapter relies on the concepts I developed in chapters 1 and 2 of my book *Instagram and Contemporary Image* (2016; available on http://manovich.net under Creative Commons License). Therefore, I will first briefly summarize these concepts.

I look at three popular types of photos shared by people on Instagram and other popular media sharing networks. I called them *casual, professional,* and *designed.* (My discussion of these types is based on quantitative analysis in my Cultural Analytics Lab of 16 million geotagged images shared on Instagram in 17 global cities in 2012–2016, as well as my own observations as an Instagram user. Certainly, there are other types; moreover, since social media platforms, their users, and their content keep evolving, I do not want to make claims about applicability of my analysis to every geographical location or other periods outside of 2012–2016.) The main purpose of *casual* images is to document an experience, a situation, or represent a person or a group of people. A person who captures and shares a casual photo does not try to control contrast, colors, and composition. Representative function dominates over aesthetic function. Historically, these images continue the practices of color "home photography" that develops in the 1950s as the costs of color film processing decreases.

Professional photos are created by people who are explicitly or implicitly aware of the rules of "professional photography" that also develop during the twentieth century. The authors of these photos try to follow these rules, conventions, and techniques, which they likely learn from either online tutorials, posts, videos, or classes. Thus, in my use, the term "professional" refers not to people who earn living from their photography but to photographs that follow particular aesthetics.

My third *designed* type refers to photos that adopt the aesthetics that go back to a different tradition of Modernist art, design, and photography of the 1920s. It was further developed in commercial fashion, advertising, and editorial photography of the 1940s–1950s. Note that I use "aesthetics" to refer to a combination of visual style, photo techniques, and types of content, because in Instagram photos they usually go together. These aesthetics (there is more than one) follow their own conventions, but because they emerged very recently, they may be still less fixed than that of professional photographs. One significant difference between professional and designed image is the treatment of space. Professional photos often show deep space, exaggerated by composition, blurred backgrounds, and choice of subjects. In contrast, designed photos often create a shallower or flat space with strong two-dimensional rhythm more similar to Modernist abstract art and design. If landscape and cityscape genre exemplifies professional photo aesthetics, still-life and "flat lay" genres exemplify design photo aesthetics.

I use the term Instagramism to refer to the *aesthetics of designed photos* on Instagram. I proposed that the key aspect of Instagramism is the focus on *mood* and *atmosphere* rather than *representation* or communication of *emotions*. I also proposed that Instagramism does not dramatically oppose "commercial" and "dominant" imagery and genres such as *lifestyle* genre of photography and videography. Instead, it establishes small and subtle *distinctions* from this imagery in terms what is shown, how it is shown, and for what purpose. In contrast to the often binary differences between "high" and "low" cultures, or the clear oppositions between "mainstream" culture and "subcultures" during the twentieth century as analyzed by Pierre Bourdieu, Dick Hebdige and others, Instagramism uses alternative mechanism. In this, it participates in the larger aesthetics movement of the early twenty-first century also exemplified in "normcore" style.

High/low and mainstream/subculture distinctions corresponded to class differences in income, types of occupations, background, and education. In contrast, I see *Instagramism* as the aesthetic of the new *global digital youth* class that emerges in early 2010s. This class partially overlaps with the global *Adobe/Behance class.*

"Adobe/Behance Class" is my term for young, professionally educated creatives working in design, video, social media, or fashion. Adobe Creative Cloud software dominates the market for design and media authoring. There are over eight million registered software users worldwide as of September 2016. Behance.com is the leading global portfolio sharing platform. It is owned by Adobe and integrated with Adobe media creation software, so a designer can directly share work on Behance from Adobe applications. Behance reported that it had six million registered users at the end of 2015.

One of the researchers in our lab contacted 24 Instagram users who have feeds of well-designed photos to ask if they had any formal education in art, design, photography, or any other creative fields, or if they work in any of these fields at present. Half of the responders had such education and/or positions; the other half did not.

Instagram *Cool*: Positioning Instagramism Aesthetic "Brand"

I noted that Instagramism does not dramatically oppose commercial visual aesthetics. For example, browsing stock and microstock photography sites such as Shutterstock, 500px, and dozens of others (Schreiber, 2016), we see many photos in lifestyle or food categories that are very similar to many personal photos on Instagram.

But how is the aesthetic of Instagram-designed photos related to aesthetics of casual and professional photo types? In modern society, where many aesthetics, styles, and cultural choices coexist, they often have to define themselves in opposition to each other. In contrast to earlier human societies, which often were completely isolated, modern culture is *structural* in Saussure's sense. Because many types of cultural "positions" (e.g., aesthetics, ideals, sensibilities, ideologies, interpretations) coexist, their creators and promoters have to define them in opposition to each other. More generally, we can say that they are being deliberately positioned sufficiently far from each in a *cultural competitive landscape.* (The metaphor of a landscape containing a number of cultural items situated at particular distances from each other is not my invention. Marketing research uses a set of methods called "perceptual mapping" to analyze and diagram customer perceptions of relations between competing products or brands. Relative positions and cognitive distances between any cultural artifacts, authors, genres, styles, and aesthetic systems can also be analyzed and visualized using this approach. In many projects of our lab, we visualize results of computational analysis of characteristics of large sets of cultural artifacts as such maps.)

So how do you define aesthetics of designed photos using Instagram affordances? How do we create Instagram *cool*? By opposing popular image aesthetics, i.e. the types of photo conventions what we think of as *normal*, *mainstream*, and *popular*. (Historically, the term *cool* and a related term *hipster* became popular in the 1960s, when they were opposed to the term *square* that today is not used that often. See Wikipedia, 2016a.)

For example, if *casual* portraits and self-portraits (e.g., selfies) show full figures of one or more people arranged symmetrically in the center, designed photos instead show parts of bodies away from center, cut by a frame (think of Degas). They also avoid showing faces directly looking into the camera (see my discussion of "anti-selfie" genre in Tifentale & Manovich, 2016).

Similarly, if *casual* and *professional* photos favor landscapes and cityscape genres and often exaggerate the perspective and sense of deep space, *designed* photos flatten the space and use large areas empty of any details. (In terms of lenses or zoom levels, this is the opposition between *wide angle* and *telephoto* view that flattens the space.)

The strategies, such as faces and bodies, cut by frame and flat space align designed Instagram photography with the first generation of "mobile photography"—Rodchenko, Lissitzky, Moholy-Nagy, and other New Vision photographers of the 1920s and early 1930s. They created the visual aesthetics of "making strange" by practicing visual strategies that similarly opposed the popular taste, e.g., symmetrical compositions, full figures, and faces looking into the camera. Using the affordances of first compact 35 mm Leica camera released in 1925, New Vision photographers developed a different visual language: looking at the subject at a 60 to 90 degree angle from below or above; diagonal compositions; showing only parts of objects and people cut by a photo frame; and using high contrast and geometric shadows that flatten the shapes and space and interfere with shape perception. In other words, they were making photography that was *defamiliarizing* the familiar reality, thus creating a visual analog of *ostranenie* effect that Viktor Shklovsky described in 1917 in relation to literature. As many other avant-garde visual movements of the 1910s and 1920s, they were *making perception difficult*—by not using visual strategies of "normal" photography. That is, I think that simply understanding the content of many of their photos required more cognitive effort, since the compositions and subjects of these photos did not immediately trigger familiar cognitive frames. (Of course, as these strategies were gradually adopted in commercial design such as magazine covers and layouts, they became cultural stereotypes that are predictable and therefore easier to recognize and process cognitively. On the role of stereotypes, "exposure effect," and "cognitive fluency" in cognitive processing of design, see MacKay, 2015.)

Casual and *professional* photos adopt a set of visual conventions to document events, people, and situations that follow accepted social norms—for example, taking a group photo at meetings, conferences, and trips. *Designed* photos express *urban/hipster* sensibility that opposes these norms. This opposition is constructed using another set of norms—that of contemporary (2010–) *design culture*. How does this work?

The creators of designed photos find or stage unique *moments, feelings*, and *states of being*—in space, in time, with other people, with objects important to them. But rather than directly negating *square* reality through a strong alternative aesthetics (as hippies did in the 1960s), contemporary Instagram hipsters are often happy to subscribe to the styles of *global consumer minimalism*. Their Instagram photos and *feeds* (this term refers to all photos added by a user to an account over time) represent our current historical period where the twentieth-century opposites—*art* and *commerce, individual* and *corporate, natural* and *fabricated, raw* and *edited*—are blended together. The *Instagram hipster* effortlessly navigates between these positions, without experiencing them as contradictions.

Faces and Bodies

Now, let's think about the frequent subjects of designed photos. I listed some of these subjects in Chapter 2 of my *Instagram* book (Manovich, 2016). They are "spreads" or "flat lays"; photos of separate objects, parts of a body arranged with the object spreads or separate objects; parts of a body (such as hands holding objects or pointing) with landscapes or cityscapes; or a full body positioned toward the edge or corner in a scene.

Is there any common pattern in these subjects? Yes: it is the *presence of Instagrammer's body in the photos*. But these representations do not follow the mainstream portrait conventions—instead, they deliberately oppose these conventions. Hands, fingers, feet, or complete figures that are shown in *situations*: waking up, enjoying a relaxing coffee moment, surrounded by objects, pointing toward the landscape or objects in the cityscape, from the back, and so on. This set of strategies does not appear in the commercial and advertising photography published today or earlier in the twentieth century, and it also did not exist in New Vision photography.

My suggested interpretation of these Instagramism strategies is the following. The Instagram author is not a Renaissance or Modernist observer situated *outside of the scene* who records according to perspectival rules. Instead, the author is *in the scene, in the situation, in the moment.* (See the section on "anti-selfie" in "Competitive Photography and the Presentation of the Self," see Tifentale & Manovich, 2016.)

To achieve this effect, often somebody else has to photograph the author in the scene. This is similar to a third-person narration in literature or a third-person view in video games, when the virtual camera is positioned behind the character the player currently controls.

In a certain sense, hipster life as recorded/staged in a series of Instagram photos is similar to video games that use first-person/third-person narrator. In the case of Instagram, the narrative is about the author traveling through the game world, encountering other people and objects, participating in interesting situations, and having emotionally satisfying experiences. Like a person navigating worlds in a game—and unlike a tourist observing from a distance—the contemporary Instragrammer is immersed in the experiences, moments, and situations. (On the concepts of immersion and presence in the study of video games, see Denisova & Cairns, 2015.) If a tourist is looking for the unique and exotic, the Instagrammer often enjoys the familiar and even everyday: being in the favorite cafe in the city she lives in, visiting favorite places in that city, or simply being in her well-designed apartment or even one aesthetically controlled corner of the apartment. Instead of only showing her experiences when she travels to far away locations, being in her everyday space is the most important subject! Thus, it is about *interior lifestyle* rather than tourist view outside—although, certainly, Instagram also has the popular *nomad* theme as a well, presenting a diary of a person who never stays too long in one area.

The original use of the hipster term in the 1940s was associated with hot jazz. This association, in turn, allows us to better understand the meaning of hipness in Instagramism. Lives of Instagrammers as presented in their feeds can be compared to *unique improvised experiences* of jazz players opposed to *planned and routine life* of "squares."

Today, the enhanced contrast, saturation and/or colors, the use of diagonals, the appearance of objects and bodies cut by an image frame in designed Instagram photos are signs of the immersion and of *life as improvisation.* In choosing and representing (or staging and designing) such style of existence, Instagram authors echo the behavior of the original American hipsters of 1940s–1950s:

> The hipster world that Kerouac and Ginsberg drifted in and out of from the mid-1940s to the early-1950s was an amorphous movement without ideology, more a pose than an attitude; a way of "being" without attempting to explain why… The division was *hip* and *square.* Squares sought security and conned themselves into political acquiescence. Hipsters, hip to the bomb, sought the meaning of life and, expecting death, demanded it now.
>
> (Marty Jezer, *The Dark Ages: Life in the United States 1945–1960*)

Of course, looking at many examples of contemporary Instagramism, it is possible to argue that the "life as improvisation" the authors show is completely staged and planned by them. But the reality is more complicated. The boundary between authentic and staged, improvised and planned is not always clear. For example, if the author does some basic edits to the captured photos, increasing a bit brightness, contrast, and sharpness, at what point do we declare this photo to be "calculated" rather than "authentic"?

Instagram Themes

As Instagram continued to attract more and more users, and as brands discovered Instagram, many authors learned that they can use their feeds as advertising for their small business or freelance work, as a way to supplement their income by promoting products sent to them by companies, or to completely support themselves by becoming "influencers." As this happened, the number of photos and feeds that are carefully planned has quickly increased. Multiple evidence suggests that this shift took place during 2014–2015.

One very strong example of this *structuration* of Instagram is the emergence of *strong rules* one has to follow to attract many followers. The first rule: develop a particular *style* and always use it for all the photos in your feed.

By 2015, we see even more structure. In addition to earlier term *style*, another term becomes popular dominating "how to" advice, posts, and help videos: a *theme*. A theme may combine certain subjects, a particular color palette, and contrast choice. Using Google Trends and a search phrase "instagram theme ideas," I found that the global web search traffic for this phrase started to increase in January 2014 and then flattened by June 2015.

YouTube has hundreds of thousands of "how to" videos about Instagram editing, strategies, and theme ideas. I have searched YouTube on November 19, 2016 for few relevant phrases that appear in video titles. Here are these phrases and numbers of video returned:

"how i edit my instagram photos" – 131,000 videos.
"how i edit my instagram pictures" – 48,600 videos.
"how i edit my instagram photos white theme" – 20,000 videos.
"how i edit my instagram minimal theme" – 6,130 videos.

Many of these videos have lots of views. In the following, I list a few examples videos and numbers of views (as of November 19, 2016):

"How I Edit My Instagram Pictures + My Theme," published on 07/19/2016, 421,000 views.

"How I edit my Instagram pictures! | Minimal aesthetic," published on 08/07/2016, 231,000 views.

"34 Instagram Themes," published on 06/08/2016, 187,000 views.

Using a theme does not mean that all photos in one feed should be similar. On the contrary, you have to have enough variety, but this variety also has to be structured. So this is the second rule of Instagram: establish and follow a particular temporal pattern for your feed. Never post similar photos next to each other, but instead alternate between a few types in a systematic way. Create an interesting formal, temporal rhythm, alternating between compositions, color palettes, or other variables. If the goal of your feed is to feature products, place enough photos of other subjects in between product photos.

Designing Photo Sequences

The mobile Instagram app allows users to view photo in a few different ways. (Details below refer to Instagram app interface in mid 2010s.) Gallery view shows nine photos organized a 3 × 3 grid. The order of photos corresponds to the dates and times they were shared on Instagram, with newer photos appearing first. Scrolling down reveals the earlier photos. Clicking on a single photo in a grid brings a new view. It shows this photo at a larger size along with other information: number of likes, comments, posted date and time. This screen also allows a user to perform a number of functions such as "like," comment, and share. (For the analysis of Instagram interface, see Hochman & Manovich, 2013). Finally, a user also has another view, which shows all photos shared by all authors followed. Since this timeline is also sorted by date/time, the photos of a given author appear in between photos of all other authors.

Since the time is such an important dimension of Instagram interface and user experience, many Instagrammers design their feeds accordingly as *aesthetic experiences in time*. They employ special *sequencing* techniques that respond to the ways their photos are viewed by others which I listed above.

Given the two rules for "good Instagram feeds," we can divide Instagram authors into two corresponding types. Some control the characteristics of all or at least most of their individual photos, but make no attempt to sequence them in any particular way. Others control both the aesthetics of individual photos and the overall aesthetics of a sequence.

For the latter type of authors (which can be individuals, professional bloggers, and companies), the sequence aesthetics takes priority over any individual photos. No matter how interesting a particular photo is, the author does not post it if it breaks the established rhythm and theme. The blog post called "How to Establish Your Instagram Aesthetic" (Nadine, 2015) explains this:

> Resist the urge to post things that won't fit in. It might be tempting to post something funny or beautiful that doesn't fit in with the look you've chosen. At some point, you'll have a photo you desperately want to post but it just doesn't work. Resist the urge to post it

anyway and take to Twitter. Any photos that don't fit in my Instagram aesthetic go straight to Twitter. Sometimes they are photos that followers would truly enjoy but one photo that is outside of your chosen aesthetic might look odd in your feed.

A post called "Reimaging Your Instagram Profile" (Dana, 2015) from another blog gives these suggestions:

> *Come up with a theme and stick with it.* Maybe you love colourful and bright photos, or maybe only black and white photos. Maybe you post drawings, or photos of lovely landscapes. Maybe you like styling posts or taking close ups of objects. This doesn't mean creating the same photo again and again, it just means using that basic idea to inspire your next photo. Find the formula that works for you and that can easily and quickly be adapted to your future photos... *Your formula should help your photos appear as if they are part of a set. Like they belong together.* Try not to break the chain – Breaking the chain of related photos using your formula is sometimes difficult. You don't have to post every single photo you take, just the ones that are superb... so try to at least make those ones match the rest.

One male Instagrammer explained in an interview in 2014 how he used small photo printouts to design the sequence of his photos before starting his Instagram account. He quickly gathered over 50,000 followers purely on the strength of his individual photos and his sequencing. I am highlighting this author because his feed does not include any photos with popular type content that used to get likes and followers, such as spectacular views of exotic landscapes, young women in swimsuits, or pretty female faces. In 2016, it became common among Instagrammers to have two Instagram accounts. The one is for the public; the second is private and used to lay out sequences and see if new photos fit the theme and established rhythm before they are added to the public account.

The authors who design both individual photos and their sequences may be considered as the true "Instagram professionals." They do not follow the rules of "good photography" and strategies developed well before Instagram for different photo capture and edit technologies, publication and exhibition platforms, and circulation and feedback mechanisms. Instead, they systematically exploit the specific properties, affordances, advantages, and limitations of the medium Instagram.

Learning *Instagramism*

For a few years, I have been following a number of Instagram authors who have perfectly designed individual photos and sequences of them in their feeds. I suspected that most do not have any art, photography, or design school training. The descriptions below their photos, blogs, and YouTube channels linked to their Instagram accounts and occasional statement of ages reveal that many of these authors are in school and are only 13–16 years old. So they did not yet have a chance to study art or design in a university. They are not necessary based in larger metropolitan centers—many live in smaller cities.

However, their visual sophistication, the skills in using Instagram, and overall quality of their feeds from my point of view is often superior to that of the big commercial brands or adult, professionally trained image makers. Where do these individual users learn this? A likely explanation is that at least some of these sophisticated young users learn from following and studying others who use the medium well, and by "soaking in" the design principles from numerous well-designed web sites, blogs, apps, and also well designed physical objects and spaces—although for young people who live in many small locations far from larger cities, online resources such as YouTube "how to" videos and blog posts certainly have to be the major, if not the only, source.

The volume of YouTube videos where Instagrammers show how they edit individual photos, explain how to create some theme, and give other advice, and the number of views of these videos also suggest that the number of "Instagram professionals" is very large, and it has been gradually growing during Instagram history. The authors of such videos are also often teenagers or young adults in their early twenties. One popular type of such videos, as I already mentioned above, is "How I edit my Instagram?" (131,000 videos as of November 20, 2016). In this video genre, the author demonstrates the process followed to edit each of the photos before they are posted. The author works on a single photo using a few different apps such as VSCO and Snapseed in a sequence. There are currently hundreds of third-party mobile photo editing apps available for both Apple and Android phones and thousands of articles that review and compare them. Each app is used for particular types of edits, and then a photo is taken to the next app. (For the analysis of similar professional design workflow where project is moved from one application to the next, see Manovich, 2013).

In this way, the author applies a number of edits (which may or may not include applying a filter), both to improve a photo and to make sure that it fits with the aesthetic and theme. Another popular type of video is a tour of the author's phone screens, showing all the photo-editing apps, with explanations of which photo-editing app should be used then. Some authors have 15–20 editing apps on their phone. Some are used for almost every photo; others only occasionally to add very particular effects.

In comparison to this sophistication, the creators of the types of photos I called professional (because they follow the preestablished rules of "good" professional photography) appear to be less sophisticated. They are only trying to imitate a small number of "mainstream" visual norms.

In contrast, many design authors are working hard to establish their own visual idioms and ideally independent visual languages.

In one of "how to" YouTube video from 2014, a young Russian female creator of sophisticated design photos says to her audience: "Find your filters." Her message: find your own style and use it systematically. Create your own distinct visual identity. Experiment and find your own visual voice. Even though two years later, in 2016, the use of a single filter apparently is not enough, the logic of her message remains equally relevant.

That is what hundreds of thousands, and perhaps even millions, of other Instagram creators are doing: learning from each other and from today's highly designed visual environment and exploring the unique characteristics of Instagram medium. Their designed images and narratives are their unique art and also *life form.* They use the Instagram medium to find people like them, to share their images, feelings, and thoughts with global audiences who like what they like, to form groups based on common Instagram patterns (like other bloggers do, too), to plan trips with them, to support each other in hard moments, to share discoveries, and to define themselves.

The fact that they may be copying styles and strategies from other Instagram users, fashion collections, design sites, magazines, and other sources where modern design and hip sensibilities can be observed does not make them any less *authentic* or less *real.* To them, what is real is *what they feel, their emotions, and their aesthetic preferences that generate a sense of coherence and self.*

Do We Need to "Liberate" Instagram Authors?

Originally a platform aimed at "normal" people rather than professional photographers or companies, Instagram's own popularity transformed it as it grew from 100 million monthly active users in February 2013 to 500,000 million in February 2015 (Instagram, 2016). Facebook bought Instagram in April 2012. The company started to add new features to help businesses use the platform for marketing, advertising, and to "have a dialog with their customers." Other features helped individuals integrate their Instagram posts with their other social networks, which made these posts more valuable as promotion tools.

In June 2013, Instagram added the ability to connect Instagram accounts to Facebook, Twitter, Tumblr, and Flickr (Wikipedia, 2016b). In November of the same year, the company enabled advertising via a new *sponsored post* type (Protalinski, 2013). The first company to use this was fashion designer brand Michael Kors.

A number of important features for business accounts were announced in May 2016. They include analytics and "the ability to turn Instagram posts into ads directly from the Instagram app itself" (Perez, 2016). The analytics feature called Insights shows "top posts, reach, impressions and engagement around posts, along with data on followers like their gender, age and location." According to Instagram, by that time, it already had 200,000 advertisers, and these features were designed to allow business users to understand their current and prospective customers, reach more people, and refine their profiles (Perez, 2016).

Many Instagram posts that promote products and brands emulate more personal Instagram aesthetics, with its "being in the scene" pathos. The article "Master the 4 Types of Product Instagrams" (Waldron, 2015) describes how to photograph products using these four styles: *flat lay*, *minimalist* ("Showcase a product in a natural setting" but without distracting background), *the first person*, and *the scene*. The descriptions of the last two types are very revealing (Waldron, 2015):

> *The First Person.* Give viewers a sense of being in the moment, by taking photos from a first person angle. It helps promote aspirational dreams relating to the product. Hold the camera in a spot that would resemble what someone would be seeing themselves. Centering the product is a good way to keep it feeling personal and clean.
>
> *The Scene.* Shoot the product with beautiful scenery and even a storyline in the description for viewers to envision themselves partaking in. It gives life behind the product.

The difference between pre-Instagram advertising photography and these Instagram photo types is that in the former, products or models are presented from the outside, as though looking at the shop window. But in Instagram, products appear as part the author's life. So if the people already identify themselves with this author's lifestyle and aesthetics, they may also identify with the products presented in this way.

However, as I already noted, the same "product styles" are also used by Instagram authors for a noncommercial purpose: to show their favorite objects and their latest fashion purchases, or include themselves in the photographed scene. Does every photo showing a hand holding a pretty cappuccino cup promote it? Of course not. But does it contribute to establishing or maintaining the author's personal "brand," even if this author never sells or promotes anything? Of course yes. Where does the type of photo that shows a close-up of an object or its part, thus "fetishizing" it, come from? This photo type first appeared in advertising around 1908–1913.

Are the Instagram authors who brand themselves through the use of consistent aesthetics and also practice "product styles" trapped in "ideology" (Marx)? Is Instagram's self-*branded self* always a *false self*? Do we need to "liberate" these authors?

In my view, "trapped" Instagram authors are the ones who take *professional* photos, or aspire or already enjoy their "normal" bourgeois life, and do not question the world as presented to them in advertising and in "news." Their *good photos* express this sense of *conformity*, the desire to be like everybody else, i.e. to *follow the dominant social and cultural norms*. I am using terms like "dominant" and "mainstream" to refer to behaviors, taste, and values that are being held and practiced by a significantly larger proportion of people than any alternatives. This may make these values to appear *natural* and *right*.

In contrast, I see many *designed* photos and Instagramism aesthetics as expressions of a *liberated* consciousness that is critical of the global, middle-class reality. (Note that the middle class grew substantially around the world after the 1990s, reaching 784 million in 2011, according to a recent analysis, with most growth taking place in Asia.)[1] Instagramism finds meaning in refined sensibility, rather than in blind conformity. It can mix and match elements from diverse *style and lifestyle* worlds, without the fear of "losing yourself."

In this interpretation, the authors of many designed photos carry on the original vision of Instagram from 2010. In this vision, "Instagram" was constructed via a set of differences from the "normal" *good photography*. They include a square format and filters that not only beautify photos but can also introduce artifacts, erase details, and add irregular lightness and color gradients that subvert the perfect photo realism of the lens. The *normal photography* at that time meant 3 × 4 image ratio inherited from 35 mm film cameras, having everything in focus, and also showing deep perspectival space in landscapes, cityscapes, and group portraits. These norms were common in both professional and casual photography.

Because such norms were most common, and because they were used in advertising, editorial, and corporate photography, their message is *enslavement* to the world *as it exists now*, to *the safe*, and to *the common sense*. The designed and more abstract photos, on the contrary, communicate, in my view, a different message: *having a distance*, being conscious of how social reality is constructed, and being aware of the conventions, norms, and signs of the global, middle-class ideal of our time.

The Cultural Logic of Instagramism

In contrast to the influential analysis of the styles of subcultures in Dick Hebdige's *Subculture: The Meaning of Style* (1979), I do not see Instagram aesthetic of *designed* photos as a symbolic resistance. Young Instagram hipsters *do not resist* the mainstream; they *coexist* with *it* and are not afraid to borrow its elements or show how much they enjoy commercial products and their favorite brands.

Instagramism is not about binary differences from the mainstream. It is about selection and combination of particular elements, drawn from different contemporary and historical universes, including commercial offerings. (In contemporary visual creative industry, this remix logic was best realized in my view in collections of a number of fashion designers created between 1993 and 2006. Among the top global designers in that period, these were Alexander McQueen, John Galliano, and Jean Paul Gaultier).

Our standard model of modern and contemporary cultures assumes that new styles, sounds, art forms, ways of behavior, and other cultural strategies and imaginaries are typically created by small subcultures and then later appropriated by commercial culture producers who package them into products sold to the masses. Indeed, we can easily evoke plenty of examples of such appropriation stories. The subcultures or cultural movements who figure as original inventors in these stories include European Modernists of the 1920s, Paris Surrealists of the 1930s, Beat Generation in late 1940s in NYC, Northern California Hippies in the 1960s, Hip Hop in the Bronx in the early 1970s, or Williamsburg (Brooklyn) in late 1990s.

Does Instagram hip generation fit into this model? In my view, *Instagrammers are neither a subculture creating something entirely new, nor the "masses" consuming commodified versions of aesthetics developed earlier by some subcultures.*

If creation of something *new* by small subcultures or art movement represents a first stage, and later appropriation and packaging for the masses represents a second stage in modern cultural evolution, the "cultural logic" of Instagramism represents a *third stage*: Instagrammers appropriating elements of commercial products and offerings to create their own aesthetics. Instagram and other visual global networks quickly disseminate these aesthetics worldwide.

As opposed to the movement of cultural innovation from individuals and small groups to companies and then the masses as described by the appropriation model, we now also have other types of movements enabled by networks: from individuals and groups to other individuals and groups. The industry borrows as much from these individuals and groups as it influences them. (This logic was already anticipated in the emergence of *coolhunting* research in the early 1990s. See Brodmerkel & Carah, 2016.)

On Instagram, one operates in a truly global space not constrained by local, physical, and geographical reality. Although there are many paid photo editing apps available, both Instagram and enough powerful third-party editing apps are free. Among young people in most countries in Asia, South America, and Eastern Europe today, mobile phone and social media use figures are as big as in the "developed" industrial economies. The same fashion and lifestyle magazines, perfect cappuccino and latte cups, fashion items, and brands of sport shoes can appear in photos from almost anywhere in the world where there are young people who use Instagram. Certainly, because of the differences in income, fewer people in developing countries can afford global brands like Zara or Uniqlo, but there are enough local brands that are cheaper and make products that look equally good.

In physical reality, the local norms constrain how people dress and behave. Compare New York's Chelsea and Lower East Side, Garosu-gil area in Seoul, and Harajuku area in Tokyo. You hardly see any color besides black in New York; in Seoul, white/grey/black palette is the norm; in Harajuku, it is combinations of complementary (warm and cold) bright saturated colors and pastels. Each cultural norm offers plenty of space for variations and individualization—Tokyo street fashion was the most extreme well-known example of such variations in the 2000s. *A cultural norm constrains choices only on a few dimensions but not on others.* So while my examples focused on only one type of Instagram designed aesthetics that we found in images from many countries, it would be very interesting to investigate other types of Instagram aesthetics that reflect other local aesthetic norms.

I hope my analysis has demonstrated that Instagram today offers a great platform for studying not only contemporary global photography, but also contemporary global cultural evolution and dynamics in general. As the medium of choice for the "mobile" class of young people today in dozens of countries, it provides insights into their lifestyles, imagination, and the mechanisms of existence, meaning creation, and sociality.

Note

1 The figure of 784 million members of global middle class by 2011 comes from Kochnar (2015). A much higher figure of 1.8 billion is reported in Pezzini (2012). One thing economists do agree on is that the size of the global middle class grew substantially. Kochnar, for example, claims that this size grew from 399 million to 784 million between 2001 and 2011, reaching 200 million in China alone.

References

Brodmerkel, S., & Carah, N. (2016). *Brand machines, sensory media and calculative culture*. London: Palgrave MacMillan.

Dana. (2015, January 25). Reimaging your instagram profile. Retrieved from http://www.thewonderforest.com/2015/01/reimagining-your-instagram-profile.html. Accessed on November 25, 2016.

Denisova, A., & Cairns, P. (2015). First person vs. third person perspective in digital games: Do player preferences affect immersion? *Proceedings of the 33rd Annual ACM Conference on Human Factors in Computing Systems* (pp. 145–148). New York: ACM. Retrieved from https://www-users.cs.york.ac.uk/~pcairns/papers/Denisova_CHI2015.pdf. Accessed on November 25, 2016.

Drucker, P. (1959). *The landmarks of tomorrow*. New York: Harper and Row.

Google. (2016, November 22). Search results. Retrieved from http://www.google.com/?gws_rd=cr&ei=h78zWPPgDMvbvATu9ImADQ#newwindow=1&q=%22Instagram+aesthetic%22. Accessed on November 25, 2016.

Hebdige, D. (1979). *Subculture: The meaning of style*. London: Methuen.

Hochman, N., & Manovich, L. (2013). Zooming into an Instagram City: Reading the local through social media. *First Monday, 18*(7). Retrieved from http://firstmonday.org/ojs/index.php/fm/article/view/4711/3698. Accessed on November 25, 2016.

Instagram. (2016, June 21). Instagram today: 500 million windows to the world. Retrieved from http://blog.instagram.com/post/146255204757/160621-news. Accessed on November 25, 2016.

Kochnar, R. (2015, July 15). A global middle class is more promise than reality. Retrieved from http://www.pewglobal.org/2015/07/08/a-global-middle-class-is-more-promise-than-reality/. Accessed on November 25, 2016.

MacKay, J. (2015, November 5). The psychology of simple. Retrieved from https://crew.co/blog/the-psychology-of-simple. Accessed on November 25, 2016.

Manovich, L. (2013). *Software takes command*. New York and London: Bloomsbury Academic.

Manovich, L. (2016). Instagram and contemporary image. Retrieved from http://manovich.net/index.php/projects/instagram-and-contemporary-image. Accessed on November 25, 2016.

Nadine. (2015, April 8). How to establish your Instagram aesthetic. Retrieved from http://blogbrighter.com/establish-your-instagram-aesthetic/. Accessed on November 25, 2016.

Perez, S. (2016, May 31). Instagram officially announces its new business tools. Retrieved from https://techcrunch.com/2016/05/31/instagram-officially-announces-its-new-business-tools/. Accessed on November 25, 2016.

Pezzini, M. (2012). An emerging middle class. *OECD 2012 yearbook*. Retrieved from http://oecdobserver.org/news/fullstory.php/aid/3681/An_emerging_middle_class.html. Accessed on November 25, 2016.

Protalinski, E. (2013, October 3). Instagram confirms 'occasional' in-feed image and video ads are coming to the US in the next couple of months. Retrieved from http://thenextweb.com/facebook/2013/10/03/instagram-confirms-occasional-in-feed-ads-are-coming-to-the-us-in-the-next-couple-months/. Accessed on November 25, 2016.

Schreiber, T. (2016). 22 Awesome websites with stunning free stock images. *Shopify.com*. Retrieved from https://www.shopify.com/blog/17156388-22-awesome-websites-with-stunning-free-stock-images. Accessed on November 25, 2016.

Tifentale, A. (2017). Rules of the photographers' universe. *Photoresearcher journal*, no. 27 (2017).

Tifentale, A., & Manovich, L. (2016). Competitive photography and the presentation of the self. In J. Ruchatz, S. Wirth, & J. Eckel (Eds.), *Exploring the selfie: Historical, analytical, and theoretical approaches to digital self-photography*. New York: Palgrave Macmillan, forthcoming. Retrieved from http://manovich.net/index.php/projects/competitive-photography-and-the-presentation-of-the-self. Accessed on November 25, 2016.

Waldron, Z. (2015, August 13). Master the 4 types of product Instagrams. Retrieved from https://hellosociety.com/blog/master-the-4-types-of-product-instagrams/. Accessed on November 25, 2016.

Wikipedia. (2016a). Hipster. Retrieved from https://en.wikipedia.org/wiki/Hipster_(1940s_subculture). Accessed on November 25, 2016.

Wikipedia. (2016b). Instagram. Features and Tools. Retrieved from https://en.wikipedia.org/wiki/Instagram#Features_and_tools. Accessed on November 25, 2016.

YouTube. (2016, November 22). Search results. Retrieved from https://www.youtube.com/results?search_query=instagram+aesthetic+feed. Accessed on November 25, 2016.

Part VI

The Empowered User and the Media

15 Active Audiences

User Participation in Online Media Content

Koldo Meso and Simón Peña

Journalism and Active Audiences

Journalism's legitimacy rests upon its democratizing function and defense of civil liberties (Price et al. 2003). Kovach and Rosentiel (2007) have observed that the main objective of journalism is giving people the information they need to be free and self-governing. Nevertheless, this role has been increasingly questioned in the wake of the emergence of information technology, which has undermined newspapers' symbolic monopoly on "the capacity ... to intervene in the course of events, to influence the actions of others and indeed create events ..." (Thompson 1998, pp. 33–35). Some experts, in contrast, assert that the media continue to play a relevant democratizing role (Masip and Suau 2014).

Audiences are tapping into alternative news sources and developing nontraditional consumption habits. The once-ubiquitous supply-side model has given way to another, focused on demand. Users now decide not only what they consume but also how and where they access that content. Mobility and interactivity play an integral role in today's media consumption (Masip et al. 2015b). The media are constantly experimenting with new ways of interacting with their audiences. The integration of technology into every sphere of human existence has given rise to new habits that are having a direct impact on the relationships between the media and consumers.

Today's media organizations are grappling with a paradoxical situation. Media consumption has reached historic dimensions and the channels, devices, and applications by means of which audiences access media content, as well as the forms and genres in which it is presented, continue to proliferate at a steady pace. However, as audience engagement with and interconnection via digital media has intensified, the environment in which media professionals operate has eroded in terms of business models, effective regulatory practices, and the ways in which working conditions are structured (Deuze 2014).

In this context, the dawn of the twenty-first century marked a sea of change in terms of the preferences, habits, and behavior of consumers, who have become noticeably more proactive. Media audiences are no longer satisfied with assuming a passive role; they are interested in getting involved and having the option of participating (at least theoretically) in the entire news production process (Meso Ayerdi et al. 2014). The media's symbolic power is progressively passing into the hands of its increasingly active audiences (Guallar et al. 2015).

Interaction between the media and media users is nothing new (Richardson and Franklin 2004; da Silva 2012). It dates back to public journalism initiatives launched toward the end of the twentieth century, intended to forge closer connections between citizens and the news-making process (Dahlgren and Sparks 1993; Haas and Steiner 2006; Haas 2007; Ahva 2011). Advocates of public journalism seek to reestablish the notion that journalism is a public-interest profession with strong ties to the community and a clear commitment to democratic values and principles (Rosen 1999; Nip 2006; Paulussen et al. 2007).

Many analyses of the impact of new media on democracy are underpinned by optimistic discourses centered on the vast potential of citizen participation to democratize both journalism and society as a whole (Grossman 1995; Negroponte 1996; Castells 2001; Costera Meijer 2010; Borger et al. 2013; Domingo et al. 2015).

Newspapers have rushed to add features that facilitate proactive reader engagement to their online editions. Most have justified this move on the basis of the democratizing potential that such interactivity supposes. Nevertheless, the incorporation of elements designed to foster user participation has been driven more by economic incentives than any interest in blazing new paths for journalism or a culture of democracy (Masip and Micó 2010; Vujnovic et al. 2010; Rosenstiel and Michell 2011; Singer et al. 2011; Suau and Masip 2014). Newspapers view audience participation as a means of generating traffic, attracting new readers, and, to the degree possible, building user loyalty. To these ends, they have embedded a wide range of interactive features (Hermida and Thurman 2008; Thurman 2008) into their digital editions (Domingo 2008). Such mechanisms allow the editors of online dailies to gain a better understanding of what their readers are really interested in—information of crucial importance, given the significant gap between what is published and what readers consider relevant (Lee and Chyi 2014).

However, it appears that the news digital newspapers publish isn't the only thing that is falling short of public expectations. The mechanisms they have developed to promote interactivity on their sites have also failed to fulfill the objectives originally set out for them, which were to provide fora for debate between citizens and journalists and drive reader loyalty (Olmstead et al. 2011; Masip and Suau 2014). Fora for public dialogue constitute the keystone of democracy (Dahlgren 2001), and the current scarcity of such spaces partly explains why modern democracies are simply not functioning (Barber 2006).

It appears that breaking down the wall of distrust that presently divides the media and the public will require a higher level of interaction between them (Bohman 2000). Media organizations should reinvigorate the public sphere (Dahlgren and Sparks 1993; Dahlgren 2005; Papacharissi 2010; Heise et al. 2014) by providing fora for public debate and channels through which citizens can interact and exchange perceptions and opinions (Mouffe 2005; Couldry 2010; Springer et al. 2015). This would seem to be the inevitable conclusion of anyone who believes that fostering dialogue is one of the principal functions of the media in democratic societies.

The growing proactivity of readers has prompted some to question the role of journalists and journalism. A number of researchers (Chung 2007; Bakker and Pantti 2009; Masip and Micó 2010; Usher 2011; Williams et al. 2011) have examined journalists' attitudes regarding the incorporation of spaces devoted to public participation into the format of digital newspapers. Others who have focused on the Internet's potential as a vehicle for disseminating a broad range of content have hailed it as a modern agora (Bowman and Willis 2003; Gillmor 2004). New players such as social networks, blogs, and news portals not associated with legacy media outlets now form a part of the media landscape. The multimedia convergence in the sector now underway is also blurring the boundaries between mass media outlets and other types of communication services (Fernández 2013). Content can now be distributed via any of the new platforms now available and accessed via an equally varied range of consumer devices (Jenkins 2006; Cabrera 2009; Carlón 2015).

Some experts have developed theories regarding the paradigm shift from traditional journalistic gatekeeping to collective gatewatching (Bruns 2005). This change within the media ecosystem has been accelerated by the emergence of social media, which have contributed heavily to the proliferation of news sources and the burgeoning volume of news and information in circulation that have supposed new challenges for the world of journalism (Bruns 2011). The media are now faced with the challenge of striking a balance between the public interest and the interests of the public, not to mention the differing logics of business and journalism (Guallar et al. 2014). Should the scales tip too far in favor of business incentives and consumer demand, the democratic function of the media as a public service—as well as one of journalism's guiding principles—will be undermined (Ruiz et al. 2011).

There is a growing breach between the priorities of journalists and news consumers (Boczkowsky and Mitchelstein 2013; Lee and Chyi 2014). The former focus on hard news and the latter overwhelmingly prefer soft news. This gap should not, however, be viewed exclusively from the perspective of what appeals most to readers or does not merit their attention; although public interest articles attract fewer readers, they tend to generate more reader commentaries and higher levels of public debate (Guallar et al. 2014). Although they may be in the position to decide initially what is or isn't newsworthy, journalists are no longer the sole gatekeepers of the news. Today's readers not only decide what is and what is not of interest to them personally; they also have the collective power to determine the degree of visibility of what newspapers publish. Modern technology has made average citizens the secondary gatekeepers of online news content (Singer 2013).

Social networks have proved to be effective tools for launching and organizing social movements in the era of Web 2.0 and citizen engagement (Langman 2005; Wasserman 2007; Martin 2015). Social networks, which foster the formation of collective identities and provide channels for people involved in common causes to connect, have allowed formerly silent segments of society to publicly articulate their concerns (Della Porta and Mosca 2005; Della Porta 2015). They have played a pivotal role in mobilization related to the M-15 social movement in Spain (Hernández, Robles, and Martínez 2013), the Arab Spring, and public opposition to the Iraq war.

It is patently clear that social networks have had an impact on democratic practices and the ways in which people relate to each other (Harcup 2016a). Numerous studies on their communications and democratizing potential have been conducted during the last ten years (Hindman 2008; Carpentier and Scifo 2010; Díez, Fernández, and Anguita 2011). However, some scholars such as Koku, Nazer, and Wellman (2001), Díez-Rodríguez (2003), and Castells (2004) have downplayed the idea that social networking enriches the tone of citizen participation.

In spite of the pessimism that often permeates any discussion of the future of journalism, recent studies point to promising trends. Readers continue to want to keep abreast of the news, especially regarding issues of public importance, and they are interested in sharing the articles they read with others. What has fundamentally changed is the manner in which they access and relate to the news, which is no longer unidirectional. People today receive news content via multiple channels and sources (Masip et al. 2015).

Furthermore, readers in the digital era are not shy about pointing out factual errors or ways in which content could be improved and are interested in debating the issues behind the news. The media must therefore develop more comprehensive interactivity strategies that not only include fora for public debate but also foster user involvement in the news production process (Esteinou 2003).

Entrepreneurial Journalism

As mentioned previously, traditional journalism has been under intense pressure for the better part of the last decade. The newspaper business has been besieged on several fronts. The international economic crisis that began in 2008 has had a devastating impact on the sector and greatly harmed the hegemonic model that journalism enterprises followed throughout the second half of the twentieth century (Larrañaga 2009; Guallar 2011; Casero and Izquierdo 2013; Dowling 2016; Evens and Van Damme 2016). Sales and advertising—traditionally the two main means of financing newspapers—have both been adversely affected by the prolonged economic downturn. Two other equally problematic processes have been taking place as newspapers' traditional revenue sources have deteriorated. The first is a structural crisis dating back to the mid-1990s (Casero 2010) caused by young people's progressively diminishing interest in reading newspapers (Casero 2012), an uptick in online news consumption, and newspapers' diminishing audience share and power to influence public opinion in comparison to television and the Internet. The second of these factors is a direct result of the digitalization and media convergence that is transforming journalism (Díaz Noci 2010; Usher 2015).

Journalism around the world is undergoing a profound transformation. Newspaper publishers are attempting to overhaul their business models in an attempt to survive (Holm et al. 2013; Schlesinger and Doyle 2015; Adams 2016). Their response to the challenges they face—which has focused on cost reductions, staff downsizing, and the elimination of media outlets, overseas correspondent positions, and other services, rather than on the improvement of news formats or the quality of the product they offer—has made journalism in an increasingly precarious career (Levy and Nielsen 2010; Picard 2010). As Casero and Cullell have noted (2013, p. 681), the effects of the crisis have seriously undermined the conditions under which professional journalists work and their expectations for the future. News organizations' failure to develop a suitable model for digital publishing is making the situation even worse (Curran 2010; Siles and Boczkowski 2012; Alexander et al. 2016). None have been able to come up with a formula for making Internet-based journalism financially viable (Casero 2010). Despite of these negative trends, the audience for online news continues to grow.

Given these circumstances, there is a pressing need to explore new ways of financing news production (Campos 2010; Yuste and Cabrera 2014). Entrepreneurship has become one of the viable alternatives open to journalists.

We are witnessing a transition from the monopoly that legacy media have long enjoyed over the distribution of news and information to a more open and pluralistic market for this commodity (Picard 2014; Miranda et al. 2016). The reduction of cost barriers associated with journalism made possible by the emergence of digital technology has paved the way for new players to enter the news sector (Casero 2015; Harcup 2016b).

Much discussion on future job creation is focused on entrepreneurial journalism. Spain is a paradigmatic example of this phenomenon.

Between 2008 and 2014, some 454 news media outlets were created in Spain (Casero-Ripollés et al. 2016).

Entrepreneurial journalism is a term used to describe media ventures launched by professional journalists. One of the distinguishing characteristics of such enterprises is their use of digital, rather than analogue, technology (Manfredi, Rojas, and Herranz de la Casa 2015a).

Fátima Martínez qualifies any project developed by individuals or groups of individuals seeking to establish a viable and sustainable model for digital media as entrepreneurial journalism (2013, p. 85). Nonetheless, setting up a digital media outlet entails more than simply practicing journalism. According to Briggs (2011), it also supposes building an audience, identifying a target market, creating a product that will appeal to this segment of news consumers, establishing visibility, and understanding the competition.

The objective seems clear: exploit the ample opportunities the Internet offers to change the structure, content, and user base of the Web by means of new technologies and new distribution channels such as social networks and mobile devices (Breiner 2013; Carlson and Usher 2016). Everything points to the emergence of a new and completely different model that supposes a rupture with the past and a firm commitment to new technologies that may emerge at any given moment, forcing all other players in a media ecosystem to reposition themselves and sometimes even threatening their survival (Scolari 2012; Pavlik 2015).

The innovative new journalistic projects being launched today rely on digital rather than analogue technology. Their commitment to digital technology not only makes them more flexible, more dynamic, and better equipped to adapt quickly to change; it also dramatically lowers their production costs (Manfredi and Artero 2014).

According to Manfredi, Rojas, and Herranz de la Casa (2015b), entrepreneurial journalistic enterprises differ from their traditional counterparts on five key points: ownership and title, total commitment to digital technology, journalist branding, value propositions, and narrative structure.

These trends have fueled a dramatic rise in the number of freelance professionals working in the sector. Given the prevailing circumstances, it is not at all surprising that fewer and fewer media professionals are finding traditional salaried positions and an ever-increasing number are forging careers as self-employed contractors who provide remote, digital services to media outlets.

This new breed of digital professionals must be ready and able to take a proactive approach to social network engagement, create interactive content, improve the visibility of news stories by means of positioning techniques, manage online communities, and handle a large volume of information.

Technological advances and the emergence of new media have changed the rules of the game (Manfredi, Rojas, and Herranz de la Casa 2015b).

Journalism has lost the relevance it once had in the public arena and numerous audience segments are no longer interested in news published by traditional media. Social networks, blogs, and self-publishing platforms (Castells 2009) have become substitutes for newspapers. The rise of the Internet and the many possibilities it offers have supposed a revolution that is shaking the foundations of professional journalism.

In 2010, Jarvis made the prescient and timely prediction that an influx of new players employing a wide variety of alternative models would soon coalesce into a highly diversified news ecosystem that would provide the new framework under which media would function going forward (Jarvis 2011; Holton 2016). Such a perspective paves the way for the next logical step, which is to explore and promote forms of collaboration and audience participation that enrich and round out (rather than dilute) the journalism a news organization produces.

One of the latest resources to be used to finance the launch of new journalism projects is crowdfunding (Jian and Usher 2014), a community-based system that allows individuals to make monetary contributions toward the realization of specific projects of interest to them. Nevertheless, the overlap of the roles of publisher, fundraiser, and journalist inherent to this form of entrepreneurial journalism raises questions about conflicts of interest, accountability, and transparency (Porlezza and Splendore 2016).

Another phenomena having a significant impact on how journalism is being conducted is crowdsourcing, a new approach to content production that has transformed previously passive users into active participants in the newsmaking process. A number of motivational factors have driven the rapid acceptance of this form of journalism (Aitamurto 2015), which is currently being applied successfully in various contexts by major dailies such as *USA Today*, the *New York Times*, and the *Guardian*. Experts on the topic stress that news organizations must routinely check sources and verify the veracity of information obtained via this method of journalism (Aitamurto 2016; Handler and Conill 2016).

The rapid technological change that has occurred over the past few decades (Rodríguez de las Heras 2013) has changed the nature of media organizations' relationships with their audiences. Interactivity, audience participation, and the personalization of content have become popular means of attracting and retaining users. The Internet, social networks, and net-friendly mobile devices have all enhanced the appeal of news and entertainment, their protagonism in people's daily lives, and the various ways in which both can be consumed.

Concepts such as "active audiences" (Masip and Suau 2014; Meso et al. 2015), "interactive audiences" (Kammer 2013), "prosumers" (people who consume and produce media content) (Bruns 2008; Wahl Jorgensen et al. 2010; Sarsa 2014), and "social audiences" (Quintas and González 2014) have spawned a series of new roles and functions that media users now assume and fulfill, one of which is becoming promoter/funders of new journalistic enterprises via crowdfunding platforms.

The Media and Mobile Devices

Over the past few years, media organizations have been forced to grapple with the various ways in which the frameworks, under which traditional journalism has always been practiced, have progressively crumbled. On one hand, the emergence of the Internet and digital technology has given rise to a process of media dispersion and hybridization, in which analogue technology has been displaced by digital technology—a seismic shift that has undermined the foundations upon which the communications industry has traditionally rested (Salaverría 2012). Independently but simultaneously, the global economic crisis that began in 2008 has had a devastating impact on traditional forms of media-sector financing.

The media ecosystem is currently trapped in a paradox. Media consumption has reached a historically high level and the number of news channels, formats, genres, platforms, and applications continues to grow. Nevertheless, the collapse of traditional business models and the failure of new revenue systems to sustain outdated corporate frameworks have produced a media landscape in which there are significantly more, but significantly weaker, players (Figure 15.1).

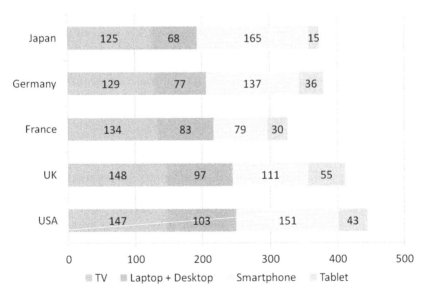

Figure 15.1 Daily distribution of screen minutes 2014.
Source: Internet Trends/World Press Trends 2014.

If emergent Internet-based media provided the impulse for the first great transformation in news distribution models and the rise of personal computers in the mid-1990s, advances in persuasive computing over the past decade (Hansmann 2003) have paved the way for the popularization of mobile devices, such as smartphones and tablets, that media organizations must now take into account. The popularity of information and communications technology (ICT) devices, which unlike home and office desktop computers are not bound by time and space and offer the possibility of permanent mobile connection, has made the media an integral part of people's daily lives (Westlund 2014).

Given the facts that smartphone sales are outpacing computer sales by a margin of three to one and there are now almost as many mobile phones (6.8 billion) in the world as people (7.1 billion), one can reliably assume that the ways in which citizens relate and interact with the media have once again radically changed (Meso Ayerdi et al. 2014).

As the connectivity of these devices has improved, the ways in which we communicate with each other and engage with media have changed and the work carried out by communications professionals has changed as well (Cebrián Herreros and Flores Vivar 2012).

Mobile Devices and Media Consumption

As their ability to provide Internet access has increased exponentially over the last decade, mobile phones and tablets have become powerful vehicles for the dissemination of online news (Wei 2013). The proliferation of these devices can be seen as a confirmation of McLuhan's assertion that technology functions as an extension of the human body and ourselves as individuals (López-García, Westlund, and Silva-Rodríguez 2015).

News media demonstrated an early interest in the potential of devices, such as personal digital assistants (PDAs), and delivery technologies, such as short messaging service (SMS) and multimedia message service (MMS), both of which supported the creation and transmission of brief bites of information that complemented other content (Westlund 2013).

Due to the limited penetration and speed of mobile networks and the compact size of mobile phones, very little content specifically conceived to be consumed via mobile devices was produced during this period. The majority of services offered took the form of pushed news alerts available on a subscriber basis that provided up-to-date information regarding sporting events, the weather, and important political and social developments (Canavilhas 2009).

Following the launch of the iPhone in 2007 and the emergence of the first tablet devices, media organizations began to create specific web content for mobile devices (Aguado and Martínez 2008) that ran parallel to what they offered in other formats. Given that consumers were already accustomed to accessing Internet content for free, they initially made no attempt to charge for mobile content.

Although innovative experimentation with mobile interfaces took place in Japan as early as the late 1990s, Internet access via mobile devices did not take off in Europe and the United States until 2008 (Westlund 2014). Since that time, the extension of 3G, 4G, and other data networks and the popularization of smartphones has led to the development of downloadable news apps.

The portability of mobile devices and the explosion in mobile Internet signal coverage have paved the way for on-the-spot citizen coverage of local events of interest to mass audiences elsewhere, such as the terrorist attacks in Boston and Paris and natural catastrophes (Sheller 2015) (Figure 15.2).

The multimedia and interactive characteristics of this ubiquitous, convergence-friendly "fourth screen" (Aguado and Martínez 2009) allow users to access news from various sources simultaneously. Although text has long been the central element of online news sites maintained by mass media enterprises across the board (even in the wake of cross-platform conversion) with the popularization of mobile devices, some audiovisual media have been gradually returning to their audiovisual roots (Canavilhas 2009). Despite the fact that the introduction of mobile technology has led to the greater incorporation of audiovisual and multimedia features in news presentation formats across the board, it has been noted that applications specifically designed for mobile devices,

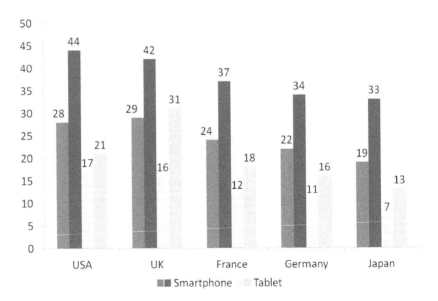

Figure 15.2 Evolution of weekly smartphone/tablet news use (2013–2015).
Source: Reuters Institute News Report, 2015.

somewhat paradoxically, fail to exploit their full potential for personalization, hypertextuality, and interactivity (Meso Ayerdi et al. 2014).

In any case, mobile technology has undoubtedly transformed newspapers into multiplatform products that users are now consuming in one or more of a broad variety of ways (print editions, computer, smartphones, tablets, etc.). Statistics confirm this new trend in consumer habits. According to a recent, comprehensive National Readership Survey (2014), 62.6% of the readers of the UK's eight main dailies access news published by these newspapers via personal computers and mobile devices. The same study notes that only one out of ten readers of such distinguished papers as *The Daily Telegraph*, *The Guardian*, and *The Independent* reads nothing but a print edition; the other 90% make use of both print and digital editions and some readers rely totally on some sort of mobile device.

Given the bourgeoning health of this new mobile ecosystem, it is not surprising that newspapers have begun to develop specific apps for mobile news consumers, which to date have largely focused on the adaptation of digital edition content for mobile devices but have also been created to provide coverage of special events, commemorate important dates, and sell commercial content.

However, not all initiatives prosper in this constantly changing landscape. The growing traction of responsive web design, an approach to web design and development that ensures website content is properly displayed on any type of device, has revealed the weaknesses and limitations of applications designed for single devices. The format specificity of the latter, which forces users to download a different app for each of the mobile devices they use, all of which require fairly frequent updates, severely limits their usefulness (Peña-Fernández, Lazkano-Arrillaga, and García González 2016). The emergence of responsive design apps that adapt website content to a wide range of tactile interfaces and formats has obviated the need to create specific apps simply to accommodate the display requirements of each type of device on the market.

In addition to offering consumers alternative ways of accessing online content, mobile technology has provided journalists with a potent means of disseminating their work. Journalists can now use mobile devices to send out reports swiftly and efficiently from locations that conventional media crews would find extremely difficult to operate in. The emergence of MoJos, as mobile journalists are known (Quinn 2009), is a good example of the impact that new technologies are having on the profession.

Mobile journalists are able to report from the scene of events without the support of extensive infrastructure: the camera, apps, and message services of their smartphones and an internet connection are all they need to do their job. Breakthroughs and collaborations that have allowed journalists to operate without expensive and labor-intensive satellite connections include CNN's citizen journalist platform iReport, the wireless mobile video transmission services provided by LiveU since 2006, the Mobile Journalism Toolkit developed jointly by Reuters and Nokia in 2007 for the Nokia N95, a more recent agreement struck between the Associated Press and Bambuser regarding direct video broadcasting from mobile devices, and Sky News reporters' use of the smartphone app Dejero (Westlund 2013; Lavín-De las Heras and Silva-Rodríguez 2015).

These initiatives have not only allowed journalists to overcome technological and political barriers and broadcast live from any point in the world but have also lowered the cost that such reporting once supposed. These innovations do have their downsides. MoJos perform a variety of tasks once covered by other colleagues, a circumstance that one assumes has an adverse effect on the quality of their work.

The Impact of Social Networks

In addition to exploring the possibilities of mobile technology, online newspapers have created their own virtual communities on social networking sites. The potential of these platforms to foster the dissemination of news content and an ongoing dialogue with readers has been widely recognized (Noguera 2010; García-de-Torres et al. 2011) (Figure 15.3).

The incorporation of social networking components into their formats has allowed legacy dailies to engage with potential new users. The never-ending flow of constantly updated information that news organizations generate meshes well with the interactivity and dynamics of

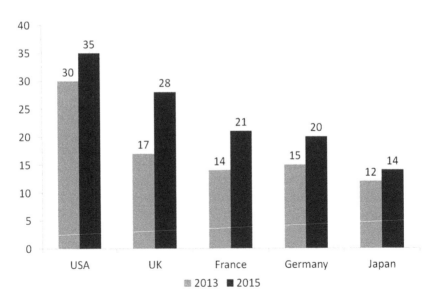

Figure 15.3 The increasing importance of social media as sources (2013–2015).
Source: Reuters Institute News Report, 2015.

social networking. The success of BuzzFeed in the United States attests to the potential of social-network based journalism.

Digital newspapers have been quick to establish a presence on the social networking sites their readers use most and to develop sharing features that take advantage of the traffic generated by these platforms (Ju, Jeong, and Chyi 2014; Said-Hung et al. 2014).

The redistribution of content via social networking platforms such as Facebook and Twitter now accounts for a significant portion of the traffic generated by digital newspapers. One out of five of the visitors to the online editions of European dailies accesses the content they publish via links posted on social networking sites. The percentage of digital natives who enter newspaper websites via these sites is even higher (Peña-Fernández, Lazkano-Arrillaga, and García González 2016).

Social networks, like mobile technology, have had a transformational effect on news content. Some experts assert that user-distributed content (UDC) is becoming more relevant than user-generated content (UGC) (Westlund 2013). Social networking sites encourage users to cruise the Web and cherry pick content from a number of sources rather than consume just one. The viralization and positioning techniques online media are using in reaction to optimize the content they produce suppose fundamental changes in the way news stories are put together. One collateral effect of this process is that online users are now tapping into content they would not otherwise consume and even visiting the websites of newspapers whose ideological standpoints may not necessarily reflect their own personal points of view (Masip et al. 2015b).

Although it has boosted their traffic in general terms, social network engagement has yet to generate significant economic returns for digital newspapers. The lackluster results of their efforts to secure the loyalty of social network users and the limited range of content this type of reader consumes both point to the need to develop new strategies for approaching and capturing this audience (Ju, Jeong, and Chyi 2014).

All of the studies published to date on newspapers' use of social networking tools indicate that, although online dailies have managed to generate a high volume of online traffic via social networks, the type of news being shared varies widely from one newspaper to another and is greatly contingent upon users' cultural and educational backgrounds and media preferences. An analysis of the news sharing habits of the readers of *The New York Times* and *The Guardian* indicates that despite the emphasis these newspapers place on sports, finance, culture, and entertainment, the type of content their readers tend to share with others is overwhelmingly related to local, national, or international issues (Toledo Bastos 2014). However, the findings of similar behavioral studies conducted in Spain have revealed that readers there tend to do the very opposite (Merino-Bobillo, Lloves-Sobrado, and Pérez Guerrero 2013).

Journalists now use social networking sites in general and Twitter in particular as sources of information. Their use of statements originally posted by political, public, cultural, and sports figures on social networking sites in the articles they write reinforces the symbiotic relationship between social networking and journalism. These platforms are also ideal vehicles for live, on-the-spot coverage of events. Social networks have become a part of most journalists' toolboxes, although their use, whether in a personal and professional context, varies according to the age and personality of each individual (Franklin 2014).

Conclusions

Journalism faces new challenges as a result of the increase in the number of information sources and the amount of data available to users. This has contributed to the emergence of social media, which have led to substantial changes in the media ecosystem.

The emergence of social networks, along with the ability to access information from multiple light and handy terminals, has led to a new situation in the field of communication. The new forms of interaction with content and changes in media consumption have favored mobility and new interfaces and have also led to significant changes in the media themselves, who have had to adapt to this new reality.

As Deuze has indicated, communications underpin the organization of contemporary society, in which every aspect of daily life "plays out in media" and "media professionals both contribute to the experience of complexity as well as providing the tools (devices and content) to manage complexity" (Deuze 2014).

Throughout the transformative changes they have undergone over the past two decades, the media have attempted to strike a balance between the classic values of journalism and the realities of a vastly altered news ecosystem. According to Pavlik, media outlets in the future will be web-based, mobile, and convergent—a mix of private and public enterprises that draw upon a variety of revenue sources, offer a balance of proprietary and user-generated content, utilize multiple sources and databases, and contextualize the news they report. They will be global in nature and will seek to make an impact, and their role in the public sphere will ultimately be oriented toward fostering public debate (Pavlik 2013).

The consumption of information through the media is greater than ever. However, this is an individualized consumption at which the user chooses the information. In this new media ecosystem, the public begins to take an active role in the production of information. Nevertheless, the selection of information remains the main form of participation in media content.

Nonetheless, studies conducted by European researchers indicate that today's journalists continue to place a greater emphasis on the traditional journalistic values than on emergent ideas such as audience participation, cross-media publishing, and entrepreneurship. Such findings reveal that practicing journalists in Europe still consider veracity, professional accountability, analytic skills, and sound judgment to be the core requisites of their profession (Drok 2012).

Therefore, there are new opportunities for the journalism industry, although neither the media nor the relationship with the audience will be again the ones before.

References

Adams, D. A. (2016). Voice, deliberation, resistance and persuasion through participatory journalism business models. *Australian Journalism Review*, *38*(1), 101.

Aguado, J. M., & Martínez, I. J. (2008). La comunicación móvil en el ecosistema informativo: de las alertas SMS al Mobile 2.0. *Trípodos*, *24*, 107–118.

Aguado, J. M., & Martínez, I. J. (2009). Construyendo la cuarta pantalla. Percepciones de los actores productivos del sector de las comunicaciones móviles. *Telos*, *83*, 62–71.

Ahva, L. (2011). What is 'public' in public journalism? *Estudos em Comunicaçao*, *9*, 119–142.

Aitamurto, T. (2015). Motivation factors in crowdsourced journalism: Social impact, social change, and peer learning. *International Journal of Communication*, *9*, 3523–3543.

Aitamurto, T. (2016). Crowdsourcing as a knowledge-search method in digital journalism: Ruptured ideals and blended responsibility. *Digital Journalism*, *4*(2), 280–297.

Alexander, J. C., Breese, & Luengo, M. (2016). *The crisis of journalism reconsidered: Democratic culture, professional codes, digital future.* Cambridge, UK: Cambridge University Press.

Bakker, P., & Pantti, M. (2009). Beyond news: User-generated content on Dutch media websites. *Proceedings of the Future of Journalism Congress.* Cardiff, Wales:Cardiff University.

Barber, B. R. (2006). ¿Hasta quépunto son democráticas las nuevas tecnologías de telecomunicación? *Revista de Internet, Derecho y Politica*, *3*, 17–27. Retrieved from http://www.uoc.edu/idp/3/dt/esp/barber.html. Accessed on May 17, 2016.

Boczkowski, P., & Mitchelstein, E. (2013). *The news gap: When the information preferences of the media and the public diverge.* Cambridge, MA: The MIT Press.

Bohman, J. (2000). The division of labour in democratic discourse. In & (Eds.), *Deliberation, democracy, and the media* (pp. 47–64). Lanham, MD: Rowman and Littlefield.

Borger, M., Van Hoof, A., Costera, I., & Sanders, J. (2013). Constructing participatory journalism as a scholary object. *Digital Journalism*, *1*(1), 117–134.

Bowman, S., & Willis, C. (2003). *We media: How audiences are shaping the future of news and information.* Reston (VA): The Media Center at The American Press Institute. Retrieved from http://www.hypergene.net/wemedia/download/we_media.pdf. Accessed on May 17, 2016.

Breiner, J. (2013). Emprendimientos periodísticos. *Revista Mexicana de Comunicación* 133. Retrieved from http://mexicanadecomunicacion.com.mx/rmc/2013/04/29/emprendimientos-periodisticos/. Accessed on May 17, 2016.

Briggs, M. (2011). *Entrepreneurial journalism: How to build What'snext for news*. London: SAGE Publications.

Bruns, A. (2005). *Gatewatching: Collaborative online news production*. New York: Peter Lang.

Bruns, A. (2008). *Blogs, Wikipedia, second life, and beyond: From production to produsage*. New York: Peter Lang.

Bruns, A.(2011). Gatekeeping, gatewatching, realimentação em tempo real: Novosdesafios para o Jornalismo. *Brazilian Journalism Research*, 7(2), 119–140.

Cabrera, M. Á. (2009). La interactividad de las audiencias enentornos de convergencia digital. *Revista Icono*, 14(15), 164–177.

Campos, F. (2010). Los nuevos modelos de gestión de las empresas mediáticas. *Estudios sobre el Mensaje Periodístico*, 16, 13–30.

Canavilhas, J. (2009). Contenidos informativos para móviles: estudio de aplicaciones para iPhone. *Textual & Visual Media*, 2, 61–80.

Carlón, M. (2015). The evolutionary concept in the development of media ecology and mediation theory: Is it time for a general theory? *Palabra Clave*, 18(4), 1111–1136.

Carlson, M., & Usher, N. (2016). News startups as agents of innovation: For-profit digital news startup manifestos as metajournalistic discourse. *Digital Journalism*, 4(5), 563–581.

Carpentier, N., & Scifo, S. (2010). Community media: The long march. *Telematics & Informatics*, 27(2), 115–118. doi:10.1016/j.tele.2009.06.006.

Casero, A. (2010). Prensaen internet: Nuevos modelos de negocio en el escenario de la convergencia. *El Profesional de la Información*, 19(6), 595–601.

Casero, A. (2012). Beyond newspapers: News consumption among young people in the digital era. *Comunicar*, 39, 151–158.

Casero, A.(2015). Nuevos proveedores de información periodística en el entorno digital: los infomediarios de segunda generación. *Anuario ThinkEPI*, 9, 172–176.

Casero, A., & Cullell, C. (2013). Periodismo emprendedor. Estrategias para incentivar el autoempleo periodístico como modelo de negocio. *Estudios sobre el Mensaje Periodístico*, 19, 681–690. doi:10.5209/rev_ESMP.2013.v19.42151.

Casero, A., & Izquierdo, J. (2013). Between decline and a new online business model: The case of the Spanish newspaper industry. *Journal of Media Business Studies*, 10(1), 63–78.

Casero-Ripollés, A., Izquierdo-Castillo, J., & Doménech-Fabregat, H. (2016). The journalists of the future meet entrepreneurial journalism: Perceptions in the classroom. *Journalism Practice*, 10(2), 286–303.

Castells, M. (2001). *The internet galaxy: Reflections on the internet, business, and society*. Oxford, UK: Oxford University Press.

Castells, M. (Ed.) (2004). *La sociedad Red: unavisión global*. Madrid, Spain: Alianza.

Castells, M. (2009). *Communication power*. Oxford, UK: Oxford University Press.

Cebrián Herreros, M., & Flores Vivar, J. (2012). *Periodismo en la telefonía móvil*. Madrid, Spain: Editorial Fragua.

Chung, D. S. (2007). Profits and perils: Online news producers' perceptions of interactivity and uses of interactive features. *Convergence: The International Journal of Research into New Media Technologies, 13*(1), 43–61.

Costera Meijer, I. (2010). Democratizing Journalism? Realizing the citizen's agenda for local news media. *Journalism Studies, 11*(3), 327–342.

Couldry, N. (2010). *Why voice matters*. London: SAGE Publications.

Curran, J. (2010). The future of journalism. *Journalism Studies, 11*(4), 464–476.

da Silva, M. T. (2012). Newsroom practices and letters to the editor. *Journalism Practice, 6*(2), 250–263.

Dahlgren, P. (2001). The public sphere and the net structure, space, and communication. In & (Eds.), *Mediated politics: Communication in the future of democracy* (pp. 33–55). New York: Cambridge University Press.

Dahlgren, P. (2005). The internet, public spheres, and political communication: Dispersion and deliberation. *Political Communication, 22*(2), 147–162.

Dahlgren, P., & Sparks, C. (1993). *Communication and citizenship: Journalism and the public sphere*. London: Routledge.

Della Porta, D. (2015). *Social movements in times of austerity: Bringing capitalism back into protest analysis*. Cambridge, UK: Polity Press.

Della Porta, D., &Mosca, L. (2005). Global-net for global movements? A network of networks for a movement of movements. *Journal of Public Policy, 25*(1), 165–190. doi:10.1017/S0143814X05000255.

Deuze, M. (2014). Journalism, media life and the entrepreneurial society. *Australian Journalism Review, 36*(2), 119–130.

Díaz Noci, J. (2010). Medios de comunicación en Internet: algunas tendencias. *El Profesional de la Información, 19*(6), 561–567.

Díez, E., Fernández, E., & Anguita, R. (2011). Haciaunateoríapolítica de la socializacióncívica virtual de la adolescencia. *RevistaInteruniversitaria de Formacióndel Profesorado, 25*(2), 73–100. Retrieved from http://www.redalyc.org/articulo.oa?id=27422047005. Accessed on May 17, 2016.

Díez Rodríguez, A. (2003). Ciudadanía cibernética. La nueva utopía tecnológica de la democracia. In J. Benedicto & M. L. Morán (Eds.), *Aprendiendo a ser ciudadanos* (pp. 193–218). Madrid, Spain: Injuve.

Domingo, D. (2008). Interactivity in the daily routines of online newsrooms: dealing with an uncomfortable myth. *Journal of Computer-Mediated Communication, 13*(3), 680–704.

Domingo, D., Masip, P., & Costera Meijer, I. (2015). Tracing digital news networks: Towards an integrated framework of the dynamics of news production, circulation and use. *Digital Journalism, 3*(1), 53–67.

Dowling, D. (2016). The business of slow journalism: Deep storytelling's alternative economies. *Digital Journalism, 4*(4), 530–546.

Drok, N. (2012). Towards new goals in European journalism education. *Journal of Applied Journalism and Media Studies, 1*(1), 55–68.

Esteinou, J. (2003). La Revolución del Ciberespacio y la Transformación de la Sociedad de Principios del Siglo XXI. *Razón y palabra, 36*, 18.

Evens, T., & Van Damme, K. (2016). Consumers' willingness to share personal data: implications for newspapers' business models. *International Journal on Media Management, 18*, 25–41.

Fernandez, P. E. (2013). Las audiencias en la era digital: interacción y participación en un sistema convergente. *Question, 1*(40), 68–82.

Franklin, B. (2014). The future of journalism. *Journalism Practice, 8*(5), 469–487.

García-de-Torres, E., Yezers'ka, L., Rost, A., Calderín, M., Edo, C., Rojano, M., Said-Hung, E., Jerónimo, P., Arcila, C., Serrano-Tellería, A., Sánchez-Badillo, J., & Corredoira, L. (2011). Uso de Twitter y Facebook por los medios iberoamericanos. *El Profesional de la Información, 20*(6), 611–620.

Gillmor, D. (2004). *We the media: Grassroots journalism by the people, for the people.* Sebastopol, CA: O'Reilly. Retrieved from http://www.oreilly.com/wethemedia/. Accessed on May 17, 2016.

Grossman, L. K. (1995). *The electronic republic: Reshaping democracy in the information age.* New York: Viking.

Guallar, J. (2011). Prensa digital en 2010. *Anuario ThinkEPI, 5,* 101–105.

Guallar, J., Orduña, E., & Olea, I. (2014). *Anuario ThinkEPI 2014.* Barcelona, Spain: Editorial UOC.

Haas, T. (2007). Public journalism: An agenda for future research. *Asia Pacific Media Educator, 18* 185–198.

Haas, T., &Steiner, L. (2006). Public journalism: A reply to critics. *Journalism, 7*(2), 238–254.

Handler, R. A., & Conill, (2016). Open data, crowdsourcing and game mechanics. A case study on civic participation in the digital age. *Computer Supported Cooperative Work (CSCW), 25*(2–3), 153–166.

Hansmann, U. (2003). *Pervasive computing: The mobile world.* Berlin, Germany: Springer.

Harcup, T. (2016a). Alternative journalism as monitorial citizenship? A case study of a local news blog. *Digital Journalism, 4*(5), 639–657.

Harcup, T. (2016b). Asking the readers: Audience research into alternative journalism. *Journalism Practice, 10*(6), 680–696.

Heise, N., Loosen, W., Reimer, J., & Schmidt, (2014). Including the audience: Comparing the attitudes and expectations of journalists and users towards participation in German TV news journalism. *Journalism Studies, 15*(4), 411–430.

Hermida, A., & Thurman, N. (2008). A clash of cultures: The integration of user-generated content within professional journalistics frameworks at British newspaper websites. *Journalism Practice, 2*(3), 343–356.

Hernández, E., Robles, & Martínez, (2013). Jóvenes interactivos y culturas cívicas: sentido educativo, mediático y político del 15M. *Comunicar, 40,* 59–67. doi:10.3916/C40-2013-02-06.

Hindman, M. (2008). *The myth of digital democracy.* Princeton, NJ: Princeton University Press.

Holm, A. B., Günzel, F., & Ulhøi, (2013). Openness in innovation and business models: Lessons from the newspaper industry. *International Journal of Technology Management, 61*(3/4), 324–348.

Holton, A. E. (2016). Intrapreneurial informants: An emergent role of freelance journalists. *Journalism Practice, 10*(7), 917–927.

Jarvis, J. (2011). *Public parts: How sharing in the digital age improves the way we work and live.* New York: Simon & Schuster.

Jenkins, H. (2006). *Convergence culture: Where old and new media collide.* New York: New York University Press.

Jian, L., &Usher, N. (2014). Crowd-funded journalism. *Journal of Computer-Mediated Communication, 19*(2), 155–170.

Ju, A., Jeong, & Chyi, (2014). Will social media save newspapers? *Journalism Practice*, *8*(1), 1–17.

Kammer, A. (2013). Audience participation in the production of online news. *Nordicom Review*, *34*, 113–126.

Koku, E., Nazer, N., & Wellman, B. (2001). Netting scholars: Online and offline. *American Behavioral Scientist*, *44*, 1752–1774. doi:10.1177/00027 640121958023.

Kovach, B., & Rosentiel, T. (2007). *The elements of journalism: What newspeople should know and the public should expect.* New York: Three Rivers Press.

Langman, L. (2005). From virtual public spheres to global justice: A critical theory of interworked social movements. *Sociological Theory*, *23*(1), 42–74. doi:10.1111/j.0735-2751.2005.00242.x.

Larrañaga, J. (2009). La crisis del modelo económico de la industria de los periódicos. *Estudios sobre el Mensaje Periodístico*, *15*, 61–80.

Lavín-De las Heras, E., & A. Silva-Rodríguez. (2015). Los smartphones revolucionan el periodismo. 10th Iberian Conference on Information Systems and Technologies—CISTI'2015, July 17–20, Aveiro, Portugal.

Lee, A. M., & Chyi, (2014). When newsworthy is not noteworthy: Examining the value of news from the audience's perspective. *Journalism Studies*, *15*(6), 807–820.

Levy, D. A. L., & Nielsen, R. K. (2010). *The changing business of journalism and its implications for democracy.* Oxford, UK: Reuters Institute for the Study of Journalism, University of Oxford.

López-García, X., Westlund, O., & Silva-Rodríguez, A. (2015). La industria de los medios impresos se sube al periodismo móvil. *Telos*, (February–May): 1–14.

Manfredi, J. L. & Artero, (2014). News business models for the media: The Spanish case. In E. Psychogiopoulou (Ed.), *Media policies revisited: The challenge for media freedom and independence* (pp. 160–174). London: Palgrave MacMillan.

Manfredi, J. L., Rojas, & Herranz de la Casa, (2015a). Innovación en el periodismo emprendedor deportivo. Modelo de negocio y narrativas. *El Profesional de la Informacion*, *24*(3), 265–273.

Manfredi, J. L., Rojas, J. L., & Herranz de la Casa, J. M. (2015b). Periodismo emprendedor: el periodismo deportivo en España. *Revista Latina de Comunicación Social*, *70*, 69–90. Retrieved from http://www.revistalatinacs.org/070/paper/1035-UC/05es.html. Accessed on May 17, 2016.

Martin, G. (2015). *Understanding social movements.* New York: Routledge.

Martínez, F. (2013). El periodismo emprendedor en España: una alternativa para contextos de crisis. In & (Eds.), *Comunicación y la Red. Nuevas formas de periodismo* (pp. 75–91). Zaragoza, Spain: Asociación de la Prensa de Aragón.

Masip, P., Guallar, J., Peralta, M., Ruiz, C., & Suau, J. (2015a). Audiencias activas y periodismo. ¿Ciudadanos implicados o consumidores motivados? *Brazilian Journalism Research*, *11*(1), 240–261.

Masip, P., Guallar, J., Suau, J., Ruiz, C., & Peralta, M. (2015b). Información de actualidad y redes sociales: comportamiento de las audiencias. *El profesional de la información*, *24*(4), 363–370.

Masip, P., & Micó, (Eds.). (2010). *La convergència comunicativa a la premsa local i comarcal: noves perspectives per a la informació.* Barcelona, Spain: Generalitat de Catalunya.

Masip, P., & Suau, J. (2014). Audiencias activas y modelos de participación en los medios de comunicación españoles. *Hipertext.net* 12. Retrieved from http://raco.cat/index.php/Hipertext/article/view/274308/364578. Accessed on May 17, 2016.

Merino-Bobillo, M., Lloves-Sobrado, B., & Pérez Guerrero, (2013). La interacción de los usuarios en los perfiles de Facebook de la prensa española. *Palabra clave, 16*(3), 842–872.

Meso, K., Agirreazkuenaga, I., & Larrondo, A. (Eds.). (2015). *Active audiences and journalism. Analysis of the quality and regulation of the user generated contents.* Bilbao, Spain: UPV/EHU.

Meso Ayerdi, K., Larrondo Ureta, A., Peña Fernández, S., & Rivero Santamarina, D. (2014). Active audiences in the mobile ecosystem: Analysis of the interaction options in Spanish cyber media through websites, mobile telephones and tablets. *Hipertext.net* 12. Retrieved from http://raco.cat/index.php/Hipertext/article/view/274309/364491. Accessed on May 17, 2016.

Miranda, S. M., Young, A., & Yetgin, E. (2016). Are social media emancipatory or hegemonic? Societal effects of mass media digitization. *Management Information Systems Quarterly, 40*(2), 303–329.

Mouffe, C. (2005). *On the political.* London: Routledge.

National Readership Survey. (2014). Newsbrands and newspaper supplements. Retrieved from http://goo.gl/fjU07F. April 03, 2015. Accessed on May 17, 2016.

Negroponte, N. (1996). *Being digital.* London: Hodder and Stoughton.

Nip, J. (2006). Exploring the second phase of public journalism. *Journalism Studies, 7*(2), 212–236.

Noguera, J. M. (2010). Redes sociales como paradigma periodístico. *Revista Latina de Comunicación Social, 65,* 176–186.

Olmstead, K., Mitchell, A., & Rosentiel, T. (2011). How users interact with news. *Pew Research Center Journalism & Media.* Retrieved from http://www.journalism.org/2011/05/09/how-users-interact-news/. Accessed on May 17, 2016.

Papacharissi, Z.A. (2010). *A Private Sphere: Democracy in a Digital Age.* Cambridge (UK): Polity Press.

Paulussen, S., Heinonen, A., Domingo, D., & Quandt, T. (2007). Doing it together: Citizen participation in the professional news making process. *Observatorio (OBS) Journal, 1*(3), 131–154.

Pavlik, J. V. (2013). Innovation and the future of journalism. *Digital Journalism, 1*(2), 181–193.

Pavlik, J. V. (2015). Transformation: Examining the implications of emerging technology for journalism, media and society. *Athens Journal of Mass Media and Communications, 1*(1), 9–24.

Peña-Fernández, S., Lazkano-Arrillaga, I., & García González, D. (2016). La transición digital de los diarios europeos: nuevos productos y nuevas audiencias. *Comunicar, 24*(46), 27–36.

Picard, R. G. (2010). The future of the news industry. In J. Curran (Ed.), *Media and society* (pp. 366–379). London: Bloomsbury Academic.

Picard, R. (2014). Twilight or new dawn of journalism? Evidence from the changing news ecosystem. *Journalism Studies, 15*(5), 500–510.

Porlezza, C., & Splendore, S. (2016). Accountability and transparency of entrepreneurial journalism: Unresolved ethical issues in crowdfunded journalism projects. *Journalism Practice*, 10(2), 196–216.

Price, M. E., Rozumilowicz, B., & Verhulst, (Eds.). (2003). *Media reform: Democratizing the media, democratizing the state.* London: Routledge.

Quinn, S. (2009). *MoJo: Mobile journalism in the Asian region.* Singapore: Konrad-Adenauer-Stiftung.

Quintas, N., & González, A. (2014). Audiencias activas: participación de la audiencia social en la televisión. *Comunicar, 43*, 83–90.

Richardson, J. E., & Franklin, B. (2004). Letters of intent: Election campaigning and orchestrated public debate in local newspapers' letters to the editor. *Political Communication*, 21(4), 459–478.

Rodríguez de las Heras, T. (2013). El crowdfunding: una forma de financiación colectiva, colaborativa y participativa de proyectos. *Revista Pensar en Derecho, 3*, 101–123.

Rosen, J. (1999). *What are journalists for?* New Haven, CT: Yale University Press.

Rosentiel, T., &Mitchell, A. (2011). The state of news media 2011. Retrieved from http://www.stateofthemedia.org/2011/overview-2/. Accessed on May 17, 2016.

Ruiz, C., Domingo, D., Micó, Díaz Noci, J., Masip, P., & Meso, K. (2011). Public sphere 2.0? The democratic qualities of citizen debates in online newspapers. *The International Journal of Press/Politics*, 16(4), 463–487.

Said-Hung, E., Serrano-Tellería, A., Garcia-De-Torres, E., Calderín, M., Rost, A., Arcila-Calderón, C., Yezers'ka, L., Edo, C., Rojano, M., Jerónimo, P., & Sánchez-Badillo, J. (2014). Ibero-American online news managers' goals and handicaps in managing social media. *Television & New Media, 15*(6), 577–589.

Salaverría, R. (2012). Medios y periodistas. ¿Un futuro compartido? In *Cuadernos de comunicación Evoca. El futuro del periodismo* edited by Julio Cerezo Gilarranz (pp. 11–15). Madrid, Spain: Evoca Comunicación e Imagen.

Sarsa, J. (2014). El perfil prosumidor de los estudiantes en la web 2.0. *Journal for Educators, Teachers and Trainers, 5*(2), 74–87.

Schlesinger, P., & Doyle, G. (2015). From organizational crisis to multi-platform salvation? Creative destruction and the recomposition of news media. *Journalism*, 16(3), 305–323.

Scolari, C. A. (2012). Are tablets killing the newspaper star? *Hipermediaciones. com.* Retrieved from https://hipermediaciones.com/2012/11/14/tablets-killing-paper-star/. Accessed on May 17, 2016.

Sheller, M. (2015). News now. *Journalism Studies*, 16(1), 12–26.

Siles, I., & Boczkowski, (2012). Making sense of the newspaper crisis: A critical assessment of existing research and an agenda for future work. *New Media & Society*, 14(8), 1375–1394.

Singer, J. B., Domingo, D., Heinonen, A., Hermida, A., Paulussen, S., Quandt, T., Reich, Z., & Vujnovic, M. (2011). *Participatory journalism: Guarding open gates at online newspapers.* New York: Wiley-Blackwell.

Singer, J. B. (2013). "User-generated visibility: Secondary gatekeeping in a shared media space". *New media & society*, 16(1), pp. 55–73.

Springer, N., Engelmann, I., & Pfaffinger, C. (2015). User comments: Motives and inhibitors to write and read. *Information, Communication & Society*, 18(7), 798–815.

Suau, J., & Masip, P. (2014). Exploring participatory journalism in mediterranean countries: Political systems and national differences. *Journalism Practice*, 8(6), 670–687.

Thompson, J. B. (1998). *Los Media y la modernidad: una teoría de los medios de comunicación*. Barcelona, Spain: Paidós.

Thurman, N. (2008). Forums for citizen journalists? Adoption of user generated content initiatives by online news media. *New Media & Society*, 10(1), 139–157.

Toledo Bastos, M. (2014). Shares, pins and tweets: News readership from daily papers to social media. *Journalism Practice*, 6(5–6), 627–637.

Usher, N. (2011). Professional journalists—Hands off! Citizen journalism as civic responsibility. In & (Eds.), *Will the last reporter please turn out the lights: The collapse of journalism and what can be done to fix it* (pp. 264–276). New York: The New Press.

Usher, N. (2015). Newsroom moves and the newspaper crisis evaluated: Space, place, and cultural meaning. *Media, Culture & Society*, 37(7), 1005–1021.

Vujnovic, M., Singer, J., Paulussen, S., Heinonen, A., Reich, Z., Quandt, T., Hermida, A., & Domingo, D.(2010). Exploring the political-economic factors of participatory journalism: Views of online journalists in 10 countries. *Journalism Practice*, 4(3), 285–296.

Wahl Jorgensen, K., Williams, A., & Wardle, C. (2010). Audience views on user-generated content: Exploring the value of news from the bottom up. *Northern Lights. Film and Media Studies Yearbook*, 8, 177–194.

Wasserman, H. (2007). Is a new worldwide web possible? An explorative comparison of the use of ICTs by two South African social movements. *African Studies Review*, 50(1), 109–131.

Wei, R. (2013). Mobile media: Coming of age with a big splash. *Mobile Media & Communication*, 1(1), 50–56.

Westlund, O. (2013). Mobile news. *Digital Journalism*, 1(1), 6–26.

Westlund, O. (2014). The production and consumption of news in an age of mobile media. In G. Goggin & L. Hjorth (Eds.), *The Routledge Companion to Mobile Media* (pp. 135–145). New York: Routledge.

Williams, A., Wardle, C., & Wahl-Jorrgensens, K. (2011). Have they got news for us? Audience revolution or business as usual at the BBC. *Journalism Practice*, 5(1), 85–99.

Yuste, B., & Cabrera, M. (2014). *Emprender en periodismo. Nuevas oportunidades para el profesional de la información*. Barcelona, Spain: Ediciones UOC.

16 Hashtag Wars and Networked Framing

The Private/Public Networked Protest Repertoires of Occupy on Twitter

Sharon Meraz

Introduction

The Occupy movement arose from a mid-July 2011 call from the Canadian magazine Adbusters to end corporate influence on US Wall Street. With the first protest occurring in Lower Manhattan in New York City on September 17, 2011, the movement's timing and concerns co-occurred with similarly themed uprisings in Europe, the MENA region, South America, and Eastern Asia (Hardt and Negri, 2011). Through creative use of social media, Occupy mobilized and spread through offline and online locations, from New York City's Zucotti Park (#ows, #occupywallstreet) to such US cities as Boston (#occupyboston), Denver (#occupydenver), Los Angeles (#occupyla), Oakland (#occupyoakland), San Francisco (#osf), Washington DC (#occupydc), and outside the US (#occupytogether, #occupyeverywhere). The "We are the 99%" refrain resonated with a general public that shared the sense of outrage against longstanding inequities in income distribution (Pew Center for the People and the Press, 2011).

The Occupy Wall Street movement was characterized by an assemblage of mobile tools that provided freedom to frame the movement among participating publics. The Free Network Foundation provided protesters with a Freedom Tower for blanket cell phone coverage, overlaying a decentralized mesh network for Wi-Fi access in New York (Haimson, 2013). Noting that the Occupy Wall Street livestreams of persistent tweets and photos was designed to be "mined and recombined," (Occupy API), Madrigal (2011) referred to this savvy mobile adoption as an "Occupy Wall Street API" and his article sparked a national focus on how this movement's advanced technological and mobile practices enabled open source access to participants to freely define the movement in real time. Protesters, utilizing the personal empowerment of these light, mobile technologies for political purpose, engaged in personal acts of digital mediated activism (Bennett and Segerberg, 2012), to render a plurality of meaning to the essence of the Occupy

Wall Street Movement. The usage of social technologies like Facebook (Carren and Gaby, 2011), Twitter (Gleason, 2013; Penney and Dadas, 2013), and YouTube (Thorson et al., 2013) assisted the digital networking of Occupy Web publics, while facilitating the listening audience's opportunity to learn about the live events.

This current study focuses on the politics of the Occupy movement on Twitter through the study of political hashtags. Theoretically, this paper extends interest to how these personal, political acts of live tweeting the movement by supporters and dissenters can amass to larger, political meaning as expressed through Twitter hashtags. The political interest of this movement, expressed in the open signifier slogan "We are the 99%," enabled distributed protests along acts of economic and social justice as it pertained to wealth inequality. This paper questions how personalized, uncoordinated, and individualized political acts, operationalized through the tweet, can result in larger political meanings about the Occupy Wall Street movement, through an analysis of central political hashtags and the emerging theoretical framework of networked framing.

Methodologically, this study culls a random sample of approximately 300,000 tweets across a longitudinal time frame from October 8, 2011, (approximately three weeks from the movement's inception on September 17), to July 15, 2012, in order to interrogate how Twitter served as a platform for delivering diverse, political messages. This study focuses on the explicit popularity of political hashtags and the usage of these political hashtags as a network strategy for framing partisan political issue and issue sentiment agendas toward the Occupy movement. This study applies novel and sophisticated methodological inquiries of automated content analysis and semantic network analysis, in addition to network visualizations, to explore the associated research questions.

This study also provides a practical assessment of the nature of digital political participation through the lens of a concrete protest event. Statistics suggest that the majority of publics engage with Twitter via a mobile device in comparison to a desktop application (Brandt, 2015; Duggan, 2015). Occupy publics adopted a deliberate mobile stance to afford their flexible, real time self-organization across geographic localities in the US (Heintz, 2011; Madrigal, 2011); thus, this study implicitly assumes that Twitter access through the mobile phone largely facilitated the ease of tweet protest across distributed locations. This study thus makes no distinction between mobile phone usage of Twitter to desktop usage and recognizes that the portability of content and the lightweight features of Twitter can permit seamless integration between mobile and nonmobile access to Twitter. The popularity of Twitter as a vehicle for place-based protest movements is directly tied to its mobile characteristics, and for this study, it is assumed that these sociotechnical mobile affordances largely drive the rhythm of the Occupy protest cycle on Twitter.

Digital Political Participation and Personalized Action Repertoires

The increased mobilization of publics during times of social protest through social media (whether mobile or not) has been globally evidenced, from the Arab Spring protests (Papacharissi & de Fatima Oliveira, 2012; Meraz & Papacharissi, 2013), to the Idle No More movement in Canada (Callison & Hermida), to the growth of the Kony 2012 meme (Lotan et al., 2012). Publics are increasingly engaging in personal digital acts of participation within social technologies that amalgamate these participatory acts through their connective infrastructures and algorithms (Bennett & Segerberg, 2013). The shape of political participation has been altered, moving from real world participation, to third-party organizations online (Karpf, 2012), to technologies that afford personalized, private digital activism on mobile, portable devices. Though these individualized and personalized participatory acts have been derided as armchair activism, clictivism (Karpf, 2012,) or slactivism, Papacharissi (2010) noted this shift as a return to a private sphere of public engagement, while Bennett and Segerberg (2012) have referred to this shift as personalized digitally mediated activism facilitated by the sociotechnical artifice of social media technologies.

With the exception of a few studies (Monterde & Postill, 2013) in the political protest literature, the majority of critical reflections on the changing character of digital political participation purposely blur the distinction between mobile and nonmobile. This lack of distinction clearly reflects the perceived fluidity or hybridity between mobile/nonmobile social media usage, as applications effortlessly port from smartphone application to desktop usage. Yet, deeply suggestive in protest movement analysis of social media is the mobile component, for publics engage in deliberate place-based location strategies to bring tangible form to the movement (Campbell, 2013). Studies that do examine mobile technologies and smartphone usage find increased collective action by political publics through these small, agile, and lightweight tools. Monterde and Postill (2013) found mobile telephony played a significant role in the Spain Indignados (15M) movement through phases of protest preparation, explosion, and diffusion. During the Arab Spring movement, mobile media played a crucial part within the media ecology of social media to afford publics to organize and create alternative protest narratives (Howard & Hussain, 2011; Groshek, 2012; Tufekci & Wilson, 2012). Though this current study makes no explicit distinction between mobile and nonmobile access to Twitter, it recognizes that Twitter provides the unique affordances of mobility for real-time documentation of protest frames.

Social Media, Social Movements, and Occupy Wall Street

As mentioned earlier, the majority of prior studies examine mobile phone usage as part of the general ecology of social media usage in mobilization of protest. Scholars argue that social media enable social revolutions to sustain mutation, achieve sustained visibility, and create contagion, thus sustaining a new brand of network repertoires (Nielsen, 2012; Rushkoff, 2013). Social media platforms also enable social movements to embrace their nonlinear, complex narratives (Rushkoff, 2013), while enabling individuals to reflect on their individual/personalized narratives within the social glue of Web 2.0 connective architectures (Bennett and Segerberg, 2012). Twitter enables networked Web publics to share information and coordinate protests during times of social movements. For example, protests in Egypt gave rise to new elites (Lotan et al., 2010; Dunn, 2011; Khamis and Vaughan, 2011; Tufekci, 2012; Meraz and Papacharissi, 2013). Twitter has sustained new models for news production (Hermida, 2010, 2012; Lewis and Usher, 2013). News emanating from Twitter's social stream is best described as an emotive stream of strong affect mixed with issue and substance (Papacharissi and de Fatima Oliveira, 2012). Research on Twitter's usage during the Occupy movement found that Twitter was used as a source for information diffusion over and above calls to participation or organizing/coordinating protests (Theocharis et al., 2013). Twitter's brevity of form also enabled rhetorical velocity, enabling information to cascade and gain contagion more swiftly than long-form, textual narratives (Carren and Gaby, 2011). This study builds on prior work about Twitter hashtags and framing effects (Yardi & boyd, 2010; Conover et al., 2011; Pew Center for the People and the Press, 2011; Small, 2011; Meraz & Papacharissi, 2013) to examine how Twitter's sociotechnical architecture of mention signs, retweet signs, and hashtags enables new networked framing practices to emerge and be sustained.

Networked Framing and Twitter Hashtags as Frame Vehicles

The inclusive, participatory logic of social media technologies now challenges the theory of elite media framing, through its deliberate fostering of nonelite, content creation and citizen-to-citizen connectivity. Revising the prior framing theory of media effects, Meraz and Papacharissi (2013) define *networked framing* as "a process through which particular problem definitions, causal interpretations, moral evaluations, and/or treatment recommendations attain prominence through *crowdsourcing practices*." These crowdsourcing practices enable publics to engage in issue framing, with frames collated via computer algorithms that amalgamate the crowdsourced preferences of both nonelite and elite publics

(Halavais, 2009). Meraz and Papacharissi (2016) noted that the theory of networked framing is driven by such processes as collaborative filtering and homophilic tendencies. Both of these processes can reduce informational diversity in ideologically consonant networks, resulting in partisan issue framing along partisan lines within partisan political blogs (Meraz, 2009, 2011a, in press). This study specifically applies this theory to the framing that occurs through Twitter's addressivity marker of the hashtag.

Hashtags as Frame Markers

The usage of Twitter hashtags as an organic, community-level convention for annotating tweets can be viewed through the lens of networked framing (Meraz and Papacharissi, 2013, 2016). Hashtags add additional context to tweets (Bruns and Burgess, 2011; Zangerle et al., 2011), and they function as a way for users to self-curate the Web by tagging their content with lightweight, semantic annotations. As Meraz and Papacharissi (2013, 2016) note, hashtags can be utilized as outward markers of the ebb and flow of network frames as they are being negotiated by real time publics while news is in its premediated form.

Several prior studies have examined hashtags as vehicles that sustain framing effects during social movements and protest cycles. Papacharissi and de Fatima Oliveira (2012) found that during the Egyptian uprisings tags like #sidibouzid, #Algeria, #Iran, #Libya, and #Bahrain connected the #Egypt uprisings to eruptions in the Arab Spring geographical area. Meraz and Papacharissi (2013) found that publics broadcasting and listening through Twitter utilized hashtags like #jan25, #Cairo, #Mubarak, and #Tahrir to label the uprisings by key geographic locations and focal dates. During the Occupy movement, the utilization of the #wearethe-99percent operated as a floating signifier, an open container for publics to engage in fluid framing of the movement by its diverse concerns (Pew Center for the People and the Press, 2011).

Outside of protest cycles, the 2012 US presidential debates enabled nontraditional political publics to utilize the "big bird" and "horses and bayonets" phrases as memes for humoristic framing of the debates. Diverse political publics can also utilize Twitter to register their non-mainstream political sentiments: a significant body of research is now emerging on Black Twitter (more references Brock, 2012; Florini, 2013). As it relates to specific hashtags, Sharma (2013) found that racialized hashtags utilized by Black Twitter publics such as #onlyintheghetto or #ifsantawasblack enable the transmission of widespread social commentary about the possibilities of black identity online. It is thus possible to understand the arc of a political cause or issue through the most popular hashtags that emerge as frame markers of the event.

This study sought to determine what popular Twitter hashtags emerged as frame markers for the Occupy movement. Prior studies have found that Twitter hashtags can encode both content and sentiment metadata (Laniado and Mika, 2010; González-Ibáñez et al., 2011; Kouloumpis et al., 2011). Prior studies have examined the hashtag as a vehicle for content framing (for example, #economy), sentiment or affect framing (for example, #solidarity), and as sentiment and content framing conjointly (for example, #getmoneyout) (Wang et al., 2011). Several studies have suggested that affective hashtags enable crowd-centered tweets to build in intensity, lending shape and form to emotion online (Papacharissi and de Fatima Oliveira, 2012; Meraz and Papacharissi, 2013). This study advances the following research question:

RQ1: What were some of the most popular political hashtags utilized in the framing of the Occupy movement by Occupy Twitter Web publics?

The relationship of political hashtags to other hashtags within tweets can be a source of networked framing effects along issue and issue-sentiment markers. Co-occurring hashtags and nonhashtag content have been found to reflect the tweet agenda (Khabiri et al., 2012; Costa et al., 2013). Viewing hashtags and their co-occurrences as a network capable of sustaining robust, framing effects, this study advances the following research question:

RQ2: How can the politics of the Occupy movement be discerned from an analysis of political hashtag co-occurrences on Twitter as utilized by Occupy publics?

Outside networked relationships with other hashtags, prior studies on Twitter in politics have found individual political hashtags to be a powerful vehicle for sustained networked framing effects. Popular hashtags are not only characterized by high fecundity and longevity, but afford the crowd-sourcing of issue and issue-sentiment frames through replication, mutation, and refashioning of associated narratives. During the 2012 Presidential Election debates, users from polar political groups engaged in hashtag wars to reframe the political debate through carefully chosen hashtags (for example #obamacare by the Right, and #iloveobamacare by the Left) (Fineman, 2012). The persistence of political partisanship has also been observed (Conover et al., 2011; Livine et al., 2011): politically motivated individuals often inject partisan content into ideologically opposed tweet streams (Yardi and boyd, 2010; Conover et al., 2011; Bode et al., in press) in an effort to hijack or pollute the hashtag frame with cross-ideological noise. This study advanced the following, final research question:

RQ3: How do Occupy publics utilize popular political discussion hashtags #p2, #tcot, and #tlot as vehicles for engaging in partisan networked framing of the Occupy movement?

Methods

Utilizing the Twitter API through a partnership with TNS Political and Social and Vigiglobe (a company that specializes in Social Media Intelligence Services) and adopting a stratified, random sampling with #ows as a keyword, a random 10% of Occupy tweets were pulled on a weekly basis from October 8, 2011 (approximately three weeks from the movement's inception on September 17) to July 15, 2012. During this 10-month time frame, a total of 279,597 tweets were culled, thus providing a large, random sample from which to discern political issue and issue sentiment frames.

Tweets were then parsed and entered into a database, enabling queries to be written against the database for hashtag frequency (RQ1), hashtag co-occurrences (RQ2), and tweet issue and issue sentiment as emanating from select hashtags #p2, #tcot, and #tlot (RQ3). Prior studies have unveiled the ubiquitous prevalence of a power law in Web networks (Barabasi et al., 2000; Perline, 2005), defined as a scenario where a few users or items are responsible for the majority of attention (Singh and Jain, 2010; Papacharissi and Meraz, 2012; Meraz and Papacharissi, 2013). The most popular hashtags that emerged as political markers of the movement were identified and manually coded in the following manner, in keeping with the general substantive/affective frame codes as adopted in former studies (Wang et al., 2011): (1) Frames of objects and issues (includes named-entity hashtags such as persons [for example, #barackobama], organizations [for example, #wallstreet], geolocations [for example, #occupyboston], issues [for example, #economy], events [for example, #policebrutality], and political discussion communities [for example, #p2]; (2) Frames of sentiment (includes hashtags like #solidarity and #wearethe99percent); (3) Frames of sentiment and issue (includes hashtags like #getmoneyout); and (4) Other. From this coding scheme, it was possible to determine how political hashtags were popularized and utilized as a marker for the networked framing of the Occupy movement's political goals (RQ1).

This study's interest in the theoretical processes of networked framing was advanced through RQ2, which sought to determine how hashtags co-existed in networked linkages with each other. Queries were made against the database for hashtag co-occurrences as they were present within all 300,000 tweets. The result of these findings afforded networked analysis and visualizations of hashtag clusters, and thus, further interpretations of how the Occupy movement's political concerns were developed through the processes of networked framing in hashtags (RQ2).

This study provided a focused analysis on the popular hashtag political discussion communities' #p2, #tcot, and #tlot (RQ3), in order to determine how these vehicles enabled distributed framing of the Occupy movement. This question involved the automated process of semantic network analysis. In order to reduce noise and type 2 error inflation, tweets that were specifically targeted to each hashtag community (as opposed to tweets spammed across all 3 communities) were filtered for analysis. Semantic network analysis (Danowski et al., 2011; Danowski, 2012; Yuan, Feng, and Danowski, 2013), sometimes referred to as network text analysis (Danowski, 1982, Diesner and Carley, 2005), refers to automated methods for mining interrelationships among word concepts in text. This study utilized the network-based content analysis methodology called windowing, a process that mines word proximal co-occurrences in order to make emergent networked frame agendas. This study replicated former studies that have examined semantic network analysis in social media data (Yuan et al., 2013). The three tweet streams from #p2, #tcot, and #tlot were exported without addressivity markers (@, VIA, and RT signs) and URLs, and further cleaned in the text analysis program Automap through minimal reductionist techniques of applying a small stopword list. To create networked relationships among words, the program Wordij, a proximity based word pair extraction program used in several prior studies (Danowski, 1982, 1993, 2008, 2010, 2012; Danowski and Lind, 2001; Danowski et al., 2011; Yuan et al., 2013), was utilized to create the most frequently occurring word pairs in the tweets. These word co-occurences, exported as networked data matrices, were further analyzed via community detection algorithms and cluster analysis within Excel's NodeXL. These clusters enabled an automated detection to the frames and facilitated visualizations in Gephi, a network analysis program. Manual checks against a random 10% of tweets across the three ideological streams confirmed the appropriateness of this automated cluster analysis methodology as accurate for investigating the relationship between networked linkages word pairs and broad-based, networked framing effects.

Results

The Role of Politics as a Central Frame in the Occupy Movement

Of the top 200 hashtags adopted by the Occupy movement (see Figure 16.1), approximately 83% were primarily adopted for named-entity framing of persons (for example, #obama), organizations (for example, #teaparty), other political discussion groups (for example, #p21 and #topprog), or events (for example, #sopa), as opposed to being used for sentiment framing (11%) or sentiment issue framing (6%). Leading sentiment frames suggested a broad desire by Occupy publics to frame the movement through change (#revolution, #protest, #freedom, #liberty, #justice, #activism, #anarchist, #fail) as well as through positive, collective metaphors (#solidarity, #truth, #peace, #love, and #funny). An examination of the leading sentiment issue frames, or hashtags that incorporated both sentiment and issue words, were primarily focused on a few leading themes: spreading the revolution (#occupyeverything, #occupytogether,

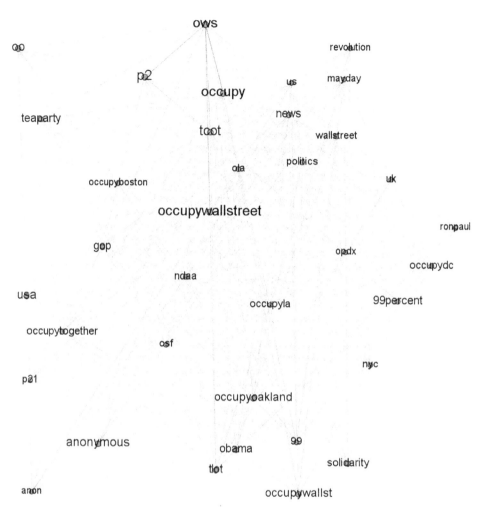

Figure 16.1 Network visualization of top 200 hashtags.

#occupymedia, #occupyflickr, #usrevolution, #globalrevolution), documenting police brutality (#ftp, #policestate, #policebrutality), cataloging economic corruption (#endthefed, #ffraud, and #nonato), and canvassing for women's rights (#waronwomen). The movement was also not without its leading humor hashtags (for example, #otb for occupy the bathroom).

RQ1 sought to determine the relative popularity of political hashtags as a political framing device for interpreting the Occupy Wall Street movement. Figure 16.1 provides a network visualization of the interrelationships among these top 200 hashtags, with node label size determined by the degree centrality (or frequency of usage). As evidenced by the size of the hashtags, #ows, #occupywallstreet, and #occupy had the high-degree centrality, suggesting that these tags operated as open or floating signifiers, connecting the fluid and diverse concerns of the movement. High-degree centrality tags also revealed the prevalence of leading political discussion tags #p2 (4th most popular tag), #tcot (5th most popular tag), #teaparty (6th most popular tag), and #tlot (8th most popular tag). Coding the top 200 hashtags for leading named-entity classifications revealed the centrality of politics. Geolocation frames or hashtags (for example, #occupywallstreet, #occupyoakland, and #occupyla) represented the majority of these hashtags, 37% of the 166 named entity hashtags cited. Both political hashtags (political discussion communities/politicians) and issue hashtags were the next popular categories, representing 16% of named-entity hashtags. Less common were organizational hashtags, such as Occupy assemblies (#nycsc), anonymous groups (#opesr), and media (#cnn), which accounted for 11% of named-entity hashtags. Occupy protest events (for example, #generalstrike) also accounted for only 8% of popular hashtag frames.

Networked Framing through Networks of Hashtags

Hashtag Co-occurrences

RQ2 sought to determine how groups of co-occurring hashtags aided in a further analysis of the framing of this movement's political concerns (RQ2). Distinct differences emerged in how leading political hashtags (#p2, #tcot, #tlot, and #teaparty) were utilized with other co-occurring hashtags (political and nonpolitical). All four hashtags most popularly recurred in a cross-ideological fashion with other political discussion communities, suggesting either (a) an attempt by Occupy publics to address all communities together or (b) an attempt by partisan Occupy publics to engage in hashtag hijacking or hashtag wars.

All four hashtags most commonly occurred with the floating signifier #ows. The next leading co-occurrence was #p2 and #tcot (present 9,626 times). The progressive hashtag #p2 was less prevalent as a co-occurrence with all other political hashtags thereafter. Other popular co-occurrences among these four leading hashtags was the pairing of #tcot and #teaparty (present 5,266 times), and #tcot and #tlot (present 5,089 times). This strong partisan homophily was mirrored in the lesser co-occurrences of #tlot and #p2 (present 3,957 times) and #teaparty and #p2 (present 3,286). The #p2 progressive hashtag appeared 56% of the time with other conservative political hashtags (#cspj, #gop, #republicans, #rnc, #sgp, #tcot, #teaparty, #tpp, #twisters, and #romney), almost twice as much as compared to its pairing with other progressive hashtags (#connecttheleft, #ctl, #dem, #democrats, #dems, #dnc, #p21, #p2b, #topprog, #tpot, #tyt, and #obama). This was unlike the #tcot political hashtag, which was almost as likely to appear with these conservative tags (38%) as progressive tags (42%). Both the #teaparty and #tlot were more likely to appear in linkages with other conservative hashtags (46% and 60% respectively) when compared with either libertarian hashtags (24% and 6% respectively) or progressive hashtags (28% and 34% respectively).

Political hashtags #tcot, #teaparty, and #tlot were also less likely to be utilized alongside other nonpolitical hashtags, suggesting a looser identification of conservative politics with the widespread goals of this movement and, furthermore, an attempt by conservative publics to pollute the Occupy stream through conscious hashtag stuffing of ideologically homophilous political hashtags in memetic linkages. For example, the progressive hashtag #p2 was also more likely to have co-occurrences with geographic hashtags documenting dispersions of the Occupy movement (37% for #p2 in comparison with 32% for #tcot, 29% for #teaparty, and 24% for #tlot) and twice as likely to co-occur with Occupy event hashtags (for example, #mayday) when compared with all other nonprogressive political discussion hashtags.

Issue and Issue Sentiment Networked Framing in Political Hashtag Memplexes

Figures 16.2 through 16.4 provide a semantic network analysis of tweets and popular hashtags as occurring through #p2, #tlot, and #tcot in an effort to analyze RQ3. These visualizations depict issue and issue-sentiment frames emerging through word proximity and cluster/ community detection algorithms (colored by similar frames), with word size determined by degree centrality or popularity of the word usage. Evident in these visualizations are strong, partisan differences in the political frames emerging around the Occupy movement, suggesting that personalized politics, encouraged through social technologies, afforded partisan networked framing of the Occupy movement.

Figure 16.2 provides a semantic network visualization of the tweets emanating from those Occupy publics directing their messages to conservative political discussion group #tcot. For these publics, the Occupy demographics were targeted as rich kids that did not want to make money, get jobs, and pay their debt. Consonant with conservative politics, they suggested that Obama was doing a poor job and that state politicians should control policy such that power should be returned to states from a federal government that is becoming too big. These publics connected this growth as a big threat to liberty and love and yearned to take back the country. Co-occurring hashtag proximities with #tcot further sought to contrast the Occupy movement (#ows) sharply with the #teaparty movement. Similar to prior studies on Tea Party politics (Armey and Kibbe, 2010; Rasmussen and Schoen, 2010), Web publics utilizing conservative political hashtags accused the Occupy movement of rape and fraud. The co-occurrence of #tcot with conservative hashtags #glennbeck (Glenn Beck) and #tpp (Tea Party Participants) links the conservative counter-framing of the Occupy movement to the backdrop of the politics of the Tea Party movement.

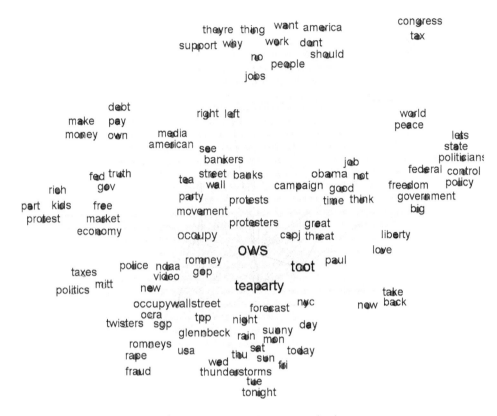

Figure 16.2 Frames arising from tweets containing #tcot hashtag.

Conversely, Occupy publics utilizing #p2 identified this movement as a source for real change in getting corporate influence and Wall Street power out of government policy and sought to influence the government in the direction of becoming more of a party for the people (Figure 16.3). Publics tweeting with the #p2 hashtag called for a redistribution of income from rich to poor by not forcing the poor to pay taxes and ending George Bush era corporate tax cuts. Sympathizing, progressive publics framed political messages of support for house democrats in standing against Wall Street corruption and banking fraud and provided calls to the Obama administration to craft new economic policy and a jobs bill, while asking Republicans to vote for these changes. Occupy publics tweeting with the #p2 tag posted information for supporters to circumvent brutality from police, specifically in Oakland and New York. Publics also utilized #p2 to engage in dialogue about the Trayvon Martin shooting, the war on women, and marriage equality. Overall, the prevalence of words like join, change, need, sign, support, vote, end, and watch, in addition to sentiments such as justice and protest, aligned the

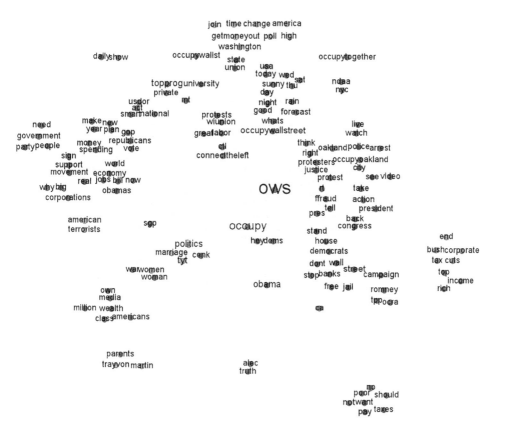

Figure 16.3 Frames arising from tweets containing #p2 hashtag.

#p2 hashtag with primarily positive messages directed at supporting the Occupy movement.

Both sets of frames contrast sharply with libertarian frames arising from #tlot and its hashtag-networked relationships. The #tlot movement showed broad concerns with largely libertarian ideals. For #tlot Web publics, Americans are not safer due to failed foreign wars and due to a government that has usurped individuals/groups/members civil liberties. Emphasis in #tlot was placed on the growth of a surveillance state, highlighted through framing the Occupy movement against the anonymous movement. Focus was placed on monetary policy discussions, which included discussing the government's failed tax policies, dollar devaluation, American unemployment growth, and American debt. Ron Paul was positioned within the network as a corrective to the concerns of both the libertarian movement and Occupy politics, evidenced by the high-degree centrality of the hashtag #ronpaul and its strong connections to global hashtags #ows and #occupywallstreet.

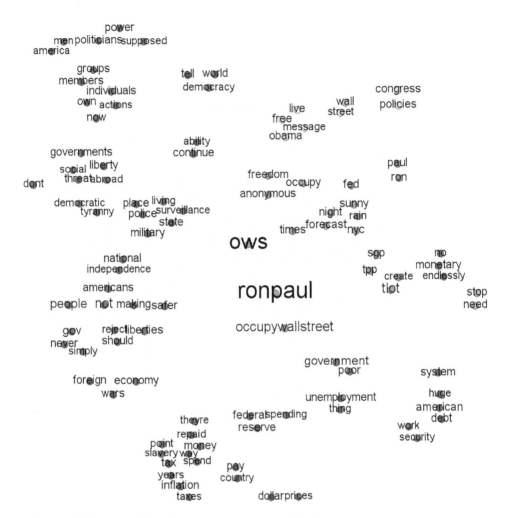

Figure 16.4 Frames arising from tweets containing #tlot hashtag.

Discussion

This paper sought to determine how the face of political participation is being altered by technologies that permit personalized digital political activism through tools that amalgamate these acts into public narratives. This study's emphasis on Twitter is meant to underscore the significance of its mobile platform as central to the infrastructure of the Occupy movement that enabled personalized digital activism among distributed publics seeking to engage with framing the movement. This study advances theoretical understanding of networked framing through emphasis on the hashtag as a lightweight marker for enabling personalized digital activism among political publics. Moreso, this study presents an interesting methodological suit of automated content analysis and semantic network analysis. Using this toolkit, this study examine how the movement's technological sophistication afforded publics frames about the Occupy movement to emerge from private usage of the technology by publics to record sentiment.

Though this study is limited by its focus on popular, emerging hashtags in a political context, its core contribution is the ability to detect the ebb and flow of a political issue through the monitoring of its popular hashtags as they coalesce in networked linkages with each other. Findings for the first research question revealed positive sentiment frames (#revolution, #protest, #freedom, #liberty, #justice, #activism, #anarchist, and #fail) and collective metaphors (#solidarity, #truth, #peace, #love, and #funny) that existed alongside the movement's desire to frame itself politically. Hashtags documenting police brutality, economic corruption, and women's rights anchored the movement in the politics of the 99%. Alongside these diverse political concerns were dense, complex hashtag linkages that broadened the reach and charge of the hashtag framing effects across a range of political communities. Evidence of strong partisan homophily, seen by co-occurences of hashtag conservative communities (#tcot, #cspj, #gop, #republicans, #rnc, #sgp, #teaparty, #tpp, #twisters, and #romney) and hashtag progressive communities (#p2, #connecttheleft, #ctl, #dem, #democrats, #dems, #dnc, #p21, #p2b, #topprog, #tpot, #tyt, and #obama), was equally counterbalanced by appearances of conservative and liberal hashtag co-occurrences.

This study also argues for the applicability of networked framing as a more suitable theoretical process for described, crowd-centered participation on Twitter. Unlike how issues were selectively framed in the past era of vertically distributed media power in an environment of limited media supply (Reese, 2001; Anderson, 2006), Web 2.0 applications now tap the wisdom of horizontal, crowd intelligence, utilizing algorithms that curate and compile audience metadata to reveal popular viewpoints that have competed in the public's marketplace of attention. Hashtags provided open calls for producer partisans to participate in the ideological crowdsourced framing of the politics of the Occupy movement. As Figures 16.2, 16.3, and 16.4 reveal, these political hashtags functioned as memetic markers for the emergence of political, partisan frames. Future studies are encouraged to further the analysis of hashtag framing through referencing contexts both within and outside the domain of social movements.

Prior studies have found a strong presence of conservatives over democrats on Twitter (Conover et al., 2011; Livine et al., 2011), and this study revealed that addressing the conservative community appeared the preoccupation of other political communities. This study's findings unearthed the persistence of a hashtag battle/frame battle in representing the political concerns of the movement. Occupy publics utilizing the #p2 hashtag were more likely to also utilize conservative hashtag networks as opposed to progressive hashtag networks. Libertarian and Tea Party publics, tweeting about the Occupy movement, also directed the majority of their political tweets toward the conservative community. These findings suggest that Twitter's open architecture, which enables interpretative flexibility (Pinch and Bijker, 1984), may not be such a good thing for listening publics, who now have more noise embedded in the signal. Though broadcasting publics may successfully advance their own ideological agendas and dilute competing ones, listening and participating publics seeking to learn about movements may find this media climate hostile. Hashtag wars can prove detrimental to the identity of developing social movements, as it can frustrate the ability of the movement to disseminate news and information, thus alienating or distancing supportive publics.

Future studies are encouraged to broaden the field of hashtag networked framing to incorporate other political groups that may not be so ideological. Yet, through this focused semantic network analysis, this study revives concerns about the growth of political polarization by providing solid evidence of partisan framing of the Occupy movement's political concerns. Political communication scholars have renewed fears of political polarization (Stroud 2011; Knobloch-Westerwick and Meng, 2012), specifically in relation to the growth of new media forms that encourage a heightened level of selective partisan attention (Baum and Groeling, 2008; Meraz, 2011a,b). The persistence of homophily as an organizing principle (McPherson et al., 2001) has resulted in further fragmentation of Web publics along ideological divides online. Though few studies have been conducted on Twitter that support ideological polarity (Yardi and boyd, 2010), this study's findings revealed a heightened level of ideological polarity among mobile Occupy publics that directed their political tweets toward singular, ideological communities.

Future studies are also encouraged to make further distinctions in social media technologies between mobile and nonmobile access. Mobile media affords select advantages due to its features of ubiquity, perpetual contact, instant information, location-based service, and personalization. The growing mobile youth culture (Mihailidis, 2014; Vanden Abeele, 2016), alongside the increasing significance of mobility (Campbell, 2013) to place-based social media activism, assures that mobile media studies will continue to burgeon in the upcoming years.

References

Anderson, C. (2006). The long tail: why the future of business is selling less of more. New York: Hyperion.

Armey, D., & Kibbe, M. (2010). *Give us liberty: A tea party manifesto.* New York: William Morrow.

Barabasi, A.L., Albert, R., Jeong, H., & Bianconi, G. (2000). Power law distribution of the World Wide Web. *Science, 287*(5461), 2115.

Baum, M.A., & Groeling, T. (2008). New media and the polarization of American political discourse. *Political Communication, 25*(4), 345–365.

Bennett, L. and Segerberg, A. (2013). *The logic of connective action: Digital media and the personalization of contentious politics.* Cambridge: Cambridge University Press.

Bennett, L., & Segerberg, A. (2012). The logic of connective action. *Information, Communication & Society, 15*(5), 739–768.

Bode, L., Hanna, A., Yang, J., & Shah, D. (in press). Candidate networks, citizen clusters and political expression: strategic hashtag use in the 2010 midterms. *The Annals of the American Academy of Political and Social Science, 659*(1), 149–165.

Brandt, M. (2015). 80% of Twitter users are mobile. *Statista.* Available at https://www.statista.com/chart/1520/number-of-monthly-active-twitter-users/.

Brock, A. (2012). From the blackhand side: Twitter as a cultural conversation. *Journal of Broadcasting & Electronic Media, 46*(4), 529–549.

Bruns, A. (2005). *Gatewatching: Collaborative online news production.* New York: Peter Lang.

Bruns, A., & Burgess, J. (2011). *The use of twitter hashtags in the formation of ad hoc publics.* Presented at the European Consortium for Political Research Conference, Reykjavik, Iceland, August 24–27, 2011.

Campbell, S. S. (2013). Mobile media and communication: a new field or just a new journal. *Mobile Media and Communication, 1*(1), 8–13.

Carren, N., & Gaby, S. (2011). Occupy online: Facebook and the spread of Occupy Wall Street. Available at http://papers.ssrn.com/sol3/papers.cfm?abstract_id=1943168. Accessed July 17, 2013.

Conover, M. D., Ratkiewicz, J., Francisco, M., Goncalves, B., Flammini, A., & Mencer, F. (2011). Political polarization on Twitter. Available at http://truthy.indiana.edu/site_media/pdfs/conover_icwsm2011_polarization.pdf. Accessed September 10, 2013.

Costa, J., Silva, C., Antunes, M., & Ribeiro, B. (2013). Defining semantic meta-hashtags for Twitter classification. *Adaptive and Natural Computing Algorithms 7824*, 226–235.

Danowski, J. (1982). A network-based content analysis methodology for computer-mediated communication: An illustration with a computer bulletin board. In M. Burgoon (Ed.), *Communication yearbook 5* (pp. 904–925). New Brunswick, NJ: Transaction Books.

Danowski, J. (1993). Network analysis of message content. In G. Barnett & W. Richards (Eds.), *Progress in communication sciences* XII (pp. 197–222). Norwood, NJ: Ablex.

Danowski, J. A., & Lind, R. (2001). A computer con- tent analysis linking gender language in presidential candidates' news to gender gaps in polls. In M. West (Ed.), *Applications of computer content analysis* (pp. 157–167). Westport, CT: Ablex Publishing.

Danowski, J. A. (2008). Short-term and long-term effects of a public relations campaign on semantic networks of newspaper content: Priming or framing?. *Public Relations Review 34*, 288–290.

Danowski, J. (2010). Inferences from word networks in messages. In K. Krippendorff & M. Bock (Eds.), *The content analysis reader* (pp. 421–430). Thousand Oaks, CA: Sage.

Danowski, J. (2012). Social network size and designers' semantic networks for collaboration. *International Journal of Organization Design and Engineering, 2*(4/2012), 343–361.

Danowski, J., Duran, M., Diaz, A., & Jimenez, J. (2011). Semantic networks for corporate communication concepts and crisis: Differences based on corporate reputation. *Observatorio (OBS*), 6*(2), 127–145.

Diesner, J., & Carley, K. M. (2005). Revealing social strucure from texts: Meta-matrix text analysis as a novel method for network text analysis. In V. K. Narayanan & D. J. Armstrong (Eds.), *Causal mapping for information systems and technology research* (pp. 81–108). Harrisburg, PA: Idea Group Publishing.

Duggan, M. (2015). Mobile messaging and social media 2015. Pew Research Center. Available at http://www.pewinternet.org/2015/08/19/mobile-messaging-and-social-media-2015/.

Dunn, A. (2011). Unplugging a nation: State media strategy during Egypt's January 25 uprising. *Fletcher Forum of World Affairs, 35*(2), 15–24.

Fineman, H. (2012). The hashtag campaign. In The Huffington Post. Available at: http://www.huffingtonpost.com/2012/04/27/hashtag-campaign-obama-romney-student-loans_n_1458922.html. Accessed July 17, 2013.

Florini, S. (2013). Tweets, tweeps and signifin': Communication and cultural performance on Black Twitter. *Television & New Media 15*(3), 223–237.

Gleason, B. (2013). #Occupy wall street: Exploring informal learning about a social movement on Twitter. *American Behavioral Scientist, 57*(7), 966–982.

González-Ibáñez, R., Muresan, S., & Wacholder, N. (2011). Identifying sarcasm in Twitter: A closer look. *Proceedings of the 49th annual meeting of the Association for Computational Linguistics*, Portland, Oregon, June 19–24, 2011.

Groshek, J. (2012). Forecasting and observing: A cross-methodological consideration of Internet and mobile phone diffusion in the Egyptian revolt. *International Communication Gazette, 74*(8), 750–768.

Haimson, O. L. (2013). Using information science to explore Occupy Wall Street. Ideals. Available at https://www.ideals.illinois.edu/bitstream/handle/2142/42045/353.pdf?sequence=2.

Halavais, A. (2009). *Search engine society*. Cambridge, UK: Polity Press.

Hardt, M., & Negri, A. (2011). The fight for 'real democracy' at the heart of Occupy Wall Street. *Foreign Affairs* 11. Available at: https://www.foreignaffairs.com/articles/north-america/2011-10-11/fight-real-democracy-heart-occupy-wall-street.

Heintz, L. (2011). The gadgets of #occupy. *Motherboard*. Available at http://motherboard.vice.com/blog/the-occupy-meme-phenomena-and-the-tech-side-of-a-revolution.

Hermida, A. (2010). Twittering the news. *Journalism Practice, 4*(3), 297–308.

Hermida, A. (2012). Tweets and truth: Journalism as a discipline of collaborative verification. *Journalism Practice, 6*(5–6), 659–668.

Howard, P. N., & Hussain, M. M. (2011). The upheavals in Egypt and Tunisia. *Journal of Democracy, 22*(3), 35–48.

Karpf, D. (2012). *The moveon effect: the unexpected transformation of American political advocacy.* New York: Oxford University Press.

Khabiri, E., Caverlee, J., & Kamdath, K. (2012). Predicting semantic annotations on the real time Web. *Proceedings of the 23rd Association for Computer Machinery Conference on Hypertext and Social Media*, Milwaukee, Wisconsin, June 25–28, 2012 (pp. 219–228). New York: AMC.

Khamis, S., & Vaughan, K. (2011). Cyberactivism in the Egyptian revolution: How civic engagement and citizen journalism tilted the balance. *Arab Media and Society, 13.* Available at http://www.arabmediasociety.com/?article=769.

Knobloch-Westerwick, S., & *Meng, J. (2011). Reinforcement of the political self through selective exposure to political messages. *Journal of Communication, 61,* 349–368.

Kouloumpis, E., Wilson, T., & Moore, J. (2011). Twitter sentiment analysis: The good, the bad, and the OMG! In *Proceedings of the 5th International AAAI Conference on Weblogs and Social Media*, Barcelona, Spain, July 17–21, 2011 (pp. 538–541). Menlo Park, CA: The AAAI Press.

Laniado, D., & Mika, P. (2010). Making sense of twitter. In *Proceedings of the 9th International Semantic Web Conference on the Semantic Web*, Shanghai, China, November 7–11, 2010 (pp. 470–485). Berlin: Springer-Verlag.

Lewis, S. C., & Usher, N. (2013). Open source and journalism: Toward new frameworks for imagining news innovation. *Media, Culture & Society, 35*(4), 602–619.

Livine, A., Simmons, M. P., Adar, E., & Adamic, L. A. (2011). The party is over here: structure and content in the 2010 election. Presented at: *ICWSM-11*, Barcelona, Spain, July 17–21, 2011.

Lotan, G., Graeff, E., Ananny, M., Gaffney, D., Pearce, I., & boyd, d. (2010). The revolutions were tweeted: Information flows during the 2011 Tunisian and Egyptian revolutions. *International Journal of Communications, 5,* 1375–1405.

Madrigal, A. (2011). A guide to the Occupy Wall Street API, or why the nerdiest way to think about OWS is so useful. *The Atlantic.* Available at http://www.theatlantic.com/technology/archive/2011/11/a-guide-to-the-occupy-wall-street-api-or-why-the-nerdiest-way-to-think-about-ows-is-so-useful/248562/.

McPherson, M., Smith-Lovin, L., & Cook, J. M. (2001). Birds of a feather flock together: Homophily in social networks. *Annual Review of Sociology, 27,* 415–444.

Meraz, S. (2009). 'Is there an elite hold? Traditional media to social media influence in blog networks', *Journal of Computer-Mediated Communication, 14*(3): 682–707.

Meraz, S. (2011a). Using time series analysis to measure intermedia agenda setting influence in traditional media and political blog networks. *Journalism and Mass Communication Quarterly, 88*(1), 176–194.

Meraz, S. (2011b). The fight for 'how to think': Traditional media, social networks, and issue interpretation. *Journalism: Theory, Practice, and Criticism, 12*(1), 107–127.

Meraz, S. (in press). Quantifying partisan selective exposure through network text analysis of elite political blog networks during the US 2012 Presidential Election. *Journal of Information Technology & Politics.*

Meraz, S., & Papacharissi, Z. (2013). Networked gatekeeping and networked framing on #egypt. *International Journal of Press/Politics, 18*(2), 138–166.

Meraz, S., & Papacharissi, Z. (2016). Networked gatekeeping and framing. In T. Witschge, C. W. Anderson, D. Domingo, & A. Hermida (Eds.), *The sage handbook of digital journalism.*

Mihailidis, P. (2014). A tethered generation: exploring the role of mobile phones in the daily life of young people. *Mobile Media and Communication, 2*(1), 58–72.

Monterde, A. & Postill, J. (2013). Mobile ensembles: the uses of mobile phones for social protest by Spain's indignados. In G. Goggin & L. Hjorth (Eds.), *Routledge companion to mobile media.* London: Routledge.

Nielsen, R. K. (2012). Mundane internet tools, the risk of exclusion, and reflexive movements—Occupy Wall Street and political uses of digital networked technologies. *The Sociological Quarterly, 54,* 173–177.

Papacharissi, Z. (2010). *A private sphere: democracy in a digital age.* Cambridge, UK: Policy Press.

Papacharissi, Z., & de Fatima Oliveira, M. (2012). Affective news and networked publics: The rhythms of news storytelling on #egypt. *Journal of Communication, 62*(2), 266–82.

Papacharissi, Z., & Meraz, S. (2012). The rhythms of occupy: Broadcasting and listening practices on #ows. *The Annual Convention of the Association of Internet Researchers 13,* Salford, UK, October 17–21, 2012.

Penney, J., & Dadas, C. (2013). Tweeting in the service of protest: Digital composition and circulation in the Occupy Wall Street movement. *New Media and Society.* doi:10.1177/1461444813479593.

Perline, R. (2005). Strong, weak and inverse power laws. *Statistical Science, 20*(1), 68–88.

Pew Center for the People and the Press. (2011). Public divided over occupy Wall Street movement. At http://www.people-press.org/2011/10/24/public-divided-over-occupy-wall-street-movement/. Accessed July 17, 2011.

Pinch, T. J., & Bijker, W. E. (1984). The social construction of facts and artefacts: Or how the sociology of science and the sociology of technology might benefit each other. *Social Studies of Science, 14,* 399–441.

Rasmussen, S., & Schoen, D. (2010). *Mad as hell: How the tea party movement is fundamentally remaking our two-party system.* New York: Harper.

Reese, S. (2001). Framing public life. In S. Reese, O. Gandy, & A. Grant (Eds.), *Framing public life: Perspectives on media and our understanding of the social world* (pp. 7–32). Mahwah, NJ: Lawrence Erlbaum.

Rushkoff, D. (2013). Permanent revolution: Occupying democracy. *The Sociological Quarterly 54,* 164–173.

Sharma, S. (2013). Black Twitter: Racial hashtags, networks and contagion. *New Formations: A Journal of Culture/Theory/Politics, 78,* 46–64.

Singh, V. K., & Jain, R. (2010). Structural analysis of the emerging event-web. *Proceedings of the 19th International Conference on World Wide Web,* Raleigh, NC, April 26–30, 2010 (pp. 1183–1184). New York: ACM Press.

Small, T. A. (2011). What the hashtag? *Information, Communication and Society, 14*(6), 872–895.

Stroud, N. J. (2011). *Niche news: The politics of news choice.* New York: Oxford University Press.

Theocharis, Y., Lowe, W., van Deth, J. W., & Albacete, G. M. G. (2013) Using Twitter to mobilize protest action: Transnational online mobilization patterns and action repertoires in the Occupy Wall Street movement, indignados, and aganaktismenoi movements. *The annual convention of the 41st ECPR joint sessions of workshops*, Mainz, Germany, March 11–16, 2013.

Thorson, K., Driscoll, K., Ekdale, B., Edgerly, S., Gamber, T., Schrock, A., Swartz, L., Vraga, E. K. and Wells, C. (2013). Youtube, Twitter, and the occupy movement: Connecting content and practices. *Information, Communication, and Society, 16*(3), 421–451.

Tufekci, Z. & Wilson, C. (2012). Social media and the decision to participate in political protest: Observations from Tahrir Square. *Journal of Communication, 62*(2), 363–279.

Tyler, T. (2011). *Memetics*. CreateSpace Independent Publishing Platform.

Vanden Abeele, M. M. P. (2016). Mobile youth culture: a conceptual development. *Mobile Media & Communication, 4*(1), 85–101.

Wang, X., Wei, F., Liu, X., Zhou, M., & Zhang, M. (2011). Topic sentiment analysis in Twitter: A graph based sentiment classification approach. *Proceedings of the 20th ACM International Conference on Information and Knowledge Management*, Glasgow, UK, October 24–28, 2011, (pp. 1013–1040). New York: AMC Press.

Yardi, S. and boyd, d. (2010). 'Dynamic debates: An analysis of group polarization over time on twitter', *Bulletin of Science, Technology and Society, 30*(5): 316–27.

Yuan, E., Feng, M., & Danowski, J. (2013). "Privacy" in semantic networks on Chinese social media: the case of sina weibo. *Journal of Communication, 63*(6), 1011–1031.

Zangerle, E., Gassler, W., & Specht, G. (2011). Using tag recommendations to homogenize folksonomies in microblogging environments. *Lecture Notes in Computer Science 6984*, 113–126.

17 Structural Crises of Meaning and New Technologies

Reframing the Public and the Private in the News Media through the Expansion of Voices by Social Networks

Ana Serrano Tellería, João Carlos Correia and Heitor Costa Lima da Rocha

The Crisis of Meaning

There is currently a structural crisis of meaning (Berger & Luckmann, 2004) visible in the protests that are emerging around the world, particularly thanks to the contribution of new media. These protests are mostly expressed as a general demand for increased legitimacy within the established institutional order. Most of them are trying to replace the almost exclusively vertical flow of media messages from the elites to the rest of society with a more open and dynamic public sphere. This crisis involves the emergence of new players and protagonists, the shaping of political messages, the setting of new frontiers between public and private domain, and the replacement of the traditional ideological and framing production apparatus.

Those protests have emerged from the periphery toward the center. Many of their protagonists claim that digital media are the most suitable weapons they have to fight against the hegemonic supremacy of dominant groups, which act as the primary definers. While we consider that all of reality is not merely a representation but also carries meanings and frames that shape how reality is perceived, we also believe that we are now seeing a new flow of meaningful experiences that shape the concepts of "public" and "private."

As we do not believe in a nominalist and essentialist conception of language, we try to find how discursive and symbolic practices really work within the new media ecology and establish the difference between acting in public and acting in private. The same action can be considered to be public or private in the same physical space depending on the specific situation. Heidegger's "dasein" in Castells' "space of flows" and "timeless time" (until another definition of mobile and online time appears) leads to a relationship of existence by producing an appropriation of the space that flows in a time constrained by Aakhus and Katz's "perpetual contact" (Fidalgo et al., 2013), as well as the "liquid environment" (Serrano Tellería, 2014, 2015a, 2015b, 2015c, 2015d, 2015e, 2016; Serrano Tellería & Oliveira, 2015). The issue takes on particular relevance because of many claims that the boundaries between the two realms are being blurred.

In terms of this discussion, it is believed that users' management of content and information, along with the self and social networking, has proved to be a prominent aspect to consider. First, the fluidity of identity, cellular and nomadic intimacy, network privatism, and the tethered, tutored, and quantified self should be highlighted. Second, continuous partial attention, multitasking and/or multiplexing performance, the relationship between memories and places, the limitation of the impact of users' knowledge on their actions, strong circumstantial pattern behavior, the importance of temporal priority in digital literacy, and the lack of rationality in some attitudes and performances have become ingrained in users' behavior online (Serrano Tellería, 2014, 2015a, 2015b, 2015c, 2015d, 2015e, 2016; Serrano Tellería & Oliveira, 2015).

In this context, we start with an adequate perception of the institutional role of traditional media and the changing perspectives on framing and reframing the definition of social reality. Media do not mirror reality, as so often claimed by naive positivist theories on objectivity. Instead, media output is the result of a complex process that begins with the systematic selection of events and subjects according to socially constructed categories (Hall et al. 1999).

Beyond the media's bureaucratic organization specializing in news production, there is the moment in which it is constructed, when the professional involved assumes a general stock of knowledge shared with the audience that often goes unnoticed and unquestioned; this prevents the world from being represented as cluttered and chaotic, and identifies and relates the news to other public events (Correia, 2004).

Social identification, classification, and contextualization of news events in terms of these background frames of reference form the fundamental process by which the media make the world intelligible to readers and viewers. "Making a meaningful event" is a social process, which comprises crucial assumptions about what society is and how it works (Hall et al., 1999, pp. 225–226).

The usual suitability of media ideologies and practices for dominant ideas should not be understood simply as the result of their interests being controlled by capitalists (although, in fact, this does happen frequently). It is necessary to bear in mind the relative autonomy of day-to-day professional practices and routines in relation to the direct economic, social, and cultural mechanisms of control.

Hegemony and Everyday Discursive Practices

Applying these concepts to the role of the mass media, we find that the critical problem of mediated communication is how the symbolic supremacy (in Gramsci's terms, hegemony) connects with professional knowledge, particularly in the journalism field. Using phenomenological concepts, Tuchman (1978) guarantees that the construction of informative reality is defined as the outcome of professional routines and discursive practices that function as typifications of reality. These typifications establish procedural standards, which ensure that professionals, under the pressure of time, can quickly turn an event into a media story. Typifications therefore allow journalists to act "as always" when faced with identical circumstances.

Conceptually related to typifications, frames are standard guidelines for submission, selection, and emphasis that are particularly used in journalistic discourse. The inclusion or exclusion of certain details of events and the evaluation of what is relevant or not relevant in the description of an event or public protest depends on its classification or categorization.

This approach leads to some epistemological problems. How is it possible to keep an open mind regarding new, strange things that do not coincide with the frames shared by primary definers? In an attempt to build a theoretical bridge between frame analysis and ideological critique, Reese (2001, p. 9) suggests that media studies should accentuate the ideological character of frames, considering the dimension of their relations with society.

First, there is an operative framework that allows events to be classified into stories as politics, human interest, and so on.

Second, there is a conceptual and evaluative framework that shapes the meaning of the event, making it intelligible to the ideological system and placing it implicitly in a number of ways: as legitimate or illegitimate, moral or immoral, right or wrong, patriotic or unpatriotic, in favor of community interests or against them, and so on.

This does not mean that there is a complete absence of autonomy in a determinist sense, as some theories such as the propaganda model or the mirror model suggest; the codes for using ideology are provided by the imperatives of professional journalism.

The constant conflict and hard negotiation between systemic powers and the media show that the interests of the media and the primary definers do not always coincide. However, it is undeniable that the dominant trend in the media is toward reproducing hegemonic definitions.

The privileged relationship of institutional primary definers enables them to establish how the primary topic at hand is defined and interpreted and then to coordinate the activities of all subsequent information processing by imposing the terms of reference that will guide how frameworks of future coverage and debate are built. In a closed frame, positions that go against a primary interpretation are required to argue with this dominant structure, which sets the framework for the issue by presenting the criteria based on which all subsequent contributions are labelled as relevant or irrelevant to the debate.

Thus, in this critical perspective, the media do not generally play the role of primary definers of news events. Instead, they often reproduce the ideas of those who enjoy privileged access, who are presented as credible sources.

Finally, the media are, despite all the nuances and internal contradictions, responsible for translating the statements of the primary definers into public language and making them more accessible to the public in general, giving them popular strength and making them natural, to be understood by the majority of society. The recent debt crisis and the attempt to build an overall frame that makes the use of austerity measures acceptable to public opinion was an example, because of the use of new metaphors and frames that try to mobilize citizens to understand the meaning of "fiscal responsibility," "entrepreneurship," "state accountability," and other keywords of hegemonic liberal jargon. One of the main discursive strategies was to compare the public budget management to domestic budget management.

External public references therefore ensure validity for powerful objectified frames as a public issue, giving them much greater interest than if they were expressed in reports by technical experts.

This process is a transformation, and such a change requires active media work and a hermeneutical and interpretative role performed by the public within the scope of their opportunity to intervene.

Hegemony and the Public Sphere

In societies where the majority of the population has no direct access to the central decisions that affect their lives, the media has an active institutional role in shaping public opinion, helping to diffuse perspectives held by the powerful social strata.

The chance for counter-hegemonic perspectives to achieve visibility on the media agenda depends on the existence of organized, interconnected sources to generate an alternative point of view.

In the case of contrafactual positions, this depends to some extent on the ability to represent an organized and substantial minority that is able to deliver alternative points of view.

Groups that cannot guarantee this limited access are often stigmatized as "extreme" and "populist." Their actions are systematically stigmatized as "irrational." It is quite easy to achieve symbolic supremacy over groups that are fragmented, relatively disunited, or unable to support their goals with reasonable requirements in a practical agenda for reform or to adopt extreme forms of opposition struggles to support their interests. Any of these features makes them an easy target for privileged groups to label them freely, refusing to take their counter-definitions into account (Hall et al., 1999, p. 235). The current state of affairs throughout Europe gives us plenty examples of this process of stereotyping or stigmatizing: center-left wing parties have increasing difficulty in imposing a credible alternative and they give way to new political movements (Syriza, Podemos), social movements, and spontaneous rebellions. The radical movements are increasingly labelled as populist. They perform agenda-setting and bring new frames to political discussion, but there is no evidence that the desired effects are achieved. The political comments from the mainstream media frame them as idealists and unrealistic and claim that they support solutions that lack credibility (UK, Brexit; Greece, Syriza; Spain, Podemos). The overall frame is to compare the proposals of radical Left with the so-called real economy and focus the discussion on specific issues, such as the balance of sovereign debt and the need to obtain support from the international markets.

Technologies and Political Participation: The Alert from the Chicago School

Almost a century ago (1927), Dewey made an observation that still fits well with new technologies. He alerted us to the need for tools to build audiences as protagonists of their own definitions of reality. The tools would allow audiences to become publics, overcoming the condition of manipulated masses caused by the reification, atomization, and passivity that characterizes this form of society.

In spite of the great diversity and complex evolution of thoughts involved in the Chicago School, it is possible to find a strong core of collective concerns by combining social theory with participant research and ethnographic fieldwork. First, a common emphasis is found on the symbolic nature of social life. Accordingly, with this approach, the formation of social worlds involves symbolic interaction. Language is the environment that shapes the communicative exchange. Supported by philosophical style based on American Pragmatism, with particular influence from thinkers such as Dewey (Subtil and Garcia, 2010, pp. 219–224), Mead (1969) and Blumer (1969), the Chicago School expressed the belief that interaction was a dynamic process. This dynamism involved avoiding an essentialist view of identities and instead taking into account the presence of several variables in the generation of meaning.

Additionally, there is a common concern with new communication technologies, expressed in the role of journalism in forming modern urban publics and a new public sphere.

This common theoretical approach particularly highlights "symbolic interactionism," which is visible in engagement with a specific conceptualization of democracy. Communication was not just concerned with the transmission and dissemination of signs. It was also a ritual of sharing, participating, and possessing common beliefs (see Subtil and Garcia, 2010, p. 222). This concept of political participation was a major insight and remained present in the pragmatist concept of public in its rejection of democratic elitism (Silveirinha, 2004, p. 433).

In fact, authors such as Charles Merriam and John Dewey proved influential in making critical thinking a skill that civic education would seek to develop—not only at school but also in newspapers, on the radio, and in film (Milner, 2010:32). One may find a link in this regard to the Web 2.0 revolution, which has opened up access to digital consumption and, more importantly, the tools of digital production in pedagogically vital ways. The transformative civic possibilities of new production and broadcast technologies can be seen with every YouTube video from the Arab Spring or Occupy movements, which then become part of the news environment. The same can be said of the use of videos and social networks by Portuguese *Indignados*, during the cycle of demonstrations that preceded the bailout. The increasing self-consciousness of the precarious workers' generation was built by the use of urban culture devices, such as YouTube videos and broadcasts of demonstrations and the action of their protagonists, thanks to the use of mobile phones and aggressive mobilization, thanks to previous discussion on social networks. Even the discussion about the effects of the demonstrations by their protagonists was much more visible on social media than in the mainstream media. The social media coverage brought to light the agenda of new social movements with their internal discussions and with their own memory and narrative.

Today, identity-building processes are boosted by a particular type of technology. Here, "mediated memories," "normative discursive strategies" (Van Dijck, 2007), "terministic screens" (Markham, 2013), and "normative behavior" (LinkedIn & Facebook: Van Dijck, 2013) show how social media profiles are not a reflection of one's identity or neutral stages of self-performance, nor are they a means of self-expression (Horning, 2014); they are instead the very tools for shaping identities (Van Dijck, 2013) through the "filtered reality," "the filtered world" (Walker Rettberg, 2014).

The Authority of the Public

The influence of systemic interests in mediated societies goes hand in hand with the proliferation of new digital media, a strong limitation on the attribution of authority to the public. Since the time that the public sphere began to extend far beyond the context of simple interactions, a differentiation has come into play that distinguishes between organizers, speakers and listeners, the arena and the gallery, and the stage and the viewing audience.

The political influence that the actors have over public communication must be based, ultimately, on resonance and, more precisely, on an audience of lay people who have the same rights. The audience of private individuals has to be convinced using understandable and interesting contributions on topics they feel are relevant. The public has this authority since they form the internal structure of the public sphere, within which different stakeholders can emerge (Habermas, 1997, pp. 95–96).

In communication theory, the public has always been a particular way of connecting individual people around the discussion of matters of the common good. There have always been two problems: (a) how to produce an association among individual people without them bringing nonlegitimate private interests; and (b) how to articulate the debate on questions related to intimacy and privacy (gender, domestic violence, ethnicity, identity, and religion) in the public sphere without destroying the existence of some kind of barrier between public and private, in such a way that we do not turn transparency into a tyranny of intimacy.

For Habermas (1997), ideology functions using pseudocommunicative elements as symbolic resources; by their merely strategic nature, they hinder the achievement of public debate, free from any coercion, as a regulatory element that normatively guides social, communicative, and political practices.

Despite the power of major interest groups, which are well organized and anchored in functional systems, privileged sectors cannot openly use it in the public sphere, since public opinions that are released through the use of undeclared money or organizational power lose their credibility as soon as such sources of social power become public. Public opinion can be manipulated but not publicly purchased or obtained by force without losing its normative strength. This circumstance can be clarified by the fact that no public sphere can be produced at the arbitrary will of dominant powers (Habermas, 1997, pp. 96–97).

Publicness has some strength because it implies open access and legitimacy. Finally, open access is related not only to universal access for participants but also the universal possibility of introducing issues that concern all participants. Nowadays, this involves extending public spheres to new issues. Additionally, the devices available produce new conditions for assessing what is meant to be a private issue and what is meant to be a public issue.

Will digital media be able to perform this role and turn audiences into publics?

In a wrong-footed perspective, supporters of the democratic role of ICTs (information and communication technologies) emphasize that digital interactivity turns communication from one-to-many into communication from many-to-many. We maintain that the number of producers and receivers is sociologically and politically relevant but not enough to assess a more important issue: the quality of social interactions that lie behind systemic moves and continuity between offline interactions and online interactions.

New Technologies and the Return of Publics

Studies on journalism and public communication can and should observe the changes and mutations induced by the emergence of new communicative environments and their impact on political activity. The academic debate on the political impact of digital technologies raises a theoretical division between "cyber euphoria" and "digital dystopia" (Correia, 2016, p. 9).

The "dystopian" claim is that one cannot neglect the social and political components of power over the media system, including the Internet. In fact, this perspective is accompanied by an idealized vision of the political and economic power structures that run through social networks. The societal, economic, and political constraints involved in the communicative process remain hidden and, therefore, unacknowledged.

On the other hand, the so-called optimistic approach believes that the Internet and social networks will provide social movements with opportunities to become active agents in the political process, enhancing their participatory collective action. Social networks could be a suitable and viable public sphere to communicate issues and alternative points of view (Correia, 2016, p. 101).

First, digital social media would have the ideal structure for forming political communities through the discussion of public issues on websites. Interactivity is a key concept employed to sustain the democratic role of the internet, encourage alternative and more inclusive frames, and introduce new protagonists into the agenda-setting process.

Unlike most mainstream media, new media would not exclude resource-poor groups, and movements could achieve visibility for their agendas or introduce new perspectives on issues present on the news agenda. Environmental issues, gender violence, and the recent mobilization on sexual harassment bring us a new kind of citizenship where the liquidity and fluidity of old narratives confront new chances to discuss the issue: what makes an issue a public issue?

The traditional kind of coverage presupposes a certain logical conformism regarding media representation of social and political movements, particularly those that challenge nonconventional modernity. For example, in the 1960s and 1970s, mainstream news typified the women's liberation movements by focusing on their provocative actions rather than on the movements' main goals and messages. Additionally, the media, including the Internet, have become increasingly commercial under the systemic imperatives of the global economy. News is more about entertainment than information, and while minor issues are covered hysterically, much more serious issues in our society go largely free of any critical perspective.

In spite of those intellectual reservations, which are worth bearing in mind, we can admit that the Internet brings another flexibility and porosity to public issues related to domination and power. The Habermasian public sphere was frequently accused of being too normative, too rational, and somewhat limited to public issues. Furthermore, its historical reports only make it possible to build a heuristic model, in which current changes in space and time cannot be considered as deeply as necessary at the present time. Political experiments in Brazil (the "My First Harassment" campaign, mostly carried out by activists using Twitter), in Portugal (all the major movements organizations that triggered the protests against austerity, such as "Que se Lixe a Troika: Queremos as nossas vidas" [Fuck the Troika: we want our lives back], "O Povo é Quem Mais Ordena" [Rise Up Portugal], and "Democracia e Dívida" [Democracy and Debt, Article 21]), and in Spain (*Indignados*) include an intense us of digital media and a strong cathartic element, close to the real meaning of indignation, which is much better suited to expressing feelings than to debating issues in order to achieve new proposals. However, this should be a starting point for discussing new forms of making decisions: the discussion model cannot only be institutional politics.

Additionally, it is possible to hold a normative view considering the visibility and invisibility regimes that shape the frontiers between public and private. Unconventional media, since they are more used to alternative sources and everyday life, are simultaneously facilitating public dialogue among citizens and avoiding the excessive use of typifications and routines found in traditional newsrooms, which helps them break away from the usual frames. The blurring of traditional boundaries between producers and users has opened up new modes of interaction, while the inclusion of multimedia content generates more innovative and inclusive forms of storytelling that challenge bureaucratic routines and closed frames.

In this media landscape, online everyday life becomes more reflexive, with alternatives to linear reifications of identity. Power and domination plays begin, as always, with the frontier between the public and individual people, issues and identities. As Hannah Arendt (1997) stated, domestic issues were not public in ancient Greece because they did not belong to the Agora, where free men fought for the freedom of the city, but to the home (*oikos*), the realm of necessity and domestic serfdom. In other narratives, the press, coffee houses, and pubs were chosen to be the new, open Agora, because of new conditions of publicity and visibility.

The public and the private are not universal concepts used to classify different social interactions. They are instead the outputs of new forms of social literacy and visibility (the press) and the product of the recent weakening in rigid and stratified hierarchical ties; they have become possible with new forms of mobility and new visibility regimes. Merchants were travelers and the bourgeoisie became a new rising class because of increased global trade. Any new structural transformation in public spheres is therefore a transformation of visibility and it causes, at the same time, a major transformation in privacy and intimacy.

The modern liberal public emerged at the same time as a new individual subjectivity began to appear within a new system in homes, in which members of the enlarged family each had their own private rooms, where they could write intimate letters and journals. Sometimes, the discussion of publicness seems to miss the point: every major transformation in the public sphere implies a major transformation in the private realm. During the rise of the bourgeois public sphere, individuals began to publicize their individual psychologies with new genres of literature, such as love novels or adventure literature that glorified the lonely adventurer risking his/her life searching for social mobility, fame, and fortune. Publicness and privacy mutate when the mechanisms that generate publicity and secrecy or intimacy change. Those mechanisms are often related to social and physical mobility, public attention, and the struggle for visibility and recognition.

The keystone is always the discussion of the emergence of new criteria to define the public and private domains, which is made possible by deep changes in communication devices and the new chance to diffuse alternative versions supported by counter-hegemonic groups. Thanks to this, the liberal public sphere was continuously challenged when new mechanisms of representation, visibility, and recognition brought to light players, issues, and policies that had often been confined to the private realm: gender, ethnicity, and environment. They also brought many new causes and movements caused by the rise of life politics, where small narratives occupy multifarious public spheres.

Mobile devices and their media environments have also produced a series of fluid parameters to configure online virtual communication, mainly altering space and time aspects. The research fields involved have therefore indicated a variety of concepts that underline a main area of tension to deal with: the state of "perpetual contact" (Katz & Aakhus, 2002) and "liquid environment" (Serrano Tellería, 2014, 2015a, 2015b, 2015c, 2015d, 2015e, 2016, 2017; Serrano Tellería & Oliveira, 2015). The question is about civic literacy and demands new ways of promoting it using new media: it cannot be doubted that this civic literacy may be enhanced through the Internet. In spite of the relevance of the utopian and dystopian debate, new media have come to stay and civic literacy is a synthesis of conventional and unconventional youth political participation (Milner, 2010, p. 217).

Some data on political participation in the US are worth analyzing. In a survey for the MacArthur Foundation Research Network on

Participatory Politics, 41% of youths aged 15 to 25 reported that they had participated in a new political group online, written or disseminated a blog article about a political issue, forwarded a political video to their social network, or taken part in a poetry slam during the past year. "Unlike traditional political activity, participatory politics are interactive, peer based, and not guided by traditional institutions like political parties or newspaper editors"—and they rely on social media (Kahne & Middaugh, 2012). This survey also found that young people who frequently engage in nonpolitical communities driven by their interests are five times as likely to engage in participatory politics as young people who are less frequently engaged. Online communities seem to foster social capital and spur civic engagement, just as in-person gatherings such as town hall meetings did for previous generations.

The Change in Publics

With new technologies, relations between social movements, public spheres, and excluded groups and the traditional media become more complex.

Agenda-setting becomes less focused on primary definers (at least rigidly) and framing becomes less dependent on the usual sources. This is especially true for groups such as the *Occupy Wall Street* movement, *MoveOn.org*, the March 12th Movement, and anti-globalization political movement groups, which have been successfully using digital communication technologies, especially websites and social networks, to frame their activities on their own and mobilize the public to support their goals and missions. With their ease of access and increasing repertoire of tools for self-expression and communication, websites of Portuguese *Indignados* groups such as "Fuck the Troika" have become one of the many ways for young people and others to engage each other in social and political interaction and define the political agenda (Nah, 2009, p. 1296).

Additionally, there is a new kind of rationality: these types of technologies were previously described as "extensions of the nervous system" by Vilém Flusser (1988), when he defined them as a revolution. To paraphrase him (1990), the human being is seen here as a media user, not just as someone who "works" with information (*Homo Faber*), but one who "plays" with information (*Homo Ludens*).

Media is everywhere and we live immersed "in" it (*Media Life*, Deuze, 2012). Thus, it can be seen how interface design works to dilute the boundaries between humans and machines (human computer interaction; HCI), incorporating these mobile devices into our daily life by fulfilling our motivations and, at the same time, generating interactions to produce them (Serrano Tellería, 2014, 2015a, 2015b, 2015c, 2015d, 2015e, 2016, 2017; Serrano Tellería & Oliveira, 2015). Wonder, love, hate, desire, joy, and sadness, the six primary passions of the soul de-scribed by Descartes (1649), are increasingly incorporated into mobile interface design and the construction of messages, altering the way our brain, and specifically our memory, deals with general content and per-sonal data (Serrano Tellería, 2014, 2015a, 2015b, 2015c, 2015d, 2015e, 2016, 2017; Serrano Tellería & Oliveira, 2015).

This means a significant diversification of symbolic and expressive pub-lic discourse that, naturally, changes the existence of one hegemonic kind of rational expression. *Indignados* and anti-austerity movements include this affective and passionate dimension. For instance, the YouTube videos and street art (rap music, improvised songs, street theater, and graffiti) extensively used during March 12th events, together with the provoca-tive, ironic, and sometimes poetic tune of the messages delivered provides the irreverence, humor, and unpredictability necessary for rejuvenating a political conversation trapped in conventional forms. It illustrates a con-temporary take of editorial cartoons and satire, elements of reporting that are popular and typically generate more emotional reactions.

The informal public spheres formed in those movements can hardly be presented as an ideal type of dialogical and argumentative rationality. From an analytical point of view, it seems that these kinds of movements are better understood if one takes into account the multimodality of a discourse, including irony, stories, comparisons, parables, silent dis-agreements, the abrupt breakdown of talks, and countless other prac-tices that constitute the diversity of language games.

The *Indignados* Case

The *Indignados* movement, flourishing particularly in Spain and Portugal, is the expression of middle-class strata fighting against aus-terity measures. The structural changes seen in the labor market with the so-called new economy has accelerated the phenomenon of a white-collar labor force that had been growing since the 1970s (in Portugal).

The great recession of 2008, followed by the national debt crisis, caused a new wave of social movements and, in Portugal, the March 12th movement would be the first real expression of this.

In 2011, the March 12th movement was triggered by students, train-ees, and colleagues who had limited prospects for obtaining well-paid, sustainable, and high-quality jobs. Despite the lack of a tradition of new social movements, the events brought to light symptoms of a new per-ception of reality that has its roots in middle-class resistance against the threat of precariousness, impoverishment, and proletarianization.

The events culminated in demonstrations in Portugal on March 12, 2011, prior to the dramatic intervention of the EU, ECB, and IMF.

The course of events continued until January 2011, when a popular music group called Deolinda performed a song in Lisbon and Oporto called *Que parva eu sou* (How silly I am). The lyrics described the drama of "never-ending students" who would never achieve stability and well-paid jobs. The song would become an anthem against the crisis, austerity measures, and employment insecurity.

The song quickly spread everywhere and the issue rose to the top of media agenda, particularly on social media.

On February 21, 2011, four days after one public call, the number of people who said they would attend the demonstration on the movement's Facebook page was about 18,700. On March 3, this number had doubled to 37,000 people. The number of demonstrators discussed by most newspapers suggested 300,000 participants in Lisbon and Oporto, the two largest Portuguese cities (Correia, 2011).

The demonstrations had some unusual characteristics that defy the central principles of the collective action paradigm, also concerning the use of media. There are some common elements, such as:

a   Frequent use of new information and communication technologies. In the creation of a common world, reality is not guaranteed by the "common nature" of humanity, but because all are interested in the same subject (Arendt, 1997). The perspective of "Human Being as a Communication Portal" (Fidalgo et al., 2013), in which the human condition is defined by attitude and ways of dealing with the human ecosystem (see for example Bateson, 1979, 1991), has been a constant presence. This concept of relationship and interdependence had, in fact, been addressed by authors such as Elias (1980:134): "The image of man in relationships has to be before the people in the plural. Obviously, we have to start with the image of a crowd of people, each one establishing an open and interdependent process." Later, "hyper-coordination" was described (Ling & Yttri, 2001; Ling, 2004, 2008).

b   Strategic communication based on ritualistic performances of urban culture, including design, the use of social networks, rap music, street art, and street assemblies to make decisions. We also find a strong cathartic element close to the real meaning of indignation, much better suited to expressing feelings than to debating solutions. Emotion and motivation therefore seem to be key elements, and technologies must work like our brain to establish the proper connection between users and interfaces and public actions (Serrano Tellería, 2014, 2015a, 2015b, 2015c, 2015d, 2015e, 2016; Serrano Tellería & Oliveira, 2015). The blurring of the old barriers between public and private realms and the arrival of new kinds of rationality are also expressed by these demonstrations: at public events, the old, white, male, middle-class oriented protocols of speech are replaced by existential self-portraits (selfies, autobiographical reports of precariousness and unemployment, life stories and cries of indignation or celebration—"yeah, here we are"). New aesthetic styles that favor the everyday sense of belonging to a giant connected multitude of individual narratives takes the place of a delegated representation of elected official representatives, which seems too rigid, too plastic, and too inauthentic.

This particular feature leads us to the issue of the privatization of the public sphere. The geometric metaphor of the sphere is probably influenced by the idea of the square. Since the beginning of the telecommunications and transport revolution, the sociology of mobility requires us to bear in mind the idea of an increasingly fluid conception of the public, no longer confined to a common public sphere. Of course, we should remember to consider the quality of interactions in common spaces. However, we must bear in mind that there are many kinds of presence and, consequently, there are many kinds of shared meaning. In the personalized environment of social networks and mobile devices, there is in many ways an obvious tendency toward the polarization that occurs in interactions with like-minded groups.

However, as we have shown, even the public is made by private people and the transformation of the public sphere involves a new subjectivity and a greater emphasis on privacy and intimacy. So we must admit that the freedom to construct our personal identities online is no longer the freedom of anonymity; instead, it is the freedom associated with self-determination and autonomy, insofar as users can manage it, as well as uncontrolled searching of huge amounts of data. The online experience is similar to Proust's account book, but with us as coauthors (Fidalgo et al., 2013; Floridi, 2014): a collective sharing of subjective memories in an intersubjective but also fluid and liquid collective memory, which no longer works as a tradition in the old sense of the term. It could be what Hardt and Negri (2004) were thinking when they talked about connected multitude.

> Privacy, precisely because it ensures we're never fully known to others or to ourselves, provides a shelter for imaginative freedom, curiosity and self-reflection. So to defend the private self is to defend the very possibility of creative and meaningful life
>
> (Preston, 2014)

Coauthorship is also available in social network reports of antiausterity demonstrations. There is no individual authorship on social networks, but the collaborative process of meaning building is not necessarily a road to reification. So, it is reasonable to highlight the need for critical digital literacy focusing on: where one finds attention; the ability to detect trash; participation; collaboration; and the clever use of networks. Also, the properties of any social network have been identified as: persistence, replicability, scalability, and the ability to be searched, including the importance of being aware of what we share and with whom we share it (to the extent that, behind networks, there are invisible and potential audiences that lie, unsuspected, between the public and the private) (Rheingold, 2012; boyd, 2014; who also discusses "digital naïves," youths).

These are joined by the relevance of time and memory on social media, in which accessibility, durability, comprehensiveness, inequality, and evolution are the main features to bear in mind (Brake, 2014) and the natural and inner disposition of humans to share (Hermida, 2014). In fact, it is not difficult to accept that those features can create some level of political literacy, understood as a minimal familiarity with relevant decision-making institutions (Milner, 2010, p. 13).

Finally, in spite of all the reservations and criticism related to the political relevance of digital media, as regards working in public, they involve the constant negotiation of rules in which norms and values are not clear; a decentralized model that has a multimedia, flexible format and is constantly changing, being updated, corrected, and revised; nonlinear content that is indifferent to distance; and diverse resource sources with fragmented audiences whose feedback is extremely important (Kawamoto, 2003). It is further characterized by spreadability and the tension between mass and collaborative culture within it (Jenkins, Ford & Green, 2013).

Those features are intertwined with Bauman's metaphor of modern life, i.e., liquid life: fluidity, transience, reticula, and the dissolution of defined borders and boundaries (Bauman, 2005; Aguado, Feijóo, & Martínez, 2013; Serrano Tellería & Oliveira, 2015; Serrano Tellería, 2015a, 2016, 2017) in a society where a "curious reversal" has redefined the private sphere characterized by the right to confidentiality as a sphere that has fallen prey to the right to publicity (Bauman, 2008).

c   Use of alternative mobilization channels (personal contact and online social networks, rather than broadcast media). The emerging literature on online social media has so far mostly concluded that these complement rather than substitute traditional mobilization organizations, such as unions, parties, or mass media (Bekkers, Moody, & Edwards, 2011; Bekkers et al., 2011; Skoric et al., 2011).

In conclusion, the new information and communication technologies are much more widely used by voices that are excluded from public visibility to build their own identity and create a self-portrait of their political and cultural agency.

Frames and typifications used by primary definers lose some of their ability to be naturalized as the "single, good old" world vision, acceptable as a reasonable and sensitive diffuser. In spite of institutional and commercial commitments, the open architecture of the Internet has challenged the old routines and frames involved in the social construction of reality. However, they are far from performing the miracle of a full deliberative and participative public sphere, despite bringing the public sphere closer to a new online life. Naturally, there are no guarantees that this search for authenticity will not bring with it demagogy and populism, but it certainly creates more diverse frames and discourses in the informal public sphere.

Conclusion

New technologies and new interactive and participative environments create the possibility of a more participative and inclusive public sphere, opening the path to a confident presence of subjectivity, not in the classical sense of the solipsist self, but in a postconventional sense of a starting point where many networked actions and interactions begin and end. The sociological subject is no longer an isolated one. The sociological subject is a multitude open to multifarious connections. The image we need to explain the network is no longer the image of a solitary essentialist human identity. Each part of the network is understandably in actual connection with all the others.

Public and private can no longer be analyzed in terms of a strictly rigid separation between the realm of intimacy and the collective realm. Public and private realms are always fully comprehensible when understood in the context of the pragmatic use of the tools and devices that shape publicity and intimacy. Those tools and devices are more than ever mobile and spreadable media that shape time, space, and social and cultural uses.

With the change in the meaning of public, the meaning of the polis as sphere of production and sharing of political meaning also changes: it is more fluid, more open to ritualistic forms of expression, involves new performative dimensions, and is much more open to multifarious forms of deliberation.

These sociocultural changes, finally, demand a strong grounding in a new media literacy founded on new epistemological, communicative bases.

References

Aguado, J. M., Feijóo, C., & Martínez, I. J. (Cords.). (2013). *La comunicación móvil. Hacia un nuevo ecosistema digital*. Barcelona: Gedisa.

Arendt, H. (1997). *A Condição Humana*. Rio de Janeiro: Forense Universitária.

Bateson, G. (1979). *Espíritu y naturaleza: una unidad necesaria (avances en teoría de sistemas, complejidad y ciencias humanas)*. New York: Bantam Books.

Bateson, G. (1991). *Una unidad sagrada: nuevos pasos hacia una ecología de la mente*. Barcelona Gedisa.

Bauman, Z. (2005). *Liquid life.* Cambridge: Polity.

Bauman, Zygmunt (2008). *Vida para consumo: A transformação das pessoas em mercadoria.* Rio de Janeiro: Jorge Zahar Ed.

Bekkers, Victor; Moody, Rebecca; and Edwards, Arthur (2011). "Micro-Mobilization, Social Media and Coping Strategies: Some Dutch Experiences," *Policy & Internet: Vol. 3:* Iss. 4, Article 6. DOI: 10.2202/1944-2866.106

Berger, P., & Luckmann, T. (2004). *Modernidade, pluralismo e crise de sentido.* Petropolis: Vozes.

Blumer, H. (1969). *Symbolic interactionism. Perspective and method.* Englewood Cliffs, NJ: Prentice Hall.

boyd, d. (2014). *It's complicated. The social lifes of networked teens.* New Haven and London: Yale University Press.

Brake, D. R. (2014). *Sharing our lives online. Risks and exposure in social media.* New York: Palgrave Macmillan.

Correia, J. C. (2004). *Comunicação e Cidadania: os media e a fragmentação do espaço público nas sociedades pluralistas.* Lisbon: Livros Horizonte.

Correia, J. C. (2011). *12 de Março de 2011: que 'causas' suportam as redes sociais.* Conference delivered at the Political Communication Working Group of the 7th Congress of Portuguese Society of Communication (SOPCOM), Lisbon, December 15–17, 2011.

Correia, J. C. (2016). Social media and political participation: The Portuguese Indignados case. In R. Figueiras & P. Espírito Santo (Ed.), *Beyond the Internet: unplugging the protest movement wave* (pp. 99–122). London: Routledge.

Deuze, M. (2012). *Media Life.* Cambridge: Polity Press.

Elias, N. (1980). *Introdução à sociologia.* Lisbon: Edições 70.

Fidalgo, A., Serrano Tellería, A., Carvalheiro, J. R., Canavilhas, J., & Correia, J. C. (2013). Human being as a communication portal: The construction of the profile on mobile phones. *Revista Latina de Comunicación Social, 68.* Retrieved from http://www.revistalatinacs.org/068/paper/989_Covilha/23_Telleriaen.html. Accessed on February 10, 2017.

Floridi, L. (2014). The Facebook-ification of everything! Sex, authenticity and reality for the status update era. *Salon.* Retrieved from http://www.salon.com/2014/08/31/the_facebook_ification_of_everything_sex_authenticity_and_reality_for_the_status_update_era/?utm_source=twitter&utm_medium=socialflow. August 31. Accessed on December 12, 2016.

Flusser, V. (1988). On writing, complexity and the technical revolutions. Interview in *Onasbrück, European Media Art Festival.* Retrieved from https://www.youtube.com/watch?v=lyfOcAAcoH8&app=desktop. September 1988.

Habermas, J. (1997). *Direito e democracia: entre facticidade e validade* (Vol. II). Rio de Janeiro: Tempo Brasileiro.

Hall, S., Chrichter, C. C., Jefferson, T., Clarke, J., & Roberts, B. (1993). A produção social das notícias: o mugging nos media. In N. Traquina (org.) (1999), *Jornalismos: Questões, Teorias e "Estórias",* (pp. 224–228). Lisbon: Vega.

Hardt, M., & Negri, A. (2004). *Multitude: War and democracy in the age of empire.* New York: Penguin Press.

Hermida, Alfred (2014). *Tell Everyone: Why We Share and Why It Matters,* DoubleDay Canada. Henry.

Horning, R. (2014). Social media is not self-expression. *The New Inquiry*. Retrieved from http://thenewinquiry.com/blogs/marginal-utility/social-media-is-not-self-expression/. November 14. Accessed on December 12, 2016.

Jenkins, H., Ford, S., & Green, J. (2013). *Spreadable media. Creating value and meaning in a networked culture*. New York: New York University Press.

Kahne, J., & Middaugh, E. (2012, November). Digital media shapes youth participation in politics. *Kappen, 94*:3. Retrieved from http://ypp.dmlcentral.net/sites/default/files/publications/Digital_Media_Shapes_Participation.pdf.

Katz, J. (Ed.). (2008). *Handbook of Mobile Communication*. MIT Press.

Katz, J. E., & Aakhus, M. (Eds.). (2002). *Perpetual contact. Mobile communication, private talk, public performance*. Cambridge: Cambridge University Press.

Kawamoto, K. (2003). *Media and society in the digital age*. New York: University of Washington.

Ling, R. (2004). *The mobile connection: The cell phone's impact on society*. San Francisco: Elsevier.

Ling, R. (2008). *The mediation of ritual interaction via the mobile telephone*. Handbook of mobile communication studies. ed. / James E. Katz. MIT Press, Cambridge, 2008. pp. 317–344.

Ling, R., & Yttri, B. (2001). Hyper-coordination via mobile phones in Norway, nobody sits at home and waits for the telephone to ring: Micro and hyper-coordination through the use of mobile telephones. In J. Katz & M. Aakhus (Eds.), *Perpetual contact*. Cambridge: Cambridge University Press. 139–169.

Markham, A. (2013). Undermining "data": A critical examination of a core term in scientific inquiry. *First Monday, 18*(10). Retrieved from http://uncommonculture.org/ojs/index.php/fm/article/view/4868/3749. 7 October. Accessed on December 12, 2016.

Mead, G. H. (1969). *Mind, self and society*. Chicago: The Chicago University Press.

Milner, H. (2010). *The internet generation. Engaged citizens or political dropout*. Hannover and London: University Press of New England and London: Routledge.

Nah, S. (2009). Social movements and journalism In C. H. Sterling (Ed.), *Encyclopedia of journalism*, (pp. 1294–1296). London: Sage.

Reese, S. D. (2001). Prologue—Framing public life: A bridging model for media research. In S. D. Reese, O. H. Gandy, & A. E. Grant (Ed.), *Framing public life: Perspectives on media and our understanding of the social world* (pp. 7–32). Mahwah, NJ: Lawrence Erlbaum Associates.

Rheingold, H. (2012). *Net smart. How to thrive online*. Cambridge: MIT Press.

Serrano Tellería, A. (2014). Interface design on mobile phones: The delimitation of the public and private spheres. In F. Paiva, C. Moura (Orgs.) *Designa: Interface* International Conference on Design Research, (pp. 87–108). Portugal: LabCom, Beira Interior University. Retrieved from http://www.livroslabcom.ubi.pt/book/111. Accessed on December 12, 2016.

Serrano Tellería, A. (2015a). The role of the profile and the digital identity on the mobile content. In J. M. Aguado, C. Feijóo, I. J. Martínez (Eds.), *Emerging perspectives on the mobile content evolution*. IGI Global. Idea group. Retrieved from http://www.igi-global.com/chapter/the-role-of-the-profile-and-the-digital-identity-on- the-mobile-content/138000. Accessed on December 12, 2016.

Serrano Tellería, A. (2015b). Liquid spheres or constellations: Reflections towards mobile devices. In J. R. Carvalheiro, A. Serrano Tellería, (Eds.), *Mobile and digital communication: Approaches to public and private*, (pp. 173–198). Covilhã, Portugal: LabCom Books, University of Beira Interior. Retrieved from http://www.livroslabcom.ubi.pt/book/141. Video of the international conference 'public and private in mobile communications': https://www. youtube.com/watch?v=q39TPaq8tBo. Accessed on December 12, 2016.

Serrano Tellería, A. (2015c). Emotion and mobile devices. In F. Paiva, C. Moura, (Ogrs.), *Designa: Desire*, International Conference on Design Research. Portugal: LabCom.IFP, Beira Interior University. Retrieved from http://www. labcom-ifp.ubi.pt/book/253. Accessed on December 12, 2016.

Serrano Tellería, A. (2015d). Twitter e a privacidade: a partilha de estratégias e ferramentas. In *IX Congresso SOPCOM: Associação Portuguesa de Ciências da Comunicação: Comunicação e Transformações Sociais*. University of Coimbra, Portugal. Retrieved from http://sopcom2015.com/. November 12–14, 2015.

Serrano Tellería, A. (2015e). Reddit e a privacidade: uma análise das interacções e conversas. In *IX Congresso SOPCOM: Associação Portuguesa de Ciências da Comunicação: Comunicação e Transformações Sociais*. University of Coimbra, Portugal. Retrieved from http://sopcom2015.com/. November 12–14, 2015.

Serrano Tellería, A. (2016). Liquid communication in mobile devices: Affordances and risks. In B. Baggio (Eds.), *Analyzing digital discourse and human behavior in modern virtual environments*. EEUU: IGI Global. Idea Group. doi:10.4018/978-1-4666-9899-4.ch011. Retrieved from http://www. igi-global.com/chapter/liquid-communication-in-mobile-devices/145920. Accessed on December 12, 2016.

Serrano Tellería, A. (2017). Innovations in mobile interface design: Affordances and risks. In: *EPI, el profesional de la información*. v. 26, n. 2 (March–April). Special number 'Ethics, research and communication' (Ética, investigación y comunicación). ISSN 1386-6710. Retrieved from https://recyt.fecyt.es/index. php/EPI/issue/view/2999/showToc.

Serrano Tellería, A., & Branco, M. L. (2015). Educação para a privacidade no espaço digital: de subsídios para uma proposta curricular. In J. R. Carvalheiro, (org), *A Nova Fluidez de Uma Velha Dicotomia: Publico e Privado nas Comunicações Móveis* (pp. 163–194). Covilhã, Portugal: Labcom books, University of Beira Interior. Retrieved from http://www.livroslabcom.ubi.pt/ book/133. Accessed on December 12, 2016.

Serrano Tellería, A., & Oliveira, M. (2015). Liquid spheres on smartphones: The personal information policies. *International Journal of Interactive Mobile Technologies*. 9(1). ISSN: 1865-7923. Retrieved from http://online-journals. org/index.php/i- jim/article/view/4065. Accessed on December 12, 2016.

Serrano Tellería, A. & Pereira, P. (2015). Instagram e a visibilidade das imagens dos utilizadores. In J. R. Carvalheiro (Ed.), *Público e privado nas comunicações móveis*, (pp. 297–316). Coimbra, Portugal: Minerva Coimbra.

Serrano Tellería, A., Portovedo, S., & Albuquerque, A. L. (2015). Negociações da privacidade nos dispositivos móveis. In J. R. Carvalheiro, *Público e privado nas comunicações móveis* (pp. 119–158). Coimbra, Portugal: Minerva Coimbra.

Silveirinha, M. J. (2004). Opinião Pública. In A. Rubim (org.), *Comunicação Política: Conceitos e Abordagens*. Salvador: Editora da Universidade Federal da Bahia e Unesp.

Skoric M. M., Teo L. L. C., Neo R. L. (2009). Children and video games: Addiction, engagement and scholastic achievement. *Cyberpsychology & Behavior*. 12:567–572.

Subtil, F., & Garcia, J. L. (2010). Communication: An inheritance of the Chicago school of social thought. In C. Hart (Ed.), *Legacy of chicago school. A collection of essays in honour of Chicago school of sociology during the first half of the 20th century*. Manchester: Midresh Publisher.

Tuchman, G. (1978). *Making news: A study in the construction of reality*. New York: Free Press.

Van Dijck, J. (2007). *Mediated memories in the digital age*. Stanford, CA: Stanford University Press.

Van Dijck, J. (2013). You have one identity: Performing the self on Facebook and LinkedIn. *Media, Culture & Society, 35*, 199. Retrieved from http://mcs.sagepub.com/content/35/2/199. Accessed on December 12, 2016.

Walker Rettberg, J. (2014). *Seeing ourselves through technology: How we use selfies, blogs and wearable devices to see and shape ourselves*. Palgrave Macmillan. Retrieved from http://www.academia.edu/8482366/Seeing_Ourselves_Through_Technology_How_ We_Use_Selfies_Blogs_and_Wearable_Devices_to_See_and_Shape_Ourselves. Accessed on December 12, 2016.

18 A Starting Path for a Great Future

Ana Serrano Tellería

Thanks to all authors involved and their enriching contributions, we have been able to approach the public and private, intimate and personal spheres within the mobile ecosystem successfully. We hope the reader agrees.

The risks involved are broad as well as the affordances are wide. To manage the right balance between the mentioned spheres implies a formed definition of them, which has been proved to be constantly ever changing because of the liquidity perceived in this ecosystem. Thus, delimiting an appropriate methodology to analyze this ecology raises a series of relevant questions that question, as well, the paradigm followed previously.

Both the state of the art review and the studies showed core areas researches have delved into: the redefinition of mobile devices as proves in the method, its implications, and the series of following questions and hypothesis implied in the process; the changing concepts and notions about how users define main communicative patterns and structures; and the extending parameters to embrace the affordances and the risks involved.

Therefore, this volume covers humbly a starting path for a great future. Why? The reason to support this proactive perspective relies on a global coverage. Results from an extended view of intrinsic cultural perceptions suggest a stronger tendency of positive affordances over worrying risks. The *Human Being as a Communication Portal* seems to offer infinitive possibilities to overcome past constraints in users' empowerment.

"First we shape our tools, thereafter they shape us." As long as we users are aware of this appropriation stage, we should be able to reshape the same tools again too. Within this ever-changing, intermittent, and infinitive process, we *human beings* have been able to reach outstanding picks: some discovered on the way, some planned, and some never even thought about. Then, a profitable development of mobile devices just relies on us.

We academic and professional researches have the opportunity to raise worldwide partners; to analyze, conclude, and understand in collaboration global challenges, while defining unique cultural features; to draw, delimit, and frame its specific characteristics.

Always and everyday we *human beings* face constant, new, and persistent risks, whereas exciting affordances open precedent delimitations for a brighter future to come. "If we know what we are doing, it would not be referred to as research," A. Einstein said.

List of Contributors

Juan Miguel Aguado is Assistant Professor of Communication Theory at the School of Communication and Information Studies of the University of Murcia, Spain. He is also the head of the Master's Program in Mobile Communication and Digital Media at the University of Murcia and the Technical University of Cartagena, Spain. His publications include *Emerging Perspectives on the Mobile Content Evolution* (2015), *Mobile Communications: Towards a New Ecosystem* (2013), *Mobile Society: Culture, Identity and Technology* (edited with Inmaculada J. Martínez, 2008), *Movilizad@s: Women and Mobile Communication in the Information Society* (with Inmaculada J. Martinez and Iolanda Tortajada, 2009), *Technology and Social Complexity* (edited with Eva Buchinger and Bernard Scott, 2010) and *Mobile Communications: Towards a New Digital Ecosystem* (Edited with Claudio Feijóo and Inmaculada J. Martínez, 2013).

Naomi S. Baron is Executive Director, Center for Teaching, Research and Learning World Languages and Cultures, College of Arts and Sciences, American University, Washington, USA. Professor Baron has a Ph.D. in Linguistics from Stanford University and is interested in electronically mediated communication, writing and technology, the history of English, and higher education. A former Guggenheim Fellow and Fulbright Fellow, she has published seven books. *Always On: Language in an Online and Mobile World* won the English-Speaking Union's Duke of Edinburgh English Language Book Award for 2008. Her most recent book is *Words Onscreen: The Fate of Reading in a Digital World* (Oxford University Press, 2015). Professor Baron taught at Brown University, Emory University, and Southwestern University before going to AU, where she has served in CAS as Associate Dean for Undergraduate Affairs, Associate Dean for Curriculum and Faculty Development, Chair of the Department of Language and Foreign Studies, and director of the TESOL Program. She was named University Honors Program Professor of the Year and received an AU Presidential Research Fellowship.

María Luisa Branco is Associate Professor in the Department of Psychology and Education and full member of the R&D Research Center LabCom. IFP, of the University of Beira Interior, Covilhã, Portugal. She has has a Ph.D. in Education Sciences and has taught at Beira Interior University since 1997, where she is director of postgraduate education. Her research interests are democracy and education, citizenship, and teacher training.

Laura Cañete Sanz is a Doctoral Research fellow at the Project "Mobile Communication and Personal Data: Impact in Creative Industries, Advertising System and Users' Perceptions" supported by the Spanish Ministry of Economy and Innovation (CSO2013-47394-R). She has a BA in Journalism and in Advertising, and holds a MA in Advanced Communication Studies at the School of Communication and Information Studies, University of Murcia (Spain). She is member of the Research Subject Group in Social Communication, Culture and Technology at the University of Murcia (Spain), and visitor fellow at the "Games and Play" research subject group at the Institute for Cultural Inquiry (ICON), Utrecht University (The Netherlands).

Ruepert Jiel Cao is Lecturer at the Multimedia Arts Program of De La Salle, College of Saint Benilde and graduate student in Applied Media Studies at the Department of Communication, De La Salle University, Philippines. His graduate thesis revolves around the performance of gender through cross-dressing and cross-gender acting in popular culture. He has also published research on ethnicity, gender, and activist media.

João Carlos Correia is Associate Professor at Beira Interior University, Portugal, where he teaches media studies, cultural theories, and journalism studies. His current fields of research are new media, public spheres, and social movements. His works include the following: Giving Sense and Making Choices: Supporting Ethnographic and Discursive Approach to the News, in The Journal of Transnational 'Worlds of Power': Proliferation of Journalism & Professional Standard, Volume 1, n°1 Publisher: Cambridge Scholars Publishing, 2015. ISSN No: 2057–5866, 69–84 (in *The Journal of Transnational*, 2015); 'Le rôle des réseaux socionumériques dans la configuration épistémologique des societés', *La contribution en ligne: Participatives pratiques à l'ère du informationnel capitalisme*, 2014); 'Online Journalism and Civic Life' (in *The Handbook of Global Online Journalism*, 2012); *The Admirable World of News: Theories and Methods* (2011); and *Communication and Citizenship: The Media and the Fragmentation of Public Sphere in Pluralist Societies* (2004).

Heitor Costa Lima da Rocha is an Associate Professor at the Federal University of Pernambuco, Brazil. Dr. Costa da Lima Rocha has a Ph.D.

on Sociology from the University of Pernambuco (2004) where he also studied a Master's in Political Science (1989). He has been teaching since then at Escola Superior de Relações Públicas (1989–1998), Universidade Católica de Pernambuco (1998–2009) and Universidade Federal Rural de Pernambuco (2008–2009) in Brazil.

He has a B.A. in Journalism (1983), and has extensive experience as journalist mainly in the political field. He has worked at Rádio Clube de Pernambuco (1981–1982); Rádio Tamandaré (1983–1985); TV Globo Nordeste (1984); Jornal do Commercio (1985–1987) and Diário Oficial da Assembleia Legislativa do Estado de Pernambuco (1986–2000) in Brazil.

Elisabeth Thomas Crocker is a graduate student in cultural anthropology at Boston University, USA. She holds a Master's in Anthropology from Louisiana State University and is currently working on her PhD at Boston University. She is a graduate research assistant for Professor James E. Katz, and together they have explored social media practice and visual communication with mediums such as Skype and Snapchat.

Leopoldina Fortunati teaches Sociology of Communication and Sociology of Cultural Processes at the Faculty of Education of the University of Udine, Italy. Professor Fortunati has conducted extensive research in the field of gender studies, cultural processes, and communication and information technologies. She is the author of many books and is the editor, with J. Katz and R. Riccini, of *Mediating the Human Body: Technology, Communication and Fashion* (2003); with P. Law and S. Yang of *New Technologies in Global Societies* (2006); and with Jane Vincent of *Electronic Emotion: The Mediation of Emotion via Information and Communication Technologies* (2009). She is very active at European level, especially in COST networks, and is the Italian representative in the COST Domain Committee (ISCH, Individuals, Societies, Cultures and Health). She has participated in and led several national and international research projects in these fields. She is the associate editor of the journal *The Information Society*, a member of the advisory board for *New Media and Society*, and a referee for many outstanding journals such as *Communication, Information, Society* and the *Journal for the Theory of Social Behavior*. She and Rich Ling co-chair the international association The Society for the Social Study of Mobile Communication (SSSMC), which intends to facilitate the international advancement of cross-disciplinary mobile communication studies. She has published many articles in journals such as *The Information Society, Information, Communication, Society, Réseaux, Trends in communication, Revista de Estudios de Juventud, Widerspruche, Personal and Ubiquitous computing, Gazette, The International Journal for*

Communication Studies, *Sociologia dell'informazione*, and *Problemi dell'informazione*.

Sandra Carina Guimarães is Assistant Professor in the Department of Psychology and Education of the University of Beira Interior, Covilhã, Portugal. She has a Ph.D. in Psychology of Education and her main research interest focus is self-regulation learning processes, with a range of publications in this field. She teaches courses in psychology of education, educational supervision, and curriculum development.

Leslie Haddon is Senior Researcher and visiting Lecturer at the Department of Media and Communications of the London School of Economics, UK, where he teaches the course Media, Technology and Everyday Life. He has authored, coauthored, edited, and coedited eight books in this field and was series editor for the Berg New Media series. He has researched the consumption and social shaping of ICTs for over 25 years, with projects on home computers, telephony, cable TV, intelligent homes, mobile phones, and the Internet—including academic projects, EC-funded projects, and projects for a range of companies.

Larissa Hjorth is Professor on the Games Program at the School of Media & Communication, Royal Melbourne Institute of Technology, Australia. She is also codirector (with Heather Horst) of the Digital Ethnography Research Centre (DERC). Since 2000, Professor Hjorth has been researching the gendered and sociocultural dimensions of mobile, social, locative, and gaming cultures in the Asia–Pacific—these studies are outlined in her books: *Mobile Media in the Asia-Pacific* (Routledge, 2009); *Games & Gaming* (2010); *Online@AsiaPacific: Mobile, Social and Locative in the Asia– Pacific region* (with Michael Arnold, Routledge, 2013); *Understanding Digital Media in the Age of Social Networking* (with Sam Hinton, 2013); and *Gaming in Locative, Social and Mobile Media* (with I. Richardson, 2014). She has also coedited four Routledge anthologies: *Gaming Cultures and Place in the Asia–Pacific region* (with Dean Chan, 2009); *Mobile technologies: from Telecommunication to Media* (with Gerard Goggin, 2009); *Studying the iPhone: Cultural Technologies, Mobile Communication, and the iPhone* (with Jean Burgess and Ingrid Richardson, 2012); and *Mobile Media Practices, Presence and Politics: The Challenge of Being Seamlessly Mobile* (with Katie Cumsikey).

Kenichi Ishii is currently Associate Professor at the University of Tsukuba, Japan. He received his Ph.D. from the University of Tsukuba in 2000. His research interests include effects of communication technology, nation branding, and transnational flow of cultural products. He has contributed to such journals as *Journal of Communication*,

Telecommunications Policy, Telematics and Informatics, Journal of Broadcasting & Electronic Media, Journal of International Consumer Marketing, and *Computers in Human Behavior.*

James E. Katz is Feld Professor of Emerging Media at Boston University's College of Communication, USA. He also directs its Division of Emerging Media Studies. Among his books are *Magic in the Air: Mobile Communication and the Transformation of Social Life, Social Consequences of Internet Use: Access, Involvement, Expression* (with Ronald E. Rice), and *Handbook of Mobile Communication Studies.*

Derrick de Kerckhove is director of the McLuhan Program in Culture & Technology at the University of Toronto, Canada, where he is professor emeritus in the Department of French. He subsequently joined the Faculty of Sociology of the University Federico II in Naples. Presently, he is also the scientific director of the Rome-based monthly "Media Duemila" and is the research director at the "Interdisciplinary Internet Institute (IN3"' of l'Universitat Oberta de Catalunya in Barcelona, Spain.

Amparo Lasén is Professor of Sociology at the University Complutense of Madrid, Spain. Her publications include *A contratiempo. Un estudio de las temporalidades juveniles* (CIS-SXXI-2000); *Le temps des jeunes: rythmes, durées, virtualités* (2001); *Understanding Mobile Phone Users and Usages* (2005); *Lasen and Hamill Mobile World. Past, Present and Future* (2005); Gebhardt, Greif, Raycheva, Lobet-Maris and Lasen (eds.), *Experiencing Broadband Society* (2010); Greif, Hjorth, Lasén et Lobet-Maris (eds.), *Cultures of Participation. Media Practices, Politics and Literacy* (2011). She has participated and led several national and international research projects in these fields.

Rich Ling is Shaw Foundation Professor of Media Technology, Wee Kim Wee School of Communication and Information, Nanyang Technological University, Singapore. He is a founding coeditor of the Sage journal *Mobile Media and Communication*, coeditor of the Oxford University Press series *Studies in Mobile Communication* with Gerard Goggin and Leopoldina Fortunati, founding editor of *The Mobile Communication Research Series* with Scott Campbell, and an associate editor for *The Information Society, Information Technology* and *International Development* and *Norsk Medietidsskrift.*

Lev Manovich is Professor of Computer Science at The Graduate Center and director of the Software Studies Initiative at City University of New York, USA. Professor Manovich is the author and editor of eight books, including *Data Drift* (RIXC, 2015), *Software Takes Command* (2013), *Soft Cinema: Navigating the Database* (2005), and *The Language of New Media* (2001), which was described as "the most suggestive and broad ranging media history since Marshall McLuhan." As director of the Software Studies Initiative, he works on the analysis and visualization of big cultural data. His website is manovich.net.

Inmaculada J. Martínez is an Assistant Professor at the School of Communication and Information Studies, University of Murcia, Spain, where she teaches Advertising Ecosystem. Her publications include *Mobile Society: Culture, Identity & Technology* (2008), *Mobilized: Women & Mobile in the Information Society* (2010); *Mobile Communications: Towards a New Digital Ecosystem* (2013) and *Emerging Perspectives on the Mobile Content Ecosystem* (2015).

Sharon Meraz is Associate Professor and Director of Graduate Studies, Department of Communication, College of Liberal Arts & Sciences, University of Illinois at Chicago, USA. She was an assistant professor at the same university (2008–15); previously, she was assistant instructor at the School of Journalism, College of Communication of the University of Texas at Austin (2005–06); member of the Social Media Editorial Team, BlogBurst, Pluck Cooperation, Austin (2006–07); Web Developer/Webmaster in the Department of Continuing Education, University of Texas at Austin (2001–05); and member of Graphic Design Production, Publisher's Resource Group, Austin, Texas (1999–2001).

Koldo Meso is Associate Professor in the Department of Journalism II at the Faculty of Social and Communication Sciences of the University of the Basque Country (UPV/EHU), Spain. He has a Ph.D. in Communication and was director of the Digital Journalism course at the Asmoz Fundation, organized by the Basque Studies Society and the Department of Journalism II of the Faculty of Communication (UPV-EHU). He currently directs research projects about cyberjournalism and is the director of the Department of Journalism II and the International Congress of Cyberjournalism and Web 2.0 (UPV-EHU, 6 congresses).

Javier Díaz Noci is Full Professor at Pompeu Fabra University, Spain. He has his MA in Law, Ph.D. in History, and Bachelor's degree in Journalism. With Professor Marcos Palacios, he coordinated the International Cooperation Program in Online Journalism between Spain and Brazil involving 50 postdoctoral researchers. He is specializes in communication, history, intellectual property, journalism, and journalism history. He is considered a pioneer and outstanding academic in online journalism in Spain and South America and has been awarded with five stays abroad.

Simón Peña is Assistant Professor in the Department of Journalism II at the Faculty of Social and Communication Sciences of the University of the Basque Country (UPV/EHU), Spain. He has a Ph.D. in Journalism and has published more than 30 journal articles on online journalism, communication and social networks, and social innovation. He has also participated in 20 research projects at international, national, and regional level. Together with Koldo Meso and other colleagues, he edits the academic journal they publish (Mediatika) and teaches on various master's programs.

Cheryll Ruth R. Soriano is Associate Professor and Chair of the Department of Communication at De La Salle University, Philippines. Her research interests lie in community, alternative, and activist new media, focusing on the media used and produced by cultural activists and marginal populations and the political, social, and spatial contexts underlying these new media engagements. Her research works appear in journals such as *Media, Culture and Society*, *The Information Society*, and *Communication, Culture & Critique*, among others. Her coedited book, *Asian Perspectives on Digital Culture: Emerging Phenomena, Enduring Concepts* (with A/P Sun Sun Lim) was published by Routledge. Cheryll is also a 2016 Australia Women in Research Fellow based in RMIT University.

Ishita Shruti is part-time faculty in the Department of Public Health, State University of Bangladesh, Dhaka. She holds a Ph.D. from the Department of Humanities and Social Sciences, Indian Institute of Technology Delhi. Her areas of interest are migration and gender. She has coauthored a chapter on "Mobile Technology and 'Doing Family' in a Global World" in Lim, S. S. (Ed.) (2016) *Mobile Communication and the Family: Asian Experiences in Technology Domestication*. She has also published a book review of Beatrix Hauser's book "Promising Rituals: Gender and Performativity in Eastern India" (2012, Routledge) in *Interactions: Gender and Sexuality in Asia and Pacific*. Issue 39, July 2016.

Ana Serrano Tellería is Assistant Professor (ANECA, Spanish Official State Agency), at University of Castilla La Mancha, Spain, and postdoctoral researcher at the R&D Research Center LabCom. IFP, University of Beira Interior, Portugal. She has over 72 publications and has also participated in several national and international research projects on journalism, media studies, digital/mobile/online communication and design, and performing & stage arts. She is a member of the Communication Studies editorial board and reviewer for ICA, IAMCR, IGI Global, iJIM, Derecom, Ciaiq.org, etc.

Index

For Product Safety Concerns and Information please contact our EU
representative GPSR@taylorandfrancis.com
Taylor & Francis Verlag GmbH, Kaufingerstraße 24, 80331 München, Germany